NYSTCE
007

CST
Chemistry
Teacher Certification Exam

By: Sharon Wynne, M.S.
Southern Connecticut State University

"And, while there's no reason yet to panic, I think it's only prudent that we make preparations to panic."

XAMonline, INC.
Boston

Library of Congress Cataloging-in-Publication Data

Wynne, Sharon A.
    CST Chemistry 007: Teacher Certification / Sharon A. Wynne. -2nd ed.
    ISBN 978-1-58197-855-1
    1. CST Chemistry 007.   2. Study Guides.   3. NYSTCE
    4. Teachers' Certification & Licensure.   5. Careers

Disclaimer:
The opinions expressed in this publication are the sole works of XAMonline and were created independently from the National Education Association, Educational Testing Service, or any State Department of Education, National Evaluation Systems or other testing affiliates.

Between the time of publication and printing, state specific standards as well as testing formats and website information may change that is not included in part or in whole within this product. Sample test questions are developed by XAMonline and reflect similar content as on real tests; however, they are not former tests. XAMonline assembles content that aligns with state standards but makes no claims nor guarantees teacher candidates a passing score. Numerical scores are determined by testing companies such as NES or ETS and then are compared with individual state standards. A passing score varies from state to state.

Printed in the United States of America   œ-1

NYSTCE: CST Chemistry 007
ISBN: 978-1-58197-855-1

Massachusetts Tests for Educator Licensure®

Test Date: March 4, 2006

See reverse side for an explanation of how to read your score report.

MARC SHELIKOFF has met the qualifying score on the following test(s) as of March 4, 2006:
12 Chemistry

MARC SHELIKOFF

Your scores have been reported to the Massachusetts Department of Education.

---

12 Chemistry

Your Score: 94   **Minimum Qualifying Score: 70**   **Status: Met the Qualifying Score**

Number of Questions	Subarea Name	Graphic Display
1 to 10	The Nature of Chemical Inquiry..	
11 to 20	Matter and Atomic Structure..	
11 to 20	Energy/Chemical Bonds/Molecular Struct..................................	
11 to 20	Chemical Reactions...	
1 to 10	Quantitative Relationships...	
11 to 20	Chemistry, Society, and the Environment...................................	
2	Open-Response Items..	

Table of Contents

Great Study and Testing Tips!

What to study in order to prepare for the subject assessments is the focus of this study guide but equally important is *how* you study.

You can increase your chances of truly mastering the information by taking some simple, but effective steps.

Study Tips:

1. <u>Some foods aid the learning process.</u> Foods such as milk, nuts, seeds, rice, and oats help your study efforts by releasing natural memory enhancers called CCKs (*cholecystokinin*) composed of *tryptophan*, *choline*, and *phenylalanine*. All of these chemicals enhance the neurotransmitters associated with memory. Before studying, try a light, protein-rich meal of eggs, turkey, and fish. All of these foods release the memory enhancing chemicals. The better the connections, the more you comprehend.

Likewise, before you take a test, stick to a light snack of energy boosting and relaxing foods. A glass of milk, a piece of fruit, or some peanuts all release various memory-boosting chemicals and help you to relax and focus on the subject at hand.

2. <u>Learn to take great notes.</u> A by-product of our modern culture is that we have grown accustomed to getting our information in short doses (i.e. TV news sound bites or USA Today style newspaper articles.)

Consequently, we've subconsciously trained ourselves to assimilate information better in <u>neat little packages</u>. If your notes are scrawled all over the paper, it fragments the flow of the information. Strive for clarity. Newspapers use a standard format to achieve clarity. Your notes can be much clearer through use of proper formatting. A very effective format is called the *"Cornell Method."*

Take a sheet of loose-leaf lined notebook paper and draw a line all the way down the paper about 1-2" from the left-hand edge.

Draw another line across the width of the paper about 1-2" up from the bottom. Repeat this process on the reverse side of the page.

Look at the highly effective result. You have ample room for notes, a left hand margin for special emphasis items or inserting supplementary data from the textbook, a large area at the bottom for a brief summary, and a little rectangular space for just about anything you want.

3. Get the concept then the details. Too often we focus on the details and don't gather an understanding of the concept. However, if you simply memorize only dates, places, or names, you may well miss the whole point of the subject.

A key way to understand things is to put them in your own words. If you are working from a textbook, automatically summarize each paragraph in your mind. If you are outlining text, don't simply copy the author's words.

Rephrase them in your own words. You remember your own thoughts and words much better than someone else's, and subconsciously tend to associate the important details to the core concepts.

4. Ask Why? Pull apart written material paragraph by paragraph and don't forget the captions under the illustrations.

Example: If the heading is "Stream Erosion", flip it around to read "Why do streams erode?" Then answer the questions.

If you train your mind to think in a series of questions and answers, not only will you learn more, but it also helps to lessen the test anxiety because you are used to answering questions.

5. Read for reinforcement and future needs. Even if you only have 10 minutes, put your notes or a book in your hand. Your mind is similar to a computer; you have to input data in order to have it processed. *By reading, you are creating the neural connections for future retrieval.* The more times you read something, the more you reinforce the learning of ideas.

Even if you don't fully understand something on the first pass, *your mind stores much of the material for later recall.*

6. Relax to learn so go into exile. Our bodies respond to an inner clock called biorhythms. Burning the midnight oil works well for some people, but not everyone.

If possible, set aside a particular place to study that is free of distractions. Shut off the television, cell phone, pager and exile your friends and family during your study period.

If you really are bothered by silence, try background music. Light classical music at a low volume has been shown to aid in concentration over other types. Music that evokes pleasant emotions without lyrics are highly suggested. Try just about anything by Mozart. It relaxes you.

7. Use arrows not highlighters. At best, it's difficult to read a page full of yellow, pink, blue, and green streaks. Try staring at a neon sign for a while and you'll soon see that the horde of colors obscure the message.

A quick note, a brief dash of color, an underline, and an arrow pointing to a particular passage is much clearer than a horde of highlighted words.

8. Budget your study time. Although you shouldn't ignore any of the material, *allocate your available study time in the same ratio that topics may appear on the test.*

Testing Tips:

1. Get smart, play dumb. Don't read anything into the question. Don't make an assumption that the test writer is looking for something else than what is asked. Stick to the question as written and don't read extra things into it.

2. Read the question and all the choices *twice* before answering the question. You may miss something by not carefully reading, and then re-reading both the question and the answers.

If you really don't have a clue as to the right answer, leave it blank on the first time through. Go on to the other questions, as they may provide a clue as to how to answer the skipped questions.

If later on, you still can't answer the skipped ones . . . *Guess.* The only penalty for guessing is that you *might* get it wrong. Only one thing is certain; if you don't put anything down, you will get it wrong!

3. Turn the question into a statement. Look at the way the questions are worded. The syntax of the question usually provides a clue. Does it seem more familiar as a statement rather than as a question? Does it sound strange?

By turning a question into a statement, you may be able to spot if an answer sounds right, and it may also trigger memories of material you have read.

4. Look for hidden clues. It's actually very difficult to compose multiple-foil (choice) questions without giving away part of the answer in the options presented.

In most multiple-choice questions you can often readily eliminate one or two of the potential answers. This leaves you with only two real possibilities and automatically your odds go to Fifty-Fifty for very little work.

5. Trust your instincts. For every fact that you have read, you subconsciously retain something of that knowledge. On questions that you aren't really certain about, go with your basic instincts. **Your first impression on how to answer a question is usually correct.**

6. Mark your answers directly on the test booklet. Don't bother trying to fill in the optical scan sheet on the first pass through the test.

7. Watch the clock! You have a set amount of time to answer the questions. Don't get bogged down trying to answer a single question at the expense of 10 questions you can more readily answer.

Periodic Table of the Elements

Group	1 IA	2 IIA	3 IIIB	4 IVB	5 VB	6 VIB	7 VIIB	8 VIIIB	9 VIIIB	10 VIIIB	11 IB	12 IIB	13 IIIA	14 IVA	15 VA	16 VIA	17 VIIA	18 VIIIA
Period 1	hydrogen 1 H 1.0079																	helium 2 He 4.0026
2	lithium 3 Li 6.941	beryllium 4 Be 9.0122											boron 5 B 10.811	carbon 6 C 12.011	nitrogen 7 N 14.007	oxygen 8 O 15.999	fluorine 9 F 18.998	neon 10 Ne 20.180
3	sodium 11 Na 22.990	magnesium 12 Mg 24.305											aluminum 13 Al 26.982	silicon 14 Si 28.086	phosphorus 15 P 30.974	sulfur 16 S 32.065	chlorine 17 Cl 35.453	argon 18 Ar 39.948
4	potassium 19 K 39.098	calcium 20 Ca 40.078	scandium 21 Sc 44.956	titanium 22 Ti 47.867	vanadium 23 V 50.942	chromium 24 Cr 51.996	manganese 25 Mn 54.938	iron 26 Fe 55.845	cobalt 27 Co 58.933	nickel 28 Ni 58.693	copper 29 Cu 63.546	zinc 30 Zn 65.409	gallium 31 Ga 69.723	germanium 32 Ge 72.64	arsenic 33 As 74.922	selenium 34 Se 78.96	bromine 35 Br 79.904	krypton 36 Kr 83.798
5	rubidium 37 Rb 85.468	strontium 38 Sr 87.62	yttrium 39 Y 88.906	zirconium 40 Zr 91.224	niobium 41 Nb 82.906	molybdenum 42 Mo 95.94	technetium 43 Tc [98]	ruthenium 44 Ru 101.07	rhodium 45 Rh 102.91	palladium 46 Pd 106.42	silver 47 Ag 107.87	cadmium 48 Cd 112.41	indium 49 In 114.82	tin 50 Sn 118.71	antimony 51 Sb 121.76	tellurium 52 Te 127.60	iodine 53 I 126.90	xenon 54 Xe 131.29
6	cesium 55 Cs 132.91	barium 56 Ba 137.33	57-71 *	hafnium 72 Hf 178.49	tantalum 73 Ta 180.95	tungsten 74 W 183.84	rhenium 75 Re 186.21	osmium 76 Os 190.23	iridium 77 Ir 192.22	platinum 78 Pt 195.08	gold 79 Au 196.97	mercury 80 Hg 200.59	thallium 81 Tl 204.38	lead 82 Pb 207.2	bismuth 83 Bi 208.98	polonium 84 Po [209]	astatine 85 At [210]	radon 86 Rn [222]
7	francium 87 Fr [223]	radium 88 Ra [226]	89-103 **	rutherfordium 104 Rf [261]	dubnium 105 Db [262]	seaborgium 106 Sg [266]	bohrium 107 Bh [264]	hassium 108 Hs [277]	meitnerium 109 Mt [268]	darmstadtium 110 Ds [271]	roentgenium 111 Rg [272]							

*Lanthanoids

lanthanum 57 La 138.91	cerium 58 Ce 140.12	praseodymium 59 Pr 140.91	neodymium 60 Nd 144.24	promethium 61 Pm [145]	samarium 62 Sm 150.36	europium 63 Eu 151.96	gadolinium 64 Gd 157.25	terbium 65 Tb 158.93	dysprosium 66 Dy 162.50	holmium 67 Ho 164.93	erbium 68 Er 167.26	thulium 69 Tm 168.93	ytterbium 70 Yb 173.04	lutetium 71 Lu 174.97

**Actinoids

actinium 89 Ac [227]	thorium 90 Th 232.04	protactinium 91 Pa 231.04	uranium 92 U 238.03	neptunium 93 Np [237]	plutonium 94 Pu [244]	americium 95 Am [243]	curium 96 Cm [247]	berkelium 97 Bk [247]	californium 98 Cf [251]	einsteinium 99 Es [252]	fermium 100 Fm [257]	mendelevium 101 Md [258]	nobelium 102 No [259]	lawrencium 103 Lr [262]

Atomic mass values from IUPAC review (2001): http://www.iupac.org/reports/periodic_table/

SUBAREA I.   **FOUNDATIONS OF SCIENTIFIC INQUIRY**

Competency 1.0   **Understand the relationship and common themes that connect mathematic, science and technology**

Science, mathematics, and technology are interconnected. Teaching Chemistry incorporates the other sciences as well as other disciplines, such as mathematics. For example, graphs and charts are frequently used to record and analyze data. On a daily basis, we are surrounded with mathematics in the ability to make various measurements of mass and size, in the conversions betweens the numerous units, and in tabulating amounts of materials. Beyond these basic skills, mathematical and algebraic skills are used in a plethora of chemical calculations from determining the percent composition of elements in a compound to estimating the mass of reactants needed in a reaction.

The union of science, technology, and mathematics has shaped the world we live in today. Science describes the world. It attempts to explain all aspects of how nature works, from our own bodies to the tiny particles making up matter, from the entire earth to the universe beyond. Science lets us know in advance what will happen when a cell splits or when two chemicals react. Yet, science is ever-evolving. Throughout history, people have developed and validated many different ideas about the processes of the universe. Frequently, the development of new technology used in conducting experiments allows for new information and theories to emerge.

Chemistry is an everyday experience. Some facet of chemistry is involved in every aspect of our daily lives whether in the manufacture of the soaps and cosmetics one uses to get ready for the day, in the synthesis of the fabrics one wears, or in the production of the foods that are consumed daily.

Through the partnership of Chemistry and Biology, enormous advances in medicine and biotechnology have been made in the discovery of the molecular structure of the DNA molecule to the development of the field of medicinal chemistry. We have the ability to clone animals from a single adult cell and cure people of certain types of cancer. In the field of medicinal chemistry, scientists identify, synthesize, develop, and study chemicals to use for diagnostic tools and pharmaceuticals. Pharmacology is the study of how chemical substances interact with living systems. As biological knowledge has increased, the biochemical causes of many diseases have been determined and the field of pharmacology has grown tremendously. With the development of new medicines, antibiotics and vaccines, humans can be cured from common diseases and even avoid getting sick. Antibiotics are organic chemicals to kill or slow the growth of bacteria. Before antibiotics were available, infections were often treated with moderate levels of poisons like strychnine or arsenic. Antibiotics target the disease without harming the patient, and they have saved millions of lives. A baby born today in the United States is expected to live 30 years longer on average than a baby born 100 years ago. Since 1980, genetic engineering has been used to design recombinant DNA in order to produce human protein molecules in bioreactors using non-human cells. These molecules fight diseases by elevating the level of proteins made naturally by the human body or by providing proteins that are missing due to genetic disorders. Most tools in biotechnology originated from chemical technology, and with the continued partnership, better instruments and equipment will continue to be invented. With such developments, doctors can diagnose and treat patients more easily and with greater precision, so that we as a society are able to live longer and healthier lives.

In addition to a better quality of life we are able to increase the world's supply of food. Scientists have developed fertilizers, insecticides, and herbicides that enable us to grow stronger and healthier plants and to prevent diseases and pests in crops. The major breakthrough in the use of fertilizers from chemical processes occurred with the development of the Haber process for ammonia production in 1910:

$$N_2(g) + 3\ H_2(g) \rightleftharpoons 2\ NH_3(g) \text{ over Fe catalyst}$$

Millions of tons of ammonia are used worldwide each year to supply crops with nitrogen. Ammonia is either added to irrigation water or injected directly into the ground. Many other nitrogen fertilizers are synthesized from ammonia. Phosphorus in fertilizers originates from phosphate (PO_4^{3-}) in rock deposits. Potassium in fertilizers comes from evaporated ancient seabeds in the form of potassium oxide (K_2O). Pesticides are used to control or kill organisms that compete with humans for food, spread disease, or are considered a nuisance. Herbicides are pesticides that attack weeds; insecticides attack insects; fungicides attack molds and other fungus. Sulfur was used as a fungicide in ancient times. The development and use of new pesticides has exploded over the last 60 years, but these pesticides are often poisonous to humans. One example is the insecticide DDT. It was widely used in the 1940s and 1950s and is responsible for eradicating malaria from Europe and North America. It quickly became the most widely used pesticide in the world. In the 1960s, some claimed that DDT was preventing fish-eating birds from reproducing and that it was causing birth defects in humans. DDT is now banned in many countries, but it is still used in developing nations to prevent diseases carried by insects.

The herbicide *Roundup* kills all natural plants it encounters. It began to be used in the 1990s in combination with genetically engineered crops that include a gene intended to make the crop (and only the crop) resistant to the herbicide. This combination of chemical and genetic technology has been an economic success but it has raised many concerns about potential problems in the future.

Farming designed to maximize productivity is called intensive agriculture. These methods of fertilizer and pesticide use in combination with other farming techniques decreased the number of farm laborers needed and gave a growing world population enough to eat in the last 50 years. Intensification of agriculture in developing countries is known as the green revolution.

These techniques were credited with saving a billion people from starvation in India and Pakistan.

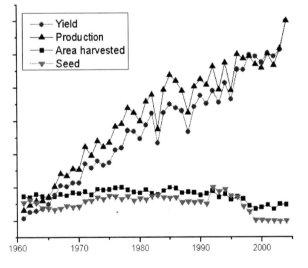

Total world production of coarse grain, 1961-2004

Source: Food and Agriculture Organization of the United Nations
(http://faostat.fao.org/)

Technology makes use of scientific knowledge to solve real-world problems. For example, science is used to study the flow of electrons but technology is required to channel the flow of electrons to create a supercomputer. **Basic research** generally refers to investigation of fundamental scientific principles. **Applied research** is oriented toward making use of basic research in technology development. Applied research is dependent on basic research, and both are necessary for technology advancement. Mathematics in turn provides the language that allows this knowledge to be communicated. It allows the creation of models for scientists to use in explaining natural phenomena and is also the language of technology and computers.

Chemical technology helps keep foods fresh longer and alters the molecules in food. Processes such as pasteurization, drying, salting, and adding preservatives all prevent microbial contamination by altering the nutritional content of food. Preservatives are substances added to food to prevent the growth of microorganisms and spoilage. For example, potassium and sodium nitrites and nitrates are often used as a preservative for root vegetables and processed meats. Another method to preserve and sterilize food is by irradiation. Gamma rays from a sealed source of ^{60}Co or ^{137}Cs are used to kill microorganisms in over 40 countries. This process is less expensive than refrigeration, canning, or additives, and it does not make food radioactive.

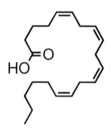

Another benefit of chemical technology is the ability to manipulate the chemical structure of molecules. Hydrogenation uses a chemical reaction to convert unsaturated to saturated oils. Many plant oils are polyunsaturated with double bonds in the **cis-** form as shown at left. These molecules contain rigid bends in them. Complete hydrogenation creates a flexible straight-chain molecule that permits more area for London dispersion forces to form intermolecular bonds. The result is that hydrogenation increases the melting point of an oil. Semi-solid fats are preferred for baking because the final product has the right texture in the mouth. Unfortunately, saturated fats are less healthy than cis- unsaturated fats because they promote obesity and heart disease. Complete hydrogenation of the molecule above is shown here:

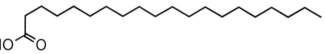

When the hydrogenation process does not fully saturate, it results in partially hydrogenated oil. Partial hydrogenation often creates a semi-solid fat in cases where complete hydrogenation would create a fat that is fully solid.

However, partial hydrogenation of cis-polyunsaturated fats results in a random isomerization, creating a mixture of *cis-* and *trans-* forms. In the structure below, the molecule has been partially hydrogenated, resulting in the saturation of two double bonds. One of the two remaining *cis-* bonds has been isomerized to a *trans-* form:

Trans-fatty acids have a slight kink in them compared to *cis-* forms, and they rarely occur in the food found in nature. Campaigns against saturated fat in the 1980s led to the increased use of partially hydrogenated oils. The health benefits of monounsaturated fat were promoted, but labels made no distinction between *cis-* and *trans-* forms. As a result, there has been an increase in consumption of *trans* fat. Unfortunately, it is now known that *trans* fat is even worse for the body than saturated fat. Some nations have completely banned the use of partially hydrogenated oils. Food labels in the United States are currently (as of 2006) required to list total, saturated, and *trans*-fat content. Fatty acids with one or more *trans* nonconjugated double bonds are labeled as *trans* fat under this rule.

In the area of material science, we are able to improve our ability to synthesize materials and compounds. We have stronger and more durable fabrics that resist staining and daily wear better than the non-synthetic counterparts. Chemists have learned to synthesize plastics, which have a high strength-to-weight ratio. For example, a given piece of structural plastic can be up to six times stronger than steel with the same mass. We can even synthesize diamonds, which at one time were only available by tedious and dangerous mining.

With the increased amount of technology in the other fields of science, basic systems and modern conveniences are also being improved to benefit society. In our ever growing need for more power, Chemistry is playing a huge role in the area energy conservation and more efficient methods of producing energy.

Besides developing alternative fuel sources, like bio-diesel, we are producing better vehicles that are more efficient at combusting the petroleum fuel, and thus producing lower carbon dioxide emissions.

This technology has even produced hybrid and electric vehicles that operate on battery power and can convert the mechanical energy of braking into stored electrochemical power to recharge and run the car continuously.

Beyond our planet, technology has enabled us to travel to the moon and beyond. By analyzing the percent composition of the rocks and minerals found on the moon and Mars and comparing them to those on earth, scientists can begin to gather more information on whether life can exist on planets in our solar system.

The technological advances, which also include the computer, plasma TV, cell phones, CAT scan, and angioplasty to name a few, have become indispensable to human beings. The impact of chemicals and of the ability to alter matter by chemical technology has created tools that have improved the industrial production of nearly every substance. A basic understanding of all the multiple disciplines makes any society well informed and knowledgeable. Chemistry, physics, earth sciences, and biology are all closely involved with society, and many times we don't even notice it. Also, mathematics is interwoven into all of these fields to a great extent. By looking at the world around us closely we can visualize the interconnectedness of all the various disciplines.

The study of the properties and behavior of systems as a whole is known as **systems theory**. It is a highly interdisciplinary field ranging from physics to philosophy. **A system is composed of parts or activities that work together to form a whole.** The most basic definition of a system is a configuration of parts joined together by various relationships. Systems theory places emphasis on the recognition of the structure of systems and the dependence of its components on one another, even if in a time-delayed fashion. Typically, **the whole has unique properties not possessed by the parts alone.** As a result, systems theory prioritizes characterizing the behavior of the system and not the individual parts. This is occasionally at odds with the more traditional approach to science in which components are isolated as much as possible for study.

Systems theory encompasses physics, chemistry, biochemistry, biology, microbiology, engineering, economics, sociology, political science, management, psychotherapy, and many other disciplines. Therefore, systems-based models have been applied to a wide variety of instances in which multiple components interact. These systems can become quite complex. For instance, consider the human body. To understand how food is used to make energy, studying a single cell (cell biology) from the wall of the small intestine might give you some information about how free nutrients are absorbed, but you must also understand how all the organs in the digestive tract work together in sequence to digest the food (anatomy and physiology). Next, you would study the equally complex process by which energy in sugar is converted to ATP (adenosine triphosphate) using biochemistry. Again, simply examining the mechanisms of addition of a phosphate group to ADP (adenosine diphosphate) would not give you a full picture of what is happening. Only when relationships between components in the systems and the relationships between the systems are clear can the entire process be understood. This illustrates that components of systems may be separated by space and time and a single system may interact with other systems to form an even more complex system.

There are certain recurring themes and overarching "rules" that seem to govern science, technolgy, and mathematics. Those overarching "rules" are the **natural laws**: the laws of gravity, inertia, conservation of energy and mass, and the various ways in which matter naturallly behaves. Understanding chemistry is central to understanding these laws and, therefore, to understanding much of science, math and technology. Once one learns how to predict the physical and chemical properties of the elements, he can better predict the reactions of one element with another. Because reactions either need energy and emit energy, the study of chemistry leads to the study of energy transformations which borders on technology, and because those transformations conserve energy and mass, the mathematics must also be understood.

Certain themes recur throughout the sciences, technology and mathematics. The tendency of a system to achieve **equilibrium** is important whether we are observing chemical reactions or all the components in an ecosystem. The effect described by **chaos theory,** the creation of recognizable order from chaotic systems, has been observed throughout the sciences. In biology, understanding the forces of **evolution** is important whether considering a single biochemical pathway or an entire organism. Closely related is the recurring theme that the **structure** of biological subsystems is almost always a result of their **function**.

Competency 2.0   Understand the historical and contemporary contexts of the study of chemistry

Identify historical contributions to the field of chemistry.

<u>Development of Modern Chemistry</u>

Chemistry emerged from two ancient roots: craft traditions and philosophy. The oldest ceramic crafts (i.e., pottery) known are from roughly 10000 BC in Japan. Metallurgical crafts in Eurasia and Africa began to develop by trial and error around 4000-2500 BC resulting in the production of copper, bronze, iron, and steel tools. Other craft traditions in brewing, tanning, and dyeing led to many useful empirical ways to manipulate matter.

Ancient philosophers in Greece, India, China, and Japan speculated that all matter was composed of four or five elements. The Greeks thought that these were: fire, air, earth, and water. Indian philosophers and the Greek **Aristotle** also thought a fifth element—"aether" or "quintessence"—filled all of empty space. The Greek philosopher Democritus thought that matter was composed of indivisible and indestructible atoms. These concepts are now known as classical elements and classical atomic theory.

Before the emergence of the scientific method, attempts to understand matter relied on alchemy: a mixture of mysticism, best guesses, and supernatural explanations. Goals of alchemy were the transmutation of other metals into gold and the synthesis of an elixir to cure all diseases. Ancient Egyptian alchemists developed cement and glass. Chinese alchemists developed gunpowder in the 800s AD.

During the height of European alchemy in the 1300s, the philosopher **William of Occam** proposed the idea that when trying to explain a process or develop a theory, the simplest explanation with the fewest variables is best. This is known as **Occam's Razor.** European alchemy slowly developed into modern chemistry during the 1600s and 1700s. This began to occur after **Francis Bacon** and **René Descartes** described the scientific method in the early 1600s.

Robert **Boyle** was educated in alchemy in the mid-1600s, but he published a book called *The Skeptical Chemist* that attacked alchemy and advocated using the scientific method. He is sometimes called the founder of modern chemistry because of his emphasis on proving a theory before accepting it, but the birth of modern chemistry is usually attributed to Lavoisier. Boyle rejected the 4 classical elements and proposed the modern definition of an element. **Boyle's law** states that gas volume is proportional to the reciprocal of pressure (see **0010).**

Blaise **Pascal** in the mid-1600s determined the relationship between pressure and the height of a liquid in a barometer. He also helped to establish the scientific method. The SI unit of **pressure** is named after him.

Isaac **Newton** studied the nature of light, the laws of gravity, and the laws of motion around 1700. The SI unit of **force** is named after him.

Daniel **Bernoulli** proposed the **kinetic molecular theory** (see **0007**) for gases in the early 1700s to explain the nature of heat and Boyle's Law. At that time, heat was thought to be related to the release of a substance called *phlogiston* from combustible material.

James **Watt** created an efficient **steam engine** in the 1760s-1780s. Later chemists and physicists would develop the theory behind this empirical engineering accomplishment. The SI unit of **power** is named after him.

Joseph **Priestley** studied various gases in the 1770s. He was the first to produce and drink **carbonated water**, and he was the first to **isolate oxygen** from air. Priestley thought oxygen was air with its normal phlogiston removed so it could burn more fuel and accept more phlogiston than natural air.

Antoine **Lavoisier** is called the father of modern chemistry because he performed quantitative, controlled experiments. He carefully weighed material before and after combustion to determine that burning objects gain weight. Lavoisier formulated the rule that chemical reactions do not alter total mass after finding that reactions in a closed container do not change weight. This disproved the phlogiston theory, and he named Priestley's substance oxygen. He demonstrated that air and water were not elements. He **defined an element** as a substance that could not be broken down further. He published the first modern chemistry textbook, *Elementary Treatise of Chemistry*. Lavoisier was executed in the Reign of Terror at the height of the French Revolution.

Additional Gas Laws in the 1700s and 1800s

These contributions built on the foundation developed by Boyle in the 1600s.

Jacque **Charles** developed **Charles's law** in the late 1700s. This states that gas volume is proportional to absolute temperature (see **0010**).

William **Henry** developed the law stating that gas solubility in a liquid is proportional to the pressure of gas over the liquid. This is known as **Henry's Law** (see **0025**).

Joseph Louis **Gay-Lussac** developed the gas law stating that gas pressure is directly proportional to absolute temperature (see **0010**). He also determined that 2 volumes of hydrogen react with one of oxygen to produce water and that other reactions occurred with similar simple ratios. These observations led him to develop the **Law of Combining Volumes.**

Amedeo **Avogadro** developed the hypothesis that equal volumes of different gases contain an equal numbers of molecules if the gases are at the same temperature and pressure. The proportionality between volume and number of moles is called **Avagadro's Law**, and the number of molecules in a mole is called **Avagadro's Number**. Both were posthumously named in his honor. See **0022.**

Thomas **Graham** developed **Graham's Law** of effusion and diffusion in the 1830s. He is called the father of colloid chemistry (see **0025**).

Electricity and Magnetism in the 1700s and 1800s

Benjamin **Franklin** studied **electricity** in the mid-1700s. He developed the concept of positive and negative electrical charges. His most famous experiment showed that lightning is an electrical process.

Luigi **Galvani** discovered **bioelectricity**. In the late 1700s, he noticed that the legs of dead frogs twitched when they came into contact with an electrical source.

In the late 1700s, Charles Augustin **Coulomb** derived mathematical equations for attraction and repulsion between electrically charged objects.

Alessandro **Volta** built the first **battery** in 1800 permitting future research and applications to have a source of continuous electrical current available. The SI unit of **electric potential difference** is named after him.

André-Marie **Ampère** created a mathematical theory in the 1820s for magnetic fields and electric currents. The SI unit of **electrical current** is named after him.

Michael **Faraday** is best known for work in the 1820s and 1830s establishing that a moving **magnetic field induces an electric potential**. He built the first **dynamo** for electricity generation. He also discovered benzene, invented oxidation numbers, and popularized the terms *electrode*, *anode*, and *cathode*. The SI unit **of electrical capacitance** is named in his honor.

James Clerk **Maxwell** derived the **Maxwell Equations** in 1864. These expressions completely describe **electric and magnetic fields** and their interaction with matter. Also see Ludwig Boltzmann below for Maxwell's contribution to thermodynamics.

Nineteenth Century Chemistry: Caloric Theory and Thermodynamics

Lavoisier proposed in the late 18th century that the heat generated by combustion was due to a weightless material substance called **caloric** that flowed from one place to another and was never destroyed.

In 1798, **Benjamin Thomson**, also known as **Count Rumford** measured the heat produced when cannon were bored underwater and concluded that caloric was not a conserved substance because heat could continue to be generated indefinitely by this process.

Sadi **Carnot** in the 1820s used caloric theory in developing theories for the **heat engine** to explain the engine already developed by Watt. Heat engines perform mechanical work by expanding and contracting a piston at two different temperatures.

In the 1820s, Robert **Brown** observed dust particles and particles in pollen grains moving in a random motion. This was later called **Brownian motion**.

Germain Henri **Hess** developed **Hess's Law** (see **0013**) in 1840 after studying the heat required or emitted from reactions composed of several steps.

James Prescott **Joule** determined the equivalence of heat energy to mechanical work in the 1840s by carefully measuring the heat produced by friction. Joule attacked the caloric theory and played a major role in the acceptance of **kinetic molecular theory** (see **0007**). The SI unit of **energy** is named after him.

William Thomson, 1st Baron of Kelvin also called **Lord Kelvin** recognized the existence of **absolute temperature** in the 1840s and proposed the temperature scale named after him. He failed in an attempt to reconcile caloric theory with Joule's discovery and caloric theory began to fall out of favor.

Hermann von **Helmholtz** in the 1840s proposed that **energy is conserved** during physical and chemical processes, not heat as proposed in caloric theory

Rudolf **Clausius** in the 1860s introduced the concept of **entropy**.

In the 1870s, Ludwig **Boltzmann** generalized earlier work by Maxwell solving the **velocity or energy distribution among gas molecules**. The final diagram in **0018** shows the Maxwell-Boltzmann distribution for kinetic energy at two temperatures. Maxwell's contribution to electromagnetism is described above.

Johannes **van der Waals** in the 1870s was the first to consider **intermolecular attractive forces** (see **0007**) in modeling the behavior of liquids and non-ideal gases.

Francois Marie **Raoult** studied colligative properties in the 1870s. He developed **Raoult's Law** (see **0025**) relating solute and solvent mole fraction to vapor pressure lowering.

Jacobus **van't Hoff** was the first to fully describe **stereoisomerism** in the 1870s. He later studied **colligative properties** and the impact of temperature on equilibria (see **0018** & **0025**).

Josiah Willard **Gibbs** studied thermodynamics and statistical mechanics in the 1870s. He formulated the concept now called **Gibbs free energy** (see **0013**) that will determine whether or not a chemical process at constant pressure will spontaneously occur.

Henri Louis **Le Chatelier** described chemical **equilibrium** in the 1880s using **Le Chatelier's Principle**. See **0018**.

In the 1880s, Svante **Arrhenius** developed the idea of **activation energy** (see **0018**). He also described the dissociation of salts—including **acids and bases** (see **0019**)—into ions. Before then, salts in solution were thought to exist as intact molecules and ions were mostly thought to exist as electrolysis products. Arrhenius also predicted that CO_2 emissions would lead to **global warming** (see **0028**).

In 1905, **Albert Einstein** created a **mathematical model of Brownian motion** based on the impact of water molecules on suspended particles. Kinetic molecular theory could now be observed under the microscope. Einstein's more famous later work in physics on **relativity** may be applied to chemistry by correlating the energy change of a chemical reaction with extremely small changes in the total mass of reactants and products.

Nineteenth and Twentieth Century: Atomic Theory

See **0008** for the contributions to atomic theory of John **Dalton**, J. J. **Thomson**, Max **Planck**, Ernest **Rutherford**, Niels **Bohr**, Louis **de Broglie**, Werner **Heisenberg**, and Erwin **Schrödinger**.

Wolfgang **Pauli** helped to develop quantum mechanics in the 1920s by forming the concept of spin and the **exclusion principle** (see **0009**). According to **Schrodinger's Equation**, each electron is unique. The Pauli Exclusion Principle states that no two electrons may have the same set of quantum numbers. Thus, for two electrons to occupy the same orbital, they must have different spins so each has a unique set of quantum numbers. The spin quantum number was confirmed by the Stern-Gerlach experiment.

Friedrich **Hund** determined a set of **rules to determine the ground state** of a multi-electron atom in the 1920s. One particular rule is called **Hund's Rule** in introductory chemistry courses. Hund's rule states that every orbital in a subshell is singly occupied with one electron before any one orbital is doubly occupied, and all electrons in singly occupied orbitals have the same spin.

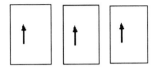

Correct "p" orbitals

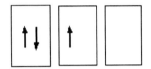

Incorrect "p" orbitals

Discovery and Synthesis: Nineteenth Century:

Humphry **Davy** used Volta's battery in the early 1800s for **electrolysis of salt solutions**. He synthesized several pure elements using electrolysis to generate non-spontaneous reactions.

Jöns Jakob **Berzelius** isolated several elements, but he is best known for inventing modern **chemical notation** by using one or two letters to represent elements in the early 1800s.

Friedrich **Wöhler** isolated several elements, but he is best known for the chemical **synthesis of an organic compound** in 1828 using the carbon in silver cyanide. Before Wöhler, many had believed that a transcendent "life-force" was needed to make the molecules of life.

Justus **von Liebig** studied the chemicals involved in agriculture in the 1840s. He has been called the **father of agricultural chemistry**.

Louis **Pasteur** studied **chirality** in the 1840s by separating a mixture of two chiral molecules. His greater contribution was in biology for discovering the germ theory of disease.

Henry **Bessemer** in the 1850s developed the **Bessemer Process** for mass producing steel by blowing air through molten iron to oxidize impurities.

Friedrich August **Kekulé** von Stradonitz studied the chemistry of carbon in the 1850s and 1860s. He proposed the **ring structure of benzene** and that carbon was tetravalent.

Anders Jonas **Ångström** was one of the founders of the science of spectroscopy. In the 1860s, he found hydrogen and other **elements in the spectrum of the sun**. A non-SI unit of length equal to 0.1 nm is named for him.

Alfred **Nobel** invented the explosive **dynamite** in the 1860s and continued to develop other explosives. In his will he used his fortune to establish the **Nobel Prizes**.

Dmitri **Mendeleev** developed the first modern **periodic table** in 1869. See **0009**.

Discovery and Synthesis: Turn of the 20th Century

William **Ramsay** and Lord **Rayleigh** (John William Strutt) isolated the **noble gases**.

Wilhelm Konrad **Röntgen** discovered **X-rays**.

Antoine Henri **Becquerel discovered radioactivity** using uranium salts.

Marie **Curie** named the property radioactivity and determined that it was **a property of atoms** that did not depend on which molecule contained the element.

Pierre and Marie **Curie** utilized the properties of radioactivity to **isolate radium** and other radioactive elements. Marie Curie was the first woman to receive a Nobel Prize and the first person to receive two. Her story continues to inspire. See http://nobelprize.org/physics/articles/curie/index.html for a biography.

Frederick **Soddy** and William **Ramsay** discovered that **radioactive decay can produce helium** (alpha particles).

Fritz **Haber** developed the **Haber Process** for synthesizing ammonia from hydrogen and nitrogen using an iron **catalyst** (see **0017**). Ammonia is still produced by this method to make fertilizers, textiles, and other products.

Robert Andrew **Millikan** determined the **charge of an electron** using an oil-drop experiment.

Discovery and Synthesis: 20th Century

Gilbert Newton **Lewis** described **covalent bonds** as sharing electrons in the 1910s and the **electron pair donor/acceptor theory of acids and bases** in the 1920s. Lewis dot structures (see **0015**) and Lewis acids (see **0019**) are named after him.

Johannes Nicolaus **Brønsted** and Thomas Martin **Lowry** simultaneously developed the **proton donor/acceptor theory of acids and bases** (see **0019**) in the 1920s.

Irving **Langmuir** in the 1920s developed the science of **surface chemistry** to describe interactions at the interface of two phases. This field is important to heterogeneous catalysis (see **0017**).

Fritz **London** studied the electrical nature of chemical bonding in the 1920s. The weak intermolecular **London dispersion forces** (see **0014**) are named after him.

Hans Wilhelm **Geiger** developed the **Geiger counter** for measuring ionizing radiation in the 1930s.

Wallace **Carothers** and his team first synthesized **organic polymers** (including neoprene, polyester and nylon) in the 1930s.

In the 1930s, Linus **Pauling** published his results on **the nature of the covalent bond**. Pauling electronegativity (see **0014**) is named after him. In the 1950s, Pauling determined the α-helical structure of proteins.

Lise **Meitner** and Otto **Hahn** discovered **nuclear fission** in the 1930s.

Glenn Theodore **Seaborg** created and isolated several **elements larger than uranium** in the 1940s. Seaborg reorganized the periodic table to its current form.

James **Watson** and Francis **Crick** determined the **double helix structure of DNA** in the 1950s.

Neil **Bartlett** produced **compounds containing noble gases** in the 1960s, proving that they are not completely chemically inert.

Harold **Kroto**, Richard **Smalley**, and Robert **Curl** discovered the **buckyball C_{60}** (see **0013**) in the 1980s.

Competency 3.0   Understand the process of scientific inquiry and the role of observation and experimentation in explaining natural phenomena

Modern science began around the late 16th century with a new way of thinking about the world. Few scientists will disagree with Carl Sagan's assertion that "science is a way of thinking much more than it is a body of knowledge" (Broca's Brain, 1979). Thus science is a process of inquiry and investigation. It is a way of thinking and acting, not just a body of knowledge to be acquired by memorizing facts and principles. This way of thinking, the scientific method, is based on the idea that scientists begin their investigations with observations. From these observations they develop a hypothesis, which is extended in the form of a predication, and challenge the hypothesis through experimentation and thus further observations. Science has progressed in its understanding of nature through careful observation, a lively imagination, and increasingly sophisticated instrumentation. Science is distinguished from other fields of study in that it provides guidelines or methods for conducting research, and the research findings must be reproducible by other scientists for those findings to be valid.

It is important to recognize that scientific practice is not always this systematic. Discoveries have been made that are serendipitous and others have not started with the observation of data. Einstein's theory of relativity started not with the observation of data but with a kind of intellectual puzzle.

The Scientific Method is a logical set of steps that a scientist goes through to solve a problem. The main purpose of using the Scientific Method is to eliminate, as much as possible, preconceived ideas, prejudices and biases by presenting an objective way to study possible answers to a question. Only by designing a way to study one variable at a time can each possible answer be ruled out or accepted for further study. There are as many different scientific methods as there are scientists experimenting. However, there seems to be some pattern to their work.

While an inquiry may start at any point in this method and may not involve all of the steps, here is the pattern.

Observations
Scientific questions result from observations of events in nature or events observed in the laboratory. An observation is not just a look at what happens. It also includes <u>measurements</u> and <u>careful records</u> of the event. Records could include photos, drawings, or written descriptions.

Question
The observations and **data collection** lead to a question. In chemistry, observations almost always deal with the behavior of matter.

Information Gathering / Research

Having arrived at a question, a scientist usually researches the scientific literature to see what is known about the question. This research can be done by using scientific journals, by reading papers presented at conferences, by asking scientists at other institutions and in industry, and by researching the internet. Maybe the question has already been answered. The scientist then may want to test the answer found in the literature. Or, maybe the research will lead to a new question.

Sometimes the same observations are made over and over again and are always the same. For example, you can observe that daylight lasts longer in summer than in winter. This observation never varies. Such observations are called **laws** of nature. Probably the most important law in chemistry was discovered in the late 1700s. Chemists observed that no mass was ever lost or gained in chemical reactions. This law became known as the law of conservation of mass. Explaining this law was a major topic of chemistry in the early 19th century.

Hypothesis

If the question or some aspect of the question has not been answered, the scientist may prepare for an experiment by making a hypothesis. A **hypothesis** is a statement of a possible answer to the question. It is a tentative explanation for a set of observations and must be stated in positive terms and in such a way that can be tested by experiments. Although hypotheses are usually based on observations, they may also be based on a sudden idea or intuition.

Experiment

An **experiment** tests the hypothesis to determine whether it may be a correct answer to the question or a solution to the problem. Designing an appropriate experiment can be challenging. Experiments need to have clearly defined controls (standards), variables, constants, and procedures that truly do test the variable in the question and hypothesis. Some experiments may test the effect of one thing on another under controlled conditions. Such experiments have two variables. The experimenter controls one variable, called the *independent variable.* The other variable, the *dependent variable*, is the change caused by changing the independent variable.

For example, suppose a researcher wanted to test the effect of vitamin A on the ability of rats to see in dim light. The independent variable would be the dose of Vitamin A added to the rats' diet. The dependent variable would be the intensity of light to which the rats respond. All other factors, such as time, temperature, age, water and other nutrients given to the rats would be held constant.

*[handwritten note: Q=K => no change
Q<K => shifts right (more reactants)
Q>K => shifts left (more products)]*

Chemists sometimes do short experiments "just to see what happens" or to see what products a certain reaction produces. Often, these are not formal experiments. Rather they are ways of making additional observations about the behavior of matter.

When students are involved in designing experiments, they better understand what scientists are doing as well as the difficulty of designing appropriately controlled experiments. An ideal experiment at the high school level should not last more than 12-14 days.

Data Collection

In most experiments, scientists collect **quantitative data**, which are data that can be measured with instruments. Quantitative data involves numbers and measurements against a standard. Those measurements may be taken at specified time intervals. They also collect **qualitative data**, descriptive information from observations other than measurements. Qualitative data includes any observations made with the senses of hearing or seeing such as a popping sound or a color change.

Data Analysis / Interpretation

Interpreting data and analyzing observations are important. If data are not organized in a logical manner, incorrect conclusions can be drawn. Also, other scientists may not be able to follow or reproduce the results. By placing data into charts and graphs, the scientist may see patterns or lack thereof. The scientist will also be able to understand if the experiment truly tested the hypothesis. Induction is drawing conclusions based on facts or observations. Deduction is drawing conclusions based on generalizations.

Conclusion

Finally, a scientist must draw conclusions from the experiment. A conclusion must address the hypothesis on which the experiment was based. The conclusion states in writing whether or not the data supports the hypothesis. If it does not, the conclusion should state what the experiment *did* show. If the hypothesis is not supported, the scientist uses the observations from the experiment to make a new or revised hypothesis. Then, new experiments are planned.

Effective written communication is necessary to present the research to a teacher or to a scientific journal. Effective oral communication is needed to present the research to a group whether that group is a class or other scientists. Students must recognize that, in this age of communication, those who cannot communicate effectively will be left behind. Accordingly, the evaluation system of the use of the scientific method should make provision for communication skills and activities.

Defending results

Defending results is as important as conducting an experiment. One can honestly defend one's own results only if the results are reliable, and experiments must be well-controlled and repeated at least twice to be considered reliable. It must be emphasized to the students that *honesty and integrity are the foundation for any type of investigation.*

Steps of a Scientific Method

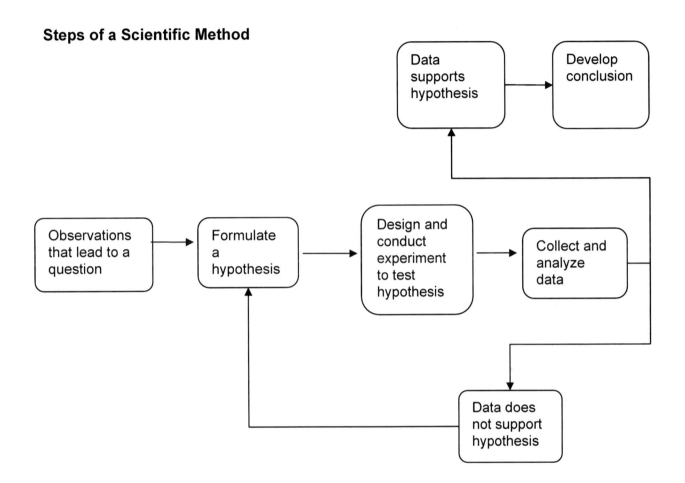

The Development of a Scientific Theory using the Scientific Method

When a hypothesis survives many experimental tests to determine its validity, the hypothesis may evolve into a **theory**. A theory explains a body of facts and laws that are based on the facts. A theory also reliably predicts the outcome of related events in nature. For example, the law of conservation of matter and many other experimental observations led to a theory proposed early in the 19th century. This theory explained the conservation law by proposing that all matter is made up of atoms which are never created or destroyed in chemical reactions, only rearranged. This atomic theory also successfully predicted the behavior of matter in chemical reactions that had not been studied at the time. As a result, the atomic theory has stood for 200 years with only small modifications.

A theory also serves as a scientific **model**. A model can be a physical model made of wood or plastic, a computer program that simulates events in nature, or simply a mental picture of an idea. A model illustrates a theory and explains nature. In your chemistry course, you will develop a mental (and maybe a physical) model of the atom and its behavior. Outside of science, the word theory is often used to describe someone's unproven notion about something. In science, theory means much more. It is a thoroughly tested explanation of things and events observed in nature.

A theory can never be proven true, but it can be proven untrue. All that is required to prove a theory untrue is to show *one exception* to the theory.

Competency 4.0   Understand the processes of gathering, organizing, reporting and interpreting scientific data, and apply this understanding in the context of chemistry investigations

The design of chemical experiments must include every step to obtain the desired data. In other words, the design must be **complete** and it must include all required **controls**.

Complete design

Familiarity with individual experiments and equipment will help you evaluate if anything is missing from the design. For data requiring a difference between two values, the experiment **must determine both values**. For data utilizing the ideal gas law, the experiment **must determine three values of** *P, V, n,* **or** *T* in order to determine the fourth or one value and a ratio of the other two in order to determine the fourth.

Example: In a mercury manometer, the level of mercury in contact with a reaction vessel is 70.0 mm lower than the level exposed to the atmosphere. Use the following conversion factors:

$$760 \text{ mm Hg} = 1 \text{ atm} = 101.325 \text{ kPa.}$$

What additional information is required to determine the pressure in the vessel in Pa?

Solution: The barometric pressure is needed to determine vessel pressure from an open-ended manometer. A manometer reading is always a <u>difference</u> between two pressures. See **0005**. One standard atmosphere is 760 mm mercury, but on a given day at a given location, the actual ambient pressure may vary. If the barometric pressure on the day of the experiment is 104 kPa, the pressure of the vessel is:

$$104 \text{ kPa} + 70.0 \text{ mm Hg} \times \frac{101.325 \text{ kPa}}{760 \text{ mm Hg}} = 113 \text{ kPa.}$$

Controls

Experimental **controls** prevent factors other than those under study from impacting the outcome of the experiment. An **experimental sample** in a controlled experiment is the unknown to be compared against one or more **control samples**. These should be nearly identical to the experimental sample except for the one aspect whose effect is being tested.

A **negative control** is a control sample that is known to lack the effect. A **positive control** is a control sample that is known to contain the effect. Positive controls of varying strengths are often used to generate a **calibration curve** (also called a **standard curve**).

When determining the concentration of a component in a mixture, an **internal standard** is a known concentration of a different substance that is added to the experimental sample. An **external standard** is a known concentration of the substance of interest. External standards are more commonly used. They are not added to the experimental sample; they are analyzed separately

Replicate samples decrease the impact of random error. A mean is taken of the results from replicate samples to obtain a best value. If one replicate is obviously inconsistent with the results from other samples, it may be discarded as an **outlier** and not counted as an observation when determining the mean. Discarding an outlier is equivalent to assuming the presence of a systematic error for that particular observation. In research, this must be done with great caution because some real-world behavior generates sporadically unusual results.

Example: A pure chemical in aqueous solution is known to absorb light at 615 nm. What controls would best be used with a spectrophotometer (see **0005**) to determine the concentration of this chemical when it is present in a mixture with other solutes in an aqueous solution?

Solution: The other solutes may also absorb light at 615 nm. The best negative control would be an identical mixture with the chemical of interest entirely absent. Known concentrations of the chemical could then be added to the negative control to create positive controls (external standards) and develop a calibration curve of the spectrophotometer absorbance reading at 615 nm as a function of concentration. Replicate samples of each standard and of the unknown should be read.

Example: Ethanol is separated from a mixture of organic compounds by gas chromatography (see **0005**). The concentration of each component is proportional to its peak area. However, the chromatograph detector has a variable sensitivity from one run to the next. Is an internal standard required to determine the concentration of ethanol?

Solution: Yes. The variable detector sensitivity may only be accounted for by adding a known concentration of a chemical not found in the mixture as an internal standard to the experimental sample and control samples. The variable sensitivity of the detector will be accounted for by determining the ratio of the peak area for ethanol to the peak area of the added internal standard.

Using appropriate equipment and technology

Scientists use a variety of tools and technologies to perform tests, collect and display data, and analyze relationships. Examples of commonly used tools include computer-linked probes, spreadsheets, and graphing calculators.

Scientists use computer-linked probes to measure various environmental factors including temperature, dissolved oxygen, pH, ionic concentration, and pressure. The advantage of computer-linked probes, as compared to more traditional observational tools, is that the probes automatically gather data and present it in an accessible format. This property of computer-linked probes eliminates the need for constant human observation and manipulation.

Scientists use spreadsheets to organize, analyze, and display data. For example, conservation ecologists use spreadsheets to model population growth and development, apply sampling techniques, and create statistical distributions to analyze relationships. Spreadsheet use simplifies data collection and manipulation and allows the presentation of data in a logical and understandable format.

Graphing calculators are another technology with many applications to science. For example, biologists use algebraic functions to analyze growth, development and other natural processes. Graphing calculators can manipulate algebraic data and create graphs for analysis and observation. In addition, biologists use the matrix function of graphing calculators to model problems in genetics. The use of graphing calculators simplifies the creation of graphical displays including histograms, scatter plots, and line graphs. Scientists can also transfer data and displays to computers for further analysis. Finally, scientists connect computer-linked probes, used to collect data, to graphing calculators to ease the collection, transmission, and analysis of data.

Organizing and interpreting data

Scientific data are initially organized into tables, spreadsheets, or databases. However, trends or patterns in data can be difficult to identify using tables of numbers. For example, the table below presents carbon dioxide concentrations taken over many years from the Mauna Loa Observatory in Hawaii.

Atmospheric CO_2 concentrations at Mauna Loa

Year	Jan.	Feb.	March	April	May	June	July	Aug.	Sept.	Oct.	Nov.	Dec.	Annual
1958	-99.99	-99.99	315.71	317.45	317.5	-99.99	315.86	314.93	313.19	-99.99	313.34	314.67	-99.99
1959	315.58	316.47	316.65	317.71	318.29	318.16	316.55	314.8	313.84	313.34	314.81	315.59	315.98
1960	316.43	316.97	317.58	319.03	320.03	319.59	318.18	315.91	314.16	313.83	315	316.19	316.91
1961	316.89	317.7	318.54	319.48	320.58	319.78	318.58	316.79	314.99	315.31	316.1	317.01	317.65

1962	317.94	318.56	319.69	320.58	321.01	320.61	319.61	317.4	316.26	315.42	316.69	317.69	318.45
1963	318.74	319.08	319.86	321.39	322.24	321.47	319.74	317.77	316.21	315.99	317.07	318.36	318.99
1964	319.57	-99.99	-99.99	-99.99	322.23	321.89	320.44	318.7	316.7	316.87	317.68	318.71	-99.99
1965	319.44	320.44	320.89	322.13	322.16	321.87	321.21	318.87	317.81	317.3	318.87	319.42	320.03
1966	320.62	321.59	322.39	323.7	324.07	323.75	322.4	320.37	318.64	318.1	319.79	321.03	321.37
1967	322.33	322.5	323.04	324.42	325	324.09	322.55	320.92	319.26	319.39	320.72	321.96	322.18
1968	322.57	323.15	323.89	325.02	325.57	325.36	324.14	322.11	320.33	320.25	321.32	322.9	323.05
1969	324	324.42	325.64	326.66	327.38	326.7	325.89	323.67	322.38	321.78	322.85	324.12	324.62
1970	325.06	325.98	326.93	328.13	328.07	327.66	326.35	324.69	323.1	323.07	324.01	325.13	325.68
1971	326.17	326.68	327.18	327.78	328.92	328.57	327.37	325.43	323.36	323.56	324.8	326.01	326.32
1972	326.77	327.63	327.75	329.72	330.07	329.09	328.05	326.32	324.84	325.2	326.5	327.55	327.46
1973	328.54	329.56	330.3	331.5	332.48	332.07	330.87	329.31	327.51	327.18	328.16	328.64	329.68
1974	329.35	330.71	331.48	332.65	333.09	332.25	331.18	329.4	327.44	327.37	328.46	329.58	330.25
1975	330.4	331.41	332.04	333.31	333.96	333.59	331.91	330.06	328.56	328.34	329.49	330.76	331.15
1976	331.74	332.56	333.5	334.58	334.87	334.34	333.05	330.94	329.3	328.94	330.31	331.68	332.15
1977	332.92	333.42	334.7	336.07	336.74	336.27	334.93	332.75	331.58	331.16	332.4	333.85	333.9
1978	334.97	335.39	336.64	337.76	338.01	337.89	336.54	334.68	332.76	332.54	333.92	334.95	335.5
1979	336.23	336.76	337.96	338.89	339.47	339.29	337.73	336.09	333.91	333.86	335.29	336.73	336.85
1980	338.01	338.36	340.08	340.77	341.46	341.17	339.56	337.6	335.88	336.01	337.1	338.21	338.69
1981	339.23	340.47	341.38	342.51	342.91	342.25	340.49	338.43	336.69	336.85	338.36	339.61	339.93
1982	340.75	341.61	342.7	343.56	344.13	343.35	342.06	339.82	337.97	337.86	339.26	340.49	341.13
1983	341.37	342.52	343.1	344.94	345.75	345.32	343.99	342.39	339.86	339.99	341.16	342.99	342.78
1984	343.7	344.51	345.28	347.08	347.43	346.79	345.4	343.28	341.07	341.35	342.98	344.22	344.42
1985	344.97	346	347.43	348.35	348.93	348.25	346.56	344.69	343.09	342.8	344.24	345.56	345.9
1986	346.29	346.96	347.86	349.55	350.21	349.54	347.94	345.91	344.86	344.17	345.66	346.9	347.15
1987	348.02	348.47	349.42	350.99	351.84	351.25	349.52	348.1	346.44	346.36	347.81	348.96	348.93
1988	350.43	351.72	352.22	353.59	354.22	353.79	352.39	350.44	348.72	348.88	350.07	351.34	351.48
1989	352.76	353.07	353.68	355.42	355.67	355.13	353.9	351.67	349.8	349.99	351.3	352.53	352.91
1990	353.66	354.7	355.39	356.2	357.16	356.22	354.82	352.91	350.96	351.18	352.83	354.21	354.19
1991	354.72	355.75	357.16	358.6	359.34	358.24	356.17	354.03	352.16	352.21	353.75	354.99	355.59
1992	355.98	356.72	357.81	359.15	359.66	359.25	357.03	355	353.01	353.31	354.16	355.4	356.37
1993	356.7	357.16	358.38	359.46	360.28	359.6	357.57	355.52	353.7	353.98	355.33	356.8	357.04
1994	358.36	358.91	359.97	361.26	361.68	360.95	359.55	357.49	355.84	355.99	357.58	359.04	358.88
1995	359.96	361	361.64	363.45	363.79	363.26	361.9	359.46	358.06	357.75	359.56	360.7	360.88
1996	362.05	363.25	364.03	364.72	365.41	364.97	363.65	361.49	359.46	359.6	360.76	362.33	362.64
1997	363.18	364	364.57	366.35	366.79	365.62	364.47	362.51	360.19	360.77	362.43	364.28	363.76
1998	365.32	366.15	367.31	368.61	369.3	368.87	367.64	365.77	363.9	364.23	365.46	366.97	366.63
1999	368.15	368.86	369.58	371.12	370.97	370.33	369.25	366.91	364.6	365.09	366.63	367.96	368.29
2000	369.08	369.4	370.45	371.59	371.75	371.62	370.04	368.04	366.54	366.63	368.2	369.43	369.4
2001	370.17	371.39	372	372.75	373.88	373.17	371.48	369.42	367.83	367.96	369.55	371.1	370.89
2002	372.29	372.94	373.38	374.71	375.4	375.26	373.87	371.35	370.57	370.1	371.93	373.63	372.95

(Carbon Dioxide Information Analysis Center (CDIAC))

However, more often than not, the data are then compiled into graphs or charts. Graphs help scientists visualize and interpret the variations and patterns in data. Depending on the nature of the data, there are many types of graphs that may be useful. Bar graphs, pie charts and line graphs are just a few methods used to pictorially represent numerical data.

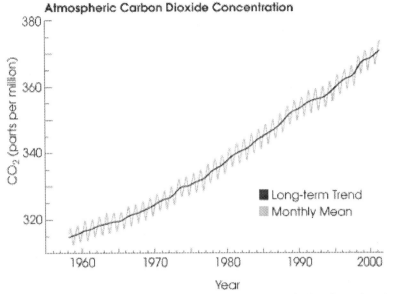

Atmospheric CO_2 measured at Mauna Loa. This is a famous graph called the Keeling Curve (courtesy NASA).

In the graph above, the x-axis represents time in units of years and the y-axis represents CO_2 concentration in units of parts per million (ppm). The best fit line (solid dark line) shows the trend in CO_2 concentrations during the time period. The steady upward-sloping line indicates a trend of increasing CO_2 concentrations during the time period of 1958 to 2002. However, the light blue line which indicates monthly mean CO_2 levels shows a periodic variation in CO_2 concentrations during each year. This periodic variation is accounted seasonal effects. In the spring and summer, deciduous trees and plants undergo increased photosynthesis and remove more CO_2 from the atmosphere in the Northern Hemisphere than in the fall and winter when they have no leaves.

The interpretation of data and the construction and interpretation of graphs are central practices in science. Graphs are effective visual tools which relay information quickly and reveal trends easily. While there are several different types of graphical displays, extracting information from them can be described in three basic steps.

1. Describe the graph: What does the title say? What is displayed on the x-axis and y-axis, including the units.
   - Determine the set-up of the graph.
   - Make sure the units used are understood.
     For example, g·cm^3 means g/cm^3
   - Notice symbols used and check for legend or explanation.

2. Describe the data: Identify the range of data. Are patterns reflected in the data?

3. Interpret the data: How do patterns seen in the graph relate to other variables? What conclusions can be drawn from the patterns?

There are seven basic types of graphs and charts.

Column Graphs

Column graphs, consist of patterned rectangles displayed along a baseline called the x-category or the horizontal axis. The height of the rectangle represents the amount of the variable shown on the y-axis.

Column graphs best show:
• changes in data over time (short time series)
• comparisons of several items (relationship between two series)

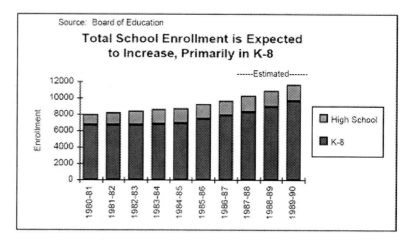

Bar Graphs

Bar graphs are column graphs in which the rectangles are arranged horizontally. The length of each rectangle represents its value. Bar graphs are sometimes referred to as histograms. Bar graphs best show data series with no natural order.

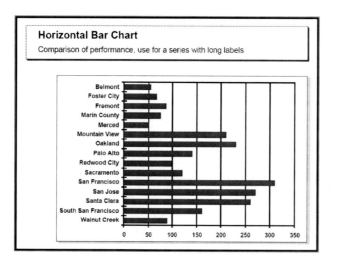

Bar graphs are good for looking at differences among similar things. If the data are a time series, a carefully chosen column graph is generally more appropriate but bar graphs can be used to vary a presentation when many column graphs of time series are used. One advantage of bar graphs is that there is greater horizontal space for variable descriptors because the vertical axis is the category axis.

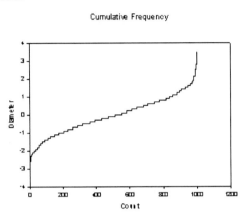

Cumulative Frequency

Line Graphs

Line graphs show data points connected by lines; different series are given different line markings (for example, dashed or dotted) or different tick marks. Line graphs are useful when the data points are more important than the transitions between them. They are best for showing the comparison of long series of data points. a general trend in the data, or changes over time.

Pie Charts

A pie chart is a circle with radii connecting the center to the edge. The area between two radii is called a slice. Data values are proportionate to the angle between the radii.

Pie charts best show parts of a whole. Be careful not to include too many slices since that results in a cluttered graph. Six slices are usually as many as can be handled on one pie.

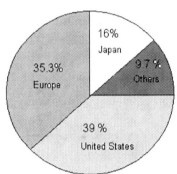

Computers
(% World Production)

16% Japan
35.3% Europe
9.7% Others
39% United States

Area Charts

Area charts show the relative contributions over time that each data series makes to a whole picture and are "stacked line graphs" in the sense that the variables are added together (e.g., principal + interest = total payment). Unlike line graphs, the space between lines is filled with shadings to emphasize variation among the variables over time.

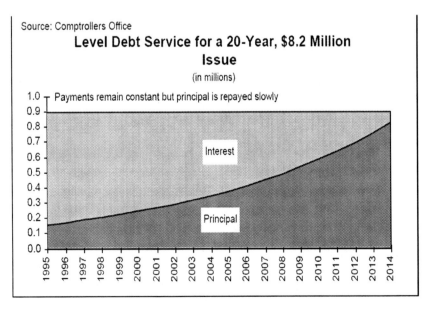

Source: Comptrollers Office
Level Debt Service for a 20-Year, $8.2 Million Issue
(in millions)

Payments remain constant but principal is repaid slowly

Interest

Principal

Scatter Graphs
A scatter plot is the simplest type of graph. It simply plots the data points against their values, without adding any connecting lines, bars or other features. The first variable is measured along the x-axis and the second along the y-axis. Because of this, scatter graphs do not have descriptors in the same sense as other graphs.

Scatter graphs best show possible relationships between two variables. The purpose of the graph is to try to decide if some partial or indirect relationship—a correlation—exists.

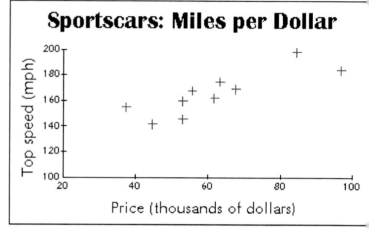

Applying appropriate methods of statistical measures and analysis

To more easily manage large amounts of data, statistical measures are employed to characterize trends in the data. In many systems, the data fits a **normal distribution**, which has a concentration of data points in the center and two equally sized tails (the ends of the distributions). This type of distribution looks like this:

A distribution is considered **skewed** if one tail is larger than the other. To further characterize these distributions, a variety of statistical measures are used. The following are the most commonly used statistical measures:

Arithmetic Mean: The arithmetic mean is the same as the arithmetic mean or **average** of a distribution – the sum of all the data points divided by the number of data points. The arithmetic mean is a good measure of the central tendency of roughly normal distributions, but may be misleading in skewed distributions. In cases of skewed distributions, other statistics such as the median or geometric mean may be more informative.

Median: The median is the **middle** of a distribution: half the scores are above the median and half are below it. Unlike the mean, the median is not highly sensitive to extreme data points. This makes the median a better measure than the mean for finding the central tendency of highly skewed distributions. The median is determined by organizing the data points from lowest to highest. When there is an odd number of numbers, the median is simply the middle number. For example, the median of 2, 4, and 7 is 4. When there is an even number of numbers, the median is the mean of the two middle numbers. Thus, the median of the numbers 2, 4, 7, 12 is (4+7)/2 = 5.5.

Mode: The mode is the **most frequently occurring** data point in a distribution and is used as a measure of central tendency. The advantage of the mode as a measure of central tendency is that its meaning is obvious. However, the mode is greatly subject to sample fluctuations and so is not recommended for use as the only measure of central tendency. Additionally, many distributions have more than one mode. Note also that in the case of a perfectly normal distribution, the mean, median, and mode are identical.

Percentile: Percentiles are similar to a median, but may represent any point in the data set. For example, the 90th percentile represents that point at which 90% of the data points are below that value and 10% of the data points are above that value. Quartiles, representing the 25th, 50th, and 75th percentiles of a data set, are often used to describe a distribution.

Variance: The variance is used to give a measure of the **variability in a distribution**. It is computed as the average squared deviation of each number from its mean. For example, for the numbers 1, 2, and 3, the mean is 2 and the variance (σ^2) is:

$$\sigma^2 = [(1-2)^2 + (2-2)^2 + (3-2)^2]/3 = 0.667$$

Standard deviation: Like variance, standard deviation is a measure of the spread of the distribution, but it is the more commonly used statistic. The standard deviation is simply the square root of the variance.

Note that the standard deviation can be used to compute the percentile rank associated with a given data point (if the mean and standard deviation of a normal distribution are known). In such a normal distribution, about 68% of the data points are within one standard deviation of the mean and about 95% of the data points are within two standard deviations of the mean.

Precision, accuracy, and sources of error

Finally, we must consider the quality of the data itself. That is, is it accurate and precise? And, if not, what is the source of error? A measurement is **precise** when individual measurements of the same quantity **agree with one another**. For example, three arrows that land very close to each other on a target are precise. A measurement is **accurate** when it **agrees with the true value** of the quantity being measured. As an example, an arrow that lands on or near the bull's-eye is accurate. An **accurate** measurement is **valid**. We get the right answer. Measurements can be both accurate and precise. A **precise** measurement is **reproducible**. We get a similar answer each time. These terms are related to **sources of error** in a measurement. Precise measurements are near the **arithmetic mean** of the values.

Random error results from **limitations in equipment or techniques**. **Random error decreases precision**. Remember that all measurements reported to proper number of significant digits contain an imprecise final digit to reflect random error. **Systematic error** results from **imperfect equipment or technique. Systematic error decreases accuracy.** Instead of a random error with random fluctuations, there is a biased result that on average is too large or small. Precision, accuracy, and errors are discussed further in **0005.**

Reporting data

Open communication among scientists fosters the advancement of knowledge for all. One scientist may want to go in a certain direction and not know how to get there, but after speaking with another scientist about experiments, results, data, etc., the seeds of an idea may be planted. Another scientist may need to solve a technical problem, and yet another may have the necessary skills in his or how own field but may require the skills of someone in a totally different field in order to build a piece of equipment or do an experiment. All of these problems may be remedied by open communication and the resulting exchange of information.

Today it is much more common for scientific disciplines to cross over into other fields than it past decades. A scientist working alone would need to be a jack-of-all-trades in order to have the best chance of making a new discovery. Generally, collaboration of numerous scientists around the globe can hasten the process of discovery. Collaboration is strongly encouraged in most academic and scientific settings.

However, if proprietary information is involved, there is no exchange of information. In the case of corporations or government laboratories who deal with patents, their scientists usually sign non-compete agreements which state they will not go to competing corporations for a set amount of time after leaving that corporation and non-disclosure agreements which state they will not say or write anything that might give away any trade secrets or new discoveries. Such laboratories would not freely exchange information or collaborate with scientists outside their organization for legal reasons.

Scientists in a military setting may be prevented from sharing any data considered classified because of national security. Other than these examples, free and open lines of communication are preferred by most scientists.

Publishing a scholarly article in a journal is the most common way for scientists to share their experimental results with the rest of the world. Writing books, attending and presenting at conferences, lectures and poster sessions are other formal methods for communication with larger groups of people. Some less formal methods with smaller groups of people are attending journal clubs, weekly or monthly lab group meetings, and corresponding via mail, e-mail, and the Internet.

Competency 5.0   **Understand principles and procedures of measurement used in chemistry**

Identify appropriate laboratory data collection procedures and equipment necessary to perform standard laboratory activities.

A **lab notebook** is used as the **record of lab work and data collection as it occurs**. Researchers often use lab notebooks to document hypotheses and data analysis. A good lab notebook should allow another scientist to follow the same steps. Electronic lab notebooks are growing in popularity.

Quantitative data involves a number, and **qualitative** data does not. Qualitative data may be a description such as a slight/moderate/intense color change or a weak/strong/explosive reaction or it may simply be the absence/presence of an event.

Basically, quantitative research is objective; qualitative is subjective. Quantitative research seeks explanatory laws; qualitative research aims at in-depth description. Quantitative research measures what it assumes to be a static reality in hopes of developing universal laws and is well suited to establishing cause-and-effect relationships. Quantitative data are measurements that are numerical in nature. "The sample had a mass of 1.15 grams" is a quantitative data point. Qualitative research is an exploration of what is assumed to be a dynamic reality. It does not claim that what is discovered in the process is universal, and thus necessarily replicable.

Simple quantitative data

Many standard lab activities use simple measuring devices such as a **thermometer**, a **clock** (or wristwatch, chronometer or stopwatch), a **ruler** (or micrometer or tape measure), or an **electrical meter** (e.g. voltmeter, ammeter). Humidity is measured with a **hygrometer**.

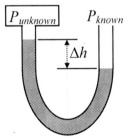

The **pressure in a vessel** is measured with a **pressure gauge** or a **manometer** (shown at left). The unknown pressure $P_{unknown}$ is applied to one side of a U-shaped tube and a known reference pressure is applied to the other. P_{known} may be another vessel or the **atmospheric pressure that is determined with a barometer**. The difference in liquid levels Δh may be converted to a pressure (e.g., 760 mm mercury = 1 atm). If the liquid level is higher on the P_{known} side, Δh is added to P_{known} to obtain $P_{unknown}$. If the liquid level is higher on the $P_{unknown}$ side as in the example shown, Δh is subtracted from P_{known} to obtain $P_{unknown}$.
Volumetric data are often found by determining the level of liquid in a **graduated cylinder** (shown at right) or a **buret** (see **0019**).

Volumetric flasks (shown on the left) are designed to hold a defined volume. A mark on the neck indicates when that volume has been reached. Volumetric containers are usually labeled with **TC** or **TD**.

TC is an abbreviation for "**To Contain.**" These are containers for measuring an unknown volume or creating a stock solution.

TD means "**To Deliver.**" These are used for pouring a known volume into another vessel.

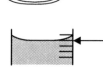

To read a volume level, position your eye **at the level of the meniscus.** The meniscus is the liquid/air interface. Read the volume level **at the bottom of the meniscus** as shown by the arrow to the left.

A graduated **pipet** (or pipette) is used to transfer small quantities of liquid. A **pipet bulb** is a rubber ball that is squeezed and released to generate the suction for drawing liquid into a pipet. A **micropipet** is used for microliters of liquid. An **automatic pipet** uses a button press to fill and discharge a defined volume of liquid. Pipets are always calibrated "to deliver."

A **eudiometer tube** contains volumetric graduations and is used to **measure the volume of gases.** The tube is filled with liquid (usually water) and is inverted in a container of the liquid (as shown at left). Gas is bubbled into the eudiometer and the volume is read. The tube sometimes contains a sparking device to create a reaction in the gases inside.

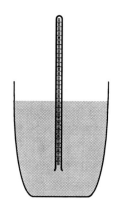

If the eudiometer is raised or lowered until the level of liquid inside and outside the tube are the same **(as shown at right) then the total pressure inside the eudiometer is** identical to atmospheric pressure as found with a barometer. Vapor pressure of the liquid may be found from its temperature.

Using Dalton's Law of partial pressures, this vapor pressure (P_{vapor}) is subtracted from the barometric pressure (P_{total}) to determine the partial pressure of the gas:

$$P = P_{total} - P_{vapor}.$$

PV=nRT

If the temperature of the gas is found, it may be used along with P and V in the ideal gas law to determine the number of moles of the gas in the eudiometer:

$$n = \frac{PV}{RT}.$$

If the mass, m, of the gas is known, then M, its **molecular weight, may be found**.

$$M = \frac{m}{n}.$$

Mass is measured with a **balance**. The terms "mass" and "weight" are often incorrectly used interchangeably in the lab. A container is placed on the **weighing pan**, and either its mass is recorded (this is called a **tare weight**) or a button is pressed to reset the balance to zero. The material is then added to the container and its weight is recorded. Tare weight must be subtracted from this gross weight to obtain the net weight of the substance. When creating a **stock solution** of known concentration, **do not try to measure out an exact mass**. First, measure a mass of the substrate as close as possible to the amount desired and then measure out the appropriate volume of liquid.

Radioactivity is measured using a **Geiger counter** or a **scintillation counter**. A **dosimeter** is any device to measure a person's exposure to a hazardous substance, but it usually refers to radioactive exposure.

Heat measurements involved in **thermochemistry** (see **0008**) are made using a thermometer in a thermally insulated device called a **calorimeter**. Food calories are determined by a **bomb calorimeter**.

Concentration, molecular weight, separation and identification

A **pH meter** or the color of a **pH indicator** is used to measure **hydrogen ion concentration** (see **0019**).

A **photometer** is any instrument that measures the intensity of light. A **spectrometer** is any instrument that separates light or mass into its component parts by a scattering process.

An unknown **concentration** of a solute in a liquid solution is typically determined using a **colorimeter** or **spectrophotometer** to measure the amount of light that passes through the solution. Concentrated solutions have a higher **absorption** of light, so less light passes through the liquid. Different solutes absorb light at different wavelengths.

This phenomenon is visible to the naked eye in the case of dilute and concentrated solutions of different food colorings or inks. The solution is placed in a clear square container called a **cuvette** (or cuvet), and the cuvette is placed in the instrument. Solutions of known concentrations are prepared first and used as **standards** to generate a **calibration curve** of light absorption as a function of concentration. The absorption of the unknown is found from the instrument, and its concentration is determined from the calibration curve. Colorimeters use color filters to separate visible light into broad components. Spectrophotometers make more detailed measurements at defined wavelengths of light. Most spectrophotometers are called **UV/Vis** because they measure light absorption at ultra-violet and visible wavelengths. Other types are **NIR** for "near infrared" and **IR** for infrared.

An unknown **concentration of a metallic element** in a sample may be found in an **atomic absorption spectrometer**. The sample is broken up into free atoms in a very hot flame, and light is passed through the flame to measure absorbance.

The **molecular weights of atoms or molecules** in a mixture are determined with a **mass spectrometer**. The sample is vaporized, this gas is ionized, and these ions are deflected towards a magnet that separates them according to their mass. There are many specialized applications of mass spectrometry so there are dozens of variations to the process. Mass spectrometry is used to determine the ratio of $^2H/^1H$ in water, for ^{14}C dating, and to characterize polymers and biological molecules with molecular weights of over a million.

Chromatography is a method for **separating mixtures** by passing the sample through a stationary material. The instrument is called a **chromatograph**. Different components of the mixture travel at different rates. After the separation, the time that component took to emerge from the instrument (or its location within the stationary phase) is found with a detector. The result is a **chromatogram** like the one shown below. The **identity of an unknown** peak is found by comparing its location on the chromatogram to standards. The **concentration** of a component is found from signal strength or peak area by comparison to calibration curves of known concentrations.

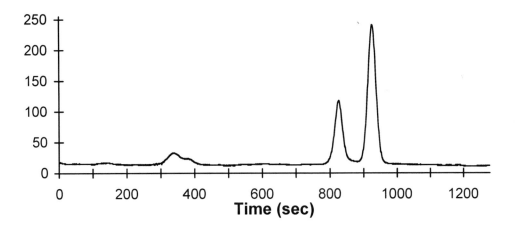

In **paper chromatography** and **thin layer chromatography (TLC)**, the sample rises up by capillary action through a solid phase.

In **gas chromatography (GC)**, the sample is vaporized and forced through a column filled with a packing material. GC is often used to separate and determine the concentration of **low molecular weight volatile organic** compounds.

In **liquid chromatography (LC)**, the sample is a liquid. It is either allowed to seep through an open column using the force of gravity or it is forced through a closed column under pressure. The variations of liquid chromatography depend on the identity of the packing material. For example, an ion-exchange liquid chromatograph contains a material with a charged surface. The mixture components with the opposite charge interact with this packing material and spend more time in the column. LC is often used to separate **large organic polymers** like proteins.

Interpret laboratory measurements and data, including SI units, significant figures, precision, and accuracy.

A large proportion of errors in research and engineering as well as in the classroom are due to treating units as if they were not part of the number. In all scientific disciplines, it is essential that a **unit be associated with every value in every calculation** unless the value is a dimensionless quantity. On September 23, 1999, NASA's $125 million Mars Climate Orbiter was lost because of a data transfer where units were not included as part of the number. Most students first learn the importance of associating numbers with units in their high school chemistry class.

SI units

SI is an abbreviation of the French *Système International d'Unités* or the **International System of Units**. It is the most widely used system of units in the world and is the system used in science.

The use of many SI units in the United States is increasing outside of science and technology. There are two types of SI units: **base units** and **derived units**. The base units are:

Quantity	Unit name	Symbol
Length	meter	m
Mass	kilogram	kg
Amount of substance	mole	mol
Time	second	s
Temperature	kelvin	K
Electric current	ampere	A
Luminous intensity	candela	cd

Amperes and candelas are rarely used in chemistry. The name "kilogram" occurs for the SI base unit of mass for historical reasons. Derived units are formed from the kilogram, but appropriate decimal prefixes are attached to the word "gram." See **0017** for reaction rate constant units.

Derived units measure a quantity that may be **expressed in terms of other units**. The derived units important for chemistry are:

Derived quantity	Unit name	Expression in terms of other units	Symbol
Area	square meter	m^2	
Volume	cubic meter	m^3	
	liter	$dm^3 = 10^{-3}\ m^3$	L or l
Mass	unified atomic mass unit	$(6.022 \times 10^{23})^{-1}\ g$	u or Da
	minute	60 s	min
Time	hour	60 min = 3600 s	h
	day	24 h = 86400 s	d
Speed	meter per second	m/s	
Acceleration	meter per second squared	m/s^2	
Temperature*	degree Celsius	K	°C
Mass density	gram per liter	$g/L = 1\ kg/m^3$	
Amount-of-substance concentration (molarity[†])	molar	mol/L	M
Molality[‡]	molal	mol/kg	m
Chemical reaction rate	molar per second[†]	$M/s = mol/(L{\cdot}s)$	
Force	newton	$m{\cdot}kg/s^2$	N
Pressure	pascal	$N/m^2 = kg/(m{\cdot}s^2)$	Pa
	standard atmosphere[§]	101325 Pa	atm
Energy, Work, Heat	joule	$N{\cdot}m = m^3{\cdot}Pa = m^2{\cdot}kg/s^2$	J
	nutritional calorie[§]	4184 J	Cal
Heat (molar)	joule per mole	J/mol	
Heat capacity, entropy	joule per kelvin	J/K	
Heat capacity (molar), entropy (molar)	joule per mole kelvin	$J/(mol{\cdot}K)$	
Specific heat	joule per kilogram kelvin	$J/(kg{\cdot}K)$	
Power	watt	J/s	W
Electric charge	coulomb	$s{\cdot}A$	C
Electric potential, electromotive force	volt	W/A	V
Viscosity	pascal second	$Pa{\cdot}s$	
Surface tension	newton per meter	N/m	

*Temperature differences in kelvin are the same as those differences in degrees Celsius. To obtain degrees Celsius from Kelvin, subtract 273.15.

[†]Molarity is considered to be an obsolete unit by some physicists (**0025**).

[‡]Molality, m, is often considered obsolete. Differentiate m and meters (m) by context.

[§]These are commonly used non-SI units.

Decimal multiples of SI units are formed by attaching a **prefix** directly before the unit and a symbol prefix directly before the unit symbol. SI prefixes range from 10^{-24} to 10^{24}. Only the prefixes you are likely to encounter in chemistry are shown below:

Factor	Prefix	Symbol	Factor	Prefix	Symbol
10^9	*giga—*	G	10^{-1}	*deci—*	d
10^6	*mega—*	M	10^{-2}	*centi—*	c
10^3	*kilo—*	k	10^{-3}	*milli—*	m
10^2	*hecto—*	h	10^{-6}	*micro—*	μ
10^1	*deca—*	da	10^{-9}	*nano—*	n
			10^{-12}	*pico—*	p

Example: 0.0000004355 meters is 4.355×10^{-7} m or 435.5×10^{-9} m. This length is also 435.5 nm or 435.5 nanometers.

Example: Find a unit to express the volume of a cubic crystal that is 0.2 mm on each side so that the number before the unit is between 1 and 1000.

Solution: Volume is length x width x height, so this volume is $(0.0002 \text{ m})^3$ or 8×10^{-12} m^3. Conversions of volumes and areas using powers of units of length must take the power into account. Therefore:

$$1\,m^3 = 10^3\,dm^3 = 10^6\,cm^3 = 10^9\,mm^3 = 10^{18}\,\mu m^3 ,$$

The length 0.0002 m is 2×10^2 μm, so the volume is also 8×10^6 μm^3. This volume could also be expressed as 8×10^{-3} mm^3, but none of these numbers is between 1 and 1000.

Expressing volume in liters is helpful in cases like these. There is no power on the unit of liters, therefore:

$$1\,L = 10^3\,mL = 10^6\,\mu L = 10^9\,nL .$$

Converting cubic meters to liters gives

$$8 \times 10^{-12}\,m^3 \times \frac{10^3\,L}{1\,m^3} = 8 \times 10^{-9}\,L .$$

The crystal's volume is 8 nanoliters (8 nL).

Example: Determine the ideal gas constant, R, in L•atm/(mol•K) from its SI value of 8.3144 J/(mol•K).

Solution: One joule is equal to one m^3•Pa (see the table of SI units).

$$8.3144\,\frac{m^3 \bullet Pa}{mol \bullet K} \times \frac{1000\,L}{1\,m^3} \times \frac{1\,atm}{101325\,Pa} = 0.082057\,\frac{L \bullet atm}{mol \bullet K}$$

Significant figures

Significant figures or **significant digits** are the digits indicating the **precision of a measurement**. There is uncertainty **only** in the last digit.

Example: You measure an object with a ruler marked in millimeters. The reading on the ruler is found to be about 2/3 of the way between 12 and 13 mm. What value should be recorded for its length?

Solution: Recording 13 mm does not give all the information that you found.

Recording $12 \frac{2}{3}$ mm implies that an exact ratio was determined.

Recording 12.666 mm gives more information than you found. A value of 12.7 mm or 12.6 mm should be recorded because there is uncertainty only in the last digit.

There are five rules for determining the **number of significant digits** in a quantity.

1) All nonzero digits are significant and all zeros between nonzero digits are significant.
   Example: 4.521 kJ and 7002 u both have four significant digits.

2) Zeros to the left of the first nonzero digit are not significant.
   Example: 0.0002 m contains one significant digit.

3) Zeros to the right of a non-zero digit and the decimal point are significant figures.
   Example: 32.500 g contains five significant digits.

4) The significance of numbers ending in zeros that are not to the right of the decimal point can be unclear, so **this situation should be avoided** by using scientific notation or a different decimal prefix. Sometimes a decimal point is used as a placeholder to indicate the units-digit is significant. A word like "thousand" or "million" may be used in informal contexts to indicate the remaining digits are not significant.
   Example: 12000 Pa would be considered to have five significant digits by many scientists, but in the sentence, "The pressure rose from 11000 Pa to 12000 Pa," it almost certainly only has only two. "12 thousand Pa" only has two significant digits, but 12000. Pa has five, indicated by the decimal point. The value should be represented as 1.2×10^4 Pa (or 1.2000×10^4 Pa). The best alternative would be to use 12 kPa or 12.000 kPa.

5) Exact numbers have no uncertainty and contain an infinite number of significant digits. These relationships are **definitions**. They are not measurements.
   Example: There are exactly 1000 L in one cubic meter.

There are four rules for **rounding off significant digits:**.

1) If the leftmost digit to be removed is a four or less, then round down. The last remaining digit stays as it was.
   Example: Round 43.4 g to two significant digits. **Answer:** 43 g.

2) If the leftmost digit to be removed is a six or more, then round up. The last remaining digit increases by one.
   Example: Round 6.772 g to two significant digits. **Answer**: 6.8 g.

3) If the leftmost digit to be removed is a five that is followed by nonzero digits, then round up. The last remaining digit increases by one.
   Example: Round 18.502 g to two significant digits. **Answer** 19 g.

4) If the leftmost digit to be removed is a five followed by nothing or by only zeros, then force the last remaining digit to be even. If it is odd then round up by increasing it by one. If it is even (including zero) then it stays as it was. **Examples:** Round 18.50 g and 19.5 g to two significant digits. **Answers:** 18.50 g rounds to 18 g and 19.5 g rounds to 20 g.

There are three rules for **calculating with significant figures.**

1) For multiplication or division, the result has the same number of significant digits as the term with the least number of significant digits.

   Example: What is the volume of a compartment in the shape of a rectangular prism 1.2 cm long, 2.4 cm high and 0.9 cm deep?
   Solution: Volume = length x height x width.
   Volume = 1.2 cm $\times$ 2.4 cm $\times$ 0.9 cm = 2.592 cm (as read on a calculator)

   Round to one digit because 0.9 cm has only one significant digit.

   Volume = 3 cm^3

2) For addition or subtraction, the result has the same number of digits after the decimal point as the term with the least number of digits after the decimal point.

   Example: Volumes of 250.0 mL, 26 μL, and 4.73 mL are added to a flask. What is the total volume in the flask?

   Solution: Only identical units may be added to each other, so 26 μL is first converted to 0.026 mL.

   Volume = 250.0 mL + 0.026 mL + 4.73 mL = 254.756 mL (calculator value)
   Round to one digit after the decimal because 250.0 mL has only one digit after the decimal. Volume = 254.8 mL.

3) For multi-step calculations, maintain all significant digits when using a calculator or computer and round off the final value to the appropriate number of significant digits *after* the calculation. When calculating by hand or when **writing down an intermediate value** in a multi-step calculation, maintain the first non-significant digit. In this text, non-significant digits in intermediate calculations are shown in italics except in the examples for the two rules above.

> **Example:** See the final example in **0016**. The last digits are italicized in the intermediate calculations after Step 1 and Step 2 because they are non-significant.

Precision and Accuracy

A measurement is **precise** when individual measurements of the same quantity **agree with one another**. A measurement is **accurate** when they **agree with the true value** of the quantity being measured. An **accurate** measurement is **valid**. We get the right answer. A **precise** measurement is **reproducible**. We get a similar answer each time. These terms are related to **sources of error** in a measurement.

Precise measurements are near the **arithmetic mean** of the values. The arithmetic mean is the sum of the measurements divided by the number of measurements. The **mean** is commonly called the **average**. It is the **best estimate** of the quantity.

Random error results from **limitations in equipment or techniques**. **Random error decreases precision**. Remember that all measurements reported to proper number of significant digits contain an imprecise final digit to reflect random error.

Systematic error results from **imperfect equipment or technique**. **Systematic error decreases accuracy**. Instead of a random error with random fluctuations, there is a biased result that on average is too large or small.

Example: An environmental engineering company creates a solution of 5.00 ng/L of a toxin and distributes it to four toxicology labs to test their protocols. Each lab tests the material 5 times. Their results are charted as points on the number lines below. Interpret this data in terms of precision, accuracy, and type of error.

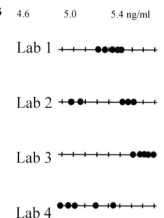

Solution: Results from lab 1 are both accurate and precise when compared to results from the other labs. Results from lab 2 are less precise than those from lab 1. Lab 2 seems to use a protocol that generates a greater random error. However, the mean result from lab 2 is still close to the known value. Lab 3 returned results that were about as precise as lab 1 but inaccurate compared to labs 1 and 2. Lab 3 most likely uses a protocol that yields a systematic error. The data from lab 4 are both imprecise and inaccurate. Systematic and random errors are larger than for lab 1.

Identify appropriate laboratory techniques.

The descriptions and diagrams in this skill are included to help you **identify** the techniques. They are **not meant as a guide to perform the techniques** in the lab. Techniques involving a measurement were considered in **0005**. These techniques are used to develop the procedures given in **0006**.

<u>Handling liquids</u>

A **beaker** (left) is a cylindrical cup with a notch at the top. They are often used for making solutions. An **Erlenmeyer** flask (center) is a conical flask. A liquid in an Erlenmeyer flask will evaporate more slowly than when it is in a beaker and it is easier to swirl about. A **round-bottom flask** (right) is also called a Florence flask. It is designed for uniform heating, but it requires a stand to keep it upright.

A **test tube** has a rounded bottom and is designed to hold and to heat small volumes of liquid. A **Pasteur pipet** is a small glass tube with a long thin capillary tip and a latex suction bulb.

A **crucible** is a cup-shaped container made of porcelain or metal for holding chemical compounds when heating them to very high temperatures.

A **watch glass** is a concave circular piece of glass that is usually used as surface to evaporate a liquid and observe precipitates or crystallization. A **Dewar flask** is a double walled vacuum flask with a metallic coating to provide good thermal insulation.

Fitting and cleaning glassware

If a thermometer or funnel must be threaded through a stopper or a piece of tubing and it won't fit, either **make the hole larger or use a smaller piece of glass**. Use soapy water or glycerol to **lubricate** the glass before inserting it. Hold the glass piece as close as possible to the stopper during insertion. It's also good practice to wrap a towel around the glass and the stopper during this time. **Never apply undue pressure**.

Glassware sometimes contains **tapered ground-glass joints** to allow direct glass-to-glass connections. A thin layer of joint **grease** must be applied when assembling an apparatus with ground-glass joints. Too much grease will contaminate the experiment, and too little will permit the components to be permanently locked together. Disassemble the glassware with a **twisting** motion immediately after the experiment is over.

Cleaning glassware becomes more difficult with time, so it should be cleaned soon after the experiment is completed. Wipe off any lubricant with paper towel moistened in a solvent like hexane before washing the glassware. Use a brush with lab soap to clean lines left by boiling liquids. Acetone may be used to dissolve most organic residues. Spent solvents should be transferred to a waste container for proper disposal.

Heating

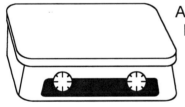

A hot plate (shown) is used to heat Erlenmeyer flasks, beakers and other containers with a flat bottom. Hot plates often have a built-in magnetic stirrer. A heating mantle has a hemispherical cavity that is used to heat round-bottom flasks. A Bunsen burner is designed to burn natural gas. Burners are useful for heating high-boiling point liquids, water, or solutions of non-flammable materials. They are also used for bending glass tubing. Smooth boiling is achieved by adding boiling **stones** to a liquid.

Boiling and melting point determination

Boiling point is determined by heating the liquid along with a boiling stone in a clamped test tube with a clamped thermometer positioned.

A melting point is determined by placing a pulverized solid in a capillary tube and using a rubber band to fasten the capillary to a thermometer so that the sample is at the level of the thermometer bulb. The thermometer and sample are inserted into a **Thiele tube** filled with mineral or silicon oil. The Thiele tube has a sidearm that is heated with a Bunsen burner to create a flow of hot oil. This flow maintains an even temperature during heating. The melting point is read when the sample turns into a liquid. Many **electric melting point devices** are also available that heat the sample more slowly to give more accurate results. These are also safer to use than a Thiele tube with a Bunsen burner.

Centrifugation

A **centrifuge** separates two immiscible phases by spinning the mixture (placed in a **centrifuge tube**) at high speeds. A **microfuge** or microcentrifuge is a small centrifuge. The weight of material placed in a centrifuge must be balanced, so if one sample is placed in a centrifuge, a tube with roughly an equal mass of water should be placed opposite the sample.

Filtration

The goal of **gravity filtration** is to remove solids from a liquid and obtain a liquid without solid particulates. Filter paper is folded, placed in a funnel on top of a flask, and wetted with the solvent to seal it to the funnel. Next the mixture is poured through, and the solid-free liquid is collected from the flask

The goal of **vacuum filtration** is usually to remove liquids from a solid to obtain a solid that is dry. An **aspirator** or a **vacuum pump** is used to provide suction though a rubber tube to a **filter trap**. The trap is attached to a **filter flask** (shown to the right) by a second rubber tube. The filter flask is an Erlenmeyer flask with a thick wall and a hose barb for the vacuum tube. Filter flasks are used to filter material using a **Büchner funnel** (shown to the right) or a smaller **Hirsch funnel**. These porcelain or plastic funnels hold a circular piece of filter paper. A single-hole rubber stopper supports the funnel in the flask while maintaining suction.

Mixing

Heterogeneous reaction mixtures in flasks are often mixed by swirling. To use a magnetic stirrer, a bar magnet coated with Teflon called a flea or a stir bar is placed into the container, and the container is placed on the stirrer. The container should be moved and the stir speed adjusted for smooth mixing. Mechanical stirring paddles, agitators, vortexers, or rockers are also used for mixing.

Decanting

When a coarse solid has settled at the bottom of a flask of liquid, **decanting** the solution simply means pouring out the liquid and leaving the solid behind.

Extraction

Compounds in solution are often separated based on their **solubility differences**. During **liquid-liquid extraction** (also called **solvent extraction**), a second solvent immiscible to the first is added to the solution in a **separatory funnel** (shown at right). Usually one solvent is nonpolar and the other is a polar solvent like water. The two solvents are immiscible and separate from each other after the mixture is shaken to allow solute exchange. One layer contains the compound of interest, and the other contains impurities to be discarded. The solutions in the two layers are separated from each other by draining liquid through the stopcock.

Titration – see **0019.**

Distillation

Liquids in solution are often separated based on their **boiling point differences**. During simple **distillation**, the solution is placed in a round-bottom flask called the **distillation flask** or **still pot**, and boiling stones are added. The apparatus shown is assembled (note that clamps and stands are not shown), and the still pot is heated using a heating mantle.

Hot vapor escapes through the **distillation head** during boiling and enters the **condenser**, where it is cooled and condensed back to a liquid. The vapor loses its heat to water flowing through the outside of the condenser. The condensate or **distillate** falls into the **receiving flask**. The apparatus is open to the atmosphere through a vent above the receiving flask. The distillate contains a higher concentration of the liquid with the lower boiling point. The less volatile liquid reaches a high concentration in the still pot. Head temperature is monitored during the process. Distillation may also be used to remove a solid from a pure liquid by boiling and condensing the liquid into the receiving flask.

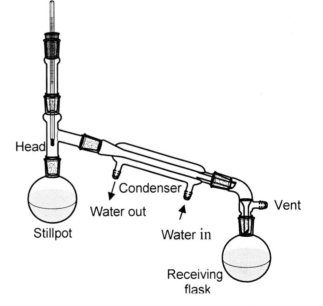

Competency 6.0   Understand equipment, materials, and chemicals used in chemistry investigations; and apply procedures for their proper, safe, and legal use.

Disclaimer: It is the responsibility of the readers of this book to consult with the school's legal counsel or other professional advisers about applicable statutes. The information presented below is intended as a starting point for statute identification purposes only and should not be regarded as a comprehensive guide for compliance.

Identify standard chemistry laboratory safety procedures.

Disclaimer: The information presented below is intended as a starting point for identification purposes only and should not be regarded as a comprehensive guide for safety procedures in the laboratory. It is the responsibility of the readers of this book to consult with professional advisers about safety procedures in their laboratory.

The following is a summary of the requirements for chemical laboratories:

1) A dousing shower and eye-wash with a floor drain are required where students handle potentially dangerous materials.

2) Accessible fully-charged fire extinguishers of the appropriate type and fire blankets must be present if a fire hazard exists.

3) There must be a master control valve or switch accessible to and within 15 feet of the instructor's station for emergency cut-off of all gas cocks, compressed air valves, water, or electrical services accessible to students. Valves must completely shut off with a one-quarter turn. This master control is in addition to the regular main gas supply cut-off, and the main supply cut-off must be shut down upon activation of the fire alarm system.

4) A high capacity emergency exhaust system with a source of positive ventilation must be installed, and signs providing instructions must be permanently installed at the emergency exhaust system fan switch.

5) Fume hoods must contain supply fans that automatically shut down when the emergency exhaust fan is turned on.

6) Rooms and/or cabinets for chemical storage must have limited student access and ventilation to the exterior of the building separate from the air-conditioning system. The rooms should be kept at moderate temperature, be well-illuminated, and contain doors lockable from the outside and operable at all times from the inside. Cabinet shelves must have a half-inch lip on the front and be constructed of non-corrosive material.

7) Appropriate caution signs must be placed at hazardous work and storage areas.

Therefore, all chemistry laboratories should be equipped with the following safety equipment. Both teachers and students should be familiar with the operation of this equipment.

Fire extinguisher

Fire extinguishers are rated for the type of fires they will extinguish. Chemical laboratories should have a combination ABC extinguisher along with a type D fire extinguisher. If a type D extinguisher is not available, a bucket of dry sand will do. Make sure you are trained to use the type of extinguisher available in your setting.

- **Class A** fires are ordinary materials like burning paper, lumber, cardboard, plastics etc.

- **Class B** fires involve flammable or combustible liquids such as gasoline, kerosene, and common organic solvents used in the laboratory.

- **Class C** fires involve energized electrical equipment, such as appliances, switches, panel boxes, power tools, hot plates and stirrers. Water is usually a dangerous extinguishing medium for class C fires because of the risk of electrical shock unless a specialized water mist extinguisher is used.

- **Class D** fires involve combustible metals, such as magnesium, titanium, potassium and sodium as well as pyrophoric organometallic reagents such as alkyllithiums, Grignards and diethylzinc. These materials burn at high temperatures and will react violently with water, air, and/or other chemicals. Handle with care!!

- **Class K** fires are kitchen fires. This class was added to the NFPA portable extinguishers Standard 10 in 1998. Kitchen extinguishers installed before June 30, 1998 are "grandfathered" into the standard.

Some fires may be a combination of these! Your fire extinguishers should have ABC ratings on them. These ratings are determined under ANSI/UL Standard 711 and look something like "3-A:40-B:C." Higher numbers mean more firefighting power. In this example, the extinguisher has a good firefighting capacity for Class A, B and C fires. NFPA has a brief description of UL 711 if you want to know more.

Fire blanket

A fire blanket can be used to smother a fire. However, use caution when using a fire blanket on a clothing fire. Some fabrics are polymers that melt onto the skin. Use of a safety shower is the best method for extinguishing clothing on fire.

Safety shower

Use a safety shower in the event of a chemical spill or fire. Pull the overhead handle and remove clothing that may be contaminated with chemicals, to allow the skin to be rinsed.

Eye protection (also see eyewash under "Facilities and Equipment")

Everyone present must wear eye protection whenever anyone in the laboratory is performing any of the following activities:
1) Handling hazardous chemicals
2) Handling laboratory glassware
3) Using an open flame.

Safety glasses do not offer protection from splashing liquids. Safety glasses appear similar to ordinary glasses and may be used in an environment that only requires protection from **flying fragments**. Safety glasses with side-shields offer additional protection from **flying fragments approaching from the side**.

Safety goggles offer protection from both flying fragments and splashing liquids. **Only safety goggles** are suitable for eye protection where **hazardous chemicals** are used and handled. Safety goggles with no ventilation (type G) or with indirect ventilation (type H) are both acceptable. Goggles should be marked "Z87" to show they meet federal standards.

In the event of an eye injury or chemical splash, use the eyewash immediately.

Help the injured person by holding their eyelids open while rinsing. Rinse copiously and have the eyes checked by a physician afterwards.

Skin protection

Wear **gloves** made of a material known to resist penetration by the chemical being handled. Check gloves for holes and the absence of interior contamination. Wash hands and arms and clean under fingernails after working in a laboratory.

Wear a **lab coat or apron**. Wear **footwear** that completely covers the feet.

Ventilation - Using a Fume Hood

A fume hood carries away vapors from reagents or reactions you may be working with. Using a fume hood correctly will reduce your personal exposure to potentially harmful fumes or vapors. When using a fume hood, keep the following in mind:

- Place equipment or reactions as far back in the hood as is practical. This will improve the efficiency of fume collection and removal.

- Turn on the light inside the hood using the switch on the outside panel, near the electrical outlets.

- The glass sash of the hood is a safety shield. The sash will fall automatically to the appropriate height for efficient operation and should not be raised above this level, except to move equipment in and out of the hood. Keep the sash between your body and the inside of the hood. If the height of the automatic stop is too high to protect your face and body, lower the sash below this point. Do not place your head inside a hood or climb inside a hood.

- Wipe up all spills immediately. Clean the glass of your hood if a splash occurs.

When you are finished using a hood, lower the sash to the level marked by the sticker on the side.

See **0005** for procedures involving fitting glassware.

Work habits
- Never work alone in a laboratory or storage area.
- Never eat, drink, smoke, apply cosmetics, chew gum or tobacco, or store food or beverages in a laboratory environment or storage area.
- Keep containers closed when they are not in use.
- Never pipet by mouth.
- Restrain loose clothing and long hair and remove dangling jewelry.
- Tape all Dewar flasks with fabric-based tape.

- Check all glassware before use. Discard it if chips or star cracks are present.
- Never leave heat sources unattended.
- Do not store chemicals and/or apparatus on the lab bench or on the floor or aisles of the lab or storage room.
- Keep lab shelves organized.
- Never place a chemical, not even water, near the edges of a lab bench.
- Use a fume hood that is known to be in operating condition when working with toxic, flammable, and/or volatile substances.
- Never put your head inside a fume hood.
- Never store anything in a fume hood.
- Obtain, read, and be sure you understand the MSDS (see below) for each chemical that is to be used before allowing students to begin an experiment.
- Analyze new lab procedures and student-designed lab procedures in advance to identify any hazardous aspects. Minimize and/or eliminate these components before proceeding. Ask yourself these questions:
  - What are the hazards?
  - What are the worst possible things that could go wrong?
  - How will I deal with them?
  - What are the prudent practices, protective facilities and equipment necessary to minimize the risk of exposure to the hazards?
- Analyze close calls and accidents to eliminate their causes and prevent them from occurring again.
- Identify which chemicals may be disposed of in the drain by consulting the MSDS or the supplier. Clear one chemical down the drain by flushing with water before introducing the next chemical.
- Preplan for possible emergencies.
  - Keep the fire department informed of your chemical inventory and its location.
  - Consult with a local physician about toxins used in the lab and ensure that your area is prepared in advance to treat victims of toxic exposure.
  - Identify devices that should be shut off if possible in an emergency.
  - Inform your students of the designated escape route and alternate route.

Substitutions

- When feasible, substitute less hazardous chemicals for chemicals with greater hazards in experiments.
- Dilute substances when possible instead of using concentrated solutions.
- Use lesser quantities instead of greater quantities in experiments when possible.
- Use films, videotapes, computer displays, and other methods rather than experiments involving hazardous substances.

Label information

Chemical labels contain safety information in four parts:
1) There will be a signal word. From most to least potentially dangerous, this word will be "Danger!" "Warning!" or "Caution."
2) Statements of hazard (e.g., "Flammable", "May Cause Irritation") follow the signal word. Target organs may be specified.
3) Precautionary measures are listed such as "Keep away from ignition sources" or "Use only with adequate ventilation."
4) First aid information is usually included such as whether to induce vomiting and how to induce vomiting if the chemical is ingested.

Chemical hazard pictorial

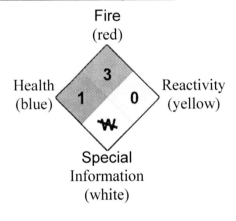

Fire
(red)

Health
(blue)

Reactivity
(yellow)

Special
Information
(white)

Several different pictorials are used on labels to indicate the level of a chemical hazard. The most common is the **"fire diamond" NFPA (National Fire Prevention Association) pictorial** shown at left. A zero indicates a minimal hazard and a four indicates a severe risk. Special information includes if the chemical reacts with water, **OX** for an oxidizer, **COR ACID** for a corrosive acid, and **COR ALK** for a corrosive base. The "Health" hazard level is for **acute toxicity only**.

Pictorials are designed for **quick reference** in emergency situations, but they are also useful as minimal summaries of safety information for a chemical. They are not required on chemicals you purchase, so it's a good idea to **add a label pictorial to every chemical** you receive if one is not already present. The entrance to areas where chemicals are stored should carry a fire diamond label to represent the materials present.

Procedures for flammable materials to minimize fire risk

The **vapors of a flammable liquid or solid** may travel across the room to an ignition source and cause a fire or explosion.
• Store flammables in an approved safety cabinet. Store in safety cans if possible.
• Minimize volumes and concentrations used in an experiment with flammables.
• Minimize the time containers are open.
• Minimize ignition sources in the laboratory.
• Ensure that there is good air movement in the laboratory before the experiment.

- Check the fire extinguishers and be certain that you know how to use them.
- Tell the students that the "Stop, Drop, and Roll" technique is best for a clothing fire *outside* the lab, but **in the lab** they should **walk calmly to the safety shower and use it**. Practice this procedure with students in drills.
- A fire blanket should not be used for clothing fires because clothes often contain polymers that melt onto the skin. Pressing these fabrics into the skin with a blanket increases burn damage.
- If a demonstration of an exploding gas or vapor is performed, it should be done behind a safety shield using glass vessels taped with fabric tape.

Procedures for corrosive materials to minimize risk of contact

Corrosive materials **destroy or permanently change living tissue** through chemical action. **Irritants** cause inflammation due to an immune response but not through chemical action. The effect is usually reversible but can be severe and long lasting. **Sensitizers** are irritants that cause no symptoms after the first exposure but may cause irritation during a later exposure to the same or a different chemical.

- Always store corrosives below eye level.
- Only diluted corrosives should be used in pre-high school laboratories and their use at full-strength in high school should be limited.
- Dilute corrosive materials by slowly and carefully **adding them to water**. Adding water to a concentrated acid or base can cause rapid boiling and splashing.
- Wear goggles and face shield when handling hazardous corrosives. The face, ears, and neck should be protected.
- Wear gloves known to be impervious to the chemical. Wear sleeve gauntlets and a lab apron made of impervious material if splashing is likely.
- Always wash your hands after handling corrosives.
- Splashes on skin should be flushed with flowing water for 15 minutes while a doctor is called.
- If a corrosive material is splashed on clothing:
    - First use the safety shower with clothing on.
    - Remove all clothing while under the safety shower including shoes and socks. This is no time for modesty.
    - Stay under the shower for 15 minutes while a doctor is called.
- Splashes in eyes should be dealt with as follows:
    - Go to the eyewash fountain within 30 seconds.
    - Have someone else hold their eyelids open with thumb and forefinger and use the eyewash.
    - Continuously move the eyeballs during 15 minutes of rinsing to cleanse the optic nerve at the back of the eye. A doctor should be called.

Procedures for toxic materials to minimize exposure

MSDS ⇒ material safety data sheet

Toxic effects are either **chronic** or **acute**. Chronic effects are seen after repeated exposures or after one long exposure. Acute effects occur within a few hours at most.

- Use the smallest amount needed at the lowest concentration for the shortest period of time possible. Weigh the risks against the educational benefits.
- Be aware of the five different routes of exposure:
  1) Inhalation-the ability to smell a toxin is not a proper indication of unsafe exposure. Work in the fume hood when using toxins. Minimize dusts and mists by cleaning often, cleaning spills rapidly, and maintaining good ventilation in the lab.
  2) Absorption through intact skin-always wear impervious gloves if the MSDS indicates this route of exposure.
  3) Ingestion – most often by eating with the hands (such as chips or sandwich) after hands are exposed to toxic materials
  4) Absorption through other body orifices such as ear canal and eye socket.
  5) Injection by a cut from broken contaminated glassware or other sharp equipment.
- Be aware of the first symptoms of overexposure described by the MSDS. Often these are headache, nausea, and dizziness.
- Get to fresh air and do not return until the symptoms have passed. If the symptom returns when you come back into the lab, contact a physician and have the space tested.
- Be aware of whether vomiting should be induced in case of ingestion
- Be aware of the recommended procedure in case of unconsciousness.

Procedures for reactive materials to minimize incompatibility

Many chemicals are **self-reactive**. For example, they explode when dried out or when disturbed under certain conditions or they react with components of air. These materials (see **0006**) generally **should not be allowed into the high school**. Other precautions must be taken to minimize reactions between **incompatible pairs**.

- Store fuels and oxidizers separately.
- Store reducing agents and oxidizing agents separately.
- Store acids and bases separately.
- Store chemicals that react with fire-fighting materials (i.e., water or carbon dioxide) under conditions that minimize the possibility of a reaction if a fire is being fought in the storage area.
- MSDSs list other incompatible pairs.
- Never store chemicals in alphabetical order by name.
- When incompatible pairs must be supplied to students, do so under direct supervision with very dilute solutions and/or small quantities.

Material Safety Data Sheet (MSDS) information

Many chemicals have a mixture of toxic, corrosive, flammable, and reactive risks. The **Material Safety Data Sheet** or **MSDS** for a chemical contains detailed safety information beyond that presented on the label. This includes acute and chronic health effects, first aid and firefighting measures, what to do in case of a spill, and ecological and disposal considerations.

The MSDS will state whether the chemical is a known or suspected carcinogen, mutagen, or teratogen. A **carcinogen** is a compound that causes cancer (malignant tumors). A **mutagen** alters DNA with the potential effects of causing cancer or birth defects in children not yet conceived. A **teratogen** produces birth defects and acts during fetal development.

There are many parts of an MSDS that are not written for the layperson. Their level of detail and technical content may be difficult for many people outside the fields of toxicology and industrial safety to understand. According to the American Chemical Society (http://membership.acs.org/c/ccs/pubs/chemical_safety_manual.pdf), an MSDS places "an over-emphasis on the toxic characteristics of the subject chemical."

In a high school chemistry lab, the value of an MSDS is in the words and not in the numerical data it contains, but some knowledge of the numbers is useful for comparing the dangers of one chemical to another. Numerical results of animal toxicity studies are often presented in the form of **LD_{50} values**. These represent the **dose required to kill 50% of animals** tested.

Exposure limits via inhalation may be presented in three ways:
1) PEL (Permissible Exposure Limit) or TLV-TWA (Threshold Limit Value-Time Weighted Average). This is the maximum permitted concentration of the airborne chemical in volume parts per million (ppm) for a **worker exposed 8 hours daily**.
2) TLV-STEL (Threshold Limit Value-Short Term Exposure Limit). This is the maximum concentration permitted for a 15-minute exposure period.
3) TLV-C (Threshold Limit Value-Ceiling). This is the concentration that should never be exceeded at any moment.

http://hazard.com/msds/index.php contains a large database of MSDSs. http://www.ilpi.com/msds/ref/demystify.html contains a useful "MSDS demystifier." Cut and paste an MSDS into the web page, and hypertext links will appear to a glossary of terms.

Facilities and equipment

- Use separate labeled containers for general trash, broken glass, and for each type of hazardous chemical waste - ignitable, corrosive, reactive, and toxic.
- Keep the floor area around safety showers, eyewash fountains, and fire extinguishers clear of all obstructions.
- Never block escape routes.
- Never prop open a fire door.
- Provide safety guards for all moving belts and pulleys.
- Instruct everyone in the lab on the proper use of the safety shower and eyewash fountain (see Corrosive materials above). Most portable eyewash devices cannot maintain the required flow for 15 minutes. A permanent eyewash fountain is preferred.
- If contamination is suspected in the breathing air, arrange for a sampling.
- Regularly inspect fire blankets, if present, for rips and holes. Maintain a record of inspection.
- Regularly check safety showers and eyewash fountains for proper rate of flow. Maintain a record of inspection.
- Keep up-to-date emergency phone numbers posted next to the telephone.
- Place fire extinguishers near an escape route.
- Regularly maintain fire extinguishers and maintain a record of inspection. Arrange with the local fire department for training of teachers and administrators in the proper use of extinguishers.
- Regularly check fume hoods for proper airflow. Ensure that fume hood exhaust is not drawn back into the intake for general building ventilation.
- Secure compressed gas cylinders at all times and transport them only while secured on a hand truck.
- Restrict the use and handling of compressed gas to those who have received formal training.
- Install chemical storage shelves with lips. Never use stacked boxes for storage instead of shelves.
- Only use an explosion-proof refrigerator for chemical storage.
- Have appropriate equipment and materials available in advance for spill control and cleanup. Consult the MSDS for each chemical to determine what is required. Replace these materials when they become outdated.
- Provide the appropriate first aid equipment and instruction on its proper use.

Additional comments: Teach safety to students

- Weigh the risks and benefits inherent in lab work, inform students of the hazards and precautions involved in their assignment, and involve students in discussions about safety before every assignment.

- If an incident happens, it can be used to improve lab safety via student participation. Ask the student involved. The student's own words about what occurred should be included in the report.
- Safety information supplied by the manufacturer on a chemical container should be seen by students who actually use the chemical. If you distribute chemicals in smaller amounts in appropriate containers to be used by students, copy the hazard and precautionary information from the original label onto the labels for the students' containers. Students interested in graphic design may be able to help you perform this task. Labels for many common chemicals may be found here: http://beta.ehs.cornell.edu/labels/cgi-bin/label_selection.pl
- Organize a student safety committee whose task is to conduct one safety inspection and present a report. A different committee may be organized each month or every other month.

Additional comments: General

- Any chemical can be hazardous. The way it is used determines the probability of harm.
- Every person is individually and personally responsible for the safe use of chemicals.
- If an accident might happen, it will eventually happen. Proper precautions will ensure that the consequences are minimized when it does occur.
- Accidents are often predicted by one or more **close calls** in which nobody is injured and no property is damaged but something out of the ordinary occurrs.
  Examples might be a student briefly touching a hot surface and saying "Ouch!" with no injury, two students engaged in horseplay, or a student briefly removing safety goggles to read a meniscus level. **Eliminate the cause of a close call to prevent a future accident.**

See: www.labsafety.org/40steps.htm, and
www.flinnsci.com/Sections/Safety/safety.asp,
and the American Chemical Society safety publications listed under References.

Chemical purchase, use, and disposal

- Inventory all chemicals on hand at least annually. Keep the list up-to-date as chemicals are consumed and replacement chemicals are received.
- If possible, limit the purchase of chemicals to quantities that will be consumed within one year and that are packaged in small containers suitable for direct use in the lab without transfer to other containers.
- Label all chemicals to be stored with date of receipt or preparation and have labels initialed by the person responsible.
- Check shelf-life of all chemicals and properly dispose of any out-dated chemicals.

- Generally, bottles of chemicals should not remain:
  - Unused on shelves in the lab for more than one week. Move these chemicals to the storeroom or main stockroom.
  - Unused in the storeroom near the lab for more than one month. Move these chemicals to the main stockroom.
  - In the main stockroom unused for more than one year. Properly dispose of these chemicals.
- Ensure that the disposal procedures for waste chemicals conform to environmental protection requirements.
- Do not purchase or store large quantities of flammable liquids. Fire department officials can recommend the maximum quantities that may be kept on hand.
- Never open a chemical container until you understand the label and the relevant portions of the MSDS.

Identify commonly recognized hazardous substances and reactions

Disclaimer: The information presented is intended as a starting point for identification purposes only and should not be regarded as a comprehensive guide for recognizing hazardous substances and reactions. It is the responsibility of the readers of this book to obtain the required information about chemical hazards in their laboratory.

Chemical storage plan for laboratories

- Chemicals should be stored according to hazard class (ex. flammables, oxidizers, health hazards/toxins, corrosives, etc.).
- Store chemicals away from direct sunlight or localized heat.
- All chemical containers should be properly labeled, dated upon receipt, and dated upon opening.
- Store hazardous chemicals below shoulder height of the shortest person working in the lab.
- Shelves should be painted or covered with chemical-resistant paint or chemical-resistant coating.
- Shelves should be secure and strong enough to hold chemicals being stored on them. Do not overload shelves.
- Personnel should be aware of the hazards associated with all hazardous materials.
- Separate solids from liquids.

A list of substances judged to have an excessive risk compared to their educational utility is found here:
http://www.govlink.org/hazwaste/publications/highrisktable.pdf

Materials that react with air or water

The risks of using these materials is considered to exceed their educational utility:
- **Picric acid** (must be kept wet, explosive when dry)
- Sodium metal (reacts with water, ignites in dry air)
- Phosphorus (white form reacts with air. Red form becomes white upon heating)

Extremely corrosive materials

These materials should not be in high school laboratories.
- **Hydrofluoric acid** (even dilute solutions cause adverse internal effects).
- **Perchloric acid** (also causes explosive products)
- Bromine

Highly toxic materials

These materials should not be in high school laboratories.
- **Carbon disulfide** (also explosive)
- Cyanide compounds
- Benzene and toluene
- Mercury and mercury compounds
- Cadmium, chromium, and arsenic compounds
- Carbon tetrachloride and chloroform

Recognize acid/base reactions and redox reactions

Many hazardous reactions are simply **acid/base reactions or redox reactions with concentrated, powerful reagents.** For acid/base reactions, see **0019.** Also see **0016** for inorganic and organic acid nomenclature. For redox reactions, see **0020.**

Recognize the impact of reagent concentration on hazard level
Recognize that a more dilute acid, base, oxidizer, or reducer presents a lower hazard level and requires a lower level of protection in the laboratory.

Organic peroxides and peroxide-forming materials

Organic peroxides have the general structure: R–O–O–R', where R and/or R' are organic substituents. These compounds are **very unstable** and may self-react in a **violent explosion** when triggered by heat, impact, friction, light, or vibration. **Benzoyl peroxide** and other organic peroxides should not be present in high school chemistry labs.

Peroxide-forming compounds are chemicals with the potential to form organic peroxides when they react with oxygen in the air (as the chemical is concentrated) and/or become vaporized either by **erroneous boiling** or over time by **evaporation from a poorly sealed container**.

A peroxide-forming compound should be treated as a **potential explosive** and the local fire chief should be called if it:
- Is discolored
- Contains layering
- Contains crystals

Peroxide crystals may **form within the threads of the cap**, and the act of removing the cap may cause a fatal detonation. A bomb squad may be required.

Many high-risk peroxide-formers were used in high school chemistry in the past. In general, the risks of using the following materials is now thought to exceed their educational utility:
- Nearly all **ethers** including diisopropyl ether (the highest risk peroxide-forming compound), **ethyl ether**, and methyl ether.
- **Potassium metal** (also reacts with water)
- Tetrohydrofuran (THF)
- Cyclohexene and cyclohexanol
- Dioxanes

Several lower-risk peroxide-forming compounds are still commonly used in high schools. These materials **should never be concentrated by boiling (i.e. distilled)**:
- Isopropanol, 2-butanol, other secondary alcohols
- Ethylene glycol
- Acetaldehyde

Below are examples of chemical groups that can be used to categorize storage. Use these groups as examples when separating chemicals for compatibility. Please note: reactive chemicals must be more closely analyzed since they have a greater potential for violent reactions. Contact Laboratory Safety if you have any questions concerning chemical storage.

Acids

- Make sure that all acids are stored by compatibility (ex. separate inorganics from organics).
- Store concentrated acids on lower shelves in chemical-resistant trays or in a corrosives cabinet. This will temporarily contain spills or leaks and protect shelving from residue.
- Separate acids from incompatible materials such as bases, active metals (ex. sodium, magnesium, potassium) and from chemicals which can generate toxic gases when combined (ex. sodium cyanide and iron sulfide).

Bases

- Store bases away from acids.
- Store concentrated bases on lower shelves in chemical-resistant trays or in a corrosives cabinet. This will temporarily contain spills or leaks and protect shelving from residue.

Flammables

- Approved flammable storage cabinets should be used for flammable liquid storage.
- You may store 20 gallons of flammable liquids per 100 sq.ft. in a properly fire separated lab. The maximum allowable quantity for flammable liquid storage in any size lab is not to exceed 120 gallons.
- You may store up to 10 gallons of flammable liquids outside of approved flammable storage cabinets.
- An additional 25 gallons may be stored outside of an approved storage cabinet if it is stored in approved safety cans not to exceed 2 gallons in size.
- Use only explosion-proof or intrinsically safe refrigerators and freezers for storing flammable liquids.

Peroxide-Forming Chemicals

- Peroxide-forming chemicals should be stored in airtight containers in a dark, cool, and dry place.
- Unstable chemicals such as peroxide-formers must always be labeled with date received, date opened, and disposal/expiration date.
- Peroxide-forming chemicals should be properly disposed of before the date of expected peroxide formation (typically 6-12 months after opening).
- Suspicion of peroxide contamination should be immediately investigated. Contact Laboratory Safety for procedures.

Water-Reactive Chemicals

- Water-reactive chemicals should be stored in a cool, dry place.
- Do not store water-reactive chemicals under sinks or near water baths.
- Class D fire extinguishers for the specific water-reactive chemical being stored should be made available.

Oxidizers

- Make sure that all oxidizers are stored by compatibility.
- Store oxidizers away from flammables, combustibles, and reducing agents.

Toxins

- Toxic compounds should be stored according to the nature of the chemical, with appropriate security employed when necessary.
- A "Poison Control Network" telephone number should be posted in the laboratory where toxins are stored. Color-coded labeling systems that may be found in your lab are shown below:

Hazard	Color Code
Flammables	Red
Health Hazards/Toxins	Blue
Reactives/Oxidizers	
Contact Hazards	White
General Storage	Gray, Green, Orange

Please Note: Chemicals with labels that are colored and striped may react with other chemicals in the same hazard class. See MSDS for more information. Chemical containers which are not color-coded should have hazard information on the label. Read the label carefully and store accordingly.

Disposal of chemical waste

Schools are regulated by the Environmental Protection Agency, as well as state and local agencies, when it comes to disposing of chemical waste. Check with your state science supervisor, local college or university environmental health and safety specialists, and the Laboratory Safety Workshop for advice on the disposal of chemical waste. The American Chemical Society publishes an excellent guidebook, *Laboratory Waste Management, A Guidebook* (1994).

The following are basic guidelines for disposing of chemical waste.

You may dispose of hazardous waste as outlined below. It is the responsibility of the generator to ensure hazardous waste does not end up in ground water, soil, or the atmosphere through improper disposal.

1. **Sanitary Sewer** - Some chemicals (acids or bases) may be neutralized and disposed to the sanitary sewer. This disposal option must be approved by the local waste water treatment authority prior to disposal. This may not be an option for some small communities that do not have sufficient treatment capacity at the waste water treatment plant for these types of wastes. Hazardous waste may NOT be disposed of in this manner. This includes heavy metals.

2. **Household Hazardous Waste Facility** - Waste chemicals may be disposed through a county household hazardous waste facility (HHW) or through a county contracted household hazardous waste disposal company. Not all counties have a program to accept waste from schools. Verify with your county HHW facility that they can handle your waste prior to making arrangements.

3. **Disposal Through a Contractor** - A contractor may be used for disposal of waste chemicals. Remember that you must keep documentation of your hazardous waste disposal for at least three years. This information must include a waste manifest, reclamation agreement or any written record which describes the waste and how much was disposed, where it was disposed and when it was disposed. Waste analysis records must also be kept when it is necessary to make a determination of whether waste is hazardous. **Any unknown chemicals should be considered hazardous!**

Competency 7.0   Understand the concept of matter, and analyze chemical and physical properties of and changes in matter

Identify characteristics and kinetic models of solids, liquids, and gases.

Molecules have **kinetic energy** (they move around), and they also have **intermolecular attractive forces** (they are attracted to each other). The relationship between these two determines whether a collection of molecules will be a gas, liquid, or solid.

A **gas** has an indefinite shape and an indefinite volume. The kinetic model for a gas is a collection of widely separated molecules, each moving in a random and free fashion, with negligible attractive or repulsive forces between them. Gases will expand to occupy a larger container so there is more space between the molecules. Gases can also be compressed to fit into a small container so the molecules are less separated.

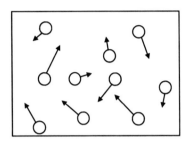

Diffusion occurs when one material spreads into or through another. Gases diffuse rapidly and move from one place to another.

A **liquid** assumes the shape of any container that it occupies and has a specific volume. The kinetic model for a liquid is a collection of molecules attracted to each other with sufficient strength to keep them close to each other but with insufficient strength to prevent them from moving around randomly. Liquids have a higher density and are much less compressible than gases because the molecules in a liquid are closer

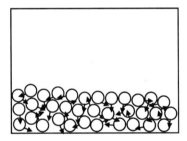

together. Diffusion occurs more slowly in liquids than in gases because the molecules in a liquid stick to each other and are not completely free to move.

A **solid** has a definite volume and definite shape; therefore, it is not dependent upon its container for its shape or volume. The kinetic model for a solid is a collection of molecules attracted to each other with sufficient strength to essentially lock them in place. Each molecule may vibrate, but it has an average position relative to its neighbors. If these positions form an ordered pattern, the solid is called **crystalline**. Otherwise, it is called **amorphous**. Solids have a high

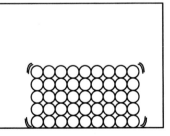

density and are almost incompressible because the molecules are very close together. Diffusion occurs extremely slowly because the molecules almost never alter their position.

Apply the kinetic molecular theory.

In a solid, the energy of intermolecular attractive forces (such as ionic or covalent bonds) is much stronger than the kinetic energy of the molecules. As temperature increases in a solid, the vibrations of individual molecules grow more intense and the molecules spread slightly further apart, decreasing the density of the solid. (See the next skill for a full discussion of solids.)

In a liquid, the energy of intermolecular attractive forces (such as dipole-dipole and London dispersion forces) is about as strong as the kinetic energy of the molecules. Therefore, both play a role in the properties of liquids. Liquids will be discussed in detail later.

In a gas, the energy of intermolecular forces is much weaker than the kinetic energy of the molecules. Kinetic molecular theory is usually applied to gases.

Gas pressure results from molecular collisions with container walls. The **number of molecules** striking an **area** on the walls and the **average kinetic energy** per molecule are the only factors that contribute to pressure. A higher **temperature** increases speed and kinetic energy. There are more collisions at higher temperatures, but the average
distance between molecules does not change, and thus density does not change in a sealed container.

Kinetic molecular theory makes the following assumptions to explain why the pressure and temperature of gases behave the way they do:

1) The energies of intermolecular attractive and repulsive forces may be neglected.
2) The average kinetic energy of the molecules is proportional to the absolute temperature.
3) Energy can be transferred between molecules during collisions and the collisions are elastic, so the average kinetic energy of the molecules doesn't change due to collisions.
4) The volume of all molecules in a gas is negligible compared to the total volume of the container.

Strictly speaking, molecules also contain some kinetic energy associated with rotation or other motions. The movement of a molecule from one place to another is called **translation**. Translational kinetic energy is the form that is transferred by collisions, and kinetic molecular theory ignores other forms of kinetic energy because they are relatively small and not proportional to temperature.

The following table summarizes the application of kinetic molecular theory to an increase in container volume, number of molecules, and temperature:

Effect of an **increase** in one variable while holding other two constant	Effect: − = decrease, 0 = no change, + = increase						
	Average distance between molecules	Density in a sealed container	Average speed of molecules	Average translational kinetic energy of molecules	Collisions with container walls per second	Collisions per unit area of wall per second	Pressure (P)
Volume of container (V)	+	−	0	0	−	−	−
Number of molecules	−	+	0	0	+	+	+
Temperature (T)	0	0	+	+	+	+	+

Additional details on the kinetic molecular theory may be found at http://hyperphysics.phy-astr.gsu.edu/hbase/kinetic/ktcon.html. An animation of gas particles colliding is located at http://comp.uark.edu/~jgeabana/mol_dyn/.

Identify the forces between units in a solid.

The type of attractive forces within solids depends on the identity of the unit particle and the chemical bonds it can form. The forces between atoms in a covalent network solid (such as carbon in diamond) are **covalent bonds**. These bonds result when at least one pair of electrons is shared by two atoms. The forces between atoms within metallic elements (such as iron) are **metallic bonds**. Electrostatic attractions—also called **ionic bonds**—are the forces between ions, atoms which have lost one or more electrons to become positively charged ions or which have gained one or more electrons to become negatively charged ions (such as those found in NaCl). Ionic compounds are often known as salts. Covalent, metallic, and ionic bonds are strong chemical bonds.

The intermolecular forces between polar molecules are known as **dipole-dipole interactions**. The partial positive charge of one molecule is attracted to the partial negative charge of its neighbor. Polar molecules (such as CH_3Cl) form molecular solids with dipole-dipole bonds between units. Polar molecules with H on one molecule attracted to O, N, or F on an adjacent molecule (like H_2O) form relatively strong dipole-dipole bonds known as **hydrogen bonds** between molecules.

[handwritten note:] Covalent, metallic and ionic bonds are strong chemical bonds.

[handwritten note:] Covalent bond: one pair of e⁻ is shared by two atoms.

[handwritten note:] metallic bond: forces between atoms within metallic elements

[handwritten note:] ionic bonds: electrostatic attractions are the forces between ions, atoms which have lost one or more e⁻ to become positively charged ions or which have gained one or more e⁻ to become negatively charged ions. Ions

[handwritten note:] ∗ Ionic cmpds are salts.

When a nonpolar molecule (or a noble gas atom) encounters an ion, its electron density is temporarily distorted resulting in an **induced dipole** that will be attracted to the ion. Intermolecular attractions due to induced dipoles in a nonpolar molecule are known as **London forces** or **Van der Waals interactions**. London dispersion forces are the only attractions between the units of non-polar molecules (like saturated hydrocarbons and N_2) and the noble gases when they form solids at low temperatures. London dispersion forces are the weakest intermolecular attractions, but these attractions grow stronger for larger molecules because a larger electron cloud is more easily polarized. The strength of London dispersion forces also **increases for molecules with a larger surface area** because there is greater opportunity for electrons to influence neighboring molecules if there is more potential contact between the molecules. Paraffin in candles is an example of a solid held together by weak London forces between large molecules. These materials are soft.

Analyze how the forces between chemical species affect the properties of substances.

The impact of intermolecular forces on substances is best understood by imagining ourselves shrinking down to the size of molecules and picturing what happens when we stick more strongly to molecules nearby. It will take more energy (higher temperatures) to pull us away from our neighbors.

If two substances are being compared, the material with the **greater intermolecular attractive forces** (i.e. the stronger intermolecular bond) will require more energy to pull apart the molecules. Substances with greater intermolecular forces will have the following properties:

For solids:
Higher melting point
Higher enthalpy of fusion
Greater hardness
Lower vapor pressure

For liquids (see **0025**):
Higher boiling point
Higher critical temperature
Higher critical pressure
Higher enthalpy of vaporization
Higher viscosity
Higher surface tension
Lower vapor pressure

Compare the final three properties for liquids to the table for liquids in **0025**. Intermolecular attractive forces have the opposite effect from temperature.

For gases:
Intermolecular attractive forces are neglected for ideal gases, as they seldom have observable effects.

For example, H_2O and NH_3 are liquids at room temperature because they contain hydrogen bonds. These bonds are of intermediate strength, so the melting point of these compounds is lower than room temperature and their boiling point is higher than room temperature. H_2S contains weaker dipole-dipole interactions than H_2O because the sulfur atoms do not form hydrogen bonds. Therefore, H_2S is a gas at room temperature due to its low boiling point. Small non-polar molecules such as CO_2, N_2, or atoms such as He are gases at room temperature due to very weak London forces, but larger non-polar molecules such as octane or CCl_4 may be liquids, and very large non-polar molecules such as paraffin will be soft solids.

In **0009**, we will learn about trends along the periodic table for the same type of chemical bond. In **0015**, we will learn about which chemicals have which bonds and about the relative strengths of those different types of bonds.

Competency 8.0   Understand the various models of atomic structure, the principles of quantum theory, and the properties and interactions of subatomic particles

Identify and sequence contributions made by Dalton, Thomson, Planck, Rutherford, Bohr, de Broglie, Heisenberg, and Schrödinger to the development of atomic theory.

Dalton

The ideas that pure materials called elements existed and that these elements were composed of fundamentally indivisible units called atoms were proposed by ancient philosophers even though they had little evidence. Modern atomic theory is credited to the work of **John Dalton** published in 1803-1807. Observations made by him and others about the composition, properties, and reactions of many compounds led him to develop the following postulates:

1) Each element is composed of small particles called atoms.
2) All atoms of a given element are identical in mass and other properties.
3) Atoms of different elements have different masses and differ in other properties.
4) Atoms of an element are not created, destroyed, or changed into a different type of atom by chemical reactions.
5) Compounds form when atoms of more than one element combine.
6) In a given compound, the relative numbers and kinds of atoms are constant.

Dalton's table of atomic symbols and masses

Dalton determined and published the known relative masses of a number of different atoms. He also formulated the law of partial pressures. Dalton's work focused on the ability of atoms to arrange themselves into molecules and to rearrange themselves via chemical reactions, but he did not investigate the composition of atoms themselves. **Dalton's model of the atom** was a tiny, indivisible, indestructible **particle** of a certain mass, size, and chemical behavior, but Dalton did not deny the possibility that atoms might have a substructure.

Thomson

Joseph John Thomson, often known as **J. J. Thomson**, was the first to examine this substructure. In the mid-1800s, scientists had studied a form of radiation called "cathode rays" or "electrons" that originated from the negative electrode (cathode) when electrical current was forced through an evacuated tube. Thomson determined in 1897 that **electrons have mass**, and because many different cathode materials release electrons, Thomson proposed that the **electron is a subatomic particle**.
Thomson's model of the atom was a uniformly positive particle with electrons contained in the interior. This has been called the "plum-pudding" model of the atom where the pudding represents the uniform sphere of positive electricity and the bits of plum represent electrons. For more on Thomson, see http://www.aip.org/history/electron/jjhome.htm.

Planck

Max Planck determined in 1900 that **energy is transferred by radiation in exact multiples of a discrete unit of energy called a quantum**. Quanta of energy are extremely small, and may be found from the frequency of the radiation, v, using the equation:

$$\Delta E = hv$$

where h is Planck's constant and hv is a quantum of energy.

Rutherford

Ernest Rutherford studied atomic structure in 1910-1911 by firing a beam of alpha particles (see **0011**) at thin layers of gold leaf. According to Thomson's model, the path of an alpha particle should be deflected only slightly if it struck an atom, but Rutherford observed some alpha particles bouncing almost backwards, suggesting that **nearly all the mass of an atom is contained in a small positively charged nucleus**.
Rutherford's model of the atom was an analogy to the sun and the planets. A small positively charged nucleus is surrounded by circling negatively charged electrons and empty space. Rutherford's experiment is explained in greater detail in this flash animation:
http://www.mhhe.com/physsci/chemistry/essentialchemistry/flash/ruther14.swf.

Bohr

Niels Bohr incorporated Planck's quantum concept into Rutherford's model of the atom in 1913 to explain the **discrete frequencies of radiation emitted and absorbed by atoms with one electron** (H, He^+, and Li^{2+}). This electron is attracted to the positive nucleus and is closest to the nucleus at the **ground state** of the atom. When the electron absorbs energy, it moves into an

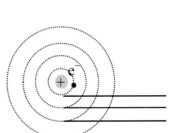

orbit further from the nucleus and the atom is said to be in an electronically **excited state**. If sufficient energy is absorbed, the electron separates from the nucleus entirely, and the atom is ionized:

$$H \rightarrow H^+ + e^-$$

The energy required for ionization from the ground state is called the atom's **ionization energy**. The discrete frequencies of radiation emitted and absorbed by the atom correspond (using Planck's constant) to discrete energies and in turn to discrete distances from the nucleus. **Bohr's model of the atom** was a small positively charged nucleus surrounded mostly by empty space and by electrons orbiting at certain discrete distances ("shells") corresponding to discrete energy levels.

Animations utilizing the Bohr model may be found at the following two URLs: http://artsci–ccwin.concordia.ca/facstaff/a–c/bird/c241/D1.html and http://www.mhhe.com/physsci/chemistry/essentialchemistry/flash/linesp16.swf

De Broglie

Depending on the experiment, radiation appears to have wave-like or particle-like traits. In 1923-1924, **Louis de Broglie** applied this **wave/particle duality to all matter with momentum**. The discrete distances from the nucleus described by Bohr corresponded to permissible distances where standing waves could exist. **De Broglie's model of the atom** described electrons as **matter waves in standing wave orbits** around the nucleus. The first three standing waves corresponding to the first three discrete distances are shown. De Broglie's model may be found here: http://artsci-ccwin.concordia.ca/facstaff/a-c/bird/c241/D1-part2.html.

Heisenberg

The realization that both matter and radiation interact as waves led **Werner Heisenberg** to the conclusion in 1927 that the act of observation and measurement requires the interaction of one wave with another. This interaction results in an **inherent uncertainty** in the location and momentum of the observed particles. This inherent limitation in the ability to measure phenomena at the subatomic level is known as the **Heisenberg uncertainty principle**, and it applies to the location and momentum of electrons in an atom. A discussion of the principle and Heisenberg's other contributions to quantum theory is located here: http://www.aip.org/history/heisenberg/.

Schrödinger

When Erwin Schrödinger studied the atom in 1925, he replaced the idea of precise orbits with regions in space called **orbitals** where electrons were likely to be found. **The Schrödinger equation** describes the **probability** that an electron will be in a given region of space, a quantity known as **electron density** or ψ^{22}. The diagrams below are surfaces of constant ψ^{22} found by solving the Schrödinger equation for the hydrogen atom $1s$, $2p_z$ and $3d_0$ orbitals (see **0009**). Additional representations of solutions may be found here: http://library.wolfram.com/webMathematica/Physics/Hydrogen.jsp.

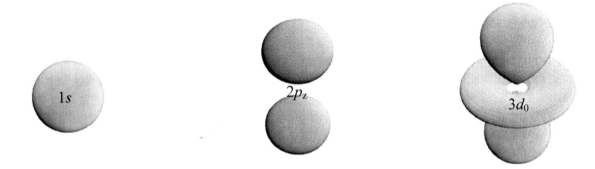

Schrödinger's model of the atom is a mathematical formulation of quantum mechanics that describes the electron density of orbitals. It is the atomic model that has been in use from shortly after it was introduced up to the present.

Pauli

Wolfgang Pauli helped develop quantum mechanics in the 1920s by developing the concept of spin and the **Pauli exclusion principle**, which states that if two electrons occupy the same orbital, they must have different spin (intrinsic angular momentum). This principle has been generalized to other quantum particles.

Hund

Friedrich Hund determined a set of **rules to determine the ground state** of a multi-electron atom in the 1920s. One of these rules is called **Hund's Rule** in introductory chemistry courses, and describes the order in which electrons fill orbitals and their spin.

Competency 9.0   Understand the organization of the periodic table

Interrelate the concepts of atomic number, mass number, and atomic mass

The first periodic table was developed in 1869 by Dmitri **Mendeleev** several decades before the nature of electron energy states in the atom was known. Mendeleev arranged the elements in order of increasing atomic mass into **columns of similar physical and chemical properties**. He then boldly **predicted the existence and the properties of undiscovered elements** to fill the gaps in his table. These interpolations were initially treated with skepticism until three of Mendeleev's theoretical elements were discovered and were found to have the properties he predicted. It is the correlation with properties—not with electron arrangements—that have placed the periodic table at the beginning of most chemistry texts.

In the modern periodic table, **the elements in a column are known as a group,** and groups are numbered from 1 to 18. Older numbering styles used Roman numerals and letters. These elements, known as a family, have similar properties due to their similar outermost electron arrangements. Each family or column as a group name. **A row of the periodic table is known as a period**, and periods of the known elements are numbered from 1 to 7. The lanthanoids are all in period 6, and the actinoids are all in period 7.

atomic # = #p+#e
atomic mass = #p+#n

atomic mass - atomic # = #n

As discussed in **0011**, the **atomic number** of an atom is the **number of protons** in the nucleus. This is the defining characteristic of an element, so, for example, all carbon has an atomic number of 6. Atomic numbers for each element may be found from the periodic table. The **mass number** of an atom is the total number of nucleons it contains. This is the **sum of the number of protons and neutrons** in the nucleus.

The number of neutrons may be found by subtracting the atomic number from the mass number. For example, uranium-235 has 235 − 92 = 143 neutrons because it has 235 nucleons and 92 protons.

As discussed in **0022**, atomic mass is a mass relative to carbon-12, and ^{12}C has an assigned value of exactly 12 u. This means that **the mass number of an atom is usually a good guess at the atom's atomic mass**, and for ^{12}C it is an exact value and not a guess at all. For example, uranium-238 has an atomic mass of 238.05 u.

But if ^{12}C is exactly 12 u, why does carbon have an atomic mass of 12.011 u in the periodic table? This is because 1.1% of carbon on Earth exists as the stable isotope carbon-13. This carbon that is heavier by 1 u and constitutes 1.1% of all carbon contributes the additional 0.011 g to the expected mass of a mole of carbon atoms that we'd find anywhere on this planet. In general, the **atomic mass** of an element is the average of the atomic masses of all stable isotopes of that element weighted by their abundance on Earth.

Atomic mass of element X = (Fraction of X as isotope A) (Atomic mass of isotope A) +

(Fraction of X as isotope B) (Atomic mass of isotope B) +

(Fraction of X as isotope C) (Atomic mass of isotope C) +

$$\vdots$$

Chlorine, for example, exists on Earth in two stable isotopes: ^{35}Cl and ^{37}Cl. 75.76% of the chlorine is ^{35}Cl which has an atomic mass of 34.969 u and 24.24% is ^{37}Cl which has an atomic mass of 36.966 u. Therefore,

Atomic mass of chlorine $= 0.7576 \times 34.969 \text{ u} + 0.2424 \times 36.966 \text{ u} = 35.453 \text{ u}$.

Elements with no stable isotopes are often listed in tables of atomic masses with a number in brackets. This value is the mass number of the isotope with the longest half-life. A list of isotopic compositions and atomic masses for all natural isotopes is at http://physics.nist.gov/cgi-bin/Compositions/stand_alone.pl.

Use quantum mechanics to identify electron arrangements and describe electron energy states.

Quantum numbers
The quantum-mechanical solutions from the Schrödinger Equation (see **0008**) utilize three quantum numbers (n, l, and m_l) to describe an orbital and a fourth (m_s) to describe an electron in an orbital. This model is useful for understanding the frequencies of radiation emitted and absorbed by atoms and chemical properties of atoms.

The **principal quantum number n** may have positive integer values (1, 2, 3, ...). n is a measure of the **distance** of an orbital from the nucleus, and orbitals with the same value of n are said to be in the same **shell**. This is analogous to the Bohr model of the atom (see **0008**). Each shell may contain up to $2n^2$ electrons. The highest quantum number n that any shell of an element has is the same as the number of the row of the periodic table in which the element is found.

The **azimuthal quantum number** *l* may have integer values from 0 to n-1. *l* describes the angular momentum of an orbital. This determines the orbital's **shape**. Orbitals with the same value of *n* and *l* are in the same **subshell**, and each subshell may contain up to $4l + 2$ electrons. Subshells are usually referred to by the principle quantum number followed by a letter corresponding to *l* as shown in the following table:

Azimuthal quantum number *l*	0	1	2	3	4
Subshell designation	*s*	*p*	*d*	*f*	*g*

Therefore, *s* subshells may have $4 \times 0 + 2 = 2$ electrons, and *p* subshells may have $4 \times 1 + 2 = 6$ electrons. Helium is in the first row of the periodic table, and has only a single *s* subshell with two electrons. This subshell would be notated as 1*s*.

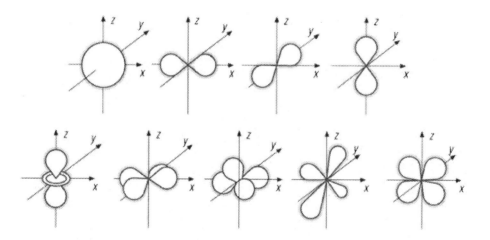

The **magnetic quantum number** m_l **or** *m* may have integer values from –*l* to *l*. m_l is a measure of how an individual orbital responds to an external magnetic field, and it often describes an orbital's orientation. In any given shell, there is only one *s* orbital with an *m* value of 0. If *p* orbitals are present in a shell there will always be 3 *p* orbitals with values of -1, 0, and 1 (usually referred to as x, y, and z to denote 3-dimensional orientation). A subscript—either the value of m_l or a function of the x-, y-, and z-axes—is used to designate a specific orbital within a subshell. (See **0008** for images of electron density regions for a few orbitals of hydrogen.) For example, $n = 3$, $l = 2$, and $m_l = 0$ would be shown as the $3d_0$ orbital. Each orbital may hold up to two electrons.

The **spin quantum number m_s or s** has one of two possible values: $-1/2$ or $+1/2$. m_s differentiates between the two possible electrons occupying an orbital. Electrons moving through a magnet behave as if they were tiny magnets themselves spinning on their axes in either a clockwise or counterclockwise direction. These two spins may be described as $m_s = -1/2$ and $+1/2$ or as down and up.

✳ The **Pauli exclusion principle** states that **no two electrons in an atom may have the same set of four quantum numbers**.

The following table summarizes the relationship among n, l, and m_l through $n=3$:

$-4l+2 = \# \max e^-$ $4l+2$

n	l	Subshell	m_l	Orbitals in subshell	Maximum number of electrons in subshell
1	0	1s	0	1	2
2	0	2s	0	1	2
	1	2p	$-1, 0, 1$	3	6
3	0	3s	0	1	2
	1	3p	$-1, 0, 1$	3	6
	2	3d	$-2, -1, 0, 1, 2$	5	10

Subshell energy levels
In single-electron atoms (H, He$^+$, and Li^{2+}) above the ground state, subshells within a shell are all at the same energy level, and an orbital's energy level is only determined by n. However, in all other atoms, multiple electrons repel each other. Electrons in orbitals closer to the nucleus create a screening or **shielding effect** on electrons further away from the nucleus, preventing them from receiving the full attractive force of the nucleus. **In multi-electron atoms, both n and l determine the energy level of an orbital**. In the absence of a magnetic field, **orbitals in the same subshell with different m_l all have the same energy** and are said to be **degenerate orbitals**.

The following list orders subshells by increasing energy level:
$1s < 2s < 2p < 3s < 3p < 4s < 3d < 4p < 5s < 4d < 5p < 6s < 4f < 5d < 6p < 7s < 5f < \ldots$

This list may be constructed by arranging the subshells according to n and l and drawing diagonal arrows as shown below:

1s

2s   2p

3s   3p   3d

4s   4p   4d   4f

5s   5p   5d   5f   5g

6s   6p   6d   6f   6g

7s   7p   7d   7f   7g

8s   8p   8d   8f   8g

Drawing electron arrangements

Electron arrangements (also called electron shell structures) in an atom may be represented using three methods: an **electron configuration**, an **orbital diagram**, or an **energy level diagram**. All three methods require knowledge of the subshells occupied by electrons in a certain atom. The **Aufbau principle** or **building-up rule** states that **electrons at ground state fill orbitals starting at the lowest available energy levels**.

An **electron configuration** is a **list of subshells** with superscripts representing the **number of electrons** in each subshell. For example, an atom of boron has 5 electrons. According to the Aufbau principle, two will fill the 1s subshell, two will fill the higher energy 2s subshell, and one will occupy the 2p subshell which has an even higher energy. The electron configuration of boron is $1s^2 2s^2 2p^1$. Similarly, the electron configuration of a vanadium atom with 23 electrons is:

$$1s^2 2s^2 2p^6 3s^2 3p^6 4s^2 3d^3.$$

Configurations are also written with their principle quantum numbers together:

$$1s^2 2s^2 2p^6 3s^2 3p^6 3d^3 4s^2.$$

Electron configurations are often written to emphasize the outermost electrons. This is done by writing the symbol in brackets for the element with a full p subshell from the previous shell and adding the **outer electron configuration** onto that configuration. The element with the last full p subshell will always be a noble gas from the right-most column of the periodic table (see **0009**). For the vanadium example, the element with the last full p subshell has the configuration $1s^2 2s^2 2p^6 3s^2 3p^6$. This is $_{18}Ar$. The configuration of vanadium may then be written as $[Ar]4s^2 3d^3$ where $4s^2 3d^3$ is the outer electron configuration.

Electron arrangements may also be written by noting the number of electrons in each shell. For vanadium, this would be:

2, 8, 11, 2.

Orbital diagrams assign electrons to individual orbitals so the energy state of individual electrons may be found. This requires knowledge of how electrons occupy orbitals within a subshell. **Hund's rule** states that **before any two electrons occupy the same orbital, other orbitals in that subshell must first contain one electron each with parallel spins**. Electrons with up and down spins are shown by half-arrows, and these are placed in lines of orbitals (represented as boxes or dashes) according to Hund's rule, the Aufbau principle, and the Pauli exclusion principle. Below is the orbital diagram for vanadium:

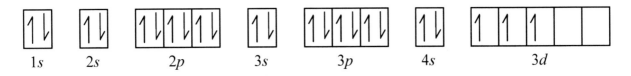

An **energy level diagram** is an orbital diagram that shows subshells with higher energy levels higher up on the page. The energy level diagram of vanadium is:

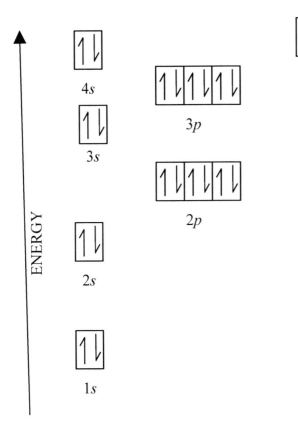

Valence shell electron arrangements and the periodic table

Electrons in the **outermost shell** are called **valence shell electrons**. For example, the electron configuration of Se is $[Ar]4s^23d^{10}4p^4$, and its valence shell electron configuration is $4s^24p^4$.

The **periodic table** may be used to write down the electron configuration of any element. The table may be divided up into **blocks corresponding to the subshell** designation of the most recent orbital to be filled by the building-up rule. Elements in the s- and p-blocks are known as **main-group elements**. The d-block elements are called **transition metals**. The f-block elements are called **inner transition metals**.

The maximum number of electrons in each subshell (2, 6, 10, or 14) determines the number of elements in each block, and the order of energy levels for subshells creates the pattern of blocks. These blocks also usually correspond to the value of l for the **outermost electron** of the atom. This has important consequences for the physical and chemical properties of the elements as shown in **0009**. The outermost shell or valence shell principle quantum number (for example, 4 for Se) is also the period number for the element in the table.

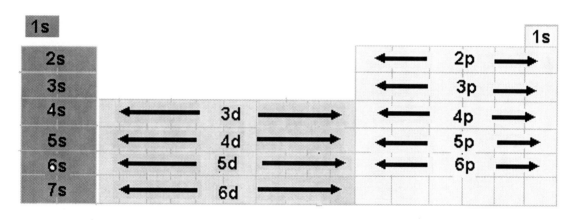

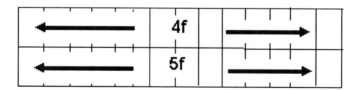

Atoms in the d- and f-blocks often have unexpected electron arrangements that cannot be explained using simple rules. Some heavy atoms have unknown electron configurations because the number of different frequencies of radiation emitted and absorbed by these atoms is very large.

http://www.cowtownproductions.com/cowtown/genchem/08_07T1.htm contains a brief tutorial on energy level diagrams.
http://www.colorado.edu/physics/2000/applets/a2.html contains (among other things) energy level diagrams and animations of electron shells and nuclei.
http://intro.chem.okstate.edu/WorkshopFolder/Electronconfnew.html animates the building up of energy level diagrams.

Apply periodic trends to physical properties of elements and compounds.

Metals, nonmetals, and atomic radius
Elements in the periodic table are divided into the two broad categories of **metals** and **nonmetals** with a jagged line separating the two as shown in the figure.

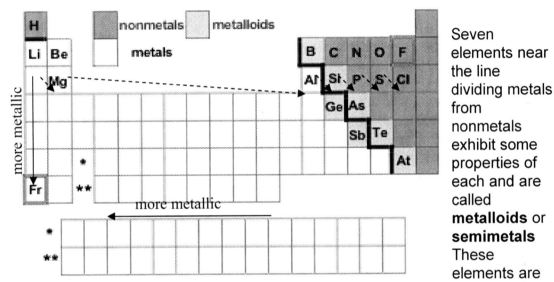

Seven elements near the line dividing metals from nonmetals exhibit some properties of each and are called **metalloids** or **semimetals** These elements are boron, silicon, germanium, arsenic, antimony, tellurium and astatine.

The **most metallic** element is **francium** at the bottom left of the table. The most **nonmetallic element** is **fluorine**. The metallic character of elements within a group increases with period number. This means that **within a column, the more metallic elements are at the bottom**. The metallic character of elements within a period decreases with group number. This means that **within a row, the more metallic elements are on the left**.

Among the main group atoms, **elements diagonal to each other** as indicated by the dashed arrows **have similar properties** because they have a similar metallic character. The noble gases are nonmetals, but they are an exception to the diagonal rule.

Physical properties relating to metallic character are summarized in the following table:

Element	Electrical/thermal conductivity	Malleable/ ductile as solids?	Lustrous ?	Melting point of oxides, hydrides, and halides
Metals	High	Yes	Yes	High
Metalloids	Intermediate. Altered by dopants (semiconductors)	No (brittle)	Varies	Varies (oxides). Low (hydrides, halides)
Nonmetals	Low (insulators)	No	No	Low

A summary of additional properties is provided in the final figure of **0009**.

Malleable materials can **be hammered into sheets**. **Ductile** materials can **be pulled into wires**. **Lustrous** materials **have a shine**. Oxides, hydrides, and halides are compounds with O, H, and halogens respectively. Measures of intermolecular attractions other than melting point (see **0007**) are also higher for metal oxides, hydrides, and halides than for the nonmetal compounds. A dopant is a small quantity of an intentionally added impurity. The controlled movement of electrons in doped silicon semiconductors carries digital information in computer circuitry.

The **size of an atom** is not an exact radius due to of the probabilistic nature of electron density (see **0008**), but we may compare radii among different atoms using a standard. As seen below, the sizes of neutral atoms **increase with period number** and **decrease with group number**. This trend is similar to the trend described above for metallic character. The smallest atom is helium.

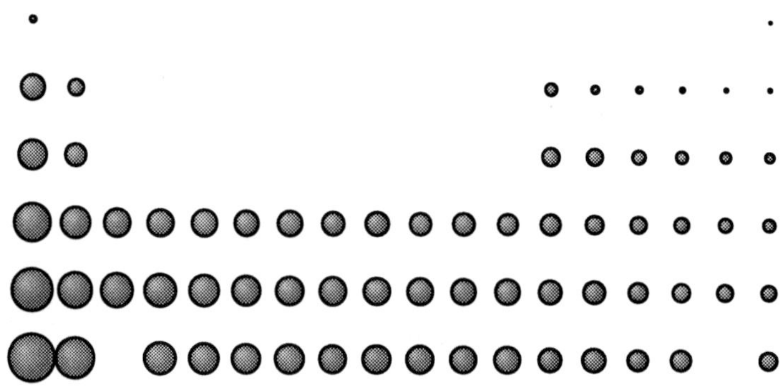

Group names, melting point, density, and properties of compounds

Groups 1, 2, 17, and 18 are often identified with a **group name**. These names are shown in the diagram below. Seven elements are found in nature only as **diatomic molecules: (H_2, N_2, O_2, and the halogens: F_2, Cl_2, Br_2, and I_2)**. Mnemonic devices to remember the diatomic elements are: "$Br_2I_2N_2Cl_2H_2O_2F_2$" (pronounced "Brinklehof") or "**Have No Fear Of Ice Cold Beer**" Another way to remember them is by using the Rule of Sevens: 7 of them which form a 7 on the Periodic Table and 4 of the 7 are from Group 7. These molecules are attracted to one another using **weak London dispersion forces**.

Note that **hydrogen** is <u>not</u> an alkali metal. Hydrogen is a colorless gas and is the most abundant element in the universe, but H_2 is very rare in the atmosphere because it is light enough to escape gravity and reach outer space. Hydrogen atoms combine with atoms of other elements to form more compounds than atoms of any other element.

Alkali metals are shiny, soft, metallic solids. They have **low melting points and low densities** compared with other metals (see squares in figures on the following page) because they have a weaker metallic bond. Measures of intermolecular attractions including their **melting points decrease going down the periodic table due to weaker metallic bonds** as the atomic radii increase. See **0014** for a discussion of metallic bonding. Common salts with an alkali metal cation are always soluble (see **0025**).

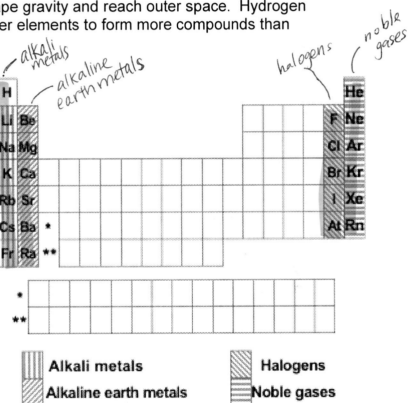

Alkaline earth metals (group 2 elements) are grey, metallic solids. They are harder, denser, and have a higher melting point than the alkali metals (see asterisks in figures on the following page), but values for these properties are still low compared to most of the transition metals. Measures of metallic bond strength such as melting points for alkaline earths do not follow a simple trend down the periodic table.

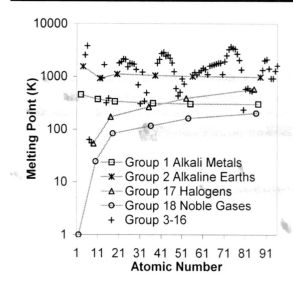

Halogens (group 17 elements) have an irritating odor. Unlike the metallic bonds between alkali metals, **London forces between halogen molecules increase in strength further down the periodic table**, increasing their melting points as shown by the triangles to the left. London forces make Br_2 a liquid and I_2 a solid at 25 °C. The lighter halogens are gases.

Noble gases (group 18 elements) have no color or odor and exist as **individual gas atoms** that experience London forces. These attractions also increase with period number as shown by the circles in the figure.

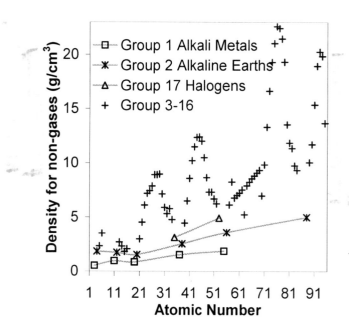

The known **densities** of liquid and solid elements at room temperature are shown to the left. **Intermolecular forces contribute to density** by bringing nuclei closer to each other, so the periodicity is similar to trends for melting point. These group-to-group differences are superimposed on a general trend in which **densities increase with period number** because heavier nuclei make the material denser. See **0007** for other properties altered by intermolecular forces.

Trends among properties of **compounds** may often be deduced from **trends among their atoms**, but caution must be used. For example, the densities of three potassium halides are 2.0 g/cm^3 for KCl, 2.7 g/cm^3 for KBr, and 3.1 g/cm^3 for KI.

We would expect this trend for increasing atomic mass within a group. We might also expect the density of KF to be less than 2.0 g/cm^3, but it is actually 2.5 g/cm^3 due to a change in crystal lattice structure.

Physics of electrons and stability of electron configurations

For an isolated atom, the **most stable system of valence electrons is a filled set of orbitals** (see **0009**). For the main group elements, this corresponds to group 18 (ns^2np^6 and $1s^2$ for helium), and, to a lesser extent, group 2 (ns^2).

The next most stable state is a set of degenerate half-filled orbitals. These occur in group 15 (ns^2np^3). The least stable valence electron configuration is a single electron with no other electrons in similar orbitals. This occurs in group 1 (ns^1) and to a lesser extent in group 13 (ns^2np^1).

An atom's first **ionization energy** is the **energy required to remove one electron** by the reaction $M(g) \rightarrow M^+(g) + e^-$. Periodicity is in the opposite direction from the trend for atomic radius. The most metallic atoms have electrons further from the nucleus, and these are easier to remove. Factors that affect ionization energy are:

    a. Nuclear charge – the larger the nuclear charge, the greater the IE
    b. Shielding effect – the greater the shielding effect, the less the IE
    c. Radius – the greater the distance between the nucleus and the outer electrons of an atom, the less the IE
    d. Sublevel – an electron from a sublevel that is more than half-full requires additional energy to be removed

An atom's **electron affinity** is the **energy released** when one **electron is added** by the reaction $M(g) + e^- \rightarrow M^-(g)$. A large negative number for the exothermic reaction indicates a high electron affinity. Halogens have the highest electron affinities.

Trends in **ionization energy and electron affinity** within a period reflect the **stability of valence electron configurations**. A stable system requires more energy to change and releases less when changed. Note the peaks in stability for groups 2, 13, and 16 to the right.

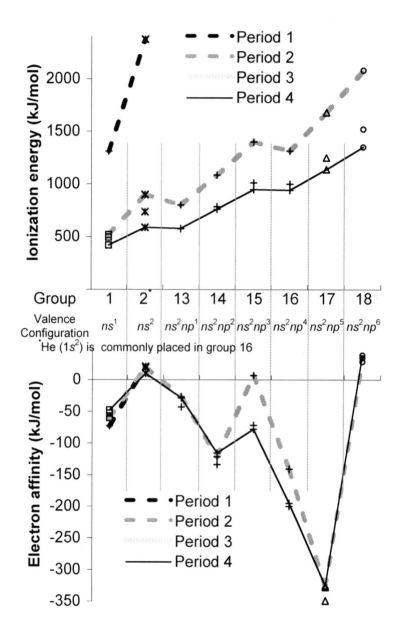

Apply periodic trends to chemical reactivities of elements and compounds.

Much of chemistry consists of atoms **bonding** to achieve stable valence electron configurations. **Nonmetals gain electrons or share electrons** to achieve these configurations and **metals lose electrons** to achieve them.

Qualitative group trends

When cut by a knife, the exposed surface of an **alkali metal or alkaline earth metal** quickly turns into an oxide. These elements **do not occur in nature as free metals**. Instead, they react with many other elements to form white or grey water-soluble salts. With some exceptions, the oxides of group 1 elements have the formula M_2O, their hydrides are MH, and their halides are MX (for example, NaCl). The oxides of group 2 elements have the formula MO, their hydrides are MH_2, and their halides are MX_2 (for example, $CaCl_2$).

Halogens form a wide variety of oxides and also combine with other halogens. They combine with hydrogen to form HX gases, and these compounds are also commonly used as acids (hydrofluoric, hydrochloric, etc.) in aqueous solution. Halogens form salts with metals by gaining electrons to become X^- ions. Astatine is an exception to many of these properties because it is an artificial metalloid.

Noble gases are **nearly chemically inert**. The heavier noble gases form a number of compounds with oxygen and fluorine such as KrF_2 and XeO_4

Electronegativity and reactivity series

Electronegativity measures the ability of an atom to **attract electrons** in a chemical bond. The most metallic elements have the lowest electronegativity, so they give up their electrons easily. The most nonmetallic have the highest electronegativity, thereby attracting electrons easily.

In a **reaction with a metal**, the **most reactive** chemicals are the **most electronegative elements** or compounds containing those elements. In a **reaction with a nonmetal**, the **most reactive** chemicals are the **least electronegative elements** or compounds containing them. The reactivity of elements may be described by a **reactivity series**: an ordered list with chemicals that react strongly at one end and nonreactive chemicals at the other. The following reactivity series is for metals reacting with oxygen:

Metal	K	Na	Ca	Mg	Al	Zn	Fe	Pb	Cu	Hg	Ag	Au
Reaction with O_2	Burns violently		Burns rapidly					Oxidizes slowly			No reaction	

Copper, silver, and gold (group 11) are known as the **noble metals** or **coinage metals** because they rarely react. The impact of electronegativity on chemical bonding is discussed in **0014**.

Valence and oxidation numbers

The term **valence** is often used to describe the number of atoms that may react to form a compound with a given atom by sharing, removing, or losing **valence electrons**. (Valence, meaning fringe, was a term used to refer to the electrons in the outermost electron level or shell.) A more useful term is **oxidation number**. The **oxidation number of an ion is its charge**. The oxidation number of an atom sharing its electrons is **the charge it would have if the bonding were ionic**.

There are four rules for determining oxidation number:

1) The oxidation number of an element (i.e., a Cl atom in Cl_2) is zero because the electrons in the bond are shared equally.

2) In a compound, the more electronegative atoms are assigned negative oxidation numbers and the less electronegative atoms are assigned positive oxidation numbers equal to the number of shared electron-pair bonds. For example, hydrogen may only have an oxidation number of −1 when bonded to a less electronegative element or +1 when bonded to a more electronegative element. Oxygen almost always has an oxidation number of −2. Fluorine always has an oxidation number of −1 (except in F_2).

3) The oxidation numbers in a compound must add up to zero, and the sum of oxidation numbers in a polyatomic ion must equal the overall charge of the ion.

4) The charge on a polyatomic ion is equal to the sum of the oxidation numbers for the species present in the ion. For example, the sulfate ion SO_4^{2-} has a total charge of -2. This comes from adding the -2 oxidation numbers for 4 oxygen atoms (total -8) and the +6 oxidation number for sulfur.

Example: What is the oxidation number of nitrogen in the nitrate ion, NO_3^- ?

Solution: Oxygen has the oxidation number of −2 (rule 2), and the sum of the oxidation numbers must be −1 (rule 3). The oxidation number for N may be found by solving for x in the equation $x + 3 \times (-2) = -1$. The oxidation number of N in NO_3^- is +5.

There is a **periodicity in oxidation numbers** as shown in the table below for examples of oxides with the maximum oxidation number. Remember that some elements occur in different compounds in several different oxidation states (see **0020**).

Group	1	2	13	14	15	16	17	18
Oxide with maximum oxidation number	Li_2O	BeO	B_2O_3	CO_2	N_2O_5		Cl_2O_7	XeO_4
	Na_2O	MgO	Al_2O_3	SiO_2	P_2O_5	SO_3	Br_2O_7	
Oxidation number	+1	+2	+3	+4	+5	+6	+7	+8

They are called "oxidation numbers" because oxygen was the element of choice for reacting with materials when modern chemistry began. The result was that Mendeleev's periodic first table looked very similar to this one.

Acidity/alkalinity of oxides

Metal oxides form basic solutions in water because the ionic bonds break apart and the O^{2-} ion reacts to form hydroxide ions:

metal oxide $\rightarrow$ metal cation$(aq) + O^{2-}(aq)$ and $O^{2-}(aq) + H_2O(l) \rightarrow 2\,OH^-(aq)$

Ionic oxides containing a large cation with a low charge (Rb_2O, for example) are most soluble and form the strongest bases.

Covalent oxides form acidic solutions in water by reacting with water. For example:

$$SO_3(l) + H_2O(l) \rightarrow H_2SO_4(aq) \rightarrow H^+(aq) + HSO_4^-(aq)$$

$$Cl_2O_7(l) + H_2O(l) \rightarrow 2HClO_4(aq) \rightarrow 2H^+(aq) + 2ClO_4^-(aq)$$

Covalent oxides at high oxidation states and high electronegativities form the strongest acids. Acids and bases are discussed in **0019**. For this skill, note that the periodic trends for acid and base strength of the oxide of an element follows the same pattern we've seen before.

Summary of Periodic Trends on the Periodic Table

A summary of periodic trends is shown below. The properties tend to decrease or increase as shown depending on a given element's proximity to fluorine in the table.

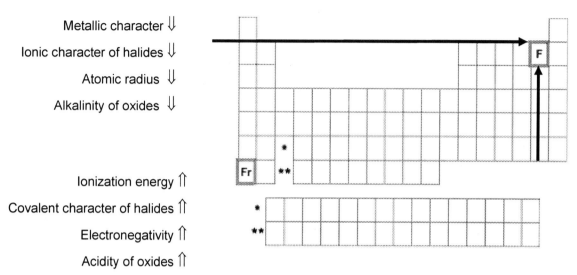

Metallic character ⇓
Ionic character of halides ⇓
Atomic radius ⇓
Alkalinity of oxides ⇓

Ionization energy ⇑
Covalent character of halides ⇑
Electronegativity ⇑
Acidity of oxides ⇑

*Note: Memorize the ones in italics; everything else increases top→bottom, left→right

Group Trends (top to bottom):

> Increases: atomic radius, nuclear charge, ionic size, shielding effect, atomic number (number of protons, number of electrons), covalent character of halides, acidity of oxides

> *Decreases: ionization energy, electron affinity, electronegativity, metallic character, ionic character of halides, alkalinity of oxides*

Period Trends (left to right):

> Increases: electronegativity, nuclear charge, ionization energy, electron affinity, atomic number (number of protons, number of electrons), acidity of oxides

> *Decreases all the way across: atomic radius, metallic character, ionic character of halides, alkalinity of oxides*

> *Decreases through cations (positive) and again through anions: ionic size Stays the same left to right: shielding effect*

http://jcrystal.com/steffenweber/JAVA/jpt/jpt.html contains an applet of the periodic table and trends.
http://www.webelements.com is an on-line reference for information on the elements.
http://www.uky.edu/Projects/Chemcomics/ has comic book pages for each element

Competency 10.0 Understand the kinetic molecular theory, the nature of phase changes, and the gas laws

Identify relationships among volume, temperature, moles, and pressure in gases.

These relationships were found by experimental observation and may be explained by the kinetic molecular theory described in **0007**.

Charles' law states that the volume of a fixed amount of gas at constant pressure is directly proportional to absolute temperature. In other words, increasing the temperature causes a gas to expand, in a mathematically proportional manner:

$$V \propto T.$$

Or V = kT where k is a constant. This gives a mathematical equation $\dfrac{V_1}{T_1} = \dfrac{V_2}{T_2}$.

Changes in temperature or volume can be found using Charles' law.

Problem: What is the new volume of a gas if 0.50 L of that gas at 25°C is heated to 35°C at constant pressure?

Solution: This is a volume-temperature change so use Charles' law. Temperature must be on the Kelvin scale. K = °C + 273.

T_1 = 25°C + 273 = 298K
V_1 = 0.50 L
T_2 = 308K
V_2 = ?

Use the equation: $\dfrac{V_1}{T_1} = \dfrac{V_2}{T_2}$ and rearrange for $V_2 = \dfrac{T_2 V_1}{T_1}$.

Substitute and solve

V_2 = 0.52L.

Boyle's law states that the volume of a fixed amount of gas at constant temperature is inversely proportional to the gas pressure. In other words, increasing the pressure causes a gas to contract in a mathematically proportional manner:

$$V \propto \dfrac{1}{P}.$$

Or V = k/P where k is a constant. This gives a mathematical equation $P_1V_1 = P_2V_2$.

Pressure or volume changes (at a constant temperature) can be determined using Boyle's law.

Problem: A 1.5 L gas has a pressure of 0.56 atm. What will be the volume of the gas if the pressure doubles to 1.12 atm at constant temperature?

Solution: This is a pressure-volume relationship at constant temperature, so using Boyle's law:

$P_1 = 0.56$ atm
$V_1 = 1.5$ L
$P_2 = 1.12$ atm
$V_2 = ?$

Use the equation $P_1V_1 = P_2V_2$, rearrange to solve for $V_2 = \dfrac{P_1V_1}{P_2}$.

Substitute and solve. $V_2 = 0.75$ L

Pressure can be in atmospheres, Pascals, or mm Hg as long as it is the same units for P_1 and P_2.

Gay-Lussac's law states that the pressure of a fixed amount of gas in a fixed volume is proportional to absolute temperature. In other words, increasing the temperature causes the pressure to increase in a mathematically proportional manner:

$$P \propto T.$$

Or $P = kT$ where k is a constant. This gives the mathematical equation $\dfrac{P_1}{T_1} = \dfrac{P_2}{T_2}$.

Changes in temperature or pressure (with a constant volume) can be found using Gay-Lussac's law.

Problem: A 2.25 L container of gas at 25°C and 1.0 atm pressure is cooled to 15°C. How does the pressure change if the volume of gas remains constant?

Solution: This is a pressure-volume change so use Gay-Lussac's law. Change the temperatures to the Kelvin scale. K = °C + 273.

$P_1 = 1.0$ atm
$T_1 = 25\ °C + 273 = 298$
$T_2 = 15\ °C + 273 = 288$

Use the equation $\dfrac{P_1}{T_1} = \dfrac{P_2}{T_2}$ to solve.

Rearrange the equation to solve for P_2, substitute and solve.

$P_2 = \dfrac{P_1T_2}{T_1} = 0.97$ atm

The **combined gas law** uses the three laws above to determine a proportionality expression that is used for a constant quantity of gas:

$$V \propto \frac{T}{P}.$$

The combined gas law is often expressed as an equality between identical amounts of an ideal gas at two different states ($n_1 = n_2$):

$$\frac{P_1 V_1}{T_1} = \frac{P_2 V_2}{T_2}.$$

Problem: 1.5 L of a gas at STP is allowed to expand to 2.0 L at a pressure of 2.5 atm. What is the temperature of the expanded gas?

Since pressure, temperature and volume are all changing, use the combined gas law to determine the new temperature of the gas. STP means "Standard Temperature and Pressure." Standard temperature is 273 K and standard pressure is 1.0 atm.

$P_1 = 1.0$ atm
$T_1 = 273$K
$V_1 = 1.5$ L
$V_2 = 2.0$L
$P_2 = 2.5$ atm
$T_2 = ?$

Using this equation, $\dfrac{P_1 V_1}{T_1} = \dfrac{P_2 V_2}{T_2}$, rearrange to solve for T_2.

$$T_2 = \frac{P_2 V_2 T_1}{P_1 V_1}$$

Substitute and solve: $T_2 = 910$ K or 637 °C

Avogadro's hypothesis states that equal volumes of different gases at the same temperature and pressure contain equal numbers of molecules.

Avogadro's law states that the volume of a gas at constant temperature and pressure is directly proportional to the quantity of gas, or:

$$V \propto n$$

where n is the number of moles of gas.

Together, Avogadro's law and the combined gas law yield

$$V \propto \frac{nT}{P}$$

The proportionality constant R - the **ideal gas constant** - is used to express this proportionality as the **ideal gas law**:

$$PV = nRT .$$

The ideal gas law is useful since it contains all the information of Charles' Law, Boyle's Law, Avogadro's Law, and the Combined Gas Law in a single equality.

Problem: What volume will 0.50 mole of an ideal gas occupy at 20.0 °C and 1.5 atm?

Solution: Since the problem deals with moles of gas as well as temperature and pressure, use the ideal gas law to find volume.

R = 0.0821 atm L/mol K. The SI value for R of **8.314 J/(mol-K)** may be used because a joule is defined as a Newton-meter. A value for R of **8.314 m^3-Pa/(mol-K)** is identical to the ideal gas constant using joules.

$$PV = nRT \qquad\qquad V = nRT/ P$$

$$V = nRT / P = 0.50 \text{ mol } (0.0821 \text{ atm L/mol K}) \, 293 \text{ K} / 1.5 \text{ atm}$$

$$V \quad = 8.0 \text{ L}$$

Problem: At STP, 0.250 L of an unknown gas has a mass of 0.429 g. Is the gas SO_2, NO_2, C_3H_8, or Ar? Support your answer.

Solution: Identify what is given and what is asked.

Given: $T_1 = 273K$
$P_1 = 1.0$ atm
$V_1 = 0.250$ L
Mass = 0.429 g

Determine: Identity of the gas. In order to do this, you must find the molar mass (MM) of the gas. $n = \dfrac{mass}{MM}$.

Find the number of moles of gas present using $PV = nRT$ and then determine the MM to compare to choices given in the problem.

Solve for $n = \dfrac{PV}{RT}$ = (1.0 atm)(0.250 L) / (0.0821 atm L/mol KI)(273 K)
$n = 0.011$ moles

$MM = \dfrac{mass}{n}$ = 0.429 g/0.011 mol = 39.0 g/mol

Compare to MM of SO_2 (96 g/mol), NO_2 (46 g/mol), C_3H_8 (44 g/mol) and Ar (39.9 g/mol). It is closest to Ar, so the gas is probably Argon.

Many problems are given at "**standard temperature and pressure**" or "**STP.**" Standard conditions are *exactly* **1 atm (101.325 kPa)** and **0° C (273.15 K)**. At STP, one mole of an ideal gas has a volume of:

$$V = \frac{nRT}{P}$$

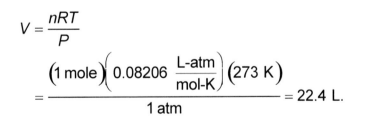

$$= \frac{\left(1\ mole\right)\left(0.08206\ \frac{L\text{-}atm}{mol\text{-}K}\right)\left(273\ K\right)}{1\ atm} = 22.4\ L.$$

This value of 22.4 L is known as the **standard molar volume** of any gas at STP.

Tutorials for gas laws may be found online at:www.chemistrycoach.com/tutorials-6.htm .

Identify the kinetic molecular description of phase change.

Kinetic models were used to describe gases, liquids, and solids in **0007**. **Phase changes** occur when the relative importance of kinetic energy and intermolecular forces is altered sufficiently for a substance to change its state.

The transition from gas to liquid is called **condensation** and from liquid to gas is called **vaporization**. The transition from liquid to solid is called **freezing** and from solid to liquid is called **melting**. The transition from gas to solid is called **deposition** and from solid to gas is called **sublimation**.

Heat removed from a substance during condensation, freezing, or deposition permits new intermolecular bonds to form, and heat added to a substance during vaporization, melting, or sublimation breaks intermolecular bonds. During these phase transitions, this **latent heat** is removed or added with **no change in the temperature** of the substance because the heat is not being used to alter the speed of the molecules or the kinetic energy when they strike each other or the container walls. Latent heat alters intermolecular bonds.

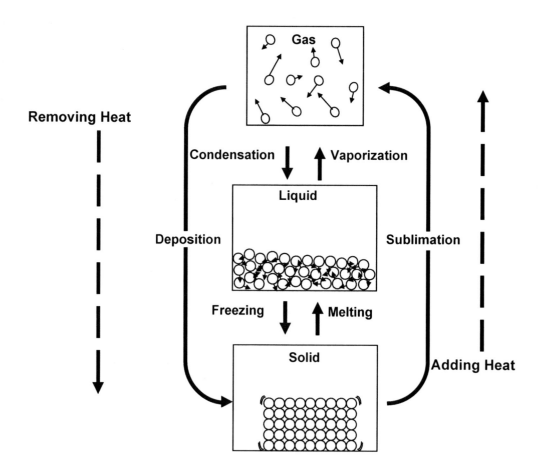

Apply kinetic molecular theory to phase changes.

The kinetic molecular theory for substances is described in **0007**. The kinetic energy of molecules is unaltered during phase changes, but the freedom of molecules to move relative to one another increases dramatically (see **0013**). The following table summarizes the application of kinetic molecular theory to the addition of heat to ice, first changing it to liquid water and then to water vapor.

Effect at 1 atm of the addition of heat to:	**0** = no change, **+** = increase, **++** = strong increase			
	Temperature	Average speed of molecules	Average translational kinetic energy of molecules	Intermolecular freedom of motion
Ice at less than 0 ºC	+	+	+	+
Ice at 0 ºC	0	0	0	++ (melting)
Liquid water at 0 ºC	+	+	+	+
Liquid water at 100 ºC	0	0	0	++ (boiling)
Water vapor at 100 ºC	+	+	+	0 (complete freedom for an ideal gas)

The term vaporization is used for any process of liquid becoming a gas. This includes evaporation and boiling. Evaporation takes place at a gas/liquid interface when temperature is less than the boiling point (as described in **0025**). Equilibrium develops between the gas and liquid phases when the rates of evaporation and condensation are equal.

An increase in the external pressure forces molecules closer to each other and may cause condensation, freezing, or deposition for most substances. Water is an exception because liquid water is denser than ice, so pressure favors the liquid state. A pressure increase for water may cause condensation, melting, or deposition.

If a time graph was made of a pure substance being heated or cooled, it would look something like this graph for the heating of water. Different changes are taking place during each interval on the graph.

When the system is heated, energy is transferred into it. In response to the energy it receives, the system changes, either by increasing its temperature or changing phase.

During the interval marked A on the graph below, energy is being absorbed by the water molecules to increase the temperature to water's melting point, 0° C. The slope of the line for this interval shows the increase in temperature and is related to the heat capacity of the substance.

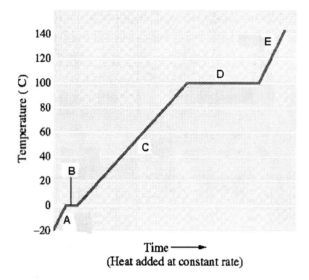

(Heat added at constant rate)

During the interval marked B on the graph, energy is still being added to the water but the temperature remains the same, at 0° C or water's melting point temperature. The additional energy is being used to overcome the intermolecular forces holding the water molecules in their solid pattern. This energy is moving the particles apart, breaking or weakening the forces of attraction that keep the water molecules aligned. The solid water (ice) is being converted to liquid water; a phase change is occurring. The temperature will not increase until every solid particle has melted and the entire sample is liquid.

Temperature again increases during interval C on the graph. Energy is being absorbed by the liquid water molecules. Notice that the slope of the line during this interval is different than the slope of the line during interval A. This is due to differences in the heat capacity of ice and liquid water.

The flat line during interval D indicates that a phase change is occurring. The additional energy is being used to overcome the attractive forces holding the liquid water molecules together. The water molecules increase their kinetic energies and move farther apart, changing to water vapor. This occurs at the boiling point temperature, or 100° C. The temperature stays at the boiling point temperature until all water molecules are converted to water vapor. Once this conversion occurs, the temperature increases as energy is added, according to the heat capacity of the substance as a vapor.

Interpret pressure/temperature phase diagrams.

Whether a substance exists as a gas, liquid, or solid depends on the nature of its intermolecular attractive forces and on its temperature and pressure. A **phase diagram** is a graphical way to summarize the environmental conditions under which the different states of a substance are stable. The diagram is divided into three areas representing the three possible states of the substance (gas, liquid, or solid). Temperature and pressure determine the phase of a substance and are shown on the x-axis and y-axis of the phase diagram, respectively.

The curves separating each area represent the boundaries of phase changes Below is a typical phase diagram. It consists of three curves that divide the diagram into regions labeled "solid," "liquid," and "gas."

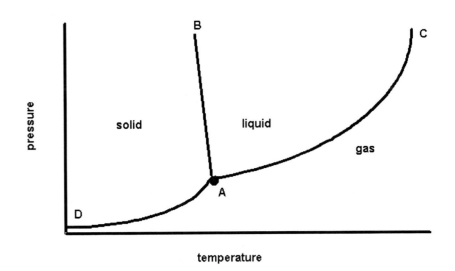

Curve **AB**, dividing the solid region from the liquid region, represents the conditions under which the solid and liquid are in equilibrium. Usually, the melting point is only slightly affected by pressure. For this reason, the melting point curve, AB, is nearly vertical.

Curve **AC**, which divides the liquid region from the gaseous region, represents the boiling point of the liquid at various pressures. This temperature is much more dependent on atmospheric pressure because of the effect of pressure on gases.

Curve **AD**, which divides the solid region from the gaseous region, represents the vapor pressure of the solid at various temperatures.

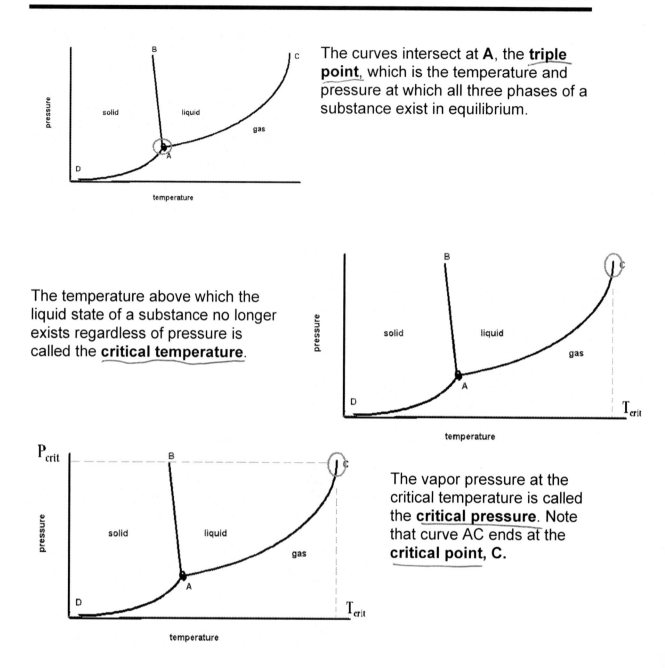

The curves intersect at **A**, the **triple point**, which is the temperature and pressure at which all three phases of a substance exist in equilibrium.

The temperature above which the liquid state of a substance no longer exists regardless of pressure is called the **critical temperature**.

The vapor pressure at the critical temperature is called the **critical pressure**. Note that curve AC ends at the **critical point, C.**

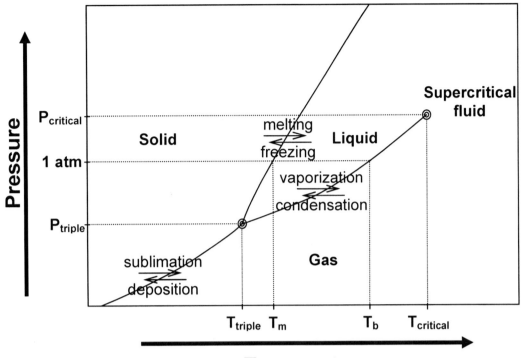

A region on the phase diagram represents each phase. Solid lines dividing these regions are located at conditions under which two phases may exist at equilibrium (see **0017** and **0018**) and a phase change may occur. All three phases may coexist at the **triple point** of a substance. The triple point pressure of CO_2 is greater than 1 atm, so dry ice sublimates at atmospheric pressure with no liquid phase. **Vapor pressure** at a given temperature is the pressure of the phase transition line to a gas at that temperature. **Normal melting point** (T_m) and **normal boiling point** (T_b) are defined at 1 atm. Note that freezing point and melting point refer to an identical temperature approached from different directions, but they represent the same concept. At temperatures and pressures above the **critical point**, the substance becomes too dense with too much kinetic energy for a gas-liquid interface to form. Matter under these conditions forms a **supercritical fluid** with properties of gases and of liquids.

The phase diagram for water (shown below) is unusual. The solid/liquid phase boundary slopes to the left with increasing pressure because the melting point of water decreases with increasing pressure. Note that the normal melting point of water is lower than its triple point. The diagram is not drawn to a uniform scale. Many anomalous properties of water are discussed here: http://www.lsbu.ac.uk/water/anmlies.html.

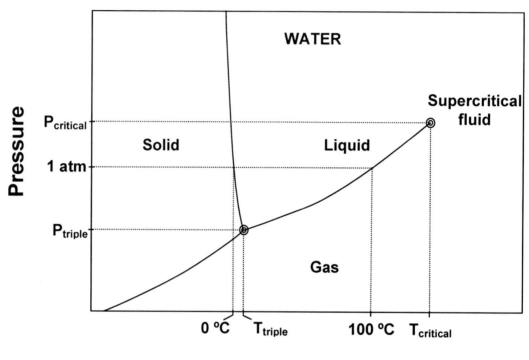

Solve mass-volume stoichiometry problems.

The progress of reactions that produce or consume a gas may be described by measuring **gas volume instead of mass**. The best way to solve these problems is to use the ideal gas equation (**0010** and **0025**) to interconvert volume and number of moles:

$$n = \frac{PV}{RT} \quad \text{and} \quad V = \frac{RT}{nP}.$$

If a volume is given, the steps are "**given volume of known (the gas) to moles of known to moles of unknown to grams of unknown**." If a mass is given, the steps will be "**given grams of known to moles of known to moles of unknown to volume of known (usually the gas)**."

Example: What volume of oxygen in liters is generated at 40 °C and 1 atm by the decomposition of 280 g of potassium chlorate in this reaction:

Solution: Start with a balanced equation

$$2KClO_3 \rightarrow 2KCl + 3O_2(g)$$

We are given a mass and asked for a volume, so the steps in the solution will be "grams to moles and then moles to volume."

Grams to moles (of given compound) uses the gram molecular mass of the compound, then compares the number of moles of the unknown (in this case the gas) on the other side of the equation with the moles of known compound using the coefficients from the balanced equation …

$$280 \text{ g KClO}_3 \times \frac{1 \text{ mol KClO}_3}{122.548 \text{ g KClO}_3} \times \frac{3 \text{ mol O}_2}{2 \text{ mol KClO}_3} = 3.427 \text{ mol O}_2.$$

…to volume using the correct constant for R, the temperature in Kelvin, the given pressure, the number of moles just calculated:

$$V = \frac{RT}{nP} = \frac{\left(0.08206 \, \frac{\text{L-atm}}{\text{mol-K}}\right)(273.15 + 40)\text{K}}{(3.427 \text{ mol O}_2)(1 \text{ atm})} = 7.50 \text{ L O}_2$$

Competency 11.0   Understand the process of nuclear transformation

Balance nuclear equations.

Subatomic particles, atomic number, and mass number

Protons and neutrons are contained in a small volume within the atom called the **nucleus**. Electrons move in the remaining space of the atom and have very little mass —about 1/1800 of the mass of a proton or neutron. Electrons are prevented from flying away from the nucleus by the attraction that exists between opposite electrical charges. This force is known as **electrostatic** or **coulombic** attraction. **Protons** have a positive charge. **Neutrons** have no charge. **Electrons** have a negative charge. Atoms have no net charge and thus have an equal number of protons and electrons.

Ions are atoms that have either gained or lost one or more electrons. **Anions** have gained at least one electron, so they have more electrons than protons which makes them negatively charged. **Cations** are positive ions because they have lost electrons and contain more protons than electrons.

The identity of an **element** depends on the **number of protons** in the nucleus of the atom. This value is called the **atomic number** and it is sometimes written as a subscript before the symbol for the corresponding element. Atoms and ions of a given element that differ in number of neutrons have a different mass and are called **isotopes**. A nucleus with a specified number of protons and neutrons is called a **nuclide**, and a nuclear particle, either a proton or neutron, may be called a **nucleon**. The total number of nucleons is called the **mass number** and may be written as a superscript before the atomic symbol.

[handwritten in margin: same #p but different #n]

$$^{14}_{6}\text{C}$$ represents an atom of carbon with 6 protons and 8 neutrons.

Different isotopes have different natural abundances and have different nuclear properties, but an atom's chemical properties are almost entirely due to electrons.

Radioactive decay, transmutation, and fusion

Some nuclei are unstable and emit particles and electromagnetic radiation. These emissions from the nucleus are known as **radioactivity**; the unstable isotopes are known as **radioisotopes**; and the nuclear reactions that spontaneously alter them are known as **radioactive decay**. Particles commonly involved in nuclear reactions are listed in the following table:

Particle	Neutron	Proton	Electron	Positron	Alpha particle	Beta particle	Gamma rays
Symbol	$^{1}_{0}\text{n}$	$^{1}_{1}\text{p}$ or $^{1}_{1}\text{H}$	$^{0}_{-1}\text{e}$	$^{0}_{1}\text{e}$	$^{4}_{2}\alpha$ or $^{4}_{2}\text{He}$	$^{0}_{-1}\beta$ or $^{0}_{-1}\text{e}$	$^{0}_{0}\gamma$

Nuclear equations are balanced by equating the sum of mass numbers on both sides of a reaction equation and the sum of atomic numbers on both sides of a reaction equation.

The electron is assigned an atomic number of –1 to account for the conversion during radioactive decay of a neutron to a proton and an emitted electron called a **beta particle**:

$$_{0}^{1}n \rightarrow {}_{1}^{1}p + {}_{-1}^{0}e .$$

Sulfur-35 is an isotope that decays by beta emission:

$$_{16}^{35}S \rightarrow {}_{17}^{35}Cl + {}_{-1}^{0}e .$$

In most cases nuclear reactions result in a **nuclear transmutation** from one element to another. Transmutation was originally connected to the mythical "philosopher's stone" of alchemy that could turn cheaper elements into gold. When Frederick Soddy and Ernest Rutherford first recognized that radioactive decay was changing one element into another, Soddy remembered saying, "Rutherford, this is transmutation!" Rutherford replied, "Soddy, don't call it transmutation. They'll have our heads off as alchemists."

Isotopes may also decay by **electron capture** from an orbital outside the nucleus:

$$_{79}^{196}Au + {}_{-1}^{0}e \rightarrow {}_{78}^{196}Pt .$$

A **positron** is a particle with the small mass of an electron but with a positive charge. A positron emission converts a proton into a neutron. Carbon-11 decays by positron emission:

$$_{6}^{11}C \rightarrow {}_{5}^{11}B + {}_{1}^{0}e .$$

Large isotopes often decay by **alpha particle** emission:

$$_{92}^{238}U \rightarrow {}_{90}^{234}Th + {}_{2}^{4}He .$$

Gamma rays are high-energy electromagnetic radiation, and gamma radiation is almost always emitted when other radioactive decay occurs. Gamma rays usually aren't written into equations because neither the mass number nor the atomic number is altered. One exception is the annihilation of an electron by a positron, an event that only produces gamma radiation:

$$_{-1}^{0}e + {}_{1}^{0}e \rightarrow 2{}_{0}^{0}\gamma .$$

Nuclear equations, whether spontaneous or induced decay, must follow the law of conservation of matter as well as obeying conservation of charge.

Example: Balance the following nuclear transmutation:

$$^{14}_{6}C \rightarrow\ ^{14}_{7}N + \underline{\ \ ^{0}_{-1}e\ \ }$$

Solution: The sum of the **mass numbers** on both the left and right side of the arrow must be the same:

Left side	Right side
14	14

They are the same so the particle emitted during decay has a mass of 0.

The sum of the **charge** must be the same on the left side and right side of the arrow.

Left side	Right side
6	7

The right side has one too many positive charges to balance 6 positive charges on the left side. The only way to balance charges is by adding electrons which are -1 each. Adding -1 to the 7 on the right side will make it balance with 6 on the left side.

So the charge of the particle emitted during decay is -1.

A particle with no mass and a -1 charge is an electron $^{0}_{-1}e$ and should be placed in the equation to complete.

$$^{14}_{6}C \rightarrow\ ^{14}_{7}N +\ ^{0}_{-1}e$$

Example: Complete the following nuclear transmutation:

$$^{234}_{90}Th \rightarrow\ ^{0}_{-1}e + \underline{\ \ ^{234}_{91}Pa\ \ }$$

Solution: Again, the sum of the mass numbers on each side of the arrow must be the same:

Left side	Right side
234	0

A mass of 234 is needed on the right side to equal the left side.

The sum of the charges must also be the same on both sides:

Left side	Right side
90	-1

A charge of 91 is needed on the right side (-1 + 91 = 90) to equal the left side (90), so the particle that forms from the decay of this isotope is $^{234}_{91}Pa$ and should be inserted to complete the transmutation equation. (Look at the Periodic Table and find which element has the atomic number of 91 to know what element to use.)

$$^{234}_{90}Th \rightarrow ^{\ \ 0}_{-1}e + ^{234}_{91}Pa$$

The same nucleons may arrange themselves within the nucleus in different ways with differing energies. This multiplicity is known as <u>nuclear isomerism</u>. Adding the letter "m" to their mass number designates nuclei with alternate arrangements. The "m" stands for "metastable," and "m1", "m2", and so on are used if additional nuclear isomers exist. Only gamma rays are produced when one nuclear isomer decays to another:

$$^{99m}_{43}Tc \rightarrow ^{99}_{43}Tc + ^{0}_{0}\gamma$$

When two nuclei collide, they sometimes stick to each other and synthesize a new nucleus. This **nuclear fusion** was first demonstrated by the synthesis of oxygen from nitrogen and alpha particles:

$$^{14}_{7}N + ^{4}_{2}He \rightarrow ^{17}_{8}O + ^{1}_{1}H.$$

Fusion can also be used to create new heavy elements, causing periodic tables to become out-dated every few years. In 2004, IUPAC (see **0016**) approved the name roentgenium (in honor of Wilhelm Roentgen, the discoverer of X-rays) for the element first synthesized in 1994 by the following reaction:

$$^{209}_{83}Bi + ^{64}_{28}Ni \rightarrow ^{272}_{111}Rg + ^{1}_{0}n.$$

A heavy nucleus may also split apart into smaller nuclei by **nuclear fission** as described in **0027**.

Solve half-life problems.

The **half-life** of a reaction is the **time required to consume half the reactant**. See **0017** for the relationship between half-life and first order rate constants. The rate of radioactive decay for an isotope is usually expressed as a half-life. Solving these problems is straightforward if the given amount of time is an exact multiple of the half-life. For example, the half-life of ^{233}Pa is 27.0 days. This means that of 200 grams of ^{233}Pa will decay according to the following table:

Day	Number of half-lives	^{233}Pa remaining	^{233}Pa decayed since day 0
0	0	200 g	0 g
27.0	1	100 g	100 g
54.0	2	50.0 g	150.0 g
81.0	3	25.0 g	175.0 g
108.0	4	12.5 g	187.5 g

Regardless of whether the given amount of time is an exact multiple of the half-life, the following equation may be used:

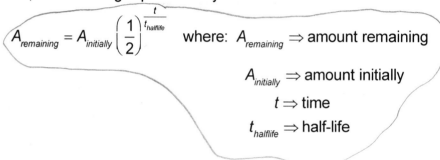

$$A_{remaining} = A_{initially}\left(\frac{1}{2}\right)^{\frac{t}{t_{halflife}}}$$ where: $A_{remaining} \Rightarrow$ amount remaining

$A_{initially} \Rightarrow$ amount initially

$t \Rightarrow$ time

$t_{halflife} \Rightarrow$ half-life

For example:

Problem: An isotope of cesium (cesium-137) has a half-life of 30 years. If 1.0 mg of cesium-137 disintegrates over a period of 90 years, how many mg of cesium-137 would remain?

Solution: Using the equation

$$A_{remaining} = A_{initially}\left(\frac{1}{2}\right)^{\frac{t}{t_{halflife}}}$$ where: $A_{remaining} \Rightarrow$ amount remaining

$A_{initially} \Rightarrow$ amount initially

$t \Rightarrow$ time

$t_{halflife} \Rightarrow$ half-life

$A_{remaining}$ = X
$A_{initially}$ = 1.0 mg
t = 90 years
$t_{1/2}$ = 30 years
then $A_{remaining}$ = 1.0 mg $(1/2)^{90/30}$ = 0.125 mg

Example: A 2.5 gram sample of an isotope of strontium-90 was formed in a 1960 explosion of an atomic bomb at Johnson Island in the Pacific Test Site. The half-life of strontium-90 is 28 years. In what year will only 0.625 grams of this strontium-90 remain?

Solution: This is a little more challenging in that substuting into the above equation gives you: $0.625\ g = 2.5\ (1/2)^{x/28}$. The solution requires simplifying and then taking the natural log of both sides:

$\ln (0.625/2.5) = \ln 0.25 = \ln (1/2^{x/28})$ $x = 56$ years

Add 56 years to 1960 and the year will be 2016 when only 0.625 grams of Sr-90 remain from that test.

$$t_{\frac{1}{2}} = 28 \qquad \frac{0.625g}{25} = \frac{2.5g}{25} \left(\frac{1}{2}\right)^{\frac{x}{28}}$$

$$\ln\left(\frac{0.625}{25}\right) = \ln\left(\frac{1}{2}^{x/28}\right)$$

$$-1.39 = \ln\left(\frac{1}{2}^{x/28}\right)$$

$$\frac{-1.39}{-0.69} = \frac{-0.69^{x/28}}{-0.69}$$

$$\frac{x}{28} = 2.01$$

$$x = 56.4 \approx 56\ years = x$$

$$1960 + 56 = \boxed{2016}$$

Competency 12.0   Understand the principles of calorimetry

Analyze the energy and entropy factors in chemical reactions.

Energy

Energy is the **driving force for change**. Energy has units of joules (J). Temperature remains constant during phase changes, so the **speed** of molecules and their **translational kinetic energy do not change** during a change in phase.

The **internal energy** of a material is the **sum of the total kinetic energy** of its molecules and the **potential energy** of interactions between those molecules. Total kinetic energy includes the contributions from translational motion and other components of motion such as rotation. The potential energy includes **energy stored in the form of resisting intermolecular attractions** between molecules.

Enthalpy

The **enthalpy** (*H*) of a material is the **sum of its internal energy and the mechanical work** it can do by driving a piston. We usually don't deal with mechanical work in high school chemistry, so the differences between internal energy and enthalpy are not important.

When a chemical reaction takes place, the enthalpies of the products will differ from the enthalpies of the reactants. There is an energy change for the reaction ΔH_{rxn}, determined by **the sum of the enthalpies of the products minus the sum of the enthalpies of the reactants**:

$$\Delta H_{rxn} = H_{product\ 1} + H_{product\ 2} + \ldots - \left(H_{reactant\ 1} + H_{reactant\ 2} + \ldots \right).$$

The enthalpy change for a reaction is commonly called the **heat of reaction**.

If the sum of the enthalpies of the products is greater than the sum of the enthalpies of the reactants, then ΔH_{rxn} **is positive** and the reaction is **endothermic**. Endothermic reactions **absorb heat** from their surroundings. The simplest endothermic reactions break chemical bonds.

If the sum of the enthalpies of the products is less than the sum of the enthalpies of the reactants, then ΔH_{rxn} **is negative** and the reaction is **exothermic**. Exothermic reactions **release heat** into their surroundings.

The heat absorbed or released by a chemical reaction often has the impact of changing the temperature of the reaction vessel and of the chemicals themselves. The measurement of these heat effects is known as **calorimetry**.

The enthalpy change of a reaction ΔH_{rxn} **is equal in magnitude but has the opposite sign to the enthalpy change for the reverse reaction**. If a series of reactions lead back to the initial reactants then the net energy change for the entire process is zero.

When a reaction is composed of sub-steps, the total enthalpy change will be the sum of the changes for each step. Even if a reaction in reality contains no sub-steps, we may still write any number of reactions in series that lead from the same reactants to the same products and their sum will be the heat of the reaction of interest. The ability to add together these enthalpies to form ultimate products from initial reactants is known as **Hess's Law**. It is used to determine one heat of reaction from others:

$$\Delta H_{net\ rxn} = H_{rxn\ 1} + H_{rxn\ 2} + \ldots$$

An example using Hess's Law is provided in **0013**. It is generally the case that exothermic reactions are more likely to occur spontaneously than endothermic reactions. Molecules usually seek the lowest possible energy state. However, entropy also plays a critical role in determining whether a reaction occurs.

A **standard** thermodynamic value occurs with all components at 25° C and 100 kPa. This *thermodynamic standard state* is slightly different from the *standard temperature and pressure* (STP) often used for gas law problems (0° C and 1 atm = 101.325 kPa). Standard thermodynamic values of common chemicals are listed in tables.

The **heat of formation** ΔH_f of a chemical is the heat taken up (positive) or emitted (negative) when elements react to form the chemical. It is also called the enthalpy of formation. The **standard heat of formation** $\Delta H_f°$ is the heat of formation with all reactants and products at 25° C and 100 kPa.

Elements in their **most stable form** are assigned a value of $\Delta H_f° = 0$ kJ/mol. Different forms of an element in the same phase of matter are known as **allotropes**.

Entropy

Entropy may be thought of as **the disorder in a system** or as a measure of the **number of states a system may occupy**. Changes due to entropy occur in one direction with no driving force. For example, a small volume of gas released into a large container will expand to fill it, but the gas in a large container never spontaneously collects itself into a small volume. This occurs because a large volume of gas has more disorder and has more places for gas molecules to be. This change occurs because **processes increase in entropy** when given the opportunity to do so. Entropy has units of Joules per Kelvin (J/K).

If two different chemicals are at the same temperature, in the same state of matter, and they have the same number of molecules, their entropy difference will depend mostly on the number of ways the atoms within the two chemicals can rotate, vibrate, and flex. Most of the time, **the more complex molecule will have the greater entropy** because there are more energetic and spatial states in which it may exist.

At zero Kelvin (0 K), there is no energy available for a chemical to sample states. The **absolute entropy**, S, of a pure crystalline solid at 0 K is zero. Absolute entropy may be measured and calculated for different substances at different temperatures.

The **entropy change of a reaction**, ΔS, is given by the sum of the absolute entropies of all the products multiplied by their stoichiometric coefficients minus the sum of all the products multiplied by their stoichiometric coefficients:

For the reaction: $aA + bB \rightleftharpoons pP + qQ$

$$\Delta S = pS(P) + qS(Q) - aS(A) - bS(B)$$

Spontaneity and Gibbs Free Energy

A reaction with a **negative ΔH and a positive ΔS** causes a decrease in energy and an increase in entropy. **These reactions will always occur spontaneously.** A reaction with a positive ΔH and a negative ΔS causes an increase in energy and a decrease in entropy. These reactions never occur to an appreciable extent because the reverse reaction takes place spontaneously.

Whether reactions with the remaining two possible combinations (ΔH and ΔS both positive or both negative) occur depends on the temperature. If $\Delta H - T\Delta S$ (known as the **Gibbs Free Energy, ΔG**) is **negative, the reaction will take place**. If it is positive, the reaction will not occur to an appreciable extent. If $\Delta H - T\Delta S = 0$ exactly, then at equilibrium there will be 50% reactants and 50% products. (Gibbs Free Energy) $\Delta G = \Delta H - T\Delta S$

A spontaneous reaction is called *exergonic*. A non-spontaneous reaction is known as *endergonic*. These terms are used much less often than *exothermic* and *endothermic*.

Spontaneous = exergonic
Non-spontaneous = endergonic

Competency 13.0   Understand thermodynamics and energy relationships in chemical bonding and chemical reactions

Analyze the energy and entropy factors in phase change.

Energy

Energy is the **driving force for change**. Energy has units of joules (J). Temperature remains constant during phase changes, so the **speed** of molecules and their **translational kinetic energy do not change** during a change in phase.

The **internal energy** of a material is the **sum of the total kinetic energy** of its molecules and the **potential energy** of interactions between those molecules. Total kinetic energy includes the contributions from translational motion and other components of motion such as rotation. The potential energy includes **energy stored in the form of resisting intermolecular attractions** between molecules.

The key concept is that a change in the **enthalpy** of a substance is the total **energy** change caused by **adding or removing heat** at constant pressure. (See **0012**). When a material is heated and experiences a phase change, **thermal energy is used to break the intermolecular bonds** holding the material together. Similarly, bonds are formed with the release of thermal energy when a material changes its phase during cooling. Therefore, **the energy of a material increases during a phase change that requires heat and decreases during a phase change that releases heat**. For example, the energy of H_2O increases when ice melts and decreases when water freezes.

Entropy

Gases are of greater entropy (disorder) than liquids, liquids are of greater entropy than solids, and matter in the same state increases in entropy with temperature. Entropy is also an extensive property of matter. **A greater number of moles will have a larger entropy.**

For phase changes, examine the graphs in **0007**. In the solid phase, each molecule may vibrate a little, but it is otherwise locked into place in an ordered position and may only be in a relatively small number of locations. In the gas phase, however, each molecule could be almost anywhere and there is greater disorder. Therefore, **the entropy of a material increases during a phase change that raises the freedom of molecular motion and decreases during a phase change that prevents molecular motion.** Entropy also increases with temperature because molecules experience more disorder when they have a wider range of energy states to occupy.

Summary

See **0010** for a description of phase changes in a pure material. Raw phase change data is often charted by recording the temperature over time when heat is added at a constant rate. A diagram for water at 1 atm from –50 °C to 150 °C is shown below. Note that temperature does not change during melting and boiling. Also note the difference in the length of time required for melting compared to boiling. This is a result of greater energy requirements to boil a substance than to melt it.

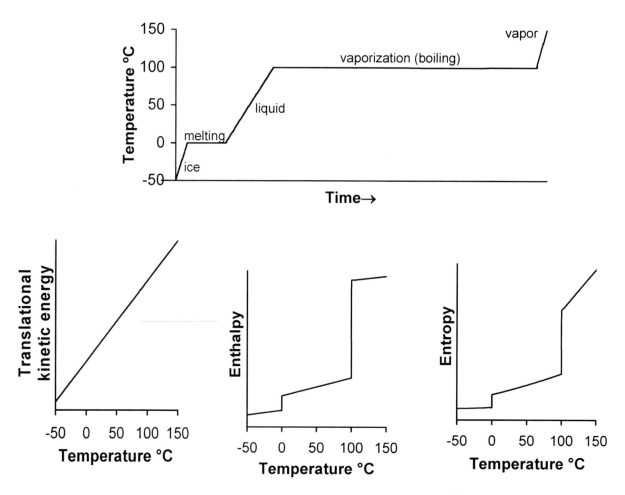

The relationship of the translational kinetic energy, enthalpy, and entropy of water to temperature is charted above under the same conditions.

Solve thermochemistry problems using heat capacity, specific heat, and phase changes.

A substance's **molar heat capacity** is the heat required to **change the temperature of one mole of the substance by one degree Celsius**. Heat capacity has units of joules per mol-kelvin or joules per mol-°C. The two units are interchangeable because we are only concerned with differences between one temperature and another. A Kelvin degree and a Celsius are the same size.

The **specific heat** of a substance (also called specific heat capacity) is the heat required to **change the temperature of one gram or kilogram by one degree.** Specific heat has units of joules per mole-gram or joules per mole-kilogram.

These terms are used to solve thermochemistry problems involving a change in temperature by applying the formula:

$q = n \times C \times \Delta T$ where $q \Rightarrow$ heat added (positive) or evolved (negative)

$n \Rightarrow$ amount of material

$C \Rightarrow$ molar heat capacity if n is in moles, specific heat if n is a mass

$\Delta T \Rightarrow$ change in temperature $T_{final} - T_{initial}$

See **0010** for a description of phase change and phase diagrams. A substance's **enthalpy of fusion** (ΔH_{fusion}) is the heat required to **change one mole from a solid to a liquid** by melting. This is also the heat released from the substance when it changes from a liquid to a solid by freezing.

A substance's **enthalpy of vaporization** ($\Delta H_{vaporization}$) is the heat required to **change one mole of a substance from a liquid to a gas** or the heat released by condensation.

A substance's enthalpy of sublimation ($\Delta H_{sublimation}$) is the heat required to change one mole directly from a solid to a gas by sublimation or the heat released by deposition.

These three values are also called "heats" or "latent heats" of fusion, vaporization, and sublimation. They have units of joules per mole, and are negative values when heat is released.

$$\text{Solid} \xrightarrow[\text{melting}]{\Delta H_{fusion}} \text{Liquid} \xrightarrow[\text{vaporization}]{\Delta H_{vaporization}} \text{Gas} \qquad \text{Solid} \xrightarrow[\text{sublimation}]{\Delta H_{sublimation}} \text{Gas}$$

$$\text{Gas} \xrightarrow[\text{condensation}]{-\Delta H_{vaporization}} \text{Liquid} \xrightarrow[\text{freezing}]{-\Delta H_{fusion}} \text{Solid} \qquad \text{Gas} \xrightarrow[\text{deposition}]{-\Delta H_{sublimation}} \text{Solid}$$

These terms are used to solve thermochemistry problems involving a change of phase by applying the formula:

$$q = n \times \Delta H_{change}$$

where $q \Rightarrow$ heat added (positive) or evolved (negative)

$n \Rightarrow$ amount of material

$\Delta H_{change} \Rightarrow$ enthalpy of fusion, vaporization, or sublimation for heat added

$\Rightarrow$ −(enthalpy of fusion, vaporization, or sublimation) for heat evolved

Example: What is the change in energy of 10 g of gold at 25 °C when it is heated beyond its melting point to 1300 °C. You will need the following data for gold:

Solid heat capacity: 28 J/mol-K

Molten heat capacity: 20 J/mol-K

Enthalpy of fusion: 12.6 kJ/mol

Melting point: 1064 °C

Solution: First determine the number of moles used: $10 \text{ g} \times \dfrac{1 \text{ mol}}{197 \text{ g}} = 0.051 \text{ mol}$.

There are then three steps. 1) Heat the solid. 2) Phase change of melting the solid. 3) Heat the liquid. All three require energy so they will be positive numbers.

1) Heat the solid:

$$q_1 = n \times C \times \Delta T = 0.051 \text{ mol} \times 28 \ \frac{J}{\text{mol-K}} \times (1064 \text{ °C} - 25 \text{ °C})$$

$$= 1.48 \times 10^3 \text{ J} = 1.48 \text{ kJ}$$

2) Melt the solid: $q_2 = n \times \Delta H_{fusion} = 0.051 \text{ mol} \times 12.6 \ \dfrac{kJ}{mol}$

$$= 0.64 \text{ kJ}$$

3) Heat the liquid:

$$q_3 = n \times C \times \Delta T = 0.051 \text{ mol} \times 20 \frac{J}{\text{mol-K}} \times (1300 \text{ °C} - 1064 \text{ °C})$$

$$= 2.4 \times 10^2 \text{ J} = 0.24 \text{ kJ}$$

The sum of the three processes is the total change in energy of the gold:

$$q = q_1 + q_2 + q_3 = 1.48 \text{ kJ} + 0.64 \text{ kJ} + 0.24 \text{ kJ} = 2.36 \text{ kJ}$$

$$= 2.4 \text{ kJ}$$

Solve chemical reaction thermochemistry problems (e.g., heat of formation, and heat of combustion).

A **standard** thermodynamic value occurs with all reactants and products at 25 °C and 100 kPa. This *thermodynamic standard state* is slightly different from the *standard temperature and pressure* (STP) often used for gas law problems, (0 °C and 1 atm=101.325 kPa). Standard properties of common chemicals are listed in tables.

The **heat of formation ΔH_f** of a chemical is the heat required (positive) or emitted (negative) when elements react to form the chemical. It is also called the enthalpy of formation. The **standard heat of formation $\Delta H_f°$** is the heat of formation with all reactants and products at 25 °C and 100 kPa.

Elements in their **most stable form** are assigned a value of $\Delta H_f° = 0$ kJ/mol. Different forms of an element in the same phase of matter are known as **allotropes**.

Example: The heat of formation for carbon as a gas is:

$\Delta H_f°$ for $C(g) = 718.4 \dfrac{kJ}{mol}$. C in the solid phase exists in three allotropes. A C_{60}

buckyball (one face is shown to the left), contains C atoms linked with aromatic bonds and arranged in the shape of a soccer ball. C_{60} was discovered in 1985. *Diamond* (below left) contains single C–C bonds in a three dimensional network. The most stable form at 25 °C is *graphite* (below right). Graphite is composed of C atoms with aromatic bonds in sheets.

$$\Delta H_f° \text{ for } C_{60}(buckminsterfullerene \text{ or } buckyball) = 38.0 \dfrac{kJ}{mol}$$

$$\Delta H_f° \text{ for } C_{\infty}(diamond) = 1.88 \dfrac{kJ}{mol}$$

$$\Delta H_f° \text{ for } C_{\infty}(graphite) = 0 \dfrac{kJ}{mol}.$$

Heat of combustion ΔH_c (also called enthalpy of combustion) is the heat of reaction when a chemical **burns in O_2** to form completely oxidized products such as **CO_2 and H_2O**. It is also the heat of reaction for **nutritional molecules that are metabolized** in the body. The standard heat of combustion **$\Delta H_c°$** takes place at 25 °C and 100 kPa. **Combustion is always exothermic**, so the negative sign for values of ΔH_c is often omitted. If a combustion reaction is used in Hess's Law, the value must be negative.

The **standard molar entropy, $S°$**, is the absolute entropy of a chemical at 1 atm and 25 °C. The molar entropy of a substance is expressed in units of J/mol-K.

Example: Determine the standard heat of formation ΔH_f° for ethylene:

$$2C(graphite) + 2H_2(g) \rightarrow C_2H_4(g).$$

Solution: Use the heat of combustion for ethylene:

$$\Delta H_c^{\circ} = 1411.2 \frac{kJ}{mol\ C_2H_4} \quad \text{for} \quad C_2H_4(g) + 3O_2(g) \rightarrow 2CO_2(g) + 2H_2O(l)$$

and the following two heats of formation for CO_2 and H_2O:

$$\Delta H_f^{\circ} = -393.5 \frac{kJ}{mol\ C} \quad \text{for} \quad C(graphite) + O_2(g) \rightarrow CO_2(g)$$

$$\Delta H_f^{\circ} = -285.9 \frac{kJ}{mol\ H_2} \quad \text{for} \quad H_2(g) + \frac{1}{2}O_2(g) \rightarrow H_2O(l).$$

Also find the standard change in entropy ΔS° for the formation of C_2H_4 given:

$$S^{\circ}(C(graphite)) = 5.7 \frac{J}{mol\ K} \quad S^{\circ}(H_2(g)) = 130.6 \frac{J}{mol\ K} \quad S^{\circ}(C_2H_4(g)) = 219.4 \frac{J}{mol\ K}.$$

Will graphite and hydrogen gas react to form C_2H_4 at 25 °C and 100 kPa?

Use Hess's Law after rearranging the given reactions so they cancel to yield the reaction of interest. Combustion is exothermic, so ΔH for this reaction is negative. We are interested in C_2H_4 as a product, so we take the opposite (endothermic) reaction. The given ΔH are multiplied by stoichiometric coefficients to give the reaction of interest as the sum of the three:

$$2CO_2(g) + 2H_2O(l) \rightarrow C_2H_4(g) + 3O_2(g) \quad \Delta H = 1411.2 \frac{kJ}{mol\ reaction}$$

$$2C(graphite) + 2O_2(g) \rightarrow 2CO_2(g) \quad \Delta H = -787.0 \frac{kJ}{mol\ reaction}$$

$$2H_2(g) + O_2(g) \rightarrow 2H_2O(l) \quad \Delta H = -571.8 \frac{kJ}{mol\ reaction}$$

$$2C(graphite) + 2H_2(g) \rightarrow C_2H_4(g) \quad \Delta H_f^\circ = 52.4 \frac{kJ}{mol}$$

-787.0 kJ/mol is found by multiplying 2 x 393.5 kJ/mol because 2 mol react.

The same is true for the -571.8 kJ/mol; 2 mol react so it becomes 2 x -285.9 kJ/mol. The value for the first equation is not multiplied by 2 because the ΔH is for the equation as it is written.

The entropy change is found from:

$$\Delta S^\circ = S^\circ(C_2H_4) - 2S^\circ(C) - 2S^\circ(H_2) = 219.4 \frac{J}{mol\ K} - 2 \times 5.7 \frac{J}{mol\ K} - 2 \times 130.6 \frac{J}{mol\ K}$$

$$= -53.2 \frac{J}{mol\ K}.$$

This reaction is endothermic with a decrease in entropy, so it is endergonic. Graphite and hydrogen gas will not react to form C_2H_4.

Competency 14   **Understand the types of bonds between atoms (ionic, covalent, and metallic bonds), the formation of these bonds, and properties of substances containing the different bonds**

Identify types and examples of ionic, polar covalent, and nonpolar covalent bonds.

An **ionic bond** occurs **between a metal and a nonmetal**. In an ionic bond, the metal "gives" an electron to the nonmetal. A **covalent bond is favored between nonmetals**. In a covalent bond both atoms attract electrons and share electrons between them. A **metallic bond is favored between metals**. In a metallic bond, atoms lose electrons to a matrix of free electrons surrounding them. Many bonds have some characteristics of more than one of the above basic bond types. Electronegativity and the location of metallic and nonmetallic elements on the periodic table are described in **0009**.

Ionic bonds

An **ionic bond** describes the electrostatic forces that exist between **particles of opposite charge**. Elements that form an ionic bond with each other have a large difference in their electronegativity. Elements that have a low ionization energy will easily allow the loss of one or more electrons. These elements, often metals, will then be

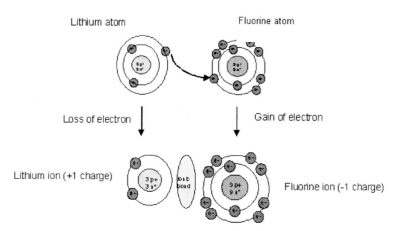

positively charged ions called cations. Elements that have a high electron affinity will gain free electrons (lost by cations) and become negatively charged ions called anions.

Metals which lose valence electrons relatively easily will form ionic bonds with non-metals which tend to gain electrons. Anions and cations pack together into a crystal **lattice** as shown to the right for NaCl. Ionic compounds are also known as **salts**.

Single and multiple covalent bonds

Nonmetals typically react with other nonmetals to form **covalent bonds**. A covalent bond is formed between two atoms by **sharing a pair of electrons**. The shared electrons are found in the outermost valence energy level and lead to a lower energy if they are shared in a way that creates a noble gas configuration (a full octet). Covalent, or molecular, bonds occur when a non-metal is bonding to a non-metal. This is due primarily to the fact that non-metals have high ionization energies and high electronegativities. Neither atom wants to give up electrons; both want to gain them. In order to fill both octets, the electrons can be shared between the two atoms.

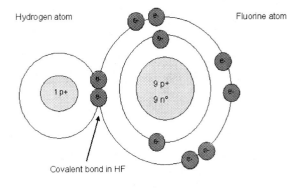

Covalent bond in HF

The simplest covalent bond is between the two single electrons of hydrogen atoms. Covalent bonds may be represented by an electron pair (a pair of dots) or a line as shown below. The shared pair of electrons provides each H atom with two electrons in its valence shell (the $1s$ orbital), so both have the stable electron configuration of helium.

$$H\cdot \ + \ \cdot H \longrightarrow \begin{array}{c} H\!:\!H \\[4pt] H\!-\!\!-\!\!-\!H \end{array}$$

Chlorine molecules have 7 electrons in their valence shell and share a pair of electrons so both have the stable electron configuration of argon.

$$:\!\overset{\cdot\cdot}{\underset{\cdot\cdot}{Cl}}\!\cdot \ + \ \cdot\!\overset{\cdot\cdot}{\underset{\cdot\cdot}{Cl}}\!: \ \longrightarrow \ \begin{array}{c} :\!\overset{\cdot\cdot}{\underset{\cdot\cdot}{Cl}}\!:\!\overset{\cdot\cdot}{\underset{\cdot\cdot}{Cl}}\!: \\[6pt] Cl\!-\!\!\!-\!Cl \ \ \overset{\cdot\cdot}{\underset{\cdot\cdot}{}}: \end{array}$$

In the previous two examples, a single pair of electrons was shared, and the resulting bond is referred to as a **single bond**. When two electron pairs are shared, two lines are drawn, representing a **double bond**, and three shared pairs of electrons represents a **triple bond** as shown below for CO_2 and N_2. The remaining electrons are in **unshared pairs**.

$$\overset{\cdot\cdot}{\underset{\cdot\cdot}{O}}\!:\!:\!C\!:\!:\!\overset{\cdot\cdot}{\underset{\cdot\cdot}{O}} \qquad :\!N\!:\!:\!:\!N\!:$$

$$O\!=\!\!=\!C\!=\!\!=\!O \ \ \overset{\cdot\cdot}{\underset{\cdot\cdot}{}} \qquad N\!\equiv\!N \ \ :$$

Electronegativity and polar/nonpolar covalent bonds

Electron pairs shared between **two atoms of the same element are shared equally (a non-polar bond)**. At the other extreme, **in ionic bonding there is no electron sharing** because the electron is transferred completely from one atom to the other. Most bonds fall somewhere between these two extremes, and the electrons are **shared unequally (a polar bond)**.

The polarity of a bond can be determined through an examination of the electronegativities of the atoms involved in the bond. The more electronegative atom will have a stronger attraction to the electrons, thus possessing the electrons more of the time. This results in a partial negative charge (δ^-) on the more electronegative atom and a partial positive charge (δ^+) on the less electronegative atom as shown below for gaseous HCl. Such bonds are referred to as **polar bonds**. A particle with a positive and a negative region is called a **dipole**. A lower-case delta (δ) is used to indicate partial charge or an arrow is draw from the partial positive to the partial negative atom.

Electronegativity is a measure of **the ability of an atom to attract electrons** in a chemical bond. Metallic elements have low electronegativities and nonmetallic elements have high electronegativities (see **0009**).

H						
2.2						
Li	Be	B	C	N	O	F
1.0	1.6	1.8	2.5	3.0	3.4	4.0
Na	Mg	Al	Si	P	S	Cl
0.9	1.3	1.6	1.9	2.2	2.6	3.2

Linus Pauling developed the concept of electronegativity and its relationship to different types of bonds in the 1930s.

A **large electronegativity difference** (greater than 1.7) results in an **ionic bond**. Any bond composed of two different atoms will be slightly polar, but for a **small electronegativity difference** (less than 0.4), the distribution of charge in the bond is so nearly equal that the result is called a **nonpolar covalent bond**. An **intermediate electronegativity difference** (from 0.4 to 1.7) results in a **polar covalent bond**. HCl is polar covalent because Cl has a very high electronegativity (it is near F in the periodic table) and H is a nonmetal (and so it will form a covalent bond with Cl), but H is near the dividing line between metals and nonmetals, so there is still a significant electronegativity difference between H and Cl. Using the numbers in the table above, the electronegativity for Cl is 3.2 and it is 2.2 for H. The difference of 3.2 – 2.2 = 1.0 places this bond in the middle of the range for polar covalent bonds.

Bond type is actually a continuum as shown in the following chart for common bonds. Note that the **C-H bond** is considered **nonpolar**.

Type of bonding	Electronegativity difference	Bond
		$Fr^+—F^-$
Very ionic		$Na^+—F^-$
	3.0	
⋮	⋮	⋮
Ionic		$Na^+—Cl^-$
	2.0	$Na^+—Br^-$
Mostly ionic		$Na^+—I^-$
Mostly polar covalent	1.5	$C^+—F^-$
		$H^+—O^-$
Polar covalent	1.0	$H^+—Cl^-$
		$C^{\delta+}{=}O^{\delta-}$
		$H^+—N^-$
		$C^+—Cl^-$
	0.5	$C^{\delta+}{\equiv}N^{\delta-}$
Mostly nonpolar covalent		$C—H$
Fully nonpolar covalent	0	$H_2, N_2, O_2,$ $F_2, Cl_2, Br_2, I_2,$ $C—C, S—S$

Increasing ionic character ⇑

Polar and nonpolar molecules

A **polar molecule** has positive and negative regions as shown above for HCl. **Bond polarity is necessary but not sufficient for molecular polarity**. A molecule containing polar bonds will still be nonpolar if the most negative and most positive location occurs at the same point. In other words, **in a polar molecule, bond polarities must not cancel**.

To determine if a molecule is polar perform the following steps.

    1) Draw the molecular structure.
    2) Assign a polarity to each bond with an arrow (remember C-H is nonpolar). If none of the bonds is polar, the molecule is nonpolar.
    3) Determine if the polarities cancel each other in space. If they do, the molecule is nonpolar. Otherwise the molecule is polar.

Examples: Which of the following are polar molecules: CO_2, CH_2Cl_2, CCl_4.

Solution: 1) Draw molecular structures of each:

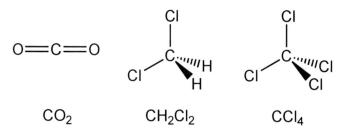

                CO_2 CH_2Cl_2 CCl_4

    2) Assign polarity to each bond within the structures:

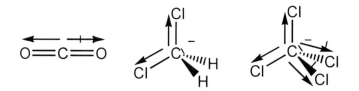

    3) Determine overall molecular polarity:

        charges cancel   net dipole   charges cancel

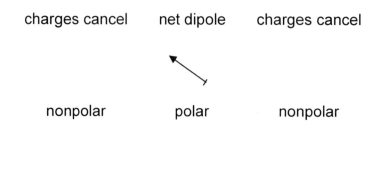

         nonpolar   polar   nonpolar

The polarity of molecules is critical for determining a good solvent for a given solute. Additional practice on the topic of polar bonds and molecules is available at http://cowtownproductions.com/cowtown/genchem/09_17M.htm.

Predict properties, including reactivity, of substances based upon the type of bonding involved.

The physical properties of substances usually result from the strength of the **intermolecular forces** at work between its molecules. Several physical consequences of this strength are listed in **0007**. The reactivity of substances is based on stability considerations that are often a result of high or low electronegativity. The reactivity of large molecules is often localized to the most polar regions or charged regions of the molecule.

The bonds in this skill are listed from strongest to weakest.

Covalent bonds in a network solid

A covalent network solid may be considered **one large molecule connected by covalent bonds**. These materials are **very hard, strong, and have a high melting point**. Diamond, C_n or C_∞, and quartz, $(SiO_2)_n$ or $(SiO_2)_\infty$, are two examples.

Ionic bonds

NaCl

All common salts (compounds with **ionic bonds**) are solids at room temperature. **Salts are brittle, have a high melting point**, and do not conduct electricity because their ions are not free to move in the crystal lattice. Salts do conduct electricity in molten form. The formation of a salt is a highly exothermic reaction between a metal and a nonmetal.
Salts in solid form are generally stable compounds, but in molten form or in solution, their component ions often react to form a more stable salt. The reactivities of these ions vary with the electronegativity of the respective element as described in **0011**.

Salts are more stable in molten form or in solution.

Some salts decompose to form more stable salts, but in molten form or in solution, their component ions often react to form a more stable salt. Some salts decompose to form more stable salts, as in the decomposition of molten potassium chlorate to form potassium chloride and oxygen:

$$2KClO_3(l) \rightarrow 2KCl(s) + 3O_2(g).$$

Metallic bonds

The physical properties of metals are attributed to the **electron sea model of metallic bonds** shown on the right. Metals **conduct heat and electricity** because electrons are not associated with the bonding between two specific atoms and they are able to flow through the material. They are called **delocalized** electrons. Metals are **lustrous** because electrons at their surface reflect light at many different wavelengths.

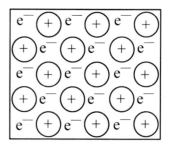

Metals are **malleable** and **ductile** because the electrons are able to rearrange their positions to maintain the integrity of the solid when the metallic lattice is deformed, acting like glue between the cations. The strengths of different metallic bonds can be related to the relative amounts and positions of electrons present.

Alkali metals contain only one valence electron ("less glue"), and that electron is a considerable distance away from the nucleus ("weaker glue") because it is shielded from nuclear attraction by the noble gas configuration of the remaining electrons. The result is a weak metallic bond and a low melting point. Heavier alkali metals contain a valence electron even further from the nucleus, resulting in a very weak metallic bond and a further lowering of the melting point. With two valence electrons and smaller atoms, alkaline earth metals have stronger metallic bonds than the alkali metals.

The metal with the weakest metallic bonds is mercury. Hg is a liquid at room temperature because Hg atoms hold on tightly to a stable valence configuration of full s, f, and d subshells. Fewer electrons are shared to create bonds than in other metals.

The reactivity of metals increases with lower electronegativity in reactions with nonmetals to form ionic bonds. See the reactivity series in **0011**.

The following bonds are usually weaker, and are called intermolecular forces.

Ion-dipole interactions

Salts tend to dissolve in several polar solvents. An ion with a full charge in a polar solvent will **orient nearby solvent molecules** so that their opposite partial charges are pointing towards the ion. In aqueous solution, certain salts react to form solid **precipitates** if a combination of their ions is insoluble. See **0025** for more about salts in solution including an example of an ion-dipole interaction for a Na^+ ion in water.

Hydrogen bonds

Hydrogen bonds are particularly **strong dipole-dipole interactions** that form between the **H-atom** of one molecule and an **F, O, or N** atom of an adjacent molecule. The partial positive charge on the hydrogen atom is attracted to the partial negative charge on the electron pair of the other atom. The hydrogen bond between two water molecules is shown as the dashed line below:

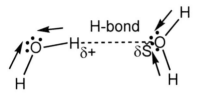

Dipole-dipole interactions

The intermolecular forces between polar molecules are known as dipole-dipole interactions. The partial positive charge of one molecule is attracted to the partial negative charge of its neighbor.

Ion-induced dipole

When a nonpolar molecule (or a noble gas atom) encounters an ion, its **electron density is temporarily distorted** resulting in an **induced dipole** that will be attracted to the ion. Intermolecular attractions due to induced dipoles in a nonpolar molecule are known as **London forces or Van der Waals interactions**. These are very weak intermolecular forces.

For example, carbon tetrachloride, CCl_4, has polar bonds but is a nonpolar molecule due to the tetrahedral symmetry of those bonds. An aluminum cation will draw the non-bonded electrons of the chlorine atom towards it, distorting the molecule (this distortion has been exaggerated in the figure) and creating an attractive force as shown by the dashed line below.

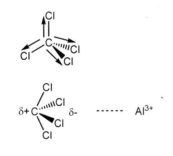

Dipole-induced dipole

The partial charge of **a permanent dipole may also induce a dipole in a nonpolar molecule** resulting in an attraction similar to—but weaker than—that created by an ion.

London dispersion force: induced dipole-induced dipole

The above two examples required a permanent charge to induce a dipole in a nonpolar molecule. A nonpolar molecule may also induce a temporary dipole on its identical neighbor in a pure substance. These forces occur because at any given moment, electrons are located within a certain region of the molecule, and **the instantaneous location of electrons will induce a temporary dipole** on neighboring molecules. For example, an isolated helium atom consists of a nucleus with a 2+ charge and two electrons in a spherical electron density cloud. An attraction of He atoms due to London dispersion forces (shown below by the dashed line) occurs because when the electrons happen to be distributed unevenly on one atom, a dipole is induced on its neighbor. This dipole is due to intermolecular repulsion of electrons and the attraction of electrons to neighboring nuclei.

The strength of London dispersion forces **increases for larger molecules** because a larger electron cloud is more easily polarized. The strength of London dispersion forces also **increases for molecules with a larger surface area** because there is greater opportunity for electrons to influence neighboring molecules if there is more potential contact between the molecules. Paraffin in candles is an example of a solid held together by weak London forces between large molecules. These materials are soft.

Competency 15.0   Understand the types of intermolecular forces and properties of substances containing the different forces between molecules

Represent ions and molecules using Lewis dot structures.

Noble gases have stable electron configurations because the subshells corresponding to their valence electrons are completely filled. Atoms often gain, lose, or share electrons in order to achieve the **same number of electrons as the noble gas nearest to them in the periodic table**. Helium has a $1s^2$ valence electron configuration, and every other noble gas has an ns^2np^6 valence electron configuration for a total of **eight valence electrons**. The observation that **many reaction products have eight valence electrons** is known as the **octet rule**.

Lewis dot structures are a method for keeping track of each atom's valence electrons in a molecule. Drawing Lewis structures is a three-step process:

1) Add the number of valence shell electrons for each atom. See **0009** for using the periodic table to do this. If the compound is an anion, add the charge of the ion to the total electron count because anions have "extra" electrons. If the compound is a cation, subtract the charge of the ion.

2) Write the symbols for each atom in a spatial arrangement, showing how the atoms connect to each other.

3) Draw a single bond (one pair of electron dots or a line) between each pair of connected atoms. Place the remaining electrons around the atoms as unshared pairs. If every atom has an octet of electrons except H atoms which have only two electrons, the Lewis structure is complete. Shared electrons count towards both atoms. If there are too few electron pairs to complete the octets with single bonds, draw multiple bonds (two or three pairs of electron dots between the atoms) until an octet is formed around each atom (except H atoms with two). If there are too many electron pairs to complete the octets with single bonds then the octet rule is broken for this compound.

Example: Draw the Lewis dot structure of HCN.

Solution:

1) From their locations in the main group of the periodic table, we know that each atom contributes the following number of electrons: H—1, C—4, N—5. Because it is a neutral compound, the molecule will have a total of 10 valence electrons.

2) The atoms are connected with C at the center and can be drawn as:

$$H - C \equiv N$$

It is impossible for H to be the central atom because H has only one valence electron. Therefore, it will always have only a single bond to one other atom. If N were the central atom then the formula would probably be written as H N C.

H : C : N (with lone pairs shown above and below)

3) First, try connecting the atoms with single bonds. This gives the structure to the right. H has two electrons to fill its valence subshells, but C and N only have six each. A triple bond between these atoms fulfills the octet rule for C and N and is the correct Lewis structure.

$$H : C ::: N :$$

Predict molecular structures using the concepts of resonance, hybridization, and molecular orbital theory.

Resonance

O_2 contains a total of 12 valence electrons and the following Lewis structure:

$$\ddot{O} = \ddot{O}$$

Ozone, O_3, has a total of 18 valence electrons, and two Lewis structures are possible for this molecule

Equivalent Lewis structures are called **resonance forms**. A double-headed arrow is used to indicate resonance. The actual molecule does not have a double bond on one bond and a single bond on the other. The **molecular structure is in an average state between the resonance forms**.

Hybridization

Electron arrangements (see **0009**) are built up by considering different energy levels for different subshells to explain spectroscopic data about individual atoms. However, when Lewis dot structures are drawn (**0015**) or molecular geometries are determined (**0015**), all valence electrons are treated identically to explain the bonding between atoms regardless of whether the electrons once belonged to the s or the p subshell of their atom. Reconciling these views of the individual and the bonded atom requires a theory known as hybridization.

Hybridization describes the pre-bonding **promotion of one or more electrons** from a lower energy subshell to a higher energy subshell followed by a **combination** of the orbitals into degenerate **hybrid orbitals**.

Example: A boron atom has the valence electron configuration $2s^2 2p^1$ as shown to the right. Before bonding to three other atoms, the capability to form three equivalent bonds is achieved by hybridization. First a $2s$ electron is promoted to an empty p orbital. Next the occupied orbitals combine into three hybrid $2sp^2$ orbitals. Now three electrons in degenerate orbitals are available to create covalent bonds with three atoms.

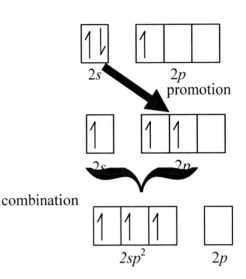

promotion

combination

$2s$ $2p$

$2sp^2$ $2p$

Hybridization occurs for atoms with a valence electron configuration of ns^2, $ns^2 np^1$, or $ns^2 p^2$. For period 2, this corresponds with Be, B, C, and N in the NH_3^+ ion.

An atom joined to its neighbor by **multiple covalent bonds** is prepared for bonding by hybridization with incomplete combination. Electrons that remain in p orbitals can contribute additional bonds between the same two atoms.

Example: An isolated carbon atom has the valence electron configuration $2s^2 2p^2$. Hybridization to four $2sp^3$ orbitals occurs before bonding to four atoms. Three hybrid sp^2 orbitals form if there is a double bond so the C atom is bonded to three atoms and one electron remains in the p orbital. Two hybrid sp orbitals occur if there is a triple bond or two double bonds. In this case, C is bonded to two atoms with two electrons remaining in p orbitals.

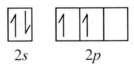

$2s$ $2p$

Bonds to 4 atoms

$2sp^3$

Bonds to 3 atoms

$2sp^2$ $2p$

Bonds to 2 atoms

$2sp$ $2p$

Note: p orbitals are shaded in the diagrams. These models are meant to illustrate the **locations** and **angles** of hybrid and p orbitals relative to the central atom. A mathematical solution would also show that each type of hybrid orbital (sp^3, sp^2, and sp) has a slightly different shape from the other two. See **0008** for an image of electron density in a p orbital.

See
http://www.mhhe.com/physsci/chemistry/essentialchemistry/flash/hybrv18.swf for a flash animation tutorial of hybridization.

Molecular Orbital Theory

The electron configurations of isolated atoms are found in atomic orbitals; the configurations of atoms about to bond are represented by atomic and hybridized atomic orbitals; and **the electron configurations of molecules are represented by molecular orbitals**. Molecular orbital theory is an advanced topic, but it may be simplified to representing the **bonds between atoms as overlapping electron density shapes from atomic orbitals**. There are two typical locations for molecular orbitals.

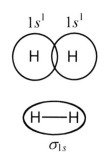

The **bonding sigma orbital** (σ) surrounds a **line drawn between the two atoms** in a bond. At least one electron pair in every bond is in a bonding σ orbital. Sigma bonds get their name from s orbitals because the spherical electron density shapes of two s orbitals overlap to form a σ orbital. A drawing of this overlap and the resulting molecular orbital is shown to the right for H_2. Hybrid or p atomic orbitals also form a σ orbital when they overlap such that the axis between the bonded atoms runs through the center of the combined electron density.

The **bonding pi orbital** (π) follows regions **separate from a line drawn between the two atoms** in a bond. Two overlapping p orbitals will form π bonds to contain the additional shared electrons in molecules with double or triple bonds. π bonds prevent atoms from rotating about the central axis between them.

In CH_4, the electron density of the four sp^3 orbitals of C each overlap with an s orbital of H to form four σ bonds. In C_2H_4 (an alkene), two sp^2 orbitals on each C overlap with H s orbitals, the remaining sp^2 orbitals overlap with each other in a σ bond, and the p orbitals (drawn as shaded shapes) overlap with each other above and beneath the carbon atoms in a π bond (also drawn as shaded shapes). In CO_2, the C atom has two sp hybrid orbitals and two p orbitals. These form one σ bond and one π bond with the two unfilled p orbitals on each O atom. In C_2H_2 (an alkyne), a triple bond forms with one σ and two π bonds.

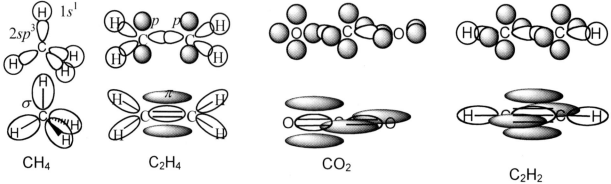

| CH_4 | C_2H_4 | CO_2 | C_2H_2 |

Molecules with double bonds next to each other and aromatic molecules based on benzene contain **more than two π orbitals on adjacent atoms**. The bonds, as well as the entire molecules, are described as being **conjugated**. Electrons in these molecules are free to move from one bond to the next **on the same molecule** and so are **delocalized**. In **0014**, we saw electron delocalization extending throughout the entire substance in materials with metallic bonds.

Benzene (C_6H_6) has the following resonance forms:

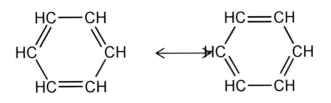

Each carbon atom in benzene bonds to three atoms, so their electrons are in three sp^2 orbitals and one p orbital as we've seen for C_2H_4. The p orbitals are shown as the shaded shapes below on the left (only the C-C bonds are shown). The p atomic orbitals combine to form molecular orbitals with delocalized electrons as shown in the bonding π molecular orbital below to the right.

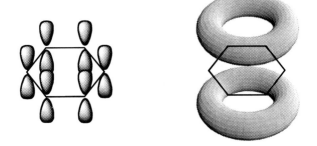

Aromatic molecules are often drawn with a circle in the center of their benzene rings (shown to the left) to show delocalized π electrons. The atoms of a benzene molecule are all located in the same plane. This is in contrast to molecules that contain 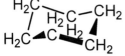 only σ bonds as shown to the right for cyclohexane, C_6H_{12}.

Molecular orbital theory also predicts **antibonding orbitals** that **prevent bonding** because they are at a higher energy level than the electrons on individual atoms. Antibonding electrons play a role in explaining why molecules like H_2 form while molecules like He_2 do not, but they are not required to predict molecular structures. For more on this aspect of molecular orbital theory, see http://www.chem.ufl.edu/~chm2040/Notes/Chapter_12/theory.html.

Predict molecular geometry.

Electron Pairs

Molecular geometry is predicted using the valence-shell electron-pair repulsion or **VSEPR** model. VSEPR uses the fact that **electron pairs around the central atom of a molecule repel each other**. Imagine you are one of two pairs of electrons in bonds around a central atom (like a bonds in BeH_2 in the table below). You want to be as far away from the other electron pair as possible, so you will be on one side of the atom and the other pair will be on the other side. There is a straight line (or a 180° angle) between you to the other electron pair on the other side of the nucleus. In general, electron pairs lie at the **largest possible angles** from each other.

Electron pairs	Geometrical arrangement		Predicted bond angles	Example
2		Linear	180°	
3		Trigonal planar	120°	
4		Tetrahedral	109.5°	
5		Trigonal bipyramidal	120° and 90°	
6		Octahedral	90°	

X represents a generic central atom. Lone pair electrons on F are not shown in the example molecules.

Unshared Electron Pairs

The **shape of a molecule is given by the location of its atoms**. These are connected to central atoms by shared electrons, but unshared electrons also have an important impact on molecular shape. Unshared electrons may determine the angles between atoms. Molecular shapes in the following table take into account total and unshared electron pairs.

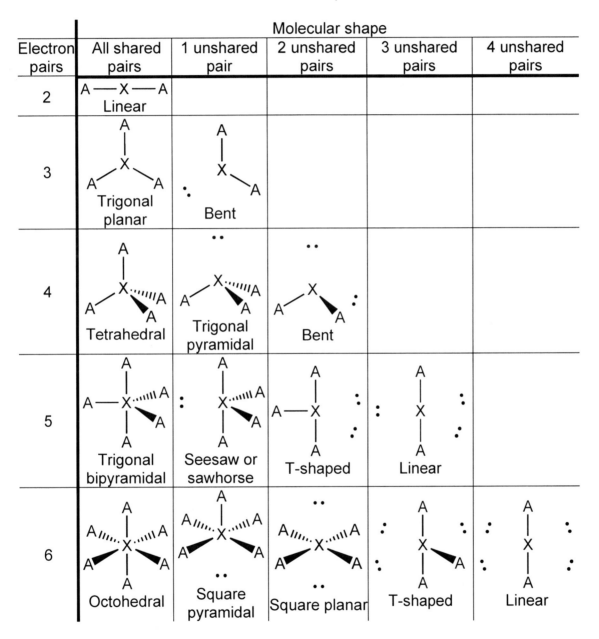

Electron pairs	Molecular shape				
	All shared pairs	1 unshared pair	2 unshared pairs	3 unshared pairs	4 unshared pairs
2	Linear				
3	Trigonal planar	Bent			
4	Tetrahedral	Trigonal pyramidal	Bent		
5	Trigonal bipyramidal	Seesaw or sawhorse	T-shaped	Linear	
6	Octohedral	Square pyramidal	Square planar	T-shaped	Linear

X represents a generic central atom bonded to atoms labeled A.

Altered Bond Angles

Unpaired electrons also have a less dramatic impact on molecular shape. The shared electron pairs are each attracted partially to the central atom and partially to the other atom in the bond, but the unpaired electrons are different. They are attracted to the central atom, but there is nothing on your their side, so they are free to expand toward the central atom. That expansion means that they take up more room than the other electron pairs, and the others are all squeezed a little closer together. Multiple bonds have a similar effect because more space is required for more electrons. In general, **unshared electron pairs and multiple bonds decrease the angles between the remaining bonds**. A few examples are shown in the following tables.

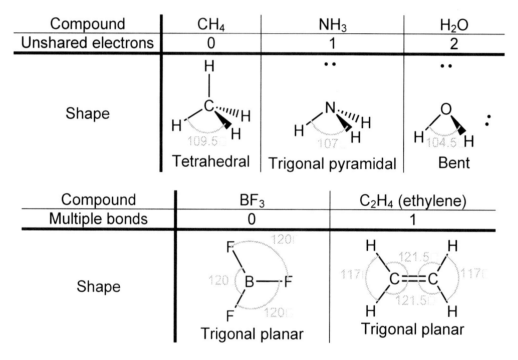

Compound	CH_4	NH_3	H_2O
Unshared electrons	0	1	2
Shape	Tetrahedral	Trigonal pyramidal	Bent

Compound	BF_3	C_2H_4 (ethylene)
Multiple bonds	0	1
Shape	Trigonal planar	Trigonal planar

Summary

In order to use VSEPR to predict molecular geometry, perform the following steps:

1) Write out Lewis dot structures.

2) Use the Lewis structure to determine the number of unshared electron pairs and bonds around each central atom counting multiple bonds as one (for now).

3) The second table of this skill gives the arrangement of total and unshared electron pairs to account for electron repulsions around each central atom.

4) For multiple bonds or unshared electron pairs, decrease the angles slightly between the remaining bonds around the central atom.

5) Combine the results from the previous two steps to determine the shape of the entire molecule.

http://www.shef.ac.uk/chemistry/vsepr/ is a good site for explaining and visualizing molecular geometries using VSEPR.

http://cowtownproductions.com/cowtown/genchem/09_16T.htm provides some practice for determining molecular shape

Competency 16.0   Understand the nomenclature and structure of inorganic and organic compounds

Apply the IUPAC system of nomenclature to common inorganic chemicals.

The IUPAC is the **International Union of Pure and Applied Chemistry**, an organization that formulates naming rules. **Organic compounds contain carbon**, and they have a separate system of nomenclature, but some of the simplest molecules containing carbon also fall within the scope of inorganic chemistry.

Naming rules depend on whether the chemical is an ionic compound or a molecular compound containing only covalent bonds. There are special rules for naming acids. The rules below describe a group of traditional "semi-systematic" names accepted by IUPAC.

Ionic compounds: Cation

Ionic compounds are named with the **cation (positive ion) first**. Nearly all cations in inorganic chemistry are **monatomic**, meaning they just consist of one atom (like Ca^{2+}, the calcium ion.) This atom will usually be a **metal ion**. For common ionic compounds, the **alkali metals always have a 1+ charge** and the **alkali earth metals always have a 2+ charge**. See **0009** for a review of these elements.

Many metals (usually transition metals) may form cations of more than one charge. In this case, a Roman numeral in parenthesis after the name of the element is used to indicate the ion's charge in a particular compound. This Roman numeral method is known as the **Stock system**. An older nomenclature used the suffix *–ous* for the lower charge and *–ic* for the higher charge and is still used occasionally.

ferrous   *ferric*

Example: Fe^{2+} is the iron(II) ion and Fe^{3+} is the iron(III) ion.

The only common inorganic **polyatomic cation** is **ammonium: NH_4^+**.

Ionic compounds: Anion

The **anion** (negative ion) is named and written last. Monatomic anions are formed from nonmetallic elements and are named by **replacing the end of the element's name with the suffix *–ide*.**

Examples: Cl^- is the chloride ion, S^{2-} is the sulfide ion, and N^{3-} is the nitride ion.

These anions also end with –*ide*:

C_2^{2-}	N_3^-	O_2^{2-}	O_3^-	S_2^{2-}	CN^-	OH^-
carbide or acetylide	azide	peroxide	ozonide	disulfide	cyanide	hydroxide

Oxoanions (also called oxyanions) **contain one element in combination with oxygen.** Many common polyatomic anions are oxoanions that **end with the suffix –ate.** If you memorize the "*-ate*" ions, you can quickly determine the corresponding "*-ite*" ions. If an element has two possible oxoanions, the one with the element at a lower oxidation state **ends with –*ite*.** This anion will also usually have **one less oxygen per atom.** See **0009** for a discussion of oxidation numbers. Additional oxoanions are named with the prefix *hypo-* if they have a lower oxidation number (and one less oxygen) than the –*ite* form and the prefix *per–* if they have a higher oxidation number (and one more oxygen) than the –*ate* form. Note the chlorate series of hypochlorite (ClO^-), chlorite (ClO_2^-), chlorate (ClO_3^-), and perchlorate (ClO_4^-).

Common examples:

					CO_3^{2-}	carbonate		
		SO_3^{2-}	sulfite	SO_4^{2-}	sulfate			
		PO_3^{3-}	phosphite	PO_4^{3-}	phosphate			
$N_2O_2^{2-}$	hyponitrite	NO_2^-	nitrite	NO_3^-	nitrate			
ClO^-	hypochlorite	ClO_2^-	chlorite	ClO_3^-	chlorate	ClO_4^-	perchlorate	
BrO^-	hypobromite	BrO_2^-	bromite	BrO_3^-	bromate	BrO_4^-	perbromate	
				MnO_4^{2-}	manganate	MnO_4^-	permanganate	
				CrO_4^{2-}	chromate	CrO_8^{3-}	perchromate	

Note that manganate/permanganate and chromate/perchromate are exceptions to the general rules because there are –*ate* ions but no –*ite* ions and because the charge changes.

Other polyatomic anions that end with –*ate* are:

$(COO)_2^{2-}$	$Cr_2O_7^{2-}$	SCN^-	HCO_2^-	$CH_3CO_2^-$
oxalate	dichromate	thiocyanate	formate	acetate

HCO_2^- and $CH_3CO_2^-$ are condensed **structural formulas** because they show how the atoms are linked together. Their molecular formulas would be CHO_2^- and $C_2H_3O_2^-$

If an H atom is added to a polyatomic anion with a negative charge greater than one, the word *hydrogen* or the prefix *bi-* are used for the resulting anion. If two H atoms are added, *dihydrogen* is used.

Examples: bicarbonate or hydrogen carbonate ion: HCO_3^-
dihydrogen phosphate ion: $H_2PO_4^-$

Ionic compounds: Hydrates

Water molecules often occupy positions within the lattice of an ionic crystal. These compounds are called **hydrates**, and the water molecules are known as **water of hydration**. The water of hydration is added after a centered dot in a formula. In a name, a number-prefix (listed below for molecular compounds) indicating the number of water molecules is followed by the root –*hydrate*.

Ionic compounds: Putting it all together

We now have the tools to name most common salts given a formula and to write a formula for them given a name. To determine a formula given a name, the number of anions and cations that are needed to achieve a neutral charge must be found.

Example: Determine the formula of cobalt(II) phosphite octahydrate.

Solution: For the cation, find the symbol for cobalt (Co) and recognize that it is the Co^{2+} ion from the Roman numerals. For the anion, remember the phosphite ion is PO_3^{3-}. A neutral charge is achieved with 3 Co^{2+} ions (3 x +2 = +6) for every 2 PO_3^{3-} ions (2 x -3 = -6 which cancels the +6). Add eight (octa- means 8) H_2O for water of hydration for the answer:

$$Co_3\left(PO_3\right)_2 \bullet 8H_2O.$$

Molecular compounds

Molecular compounds (compounds making up molecules with a neutral charge) are usually composed entirely of nonmetals and are named by placing the **less electronegative atom first**. See **0009** for the relationship between electronegativity and the periodic table. The suffix –*ide* is added to the second, more electronegative atom, and prefixes indicating numbers are added to one or both names if needed.

Prefix	mono-	di-	tri-	tetra-	penta-	hexa-	hepta-	octa-	nona-	deca-
Meaning	1	2	3	4	5	6	7	8	9	10

The final "o" or "a" may be left off these prefixes for oxides.

The electronegativity requirement is the reason the compound with two oxygen atoms and one nitrogen atom is called nitrogen dioxide, NO_2 and <u>not</u> dioxygen nitride O_2N. The hydride of sodium is NaH, sodium hydride, but the hydride of bromine is HBr, hydrogen bromide (or hydrobromic acid if it's in aqueous solution). Oxygen is only named first in compounds with fluorine such as oxygen difluoride, OF_2, and fluorine is never placed first because it is the most electronegative element.

Examples: N_2O_4, dinitrogen tetroxide (or tetraoxide)
Cl_2O_7, dichlorine heptoxide (or heptaoxide)
ClF_5 chlorine pentafluoride

Acids

There are special naming rules for acids that correspond with the **suffix of their corresponding anion** if hydrogen were removed from the acid. <u>Anions ending with –ide correspond to acids with the prefix *hydro–* and the suffix –ic.</u> Anions ending with –ate correspond to acids with no prefix that end with –ic. Oxoanions ending with –ite have associated acids with no prefix and the suffix –ous. The *hypo–* and *per–* prefixes are maintained. Some examples are shown in the following table:

anion	anion name	acid	acid name
Cl^-	chloride	$HCl(aq)$	hydrochloric acid
CN^-	cyanide	$HCN(aq)$	hydrocyanic acid
CO_3^{2-}	carbonate	$H_2CO_3(aq)$	carbonic acid
SO_3^{2-}	sulfite	$H_2SO_3(aq)$	sulfurous acid
SO_4^{2-}	sulfate	$H_2SO_4(aq)$	sulfuric acid
ClO^-	hypochlorite	$HClO(aq)$	hypochlorous acid
ClO_2^-	chlorite	$HClO_2(aq)$	chlorous acid
ClO_3^-	chlorate	$HClO_3(aq)$	chloric acid
ClO_4^-	perchlorate	$HClO_4(aq)$	perchloric acid

Example: What is the molecular formula of phosphorous acid?

Solution: If we remember that the *–ous* acid corresponds to the *–ite* anion, and that the *–ite* anion has one less oxygen than (or has an oxidation number 2 less than) the *–ate* form, we only need to remember that phosphate is PO_4^{3-}. Then we know that phosphite is PO_3^{3-} and phosphorous acid is H_3PO_3.

For additional resources, see:
<u>http://chemistry.alanearhart.org/Tutorials/Nomen/nomen-part7.html</u> has <u>thousands</u> of sample questions. Don't do them all in one sitting.

<u>http://www.iupac.org/reports/provisional/abstract04/connelly_310804.html</u> - IUPAC's latest report on inorganic nomenclature

Identify properly written or named formulas and chemical equations.

<u>Properly written and named formulas</u>

Proper formulas will follow the rules of the previous skill. Here are some ways to identify <u>improper</u> formulas that are emphasized below by underlining them.

In all common names for **ionic compounds, number prefixes are not used** to describe the number of anions and cations.

Examples: $CaBr_2$ is calcium bromide, <u>not calcium dibromide</u>.
$Ba(OH)_2$ is barium hydroxide, <u>not barium dihydroxide</u>.
Cu_2SO_4 is copper(I) sulfate, <u>not dicopper sulfate or copper(II) sulfate</u>
or
<u>dicopper sulfur tetroxide</u>.

All ionic compounds must have a **neutral charge in their formula** representations.

Example: <u>MgBr is an improperly written formula</u> because Mg ion always exists as 2+ and Br ion is always a 1− ion. $MgBr_2$, magnesium bromide, is correct.

Proper oxoanions and acids use the correct prefixes and suffixes.

Example: HNO_3 is nitric acid because NO_3^- is the nitrate ion.

In both ionic and molecular compounds, the **less electronegative element comes first**. See **0009** for electronegativity trends along the periodic table.

Example: <u>CSi is an improperly written formula</u> because Si is below C on the periodic table and therefore less electronegative. SiC, silicon carbide, is correct.

<u>Properly written chemical equations</u>

A properly written chemical equation must contain properly written formulas and must be **balanced**. Chemical equations are written to describe a certain number of moles of specific reactants becoming a certain number of moles of specific reaction products. Chemical equations obey the law of conservation of mass in that no atoms are created or destroyed, so each element has the same number of total atoms on the left of the arrow as it has on the right of the arrow when the equation is balanced. The number of moles of each compound is indicated by its **stoichiometric coefficient**. The number of atoms of an element is determined by multiplying the coefficient by the subscript, with subscripts outside of parentheses being multiplied by subscripts inside the parenthesis. This is done for each element in each compound. Then all the atoms of that element on that side of the arrow are added together.

Example: In the reaction

$$2H_2(g) + O_2(g) \rightarrow 2H_2O(l),$$

Hydrogen has a stoichiometric coefficient of two, oxygen has a coefficient of one, and water has a coefficient of two because 2 moles of hydrogen react with 1 mole of oxygen to form two moles of water. The number of atoms of hydrogen on the left is 4 which is found by multiplying the coefficient of 2 by the subscript of 2. The number of atoms of hydrogen on the right is found in the same way to be 4. The number of atoms of oxygen on the left is 2 since the coefficient of 1 is multiplied by the subscript of 2. Using the same method on the right, the coefficient of 2 is multiplied by the subscript of 1 (no subscript means there is one) to obtain a total of 2 atoms of oxygen. Therefore, this reaction is balanced.

In a balanced equation, the stoichiometric coefficients are chosen such that the equation contains an **equal number of each type of atom on each side**. In our example, there are four H atoms and two O atoms on each side. Therefore, the equation is balanced with respect to atoms.

Reactions among ions in aqueous solution may often be represented in three ways. When solutions of hydrochloric acid and sodium hydroxide are mixed, a reaction occurs and heat is produced. The **molecular equation** for this reaction is:

$$HCl(aq) + NaOH(aq) \rightarrow H_2O(l) + NaCl(aq)$$

It is called a molecular equation because the **complete chemical formulas** of reactants and products are shown. But in reality, both HCl and NaOH are strong electrolytes and exist in solution as ions. This is represented by a **complete ionic equation** that shows all the dissolved ions:

$$H^+(aq) + Cl^-(aq) + Na^+(aq) + OH^-(aq) \rightarrow H_2O(l) + Na^+(aq) + Cl^-(aq).$$

Because $Na^+(aq)$ and $Cl^-(aq)$ appear as both reactants and products, they play no role in the reaction. Ions that appear in identical chemical forms on both sides of an ionic equation are called **spectator ions** because they aren't part of the action. When spectator ions are removed from a complete ionic equation, the result is a **net ionic equation** that shows the actual changes that occur to the chemicals when these two solutions are mixed together:

$$H^+(aq) + OH^-(aq) \rightarrow H_2O(l)$$

An additional requirement for **redox** reactions (see **0020**) is that the equation contains an **equal charge on each side**. Redox reactions may be divided into half-reactions which either gain or lose electrons.

Balance properly written chemical equations.

Balancing equations is a multi-step process.

1. Determine the **correct formulas** for all compounds.

2. Write an **unbalanced equation**. This requires knowledge of the proper products which can be predicted from the reactants. Reactants are written on the left and products are written on the right.

3. Determine the **number of each type of atom on each side** of the equation to determine if the equation is already balanced. Under the reactants, list all the elements in the reactants starting with metals, then nonmetals, listing oxygen last and hydrogen next to last. Under the products, list all the elements in the same order as those under the reactants – preferably, straight across from them.

4. Count the atoms of each element on the left side and list the numbers next to the elements. Repeat for products. Don't forget that subscripts outside a parenthesis multiply subscripts inside the parenthesis. If each element has the same number of atoms on the right that it has on the left, the equation is balanced. If not, proceed to Step 5.

5. For the first element in the list that has unequal numbers of atoms, use a coefficient (whole number to the left of the compound or element) on either the left of the arrow or the right of the arrow to give an equal number of atoms. NEVER change the subscripts to balance an equation.

6. Go to the next unbalanced element and balance it, moving down the list until all are balanced.

7. Start back at the beginning of the list and actually count the atoms of each element on each side of the arrow to make sure the number listed is the actual number. Re-balance and re-check as needed.

Example: Balance the chemical equation describing the combustion of methanol in oxygen to produce only carbon dioxide and water.

Solution:

1) The structural formula of methanol is CH_3OH, so its molecular formula is CH_4O. We know from **0016** that carbon dioxide is CO_2. Therefore the unbalanced equation is:

$$CH_4O + O_2 \rightarrow CO_2 + H_2O.$$

2) On the left there are 1 C atom, 4 H atoms, and 3 O atoms. On the right, there are 1 C atom, 2 H atoms, and 3 O atoms. The equation seems close to being balanced, but there is still work to do.

3) Assuming that CH_4O has a stoichiometric coefficient of one means that the left side has 1 C atom and 4 H atoms that must be present on the right. Therefore the stoichiometric coefficient of CO_2 will be 1 to balance C and the stoichiometric coefficient of H_2O will be 2 to balance H. Now we have:

$$CH_4O + ?O_2 \rightarrow CO_2 + 2H_2O.$$

and only oxygen remains unbalanced. There are 4 O on the right and one of these is accounted for by methanol leaving 3 O to be accounted for by O_2. This gives a stoichiometric coefficient of 3/2 and a balanced equation:

$$CH_4O + \frac{3}{2}O_2 \rightarrow CO_2 + 2H_2O.$$

4) Whole-number coefficients are achieved by multiplying by two:
$$2CH_4O + 3O_2 \rightarrow 2CO_2 + 4H_2O.$$

Example: Balance the following equation:

$$Al(OH)_3 + NaOH \rightarrow NaAlO_2 + H_2O$$

Solution: List the elements, starting with metals, then nonmetals , then hydrogen, and oxygen under each side of the equation. Then list how many atoms of each are represented in the equation.

Al = 1	Al = 1
Na = 1	Na = 1
H = 3 + 1 = 4	H = 2
O = 3 + 1 = 4	O = 2 + 1 = 3

By placing a coefficient of 2 in front of H_2O on the right, a total of 4 H and 2 + 2 or 4 O will be obtained. The equation will then be balanced.

$$Al(OH)_3 + NaOH \rightarrow NaAlO_2 + 2 H_2O$$

Predict products of chemical equations.

Once we have an idea of the **reaction type**, we can make a fairly accurate prediction about the products of chemical equations, and also balance the reactions. **General reaction types** are listed in the following table. Some reaction types have multiple names.

Reaction type	General equation	Example
Combination / Synthesis	$A + B \rightarrow C$	$2H_2 + O_2 \rightarrow 2H_2O$
Decomposition	$A \rightarrow B + C$	$2KClO_3 \rightarrow 2KCl + 3O_2$
Single substitution / Single displacement / Single replacement	$A + BC \rightarrow AB + C$	$Mg + 2HCl \rightarrow MgCl_2 + H_2$
Double substitution / Double displacement / Double replacement / Ion exchange / Metathesis	$AC + BD \rightarrow AD + BC$	$HCl + NaOH \rightarrow NaCl + H_2O$
Isomerization	$A \rightarrow A'$	cyclopropane $C_3H_6 \rightarrow$ propene C_3H_6

Example: Determine the products of a reaction between Cl_2 and a solution of NaBr.

Solution: The first step is to write "$Cl_2 + NaBr(aq) \rightarrow ?$" Now examine the possible choices from the table. Decomposition and isomerization reactions require only one reactant. Since this reaction has two reactants and one of them is an element, it is not a decomposition or isomerization reaction. It also can't be a double substitution reaction because one of the reactants is an element. A synthesis reaction to form some NaBrCl compound would require very unusual valences! The most likely reaction is a single displacement reaction: Cl replaces Br in aqueous solution with Na:

$Cl_2 + NaBr(aq) \rightarrow NaCl(aq) + Br_2$. After balancing, the equation is:
$$Cl_2 + 2NaBr(aq) \rightarrow 2NaCl(aq) + Br_2.$$

Many **specific reaction types** also exist. Always determine the complete ionic equation (**0016**) for reactions in solution. This will help you determine the reaction type. The most common specific reaction types are summarized in the following table:

Reaction type	General equation	Example
Precipitation (**0025**)	Molecular: $AC(aq) + BD(aq) \rightarrow AD(s\text{ or }g) + BC(aq)$	Molecular: $NiCl_2(aq) + Na_2S(aq) \rightarrow NiS(s) + 2NaCl(aq)$
	Net ionic: $A^+(aq) + D^-(aq) \rightarrow AD(s\text{ or }g)$	Net ionic: $Ni^{2+}(aq) + S^{2-}(aq) \rightarrow NiS(s)$
Acid-base neutralization (**0019**)	Arrhenius: $H^+ + OH^- \rightarrow H_2O$	Arrhenius: $HNO_3 + NaOH \rightarrow NaNO_3 + H_2O$ $H^+ + OH^- \rightarrow H_2O$ (net ionic)
	Brønsted-Lowry: $HA + B \rightarrow HB + A$	Brønsted-Lowry: $HNO_3 + KCN \rightarrow HCN + KNO_3$ $H^+ + CN^- \rightarrow HCN$ (net ionic)
	Lewis: $A + {:}B \rightarrow A{:}B$	Lewis:
Redox (**0020**)	Full reaction: $A + B \rightarrow C + D$	$Ni + CuSO_4 \rightarrow NiSO_4 + Cu$ $Ni + Cu^{2+} \rightarrow Ni^{2+} + Cu$ (net ionic)
	Half reactions: $A \rightarrow C + e^-$ and $e^- + B \rightarrow D$	$Ni \rightarrow Ni^{2+} + 2e^-$ $2e^- + Cu^{2+} \rightarrow Cu$
Combustion	organic molecule $+ O_2 \rightarrow CO_2 + H_2O + $ heat	$2C_2H_6 + 7O_2 \rightarrow 4CO_2 + 6H_2O$

Whether precipitation occurs among a group of ions—and which compound will form the precipitate—may be determined by the solubility rules in **0025**. The possibility that oxidation numbers (**0009**) may change among the reactants indicates an electron transfer and a redox reaction (**0020**). Combustion reactants consist of an organic molecule and oxygen.

If protons are available (**0019**) for combination or substitution then it's likely they are being transferred from an acid to a base. An unshared electron pair on one of the reactants may form a bond in a Lewis acid-base reaction.

Example: Determine the products and write a balanced equation for the reaction between sodium iodide and lead(II) nitrate in aqueous solution.

Solution: This is basically a double replacement reaction. We know that sodium iodide is NaI and lead(II) nitrate is $Pb(NO_3)_2$ from **0016**. The reactants of the complete ionic equation are:

$$Na^+(aq) + Pb^{2+}(aq) + I^-(aq) + NO_3^-(aq) \rightarrow ?$$

The solubility rules indicate that lead iodide is insoluble and will form as a precipitate. The unbalanced net ionic equation is then:

$$Pb^{2+}(aq) + I^-(aq) \rightarrow PbI_2(s)$$

and the unbalanced molecular equation is:

$$NaI(aq) + Pb(NO_3)_2(aq) \rightarrow PbI_2(s) + NaNO_3(aq).$$

Balancing (**0016**) yields:

$$2NaI(aq) + Pb(NO_3)_2(aq) \rightarrow PbI_2(s) + 2NaNO_3(aq).$$

Recognize and Name Organic Molecules

Nomenclature for Organic Chemistry.

Organic compounds that **contain only carbon and hydrogen** are called **hydrocarbons**. Hydrocarbon molecules may be divided into the classes of **cyclic** and **open-chain** depending on whether they contain a ring of carbon atoms. Open-chain molecules may be divided into **branched** or **straight-chain** categories.

Hydrocarbons are also divided into classes called **aliphatic** and **aromatic**. Aromatic hydrocarbons are related to benzene and are always cyclic. Aliphatic hydrocarbons may be open-chain or cyclic. Aliphatic cyclic hydrocarbons are called **alicyclic**. Aliphatic hydrocarbons are one of three types: alkanes, alkenes, and alkynes.

Alkanes

Alkanes contain only single bonds. Alkanes have the maximum number of hydrogen atoms possible for their carbon backbone, so they are called saturated.

Straight-chain alkanes are also called **normal alkanes**. These are the simplest hydrocarbons. They consist of a linear chain of carbon atoms. The names of these molecules contain the suffix -*ane* and a **root based on the number of carbons in the chain** according to the table on the following page. The first four roots, *meth-*, *eth-*, *prop-*, and *but-* have historical origins in chemistry, and the remaining alkanes contain common Greek number prefixes. Alkanes have the general formula C_nH_{2n+2}.

A single molecule may be represented in multiple ways. Methane and ethane in the table are shown as three-dimensional structures with dashed wedge shapes attaching atoms behind the page and thick wedge shapes attaching atoms in front of the page.

Number of carbons	Name	Formula	Structure
1	Methane	CH_4	
2	Ethane	C_2H_6	
3	Propane	C_3H_8	
4	Butane	C_4H_{10}	
5	Pentane	C_5H_{12}	
6	Hexane	C_6H_{14}	
7	Heptane	C_7H_{16}	
8	Octane	C_8H_{18}	

Additional ways that pentane might be represented are:

n- pentane (the *n* represents a *normal* alkane)
$CH_3CH_2CH_2CH_2CH_3$
$CH_3(CH_2)_3CH_3$

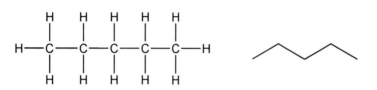

If one hydrogen is removed from an alkane, the residue is called an **alkyl** group. The *-ane* suffix is replaced by an *–yl-* infix when this residue is used as a **functional group**. Functional groups are used to systematically build up the names of organic molecules.

Branched alkanes are named using a four-step process:

1) Find the longest continuous carbon chain. This is the parent hydrocarbon.
2) Number the atoms on this chain beginning at the end near the first branch point. Number functional groups from the attachment point.
3) Determine the numbered locations and names of the substituted alkyl groups. Use *di-*, *tri-*, and similar prefixes for alkyl groups represented more than once. Separate numbers by commas and groups by dashes.
4) List the locations and names of alkyl groups in alphabetical order by their name (ignoring the *di-*, *tri-* prefixes) and end the name with the parent hydrocarbon.

Example: Name the following hydrocarbon:

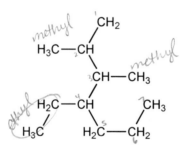

Solution:

1) The longest chain is seven carbons in length, as shown by the bold lines below. This molecule is a heptane.

2) The atoms are numbered from the end nearest the first branch as shown:

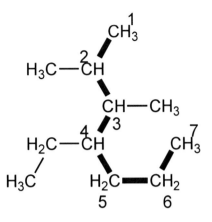

3) Methyl groups are located at carbons 2 and 3 (2,3-dimethyl), and an ethyl group is located at carbon 4.

4) "Ethyl" precedes "methyl" alphabetically. The hydrocarbon name is:
4-ethyl-2,3-dimethylheptane.

The following branched alkanes have accepted common names:

Structure	Systematic name	Common name
H_3C $CH-CH_3$ H_3C	2-methylpropane	isobutane
CH_3 H_3C CH C CH_3 H_2	2-methylbutane	isopentane
CH_3 $H_3C-C-CH_3$ CH_3	2,2-dimethylpropane	neopentane

The following alkyl groups have accepted common names. The systematic names assign a number of 1 to the attachment point:

Structure	Systematic name	Common name
H$_3$C CH CH$_3$	1-methylethyl	isopropyl
H$_3$C CH—CH$_2$ H$_3$C	2-methylpropyl	isobutyl
H$_2$C C CH$_3$ H$_3$C CH	1-methylpropyl	*sec*-butyl
CH$_3$ H$_3$C—C—CH$_3$	1,1-dimethylethyl	*tert*-butyl

Alkenes

Alkenes contain one or more double bonds. Alkenes, alkynes, and aromatics are unsaturated because they have fewer hydrogen atoms. Alkenes are also called olefins. The suffix used in the naming of alkenes is -*ene*, and the number roots are those used for alkanes of the same length.

A number preceding the name shows the location of the double bond for alkenes of length four and above. Alkenes with one double bond have the general formula C_nH_{2n}. Multiple double bonds are named using -*diene*, -*triene*, etc. The infix –*enyl*- is used for functional groups after a hydrogen is removed from an alkene. Ethene and propene have the common names **ethylene** and **propylene**. The ethenyl group has the common name **vinyl** and the 2-propenyl group has the common name **allyl**.

Examples:

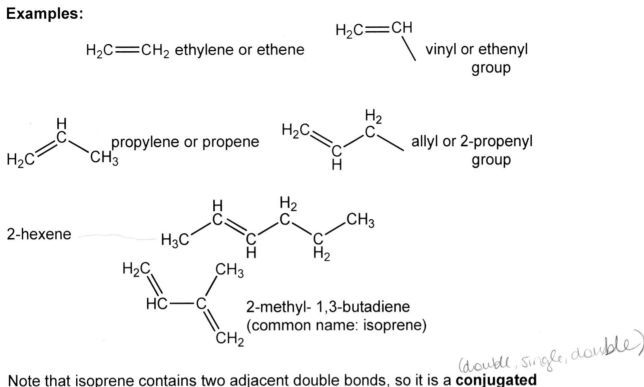

$H_2C = CH_2$ ethylene or ethene

$H_2C = CH$ vinyl or ethenyl group

propylene or propene

allyl or 2-propenyl group

2-hexene

2-methyl- 1,3-butadiene
(common name: isoprene)

(double, single, double)

Note that isoprene contains two adjacent double bonds, so it is a **conjugated** molecule.

Alkynes and alkenynes

Alkynes contain one or more triple bonds. They are named in a similar way to alkenes. The suffix used for alkynes is -*yne*. Ethyne is often called **acetylene**. Alkynes with one triple bond have the general formula C_nH_{2n-2}. Multiple triple bonds are named using -*diyne*, -*triyne*, etc. The infix –*ynyl*- is used for functional groups composed of alkynes after the removal of a hydrogen atom.

Hydrocarbons with **both double and triple bonds are known as alkenynes**. The locant number for the double bond precedes the name, and the locant for the triple bond follows the infix –*en*- and precedes the suffix -*yne*.

Examples: $HC \equiv CH$ acetylene or ethyne

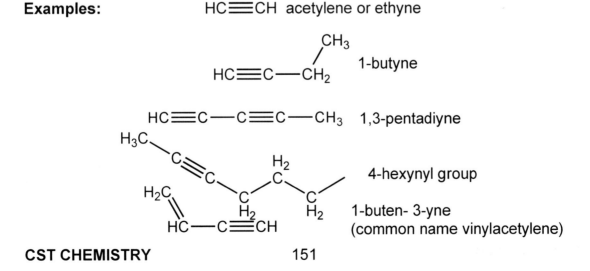

$HC \equiv C - CH_2$ ——CH₃ 1-butyne

$HC \equiv C - C \equiv C - CH_3$ 1,3-pentadiyne

4-hexynyl group

1-buten- 3-yne
(common name vinylacetylene)

Cycloalkanes, -enes, and -ynes

Alicyclic hydrocarbons use the prefix *cyclo-* before the number root for the molecule. The structures for these molecules are often written as if the molecule lay entirely within the plane of the paper even though in reality, these rings dip above and below a single plane. When there is more than one substitution on the ring, numbering begins with the first substitution listed in alphabetical order.

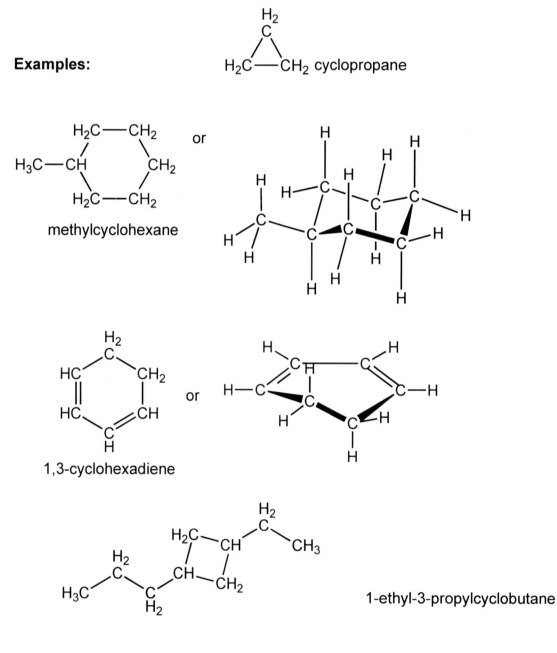

Aromatic hydrocarbons

Aromatic hydrocarbons are structurally related to benzene or made up of benzene molecules fused together. These molecules are called **arenes** to distinguish them from alkanes, alkenes, and alkynes. All atoms in arenes lie in the same plane. In other words, aromatic hydrocarbons are flat. Aromatic molecules have electrons in delocalized π orbitals that are free to migrate throughout the molecule.

Substitutions onto the benzene ring are named in alphabetical order using the lowest possible locant numbers. The prefix *phenyl-* may be used for C_6H_5- (benzene less a hydrogen) attached as a functional group to a larger hydrocarbon residue. Arenes in general form aryl functional groups. A phenyl group may be represented in a structure by the symbol Ø. The prefix *benzyl-* may used for $C_6H_5CH_2$- (methylbenzene with a hydrogen removed from the methyl group) attached as a functional group.

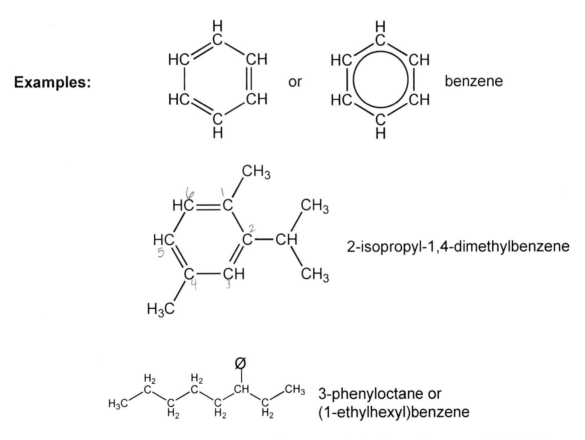

Examples: ... or ...   benzene

2-isopropyl-1,4-dimethylbenzene

3-phenyloctane or
(1-ethylhexyl)benzene

The most often used common names for aromatic hydrocarbons are listed in the table below. Naphthalene is the simplest molecule formed by fused benzene rings.

Structure	Systematic name	Common name
	methylbenzene	toluene
	1,2-dimethylbenzene	*ortho*-xylene or *o*-xylene
	1,3-dimethylbenzene	*meta*-xylene or *m*-xylene
	1,4-dimethylbenzene	*para*-xylene or *p*-xylene
	ethenylbenzene	styrene
		naphthalene

Many organic molecules contain **functional groups**, which are groups of atoms of a particular arrangement that give the entire molecule certain characteristics. Functional groups are named according to the composition of the group. For example, the carboxyl group shown at right is the arrangement of –COOH atoms that gives a molecule acidic properties.

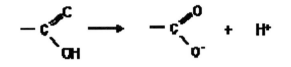

Some functional groups are polar and can ionize. For example, the hydrogen atom in the –COOH group can be removed (providing H^+ ions in solution). When this occurs, the oxygen atom retains both the electrons it shared with the hydrogen atom and this gives the molecule a negative charge:

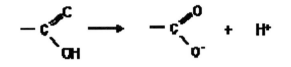

If polar or ionizing functional groups are attached to hydrophobic molecules, the molecule may become hydrophilic due to the functional group. Some ionizing functional groups are: –COOH, –OH, –CO, and $-NH_2$.

Some common functional groups are described below.

Hydroxyl group

The hydroxyl group, –OH, is the functional group identifying alcohols. The hydroxyl group makes the molecule polar, which increases the solubility of the compound.

Carbonyl group

The carbonyl group is a –C=O attached to either a carbon chain or a hydrogen atom. It is found in aldehydes and ketones.

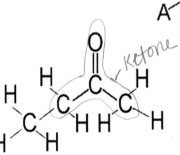

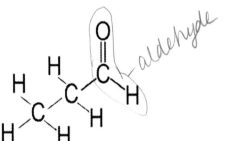

Aldehyde   Ketone

If the carbon atom is bonded to a hydrogen atom, the molecule is an aldehyde. If the carbon is attached to two carbon chains, the molecule is a ketone. The double-bonded oxygen atom is highly electronegative, so it creates a molecule that will exhibit polar properties.

Carboxyl group
The –COOH group has the ability to donate a proton (H^+ ion), giving the molecule acidic properties.

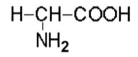

Amino group

An amino group contains an ammonia-like functional group composed of a nitrogen atom and two hydrogen atoms covalently bonded. The nitrogen atom has unshared electrons and can accept protons. This gives the molecule basic properties. An organic compound that contains an amino group is called an amine. The amines are weak bases because the unshared electron pair of the nitrogen atom can form a covalent bond with a proton. Another molecule that contains an amino group is an amino acid. It consists of the –NH_2 group of an amine and the –COOH group of an acid. The amino acid glycine is shown below.

$$H-\underset{\underset{NH_2}{|}}{C}H-COOH$$

Sulfhydryl group

A **thiol** is a compound that contains the functional group composed of a sulfur atom and a hydrogen atom (–SH). This functional group is referred to either as a *thiol group* or a *sulfhydryl group*. More traditionally, thiols have been referred to as *mercaptans*.

The small difference in electronegativity between the sulfur atom and the hydrogen atom produces a non-polar covalent bond. This does not allow hydrogen bonding, giving thiols lower boiling points and less solubility in water than alcohols of a similar molecular mass.

Phosphate group

The phosphate ion is contained in a hydrocarbon chain within the molecule. This molecule is ideal for energy transfer reactions (ATP) because of its symmetry and rotating double bond.

In biological systems, phosphates are most commonly found in the form of adenosine phosphates (AMP, ADP and ATP) and in DNA and RNA and can be released by the hydrolysis of ATP or ADP.

Derivatives utilizing other atoms are also common, as shown in the table:

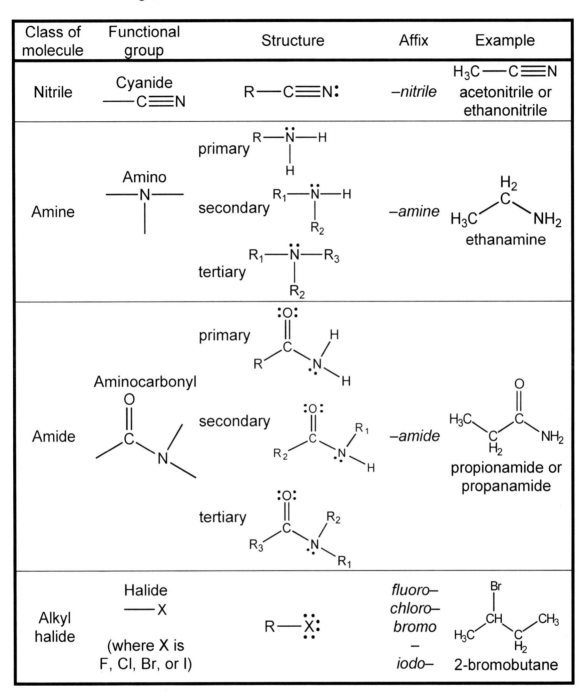

Class of molecule	Functional group	Structure	Affix	Example
Nitrile	Cyanide —C≡N	R—C≡N:	–nitrile	H₃C—C≡N acetonitrile or ethanonitrile
Amine	Amino —N—	primary, secondary, tertiary	–amine	ethanamine
Amide	Aminocarbonyl	primary, secondary, tertiary	–amide	propionamide or propanamide
Alkyl halide	Halide —X (where X is F, Cl, Br, or I)	R—X:	fluoro– chloro– bromo – iodo–	2-bromobutane

Competency 17.0   Understand factors that affect reaction rates and methods of measuring reaction rates

Derive rate laws from concentration data, rate data and simple reaction mechanisms.

Obtaining reaction rates from concentration data

The rate of any process is measured by its change per unit time. The speed of a car is measured by its change in position with time using units of miles per hour. The speed of a chemical reaction is usually measured by a change in the concentration of a reactant or product with time using units of **molarity per second** (M/s). The molarity of a chemical (see **0025**) is represented in mathematical equations using brackets.

The **average reaction rate** is the change in concentration of either a reactant or a product per unit of time during a specific time interval:

$$\text{Average reaction rate} = \frac{\text{Change in concentration}}{\text{Change in time}}$$

Reaction rates are positive quantities. Product concentrations increase and reactant concentrations decrease with time, so a different formula is required depending on the identity of the component of interest:

$$\text{Average reaction rate} = \frac{\left[\text{product}\right]_{\text{final}} - \left[\text{product}\right]_{\text{initial}}}{\text{time}_{\text{final}} - \text{time}_{\text{iniial}}}$$

$$= \frac{\left[\text{reactant}\right]_{\text{initial}} - \left[\text{reactant}\right]_{\text{final}}}{\text{time}_{\text{final}} - \text{time}_{\text{iniial}}}$$

The **reaction rate** at a given time refers to the **instantaneous reaction rate**. This is found from the absolute value of the **slope of a curve of concentration vs. time**. An estimate of the reaction rate at any time t may be found from the average reaction rate over a small time interval surrounding t. For those familiar with calculus notation, the following equations define reaction rate, but calculus is not needed to understand this skill:

$$\text{Reaction rate at time } t = \frac{d\left[\text{product}\right]}{dt} = -\frac{d\left[\text{reactant}\right]}{dt}$$

Example: The following concentration data describes the decomposition of N_2O_5 according to the reaction $2N_2O_5 \rightarrow 4NO_2 + O_2$:

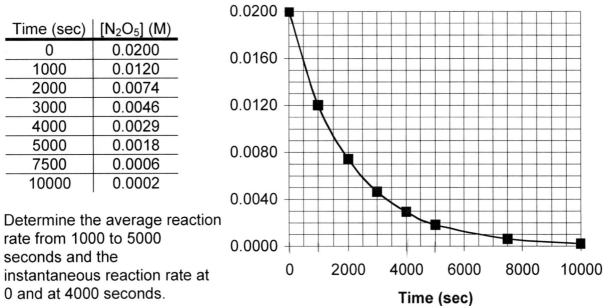

Time (sec)	$[N_2O_5]$ (M)
0	0.0200
1000	0.0120
2000	0.0074
3000	0.0046
4000	0.0029
5000	0.0018
7500	0.0006
10000	0.0002

Determine the average reaction rate from 1000 to 5000 seconds and the instantaneous reaction rate at 0 and at 4000 seconds.

Solution: Average reaction rate from 1000 to 5000 seconds is found from:

$$\frac{\left[\text{reactant}\right]_{\text{initial}} - \left[\text{reactant}\right]_{\text{final}}}{\text{time}_{\text{final}} - \text{time}_{\text{iniial}}} = \frac{0.0120\ M - 0.0018\ M}{5000\ \text{sec} - 1000\ \text{sec}} = 2.55 \times 10^{-6}\ \frac{M}{s}.$$

Instantaneous reaction rates are found by drawing lines that are tangent to the curve, finding the slopes of these lines, and forcing these slopes to be positive values.

At 0 seconds:

$$\text{rate=slope} = \frac{0.0200\ M}{2000\ s}$$

$$= 1.00 \times 10^{-5}\ \frac{M}{s}.$$

At 4000 seconds:

$$\text{rate=slope} = \frac{0.0090\ M}{6000\ s}$$

$$= 1.5 \times 10^{-6}\ \frac{M}{s}.$$

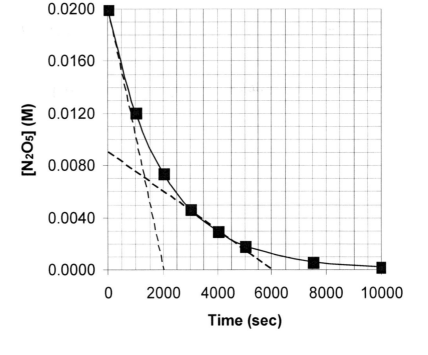

Deriving rate laws from reaction rates

A **rate law** is an **equation relating a reaction rate to concentrations of the reactants**. The rate laws for most reactions discussed in high-school level chemistry are of the form:

$$\text{Rate} = k[\text{reactant 1}]^a [\text{reactant 2}]^b \dots$$

In the above general equation, k is called the **rate constant**. a and b are called **reaction orders**. Most reactions considered in introductory chemistry have a reaction order of zero, one, or two. The sum of all reaction orders for a reaction is called the **overall reaction order**. Rate laws cannot be predicted from the stoichiometry of a reaction. They must be determined by experiment or derived from knowledge of reaction mechanisms.

If a reaction is zero order for a reactant, the concentration of that reactant has no impact on the rate as long as some reactant is present. If a reaction is first order for a reactant, the reaction rate is proportional to the reactant's concentration. For a reaction that is second order with respect to a reactant, doubling that reactant's concentration increases reaction rate by a factor of four. Rate laws are determined by finding the appropriate reaction order describing **the impact of reactant concentration on reaction rate**.

Reaction rates typically have units of M/s (moles/liter-sec) and concentrations have units of M (moles/liter). For units to cancel properly in the expression above, the units of the rate constant k must vary with overall reaction order as shown in the following table. The value of k may be determined by finding the slope of a plot charting a function of concentration against time. These functions may be memorized or computed using calculus.

Overall reaction order	Units of rate constant k	Method to determine k for rate laws with one reactant
0	M/sec	–(slope) of a chart of [reactant] vs. t
1	sec^{-1}	–(slope) of a chart of ln[reactant] vs. t
2	$M^{-1}\text{sec}^{-1}$	slope of a chart of 1/[reactant] vs. t

As an alternative to using the rate constant k, the course of **first order reactions** may be expressed in terms of a **half-life**, $t_{halflife}$. The half-life of a reaction is the time required for a reactant concentration to reach half of its initial value. First order rate constants and half-lives are inversely proportional:

$$t_{halflife} = \frac{\ln 2}{k_{first\ order}} = \frac{0.693}{k_{first\ order}}$$

The concept of half-life is applied to nuclear chemistry in **0011** and **0027**.

Example: Derive a rate law for the reaction $2N_2O_5 \rightarrow 4NO_2 + O_2$ using data from the previous example.

Solution: Three methods will be used to solve this problem.

1) In the previous example, we found the following two **instantaneous reaction rates**:

Time (sec)	$[N_2O_5]$ (M)	Reaction rate (M/sec)
0	0.0200	1.00×10^{-5}
4000	0.0029	1.5×10^{-6}

A decrease in reactant concentration to 0.0029/0.0200=14.5% of its initial value led to a nearly proportional decrease in reaction rate to 15% of its initial value. In other words, reaction rate remains proportional to reactant concentration. The reaction is first order:

$$\text{Rate} = k \left[N_2O_5 \right].$$

We may estimate a value for the rate constant by dividing reaction rates by the concentration:

$$k_{first \ order} = \frac{\text{Rate}}{\left[N_2O_5 \right]}.$$

Time (sec)	$[N_2O_5]$ (M)	Reaction rate (M/sec)	k (sec^{-1})
0	0.0200	1.00×10^{-5}	5.00×10^{-4}
4000	0.0029	1.5×10^{-6}	5.2×10^{-4}

2) We could estimate this rate constant by finding **average reaction rates** in each small time interval and assuming this rate occurs halfway between the two concentrations:

Time (sec)	$[N_2O_5]$ (M)	Average rate (M/sec)	Halfway $[N_2O_5]$ (M)	k (sec^{-1})
0	0.0200	8.00×10^{-6}	0.0160	5.00×10^{-4}
1000	0.0120	4.6×10^{-6}	0.0097	4.7×10^{-4}
2000	0.0074	2.8×10^{-6}	0.0060	4.7×10^{-4}
3000	0.0046	1.7×10^{-6}	0.0038	4.5×10^{-4}
4000	0.0029	1.1×10^{-6}	0.0024	4.7×10^{-4}
5000	0.0018	4.8×10^{-7}	0.0012	4.0×10^{-4}
7500	0.0006	2×10^{-7}	0.0004	4×10^{-4}
10000	0.0002			

3) If **concentration data** are given then no rate data needs to be found to determine a rate constant. For a first order reaction, chart the natural logarithm of concentration against time and find the slope.

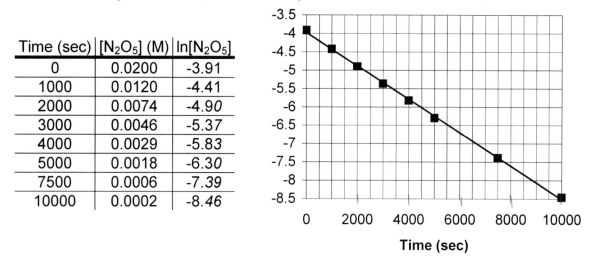

Time (sec)	$[N_2O_5]$ (M)	$\ln[N_2O_5]$
0	0.0200	-3.91
1000	0.0120	-4.41
2000	0.0074	-4.90
3000	0.0046	-5.37
4000	0.0029	-5.83
5000	0.0018	-6.30
7500	0.0006	-7.39
10000	0.0002	-8.46

The slope may be determined from a best-fit method or it may be estimated from $\dfrac{-8.46-(-3.91)}{10000} = -5 \times 10^{-4}$. The rate law describing this reaction is:

$$\text{Rate} = \left(5 \times 10^{-4} \frac{M}{\text{sec}}\right)[N_2O_5]$$

Deriving rate laws from simple reaction mechanisms

A **reaction mechanism** is a series of **elementary reactions** that explain how a reaction occurs. These elementary reactions are also called elementary processes or elementary steps. **A reaction mechanism cannot be determined from reaction stoichiometry**. Stoichiometry indicates the number of molecules of reactants and products in an **overall reaction**. Elementary steps represent a **single event**. This might be a collision between two molecules or a single rearrangement of electrons within a molecule.

The simplest reaction mechanisms consist of a single elementary reaction. The number of molecules required determines the rate laws for these processes.

For a **unimolecular process:**

$$A \rightarrow products$$

the number of molecules of A that decompose in a given time will be proportional to the number of molecules of A present. Therefore unimolecular processes are first order:

$$Rate = k[A].$$

For **bimolecular processes**, the rate law will be second order.

For $A + A \rightarrow$ products, Rate=$k[A]^2$

For $A + B \rightarrow$ products, Rate=$k[A][B]$.

Most reaction mechanisms are multi-step processes involving **reaction intermediates**. Intermediates are chemicals that are formed during one elementary step and consumed during another, but they are not overall reactants or products. In many cases one elementary reaction in particular is the slowest and determines the overall reaction rate. This slowest reaction in the series is called the **rate-limiting step**.

Example: The reaction $NO_2(g) + CO(g) \rightarrow NO(g) + CO_2(g)$ is composed of the following elementary reactions in the gas phase:

$$NO_2 + NO_2 \rightarrow NO + NO_3 \quad \rightarrow bimolecular$$
$$NO_3 + CO \rightarrow NO_2 + CO_2.$$

The first elementary reaction is very slow compared to the second. Determine the rate law for the overall reaction if NO_2 and CO are both present in sufficient quantity for the reaction to occur. Also name all reaction intermediates.

Solution: The first step is rate limiting because it is the slower step. In other words, almost as soon as NO_3 is available, it reacts with CO, so the rate-limiting step is the formation of NO_3. The first step is bimolecular.

Therefore, the rate law for the entire reaction is: Rate=$k[NO_2]^2$.

NO_3 is formed during the first step and consumed during the second. NO_3 is the only reaction intermediate because it is neither a reactant nor a product of the overall reaction.

Predicting the effect of catalysts and reaction conditions on reaction rates.

A **catalyst** is a material that increases the rate of a chemical reaction without changing itself permanently in the process. Catalysts provide an alternate reaction mechanism for the reaction to proceed in the forward and in the reverse direction. Therefore, **catalysts have no impact on the chemical equilibrium** of a reaction. They will not make a less favorable reaction more favorable.

Catalysts reduce the activation energy of a reaction. This is the amount of energy needed for the reaction to begin (see **0018**). Molecules with such low energies that they would have taken a long time to react will react more rapidly if a catalyst is present.

The impact of a catalyst may also be represented on an energy diagram. **A catalyst increases the rate of both the forward and reverse reactions by lowering the activation energy** for the reaction. Catalysts provide a different activated complex for the reaction at a lower energy state.

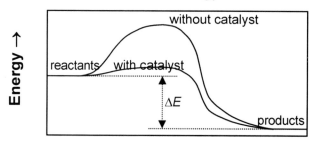

Reaction pathway →

There are two types of catalysts: **Homogeneous catalysts** are in the same physical phase as the reactants. Biological catalysts are called **enzymes**, and most are homogeneous catalysts. A typical homogenous catalytic reaction mechanism involves an initial reaction with one reactant followed by a reaction with a second reactant and release of the catalyst:

$$A + C \rightarrow AC$$
$$B + AC \rightarrow AB + C$$
$$\text{Net reaction: } A + B \xrightarrow{\text{catalyst C}} AB$$

Heterogeneous catalysts are present in a different physical state from the reactants. A typical heterogeneous catalytic reaction involves a solid surface onto which molecules in a fluid phase temporarily attach themselves in a way that favors a rapid reaction. Catalytic converters in cars utilize heterogeneous catalysis to break down harmful chemicals in exhaust.

Kinetic molecular theory (See **0007** and **0018**) may be applied to reaction rates in addition to physical constants like pressure. **Reaction rates increase with reactant concentration** because more reactant molecules are present and more are likely to collide with one another in a certain volume at higher concentrations. The nature of these relationships determines the rate law for the reaction as discussed in **0017**. For ideal gases, the concentration of a reactant is its molar density, and this varies with pressure and temperature.

Kinetic molecular theory also predicts that **reaction rate constants (values for *k*) increase with temperature** for two possible reasons:

1) More reactant molecules collide with each other per second.

2) These collisions will each occur at a higher energy that is more likely to overcome the activation energy of the reaction.

Competency 18.0   Understand the principles of chemical equilibrium

Identify the characteristics of a dynamic equilibrium.

A dynamic equilibrium consists of two **opposing reversible processes** that both occur at the **same rate**. *Balance* is a synonym for equilibrium. A system at equilibrium is stable; it does not change with time. Equilibria are drawn with a double arrow.

When a process at equilibrium is observed, it often doesn't seem like anything is happening, but at a microscopic scale, **two events are taking place that balance each other.** Arrows in this diagram represent the movement of molecules. When water is placed in a closed container, the water evaporates until the air in the container is saturated. After this occurs, the water level no longer changes, so an observer at the macroscopic scale would say that evaporation has ceased, but the reality on a microscopic scale is that both evaporation and condensation are taking place at the same rate. All equilibria between different phases of matter have this dynamic character on a microscopic scale.

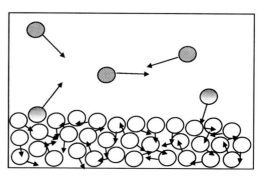

Chemical reactions often do not "go to completion." Instead, products are generated from reactants up to a certain point when the reaction no longer seems to occur, leaving some reactant unaltered. At this point, the system is in a state of **chemical equilibrium** because **the rate of the forward reaction is equal to the rate of the reverse reaction**. An example is shown to the right. Arrows in this diagram represent the chemical reactions of individual molecules. An observer at the macroscopic scale might say that no reaction is taking place at equilibrium, but at a microscopic scale, both the forward and reverse reactions are occurring at the same rate.

Homogeneous equilibrium refers to a chemical equilibrium among reactants and products that are all in the same phase of matter. **Heterogeneous equilibrium** takes place between two or more chemicals in different phases.

If a reaction at equilibrium is disturbed, changes occur to reestablish equilibrium. The nature of these changes is determined by **Le Chatelier's principle** (see **0018**).

A reaction at equilibrium contains a constant ratio of chemical species. This ratio is determined by an **equilibrium constant** (see **0018**).

Interpret energy diagrams for chemical reactions.

In order for one species to be converted to another during a chemical reaction, the reactants must collide. The collisions between the reactants determine how fast the reaction takes place. However, during a chemical reaction, only a fraction of the collisions between the appropriate reactant molecules convert them into product molecules. This occurs for two reasons:

1) Not all collisions occur with a **sufficiently high energy** for the reaction to occur.
2) Not all collisions **orient the molecules properly** for the reaction to occur.

The **activation energy**, E_a, of a reaction is the **minimum energy to overcome the barrier to the formation of products** and allow the reaction to occur. This is the minimum energy needed for the reaction to occur.

At the scale of individual molecules, a reaction typically involves a very small period of time when old bonds are broken and new bonds are formed. During this time, the molecules involved are in a **transition state** between reactants and products. A threshold of maximum energy is crossed when the arrangement of molecules is in an unfavorable intermediate state between reactants and products known as the **activated complex**. Formulas and diagrams of activated complexes are often written within brackets to indicate they are transition states that are present for extremely small periods of time.

The activation energy, E_a, is the difference between the energy of reactants and the energy of the activated complex. The energy change during the reaction, ΔE, is the difference between the energy of the products and the energy of the reactants. The activation energy of the reverse reaction is $E_a - \Delta E$. These energy levels are represented in an **energy diagram** such as the one shown below for the reaction $NO_2 + CO \rightarrow NO + CO_2$. This is an exothermic reaction because the products are lower in energy than the reactants.

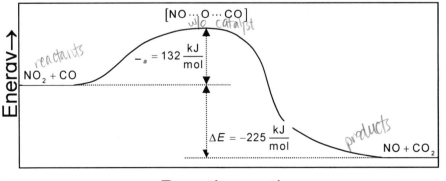

Reaction pathway→

An energy diagram is a conceptual tool, so there is some variability in how its axes are labeled. The y-axis of the diagram is usually labeled energy (E), but it is sometimes labeled "enthalpy (H)" or (rarely) "free energy (G)." There is an even greater variability in how the x-axis is labeled. The terms "reaction pathway," "reaction coordinate," "course of reaction," or "reaction progress" may be used on the x-axis, or the x-axis may remain without a label.

The energy diagrams of an endothermic and exothermic reaction (See **0012** and **0013**) are compared below.

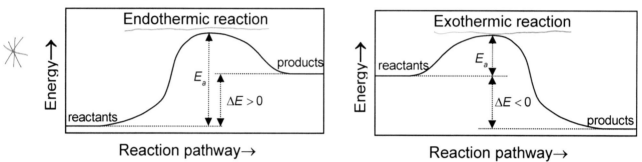

A **catalyst** is a material that increases the rate of a chemical reaction without changing itself permanently in the process. Catalysts provide an alternate reaction mechanism for the reaction to proceed in the forward and in the reverse direction. Therefore, **catalysts have no impact on the chemical equilibrium** of a reaction. They will not make a less favorable reaction more favorable.

Catalysts reduce the activation energy of a reaction. This is the amount of energy needed for the reaction to begin. Molecules with such low energies that they would have taken a long time to react will react more rapidly if a catalyst is present.

The impact of a catalyst may also be represented on an energy diagram. **A catalyst increases the rate of both the forward and reverse reactions by lowering the activation energy** for the reaction. Catalysts provide a different activated complex for the reaction at a lower energy state.

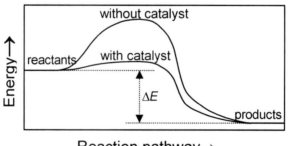

Reaction pathway→

The rate of most simple reactions **increases with temperature** because a **greater fraction of molecules have the kinetic energy** required to overcome the reaction's activation energy. The chart below shows the effect of temperature on the distribution of kinetic energies in a sample of molecules. These curves are called **Maxwell-Boltzmann distributions**. The shaded areas represent the fraction of molecules containing sufficient kinetic energy for a reaction to occur. This area is larger at a higher temperature; so more molecules are above the activation energy and more molecules react per second.

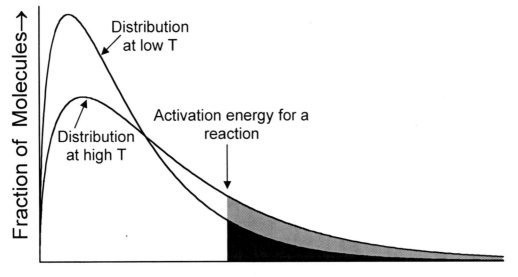

http://www.mhhe.com/physsci/chemistry/essentialchemistry/flash/activa2.swf provides an animated audio tutorial on energy diagrams.

Use Le Chatelier's principle to predict the effect that a given change will have on a system at equilibrium.

A system at equilibrium is in a state of balance because the forward and the reverse processes are taking place at equal rates. If the equilibrium is disturbed by changing concentration, pressure, or temperature, the state of balance is upset for a period of time before the equilibrium shifts to achieve a new state of balance. **Le Chatelier's principle states that equilibrium will shift to partially offset the impact of an altered condition**.

Change in reactant and product concentrations

If a chemical reaction is at equilibrium, Le Chatelier's principle predicts that **adding a substance**—either a reactant or a product—will shift the reaction so **a new equilibrium is established by consuming some of the added substance**. Removing a substance will cause the reaction to move in the direction that forms more of that substance.

Example: The reaction $CO + 2H_2 \leftrightarrow CH_3OH$ is used to synthesize methanol. Equilibrium is established, and then additional CO is added to the reaction vessel. Predict the impact on each reaction component after CO is added.

Solution: Le Chatelier's principle states that the reaction will shift to partially offset the impact of the added CO. Therefore, the CO concentration will decrease, and the reaction will "shift to the right." The H_2 concentration will also decrease and the CH_3OH concentration will increase.

Change in pressure for gases

If a chemical reaction is at equilibrium in the gas phase, Le Chatelier's principle predicts that **an increase in pressure** will shift the reaction so **a new equilibrium is established by decreasing the number of gas moles present**. A decrease in the number of moles partially offsets this rise in pressure. Decreasing pressure will cause the reaction to move in the direction that forms more moles of gas. These changes in pressure might result from altering the volume of the reaction vessel at constant temperature.

Example: The reaction $N_2 + 3H_2 \leftrightarrow 2NH_3$ is used to synthesize ammonia. Equilibrium is established. Next the reaction vessel is expanded at constant temperature. Predict the impact on each reaction component after this expansion occurs.

Solution: The expansion will result in a decrease in pressure (see Boyle's Law in **0010**). Le Chatelier's principle states that the reaction will shift to partially offset this decrease by increasing the number of moles present. There are 4 moles of gas on the left side of the equation and 2 moles of gas on the right, so the reaction will shift to the left. N_2 and H_2 concentration will increase; NH_3 concentration will decrease.

Change in temperature

Le Chatelier's principle predicts that **when heat is added** at constant pressure to a system at equilibrium, **the reaction will shift in the direction that absorbs heat** until a new equilibrium is established. For an endothermic process, the reaction will shift to the right towards product formation. For an exothermic process, the reaction will shift to the left towards reactant formation. If you understand the application of Le Chatelier's principle to concentration changes then writing "heat" on the appropriate side of the equation will help you understand its application to changes in temperature. The impact of temperature on solubility reactions was discussed in **0025**.

Example: $N_2 + 3H_2 \leftrightarrow 2NH_3$ is an exothermic reaction. First, equilibrium is established and then the temperature is decreased. Predict the impact of the lower temperature on each reaction component.

Solution: Since the reaction is exothermic, we may write it as:

$$N_2 + 3H_2 \leftrightarrow 2NH_3 + \text{heat}$$

To find the impact of temperature on equilibrium processes, we may consider heat as if it were a reaction component. Le Chatelier's principle states that after a temperature decrease, the reaction will shift to partially offset the impact of a loss of heat. Therefore more heat will be produced, and the reaction will shift to the right. N_2 and H_2 concentration will decrease. NH_3 concentration will increase.

A flash animation with audio that demonstrates Le Chatelier's principle is at http://www.mhhe.com/physsci/chemistry/essentialchemistry/flash/lechv17.swf.

Write equilibrium expressions for balanced equations.

We have seen how the concentrations of reactants and products at equilibrium remain constant because the forward and reverse reactions take place at the same rate. We have seen how this equilibrium responds to a perturbation in one concentration by altering every concentration in a well-defined way until equilibrium is reestablished. In the present skill, we will present a mathematical expression that relates these concentrations and defines the law that governs equilibrium.

A reaction at equilibrium contains a constant ratio of chemical species. This ratio is determined by an **equilibrium constant**. The mathematical relationship between the concentrations of the reactants and products of a system is called the law of mass action. It governs equilibrium expressions.

Consider the general balanced reaction:

$$mA + nB \leftrightarrow pR + qS$$

where m, n, p, and q are stoichiometric coefficients and A, B, R, and S are chemical species. An **equilibrium expression** relating the concentrations of chemical species at equilibrium is determined by the equation:

$$K_{eq} = \frac{[R]^p [S]^q}{[A]^m [B]^n}$$

where K_{eq} is a constant value called the **equilibrium constant**. Product concentrations raised to the power of their stoichiometric coefficients are placed in the numerator and reactant concentrations raised to the power of their coefficients are placed in the denominator.

Every reaction has a unique value of K_{eq} that varies only with temperature. Alternate subscripts are often given to the equilibrium constant. K_c or K with no subscript is often used instead of K_{eq} to represent the equilibrium constant. Other subscripts are used for specific reactions as described in the following skill.

Example: Write the equilibrium expression for the reaction

$$2HI \ (g) \leftrightarrow H_2 \ (g) + I_2 \ (g)$$

Solution:
$$K_{eq} = \frac{[H_2][I_2]}{[HI]^2}.$$

The units associated with equilibrium constants in the expression above are molarity raised to the power of an integer that depends on the stoichiometric coefficients of the reaction, but it is common practice to write these constants as dimensionless values. Multiplying or dividing the equilibrium expression by 1 M as needed achieves these dimensionless values. **The equilibrium expression for a reaction written in one direction is the reciprocal of the expression for the reaction in the reverse direction**.

For a heterogeneous equilibrium (a chemical equilibrium with components in different phases) , reactants or products may be pure liquids or solids. The concentration of a pure liquid or solid in moles/liter cannot change. It is a constant property of the material, and these constants are incorporated into the equilibrium constant. Therefore the concentrations of pure liquids and solids are absent from equilibrium expressions for heterogeneous equilibria.

Example: Write the equilibrium expression for the redox reaction between copper and silver:.
$$Cu \ (s) + 2Ag^+ \ (aq) \leftrightarrow Cu^{2+} \ (aq) + 2Ag \ (s)$$

Solution: $K_{eq} = \dfrac{[Cu^{2+}]}{[Ag^+]^2}$. The solids do not appear in the equilibrium expression.

Solve typical K_{eq} problems (e.g. K_{sp}, K_a, K_b, and K_w).

Calculation of unknown concentrations and concentration units

Many types of K_{eq} problems require the calculation of an unknown concentration at equilibrium from known quantities. These problems only require algebra to solve. Remember that equilibrium constants are forced to be dimensionless values. If all concentrations are represented in the same units, it is OK to be a little less cautious with units than for other problems.

Example: The reaction $N_2 (g) + 3H_2 (g) \leftrightarrow 2NH_3 (g)$ achieves equilibrium in the presence of 0.27 M H_2 and 0.094 M N_2. What is the ammonia concentration under these conditions if the reaction at the given temperature has an equilibrium constant of $K_{eq} = 0.11$?

Solution: First we will solve this problem without worrying about units because all concentrations are given in M:

$$K_{eq} = \frac{[NH_3]^2}{[N_2][H_2]^3} = \frac{[NH_3]^2}{(0.094)(0.27)^3} = 0.11.$$

Solving for [NH₃] yields: $[NH_3] = \sqrt{(0.11)(0.094)(0.27)^3} = 0.014$ M.

This is the preferred method for solving these problems.

If units are to be treated rigorously then a more explicit definition of K_{eq} is written. This assures us that we achieve a dimensionless value for K_{eq} by repeatedly multiplying by 1 M:

$$K_{eq} = \frac{[NH_3]^2 (1\,M)^2}{[N_2][H_2]^3} = \frac{[NH_3]^2 (1\,M)^2}{(0.094\,M)(0.27\,M)^3} = 0.11.$$

Solving for [NH₃] yields: $[NH_3] = \sqrt{(0.11)\frac{(0.094\,M)(0.27\,M)^3}{(1\,M)^2}} = 0.014$ M.

Determining the directionality of a reaction

Some K_{eq} problems give every concentration value for a reaction that is not at equilibrium and ask which direction the reaction will proceed for a given equilibrium constant. Solving these problems is a two step process:

1) Insert the non-equilibrium reaction concentrations into the equilibrium expression to obtain a **reaction quotient**, Q.

2) If $Q<K_{eq}$, there are too many reactant molecules for the products, and the reaction proceeds to the right. If $Q>K_{eq}$, there are too many product molecules for the reactants, and the reaction proceeds to the left. If $Q=K_{eq}$, the reaction is at equilibrium.

Example: Predict the direction in which the reaction $H_2(g)+I_2(g) \rightleftharpoons 2HI(g)$ will proceed if initial concentrations are 0.004 mM H_2, 0.006 mM I_2, and 0.011 mM HI given $K_{eq}=48$.

Solution: 1) The reactant quotient is $Q = \dfrac{\left[HI\right]^2}{\left[H_2\right]\left[I_2\right]} = \dfrac{\left(0.011\right)^2}{\left(0.004\right)\left(0.006\right)} = 5$.

2) The reactant quotient is less than K_{eq}. That is, 5<48. Therefore, the numerator (products) of the reaction quotient is too small for the denominator (reactants).

The trend towards equilibrium with time will increase the numerator relative to the denominator until a ratio of 48 is achieved. More reactants will turn into products and the reaction will proceed to the right.

Special equilibrium constants

A few equilibrium constants are used often enough to have their own unique nomenclature.

The **solubility-product constant**, K_{sp}, is the equilibrium constant for an ionic solid in contact with a saturated aqueous solution. The two processes with equal rates in this case are dissolution and crystallization.

$$\text{Ionic compound(s)} \leftrightarrow p \text{ cation}^+ (aq) + q \text{ anion}^- (aq)$$

$$K_{sp} = \left[\text{cation}^+\right]^p \left[\text{anion}^-\right]^q.$$

This is an example of a heterogeneous equilibrium, so the concentration of pure solid is not included as a variable. K_{sp} is a different quantity from solubility. K_{sp} is an equilibrium constant, and solubility is the mass of solid that is able to dissolve in a given quantity of water. See **0025** for details about solubility processes.

Example: Solid lead chloride $PbCl_2$ is allowed to dissolve in pure water until equilibrium has been reached and the solution is saturated. The concentration of Pb^{2+} is 0.016 M. What is K_{sp} for $PbCl_2$?

Solution: The reaction and solubility product are shown below:

$$PbCl_2 \ (s) \leftrightarrow Pb^{2+} \ (aq) + 2Cl^- \ (aq)$$

$$K_{sp} = \left[Pb^{2+} \right] \left[Cl^- \right]^2 .$$

The only source of both ions in solution is $PbCl_2$, so the concentration of Cl^- must be twice that for Pb^{2+}, or 0.032 M. Therefore,

$$K_{sp} = (0.016)(0.032)^2 = 1.6 \times 10^{-5} .$$

The **acid-dissociation constant**, K_a, is the equilibrium constant for the ionization of a weak acid to a hydrogen ion and its conjugate base:

$$HX \ (aq) \leftrightarrow H^+ \ (aq) + X^- \ (aq)$$

$$K_a = \frac{\left[H^+ \right]\left[X^- \right]}{[HX]} .$$

Polyprotic acids (see **0019**) have unique values for each dissociation: K_{a1}, K_{a2}, etc.

Example: Hydrofluoric acid is dissolved in pure water until $[H^+]$ reaches 0.006 M. What is the concentration of undissociated HF? K_a for HF is 6.8×10^{-4}.

Solution: The principle source of both ions is dissociation of HF (autoionization of water is negligible). Therefore $\left[F^- \right] = \left[H^+ \right] = 0.006 \ M$, and

$$[HF] = \frac{\left[H^+ \right]\left[F^- \right]}{K_a} = \frac{(0.006)^2}{6.8 \times 10^{-4}} = 0.05 \ M.$$

The **base-dissociation constant**, K_b, is the equilibrium constant for the addition of a proton to a weak base by water to form its conjugate acid and an OH^- ion. In these reactions, it is water that is dissociating as a result of reaction with the base:

$$\text{Weak base } (aq) + H_2O \ (l) \leftrightarrow \text{conjugate acid } (aq) + OH^- \ (aq)$$

$$K_b = \frac{[\text{conjugate acid}]\left[OH^- \right]}{[\text{weak base}]} .$$

The concentration of water is nearly constant and is incorporated into the dissociation constant.

For ammonia (the most common weak base), the equilibrium reaction and base-dissociation constant are:

$$NH_3\ (aq) + H_2O\ (l) \leftrightarrow NH_4^+\ (aq) + OH^-\ (aq)$$

$$K_b = \frac{\left[NH_4^+\right]\left[OH^-\right]}{\left[NH_3\right]}$$

Example: K_b for ammonia at 25 °C is 1.8×10^{-5}. What is the concentration of OH^- in an ammonia solution at equilibrium containing 0.2 M NH_3 at 25°C?

Solution: Assume $x = \left[OH^-\right]$. The principle source of both ions is NH_3 (autoionization of water is negligible). Therefore $x = [OH^-] = [NH_4^+]$.

$$K_b = \frac{\left[NH_4^+\right]\left[OH^-\right]}{\left[NH_3\right]} = \frac{x^2}{0.2} = 1.8 \times 10^{-5}.$$

Solving for x yields: $x = \sqrt{(0.2)(1.8 \times 10^{-5})} = 0.002$ M OH^-

The **ion-product constant for water**, K_w is the equilibrium constant for the dissociation of H_2O. Water molecules may donate protons to other water molecules in a process known as <u>autoionization</u>:

$$2H_2O\ (l) \leftrightarrow H_3O^{+1}\ (aq) + OH^-\ (aq)$$

A hydrated water molecule is often referred to as H^+ (aq), so the above equation may be rewritten as the following reaction that defines K_w. As with K_b, the concentration of water is nearly constant.

$$H_2O\ (l) \leftrightarrow H^+\ (aq) + OH^-\ (aq)$$

$$K_w = \left[H^+\right]\left[OH^-\right] = 1.0 \times 10^{-14}\ \text{at 25°C.}$$

$$pH + pOH = 14$$
$$[H^+] = 10^{-pH}$$
$$[OH^-] = 10^{-pOH} \quad \text{or} \quad \frac{1 \times 10^{-14}}{[H^+]} = [OH^-]$$

$$[H^+] = 1 \times 10^{-7} M$$
$$[OH^-] = 1 \times 10^{-7} M$$
$$K_w = 1.0 \times 10^{-14} M$$

Example: a) What is the concentration of OH⁻ in an aqueous solution with an H^+ concentration of 2.5×10^{-6} M?

b) What is the concentration of H^+ when pure water reaches equilibrium?

Solution: a) $K_w = \left[H^+ \right]\left[OH^- \right] = \left(2.5 \times 10^{-6} \right)\left[OH^- \right] = 1.0 \times 10^{-14}$.

Solving for $\left[OH^- \right]$ yields $\left[OH^- \right] = \dfrac{1.0 \times 10^{-14}}{2.5 \times 10^{-6}} = 4.0 \times 10^{-9}$.

b) The autoionization of pure water creates an equal concentration of the two ions:

$\left[H^+ \right] = \left[OH^- \right]$. Therefore $K_w = \left[H^+ \right]^2 = 1.0 \times 10^{-14}$.

Solving for $\left[H^+ \right]$ yields $\left[H^+ \right] = 1.0 \times 10^{-7}$.

See **0019** for details about weak acids, weak bases, their conjugates, and the nature of the H^+ ion.

Competency 19.0   Understand the theories, principles, and applications of acid-base chemistry

Identify major characteristics of acids and bases.

It was recognized centuries ago that many substances could be divided into the two general categories. **Acids** have a sour taste (as in lemon juice), dissolve many metals, and turn litmus paper red. **Bases** have a bitter taste (as in soaps), feel slippery, and turn litmus paper blue. The chemical reaction between an acid and a base is called **neutralization**. The products of neutralization reactions are neither acids nor bases. Litmus paper is an example of an **acid-base indicator**, a substance that changes color when changing from an acid to a base.

Arrhenius definition of acids and bases

Svante **Arrhenius** proposed in the 1880s that **acids form H^+ ions and bases form OH^- ions in water**.

The net ionic reaction for neutralization between an Arrhenius acid and base always produces water as shown below for nitric acid and sodium hydroxide:

$$HNO_3(aq) + NaOH(aq) \rightarrow NaNO_3(aq) + H_2O(l)$$

$$H^+(aq) + NO_3^-(aq) + Na^+(aq) + OH^-(aq) \rightarrow NO_3^-(aq) + Na^+(aq) + H_2O(l) \text{ (complete ionic)}$$

$$H^+(aq) + OH^-(aq) \rightarrow H_2O(l) \text{ (net ionic)}$$

The $H^+(aq)$ ion

In acid-base systems, **"protonated water" or "$H^+(aq)$" is shorthand for a mixture of water ions**. For example, HCl reacting in water may be represented as a dissociation:

$$HCl(aq) \rightarrow H^+(aq) + Cl^{\$}(aq).$$

The same reaction may be described as the transfer of a proton to water to form H_3O^+:

$$HCl(aq) + H_2O(l) \rightarrow Cl^{\$}(aq) + H_3O^+(aq).$$

Determining pH and % Dissociation

% dissociation = $\dfrac{[\text{ions}]}{[\text{molecules}]}$ (100)

= $\dfrac{(\text{ionized molecules})}{(\text{unionized molecules})}$ (100)

ICE Table

$K_a = \dfrac{[\text{products}]}{[\text{reactants}]}$

$[H^+]$ = some #

pH = -log(some #) = -log$[H^+]$

then to find pOH, do Kw - pH = pOH

pOH = -log$[OH^-]$

H_3O^+ is called a **hydronium ion**. Its Lewis structure is shown below to the left. In reality, the hydrogen bonds in water are so strong that H^+ ions exist in water as a mixture of species in a hydrogen bond network. Two of them are shown below at center and to the right. Hydrogen bonds are shown as dashed lines.

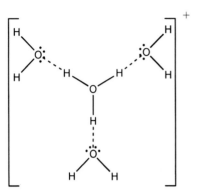

Brønsted-Lowry definition of acids and bases

In the 1920s, Johannes **Brønsted** and Thomas **Lowry** recognized that **acids can transfer a proton to bases** regardless of whether an OH^- ion accepts the proton. In an equilibrium reaction, the direction of proton transfer depends on whether the reaction is read left to right or right to left, so **Brønsted acids and bases exist in conjugate pairs with and without a proton**. Acids that are able to transfer more than one proton are called **polyprotic acids**.

Examples:

1) In the reaction:

$$HF\ (aq) + H_2O\ (l) \leftrightarrow F^-\ (aq) + H_3O^+\ (aq)$$

HF transfers a proton to water. Therefore HF is the Brønsted acid and H_2O is the Brønsted base. But in the reverse direction, hydronium ions transfer a proton to fluoride ions. H_3O^+ is the conjugate acid of H_2O because it has an additional proton, and F^- is the conjugate base of HF because it lacks a proton.

2) In the reaction:

$$NH_3\ (aq) + H_2O\ (l) \leftrightarrow NH_4^+\ (aq) + OH^-\ (aq)$$

water transfers a proton to ammonia. H_2O is the Brønsted acid and OH^- is its conjugate base. NH_3 is the Brønsted base and NH_4^+ is its conjugate acid.

3) In the reaction:

$$H_3PO_4 + HS^- \leftrightarrow H_2PO_4^- + H_2S$$

$H_3PO_4/H_2PO_4^-$ is one conjugate acid-base pair and H_2S/HS^- is the other.

4) H_3PO_4 is a polyprotic acid. It may further dissociate to transfer more than one proton:

$$H_3PO_4 \leftrightarrow H_2PO_4^- + H^+$$
$$H_2PO_4^- \leftrightarrow HPO_4^{2-} + H^+$$
$$HPO_4^{2-} \leftrightarrow PO_4^{3-} + H^+$$

Strong and weak acids and bases

Strong acids and bases are strong electrolytes (see **0025**), and weak acids and bases are weak electrolytes, so **strong acids and bases completely dissociate in water**, but weak acids and bases do not.

Example: $HCl(aq) + H_2O(l) \rightarrow H_3O^+(aq) + Cl^-(aq)$ goes to completion because HCl is a strong acid. The acids in the examples on the previous page were all weak.

The aqueous dissociation constants K_a and K_b (see **0018**) quantify acid and base strength, respectively. Another way of looking at acid dissociation is that strong acids transfer protons more readily than H_3O^+ transfers protons, so they protonate water, the conjugate base of H_3O^+. In general, **if two acid/base conjugate pairs are present, the stronger acid will transfer a proton to the conjugate base of the weaker acid**.

Acid and base **strength is not related to safety**. Weak acids like HF may be extremely corrosive and dangerous.

The most **common strong acids and bases** are listed in the following table:

Strong acid		Strong base	
HCl	Hydrochloric acid	LiOH	Lithium hydroxide
HBr	Hydrobromic acid	NaOH	Sodium hydroxide
HI	Hydroiodic acid	KOH	Potassium hydroxide
HNO_3	Nitric acid	$Ca(OH)_2$	Calcium hydroxide
H_2SO_4	Sulfuric acid	$Sr(OH)_2$	Strontium hydroxide
$HClO_4$	Perchloric acid	$Ba(OH)_2$	Barium hydroxide

A flash animation tutorial demonstrating the difference between strong and weak acids is located at http://www.mhhe.com/physsci/chemistry/essentialchemistry/flash/acid13.swf.

Trends in acid and base strength

The strongest acid in a polyprotic series is always **the acid with the most protons** (e.g. H_2SO_4 is a stronger acid than HSO_4^-). The strongest acid in a series with the same central atom is always **the acid with the central atom at the highest oxidation number** (e.g. $HClO_4 > HClO_3 > HClO_2 > HClO$ in terms of acid strength). The strongest acid in a series with different central atoms at the same oxidation number is usually **the acid with the central atom at the highest electronegativity** (e.g. the K_a of $HClO > HBrO > HIO$). This electronegativity trend stretches across the periodic table for oxides as discussed in **0009**.

Lewis definition of acids and bases

The transfer of a proton from a Brønsted acid to a Brønsted base requires that the base accept the proton. When Lewis diagrams (see **0015**) are used to draw the proton donation of Brønsted acid-base reactions, it is always clear that the base must contain an unshared electron pair to form a bond with the proton. For example, ammonia contains an unshared electron pair in the following reaction:

$$H^+ \ + \ \begin{matrix} H \\ | \\ :N-H \\ | \\ H \end{matrix} \ \longrightarrow \ \left[\begin{matrix} H \\ | \\ H-N-H \\ | \\ H \end{matrix} \right]^+$$

In the 1920s, Gilbert N. **Lewis** proposed that **bases donate unshared electron pairs to acids**, regardless of whether the donation is made to a proton or to another atom. Boron trifluoride is an example of a Lewis acid that is not a Brønsted acid because it is a chemical that accepts an electron pair without involving an H^+ ion:

$$\begin{matrix} F \\ \backslash \\ B-F \\ / \\ F \end{matrix} \ + \ \begin{matrix} H \\ | \\ :N-H \\ | \\ H \end{matrix} \ \longrightarrow \ \begin{matrix} F & H \\ | & | \\ F-B-N-H \\ | & | \\ F & H \end{matrix}$$

The Lewis theory of acids and bases is more general than the Brønsted-Lowry theory, but Brønsted-Lowry's definition is used more frequently. The terms "acid" and "base" most often refer to Brønsted acids and bases, and the term "Lewis acid" is usually reserved for chemicals like BF_3 that are not also Brønsted acids.

Summary of definitions

A Lewis base transfers an electron pair to a Lewis acid. A Brønsted acid transfers a proton to a Brønsted base. These exist in conjugate pairs at equilibrium. In an Arrhenius base, the proton acceptor (electron pair donor) is OH^-. All Arrhenius acids/bases are Brønsted acids/bases and all Brønsted acids/bases are Lewis acids/bases. Each definition is a subset of the one that comes before it.

Solve pH/pOH problems.

The concentration of $H^+(aq)$ ions is often expressed in terms of pH. **The pH of a solution is the negative base-10 logarithm of the hydrogen-ion molarity.**

$$pH = -\log\left[H^+\right] = \log\left(\frac{1}{\left[H^+\right]}\right).$$

A ten-fold increase in $[H^+]$ decreases the pH by one unit. $[H^+]$ may be found from pH using the expression:

$$\left[H^+\right] = 10^{-pH}.$$

See **0019** for a discussion about the nature of the $H^+(aq)$ ion.

In **0018**, it was shown that $\left[H^+\right] = 10^{-7}$ M for pure water with $\left[H^+\right] = \left[OH^-\right]$. Thus **the pH of a neutral solution is 7.** In an **acidic solution**, $\left[H^+\right] > 10^{-7}$ M and **pH < 7**. In a basic solution, $\left[H^+\right] < 10^{-7}$ M and **pH > 7**.

The negative base-10 log is a convenient way of representing other small numbers used in chemistry by placing the letter "p" before the symbol. Values of K_a are often represented as pK_a, with $pK_a = -\log K_a$. The concentration of OH^- (aq) ions may also be expressed in terms of pOH, with $pOH = -\log\left[OH^-\right]$.

The ion-product constant of water, $K_w = \left[H^+\right]\left[OH^-\right] = 1.0 \times 10^{-14}$ at 25 °C. The value of K_w can used to determine the relationship between pH and pOH by taking the negative log of the expression:

$$-\log K_w = -\log\left[H^+\right] - \log\left[OH^-\right] = -\log\left(10^{-14}\right).$$
$$\text{Therefore: } pH + pOH = 14.$$

Example: An aqueous solution has an H^+ ion concentration of 4.0 x 10^{-9}. Is the solution acidic or basic? What is the pH of the solution? What is the pOH?

Solution: The solution is basic because $[H^+] < 10^{-7}$ M.

$$pH = -\log\left[H^+\right] = -\log\ 4 \text{X} 10^{-9}$$
$$= 8.4.$$
$$pH + pOH = 14. \text{ Therefore } pOH = 14 - pH = 14 - 8.4 = 5.6.$$

Identify properties of buffer solutions.

A **buffer solution** is a solution that **resists a change in pH** after addition of small amounts of an acid or a base. Buffer solutions require the presence of an acid to neutralize an added base and also the presence of a base to neutralize an added acid. These two components present in the buffer also must not neutralize each other! A **conjugate acid-base pair is present in buffers** to fulfill these requirements. Buffers are prepared by mixing together **a weak acid or base and a salt of the acid or base** that provides the conjugate.

Consider the buffer solution prepared by mixing together acetic acid—$HC_2H_3O_2$—and sodium acetate—$C_2H_3O_2^-$ containing Na^+ as a spectator ion. The equilibrium reaction for this acid/conjugate base pair is:
$$HC_2H_3O_2 \leftrightarrow C_2H_3O_2^- + H^+$$

If H^+ ions from a strong acid are added to this buffer solution, Le Chatelier's principle (see **0018**) predicts that the reaction will shift to the left and much of this H^+ will be consumed to create more $HC_2H_3O_2$ from $C_2H_3O_2^-$. If a strong base that consumes H^+ is added to this buffer solution, Le Chatelier's principle predicts that the reaction will shift to the right and much of the consumed H^+ will be replaced by the dissociation of $HC_2H_3O_2$. The net effect is that **buffer solutions prevent large changes in pH that occur when an acid or base is added to pure water** or to an unbuffered solution.

The amount of acid or base that a buffer solution can neutralize before dramatic pH changes begins to occur is called its **buffering capacity**. Blood and seawater both contain several conjugate acid-base pairs to buffer the solution's pH and decrease the impact of acids and bases on living things.

An excellent flash animation with audio to explain the action of buffering solutions is found at
http://www.mhhe.com/physsci/chemistry/essentialchemistry/flash/buffer12.swf.

Interpret titration data.

Standard titration

In a typical acid-base **titration**, **an acid-base indicator** (such as *phenolphthalein*) or a **pH meter** is used to monitor the course of a **neutralization reaction**. The usual goal of titration is to **determine an unknown concentration** of an acid (or base) by neutralizing it with a known concentration of base (or acid).

The reagent of known concentration is usually used as the **titrant**. The titrant is poured into a **buret** (also spelled *burette*) until it is nearly full, and an initial buret reading is taken. Buret numbering is close to zero when nearly full. A known volume of the solution of unknown concentration is added to a flask and placed under the buret. The indicator is added or the pH meter probe is inserted. The initial state of a titration experiment is shown to the right above.

The buret stopcock is opened and titrant is slowly added until the solution permanently changes color or the pH rapidly changes. This is the titration **endpoint**, and a final buret reading is made. The final state of a titration experiment is shown to the right below. The endpoint occurs when the number of **acid and base equivalents in the flask are identical**:

$$N_{acid} = N_{base}. \text{ Therefore, } C_{acid}V_{acid} = C_{base}V_{base}.$$

The endpoint is also known as the titration **equivalence point**.

Titration data typically consist of:

$$V_{inital} \Rightarrow \text{Initial buret volume} \quad V_{final} \Rightarrow \text{Final buret volume}$$

$$C_{known} \Rightarrow \text{Concentration of known solution}$$

$$V_{unknown} \Rightarrow \text{Volume of unknown solution.}$$

To determine the unknown concentration, first find the volume of titrant at the known concentration added: $V_{known} = V_{final} - V_{initial}$.

At the equivalence point, $N_{unknown} = N_{known}$.

$$\text{Therefore, } C_{unknown} = \frac{C_{known}V_{known}}{V_{unknown}} = \frac{C_{known}(V_{final} - V_{initial})}{V_{unknown}}.$$

_Initial buret volume

Unknown with indicator

Volume added

Final volume

Color change at endpoint

Units of molarity may be used for concentration in the above expressions **unless a mole of either solution yields more than one acid or base equivalent.** In that case, concentration must be expressed using **normality** (see **0025**).

Example: A 20.0 mL sample of an HCl solution is titrated with 0.200 M NaOH. The initial buret volume is 1.8 mL and the final buret volume at the titration endpoint is 29.1 mL. What is the molarity of the HCl sample?

Solution: Two solution methods will be used. The first method is better for those who are good at unit manipulations and less skilled at memorizing formulas. HCl contains one acid equivalent and NaOH contains one base equivalent, so we may use molarity in all our calculations.

1) Calculate the moles of the known substance added to the flask:

$$0.200 \frac{mol}{L} \times \frac{1\,L}{1000\,mL} \times (29.1\,mL - 1.8\,mL) = 0.00546\ mol\ NaOH.$$

At the endpoint, this base will neutralize 0.00546 mol HCl. Therefore, this amount of HCl must have been present in the sample before the titration.

$$\frac{0.00546\ mol\ HCl}{0.0200\ L} = 0.273\ M\ HCl.$$

2) Utilize the formula: $C_{unknown} = \dfrac{C_{known}(V_{final} - V_{initial})}{V_{unknown}}$.

$$C_{HCl} = \frac{C_{NaOH}(V_{final} - V_{initial})}{V_{HCl}} = \frac{0.200\ M\ (29.1\,mL - 1.8\,mL)}{20.0\,mL} = 0.273\ M\ HCl.$$

Titrating with the unknown

In a common variation of standard titration, the unknown is added to the buret as a titrant and the reagent of known concentration is placed in the flask. The chemistry involved is the same as in the standard case, and the mathematics is also identical except for the identity of the two volumes. For this variation, V_{known} will be the volume added to the flask before titration begins and $V_{unknown} = V_{final} - V_{initial}$. Therefore:

$$C_{unknown} = \frac{C_{known}V_{known}}{V_{unknown}} = \frac{C_{known}V_{known}}{V_{final} - V_{initial}}.$$

Example: 30.0 mL of a 0.150 M HNO_3 solution is titrated with $Ca(OH)_2$. The initial buret volume is 0.6 mL and the final buret volume at the equivalent point is 22.2 mL. What is the molarity of $Ca(OH)_2$ used for the titration?

Solution: The same two solution methods will be used as in the previous example. 1 mol $Ca(OH)_2$ contains 2 base equivalents because it reacts with 2 moles of H^+ via the reaction $Ca(OH)_2 + 2HNO_3 \rightarrow Ca(NO_3)_2 + 2H_2O$. Therefore, normality must be used in the formula for solution method 2.

1) First calculate the moles of the substance in the flask:

$$0.150 \frac{mol}{L} \times 0.0300 \text{ L} = 0.00450 \text{ mol } HNO_3.$$

This acid must be titrated with 0.00450 base equivalents for neutralization to occur at the end point. We calculate moles $Ca(OH)_2$ used in the titration from stoichiometry:

$$0.00450 \text{ base equivalents} \times \frac{1 \text{ mol } Ca(OH)_2}{2 \text{ base equivalents}} = 0.00225 \text{ mol } Ca(OH)_2.$$

The molarity of $Ca(OH)_2$ is found from the volume used in the titration:

$$\frac{0.00225 \text{ mol } Ca(OH)_3}{0.0222 \text{ L} - 0.0006 \text{ L}} = 0.104 \text{ M } Ca(OH)_3.$$

2) Utilize the formula: $C_{unknown} = \dfrac{C_{known} V_{known}}{V_{final} - V_{initial}}$ using units of normality.

For HNO_3, molarity=normality because 1 mol contains 1 acid equivalent.

$$C_{Ca(OH)_2} = \frac{C_{HNO_3} V_{HNO_3}}{V_{final} - V_{initial}} = \frac{\left(0.150 \text{ M} \times \dfrac{1 \text{ N}}{1 \text{ M}}\right)(30.0 \text{ mL})}{22.2 \text{ mL} - 0.6 \text{ mL}} = 0.208 \text{ N } Ca(OH)_2.$$

This value is converted to molarity. For $Ca(OH)_2$, normality is twice molarity because 1 mol contains 2 base equivalents (See **0025**).

$$0.208 \text{ N } Ca(OH)_2 \times \frac{1 \text{ M } Ca(OH)_2}{2 \text{ N } Ca(OH)_2} = 0.104 \text{ M } Ca(OH)_2.$$

Interpreting titration curves

A **titration curve** is a plot of a solution's **pH charted against the volume of an added acid or base**. Titration curves are obtained if a pH meter is used to monitor the titration instead of an indicator. At the equivalence point, the titration curve is nearly vertical. This is the point where the most rapid change in pH occurs. In addition to determining the equivalence point, the **shape of titration curves** may be interpreted to determine **acid/base strength and the presence of a polyprotic acid.**

The pH at the equivalence point of a titration is the **pH of the salt solution obtained when the amount of acid is equal to the amount of base**. For a strong acid and a strong base, the equivalence point occurs at the neutral pH of 7. For example, an equimolar solution of HCl and NaOH will contain NaCl(*aq*) at its equivalence point.

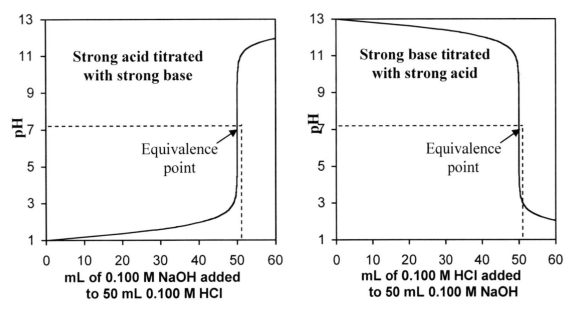

The salt solution at **the equivalence point of a titration involving a weak acid or base will not be at neutral pH**. For example, an equimolar solution of NaOH and hypochlorous acid HClO at the equivalence point of a titration will be a base because it is indistinguishable from a solution of sodium hypochlorite. A pure solution of NaClO(*aq*) will be a base because the ClO$^-$ ion is the conjugate base of HClO, and it consumes H$^+$(*aq*) in the reaction ClO$^-$ + H$^+$ $\leftrightarrow$ HClO:.

In a similar fashion, an equimolar solution of HCl and NH$_3$ will be an acid because a solution of NH$_4$Cl(*aq*) is an acid. It generates H$^+$(*aq*) in the reaction: NH$_4^+$ $\leftrightarrow$ NH$_3$ + H$^+$..

Contrast the following **titration curves for a weak acid or base** with those for a strong acid and strong base above:

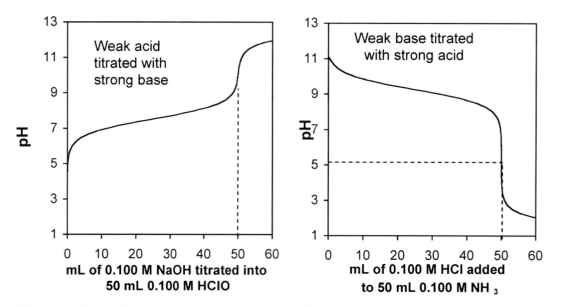

Titration of a polyprotic acid results in **multiple equivalence points** and a curve with more "bumps" as shown below for sulfurous acid and the carbonate ion.

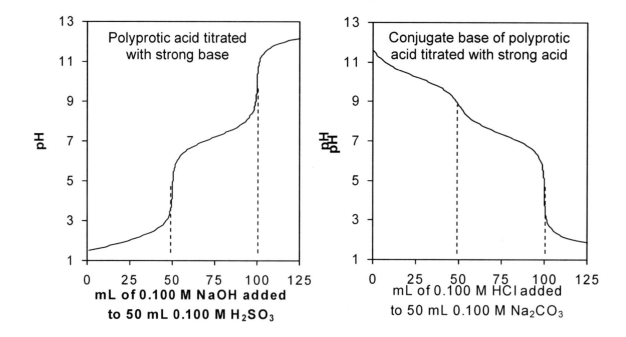

Competency 20.0 Understand redox reactions and electrochemistry

Identify redox processes.

Redox is shorthand for *reduction* and *oxidation*. **Reduction** is the **gain of an electron** by a molecule, atom, or ion. **Oxidation** is the **loss of an electron**. These two processes always occur together. Electrons lost by one substance are gained by another. In a redox process, the **oxidation numbers** of atoms are altered. Reduction decreases the oxidation number of an atom. Oxidation increases the oxidation number.

The easiest redox processes to identify are those involving monatomic ions with altered charges. For example, the reaction

$$Zn(s) + Cu^{2+}(aq) \rightarrow Zn^{2+}(aq) + Cu(s)$$

is a redox process because electrons are transferred from Zn to Cu.

However, many redox reactions involve the transfer of electrons from one molecular compound to another. For example, the reaction

$$H_2 + F_2 \rightarrow 2HF$$

is a redox process because the oxidation numbers of atoms are altered. The oxidation numbers of elements are always zero, and oxidation numbers in a compound are never zero. Fluorine is the more electronegative element, so in HF it has an oxidation number of −1 and hydrogen has an oxidation number of +1. This is a redox process where electrons are transferred from H_2 to F_2 to create HF.

In the reaction

$$HCl + NaOH \rightarrow NaCl + H_2O$$

the H-atoms on both sides of the reaction have an oxidation number of +1, the atom of Cl has an oxidation number of −1, the Na-atom has an oxidation number of +1, and the atom of O has an oxidation number of −2. **This is not a redox process because oxidation numbers remain unchanged** by the reaction.

Identify the components of redox reactions.

An **oxidizing agent** (also called an oxidant or oxidizer) has the ability to oxidize other substances by removing electrons from them. The **oxidizing agent is reduced** in the process. A **reducing agent** (also called a reductive agent, reductant or reducer) is a substance that has the ability to reduce other substances by transferring electrons to them. The **reducing agent is oxidized** in the process.

Redox reactions may also be written as **two half-reactions**, a **reduction half-reaction** with **electrons as a reactant** and an **oxidation half-reaction** with **electrons as a product**.

Example: The redox reactions:

$$Zn(s) + Cu^{2+}(aq) \rightarrow Zn^{2+}(aq) + Cu(s) \quad \text{and} \quad H_2 + F_2 \rightarrow 2HF$$

may be written in terms of the half-reactions:

$$2e^- + Cu^{2+}(aq) \rightarrow Cu(s) \qquad 2e^- + F_2 \rightarrow 2F^-$$
$$\text{and}$$
$$Zn(s) \rightarrow Zn^{2+}(aq) + 2e^-. \qquad H_2 \rightarrow 2H^+ + 2e^-.$$

An additional (non-redox) reaction, $2F^- + 2H^+ \rightarrow 2HF$, achieves the final products for the second reaction.

Determining whether a chemical equation is balanced (see **0016**) requires an additional step for redox reactions because there must be a **charge balance.**

Example: The equation:

$$Sn^{2+} + Fe^{3+} \rightarrow Sn^{4+} + Fe^{2+}$$

contains one Sn and one Fe on each side but it is not balanced because the sum of charges on the left side of the equation is +5 and the sum on the right side is +6. One electron is gained in the reduction half-reaction ($Fe^{3+} + e^- \rightarrow Fe^{2+}$), but two are lost in the oxidation half-reaction ($Sn^{2+} \rightarrow Sn^{4+} + 2e^-$).

The equation:

$$Sn^{2+} + 2Fe^{3+} \rightarrow Sn^{4+} + 2Fe^{2+}$$

is properly balanced because both sides contain the same sum of charges (+8) and electrons cancel from the half-reactions:

$$2Fe^{3+} + 2e^- \rightarrow 2Fe^{2+}$$
$$Sn^{2+} \rightarrow Sn^{4+} + 2e^-.$$

57 videos of redox experiments are presented here:
http://chemmovies.unl.edu/chemistry/redoxlp/redox000.html

Oxidation Number Method

Oxidation numbers, sometimes called oxidation states, are signed numbers assigned to atoms in molecules and ions. They allow us to keep track of the electrons associated with each atom. (See **0009**) Oxidation numbers are frequently used to write chemical formulas, to help us predict properties of compounds, and to help balance equations in which electrons are transferred. Knowledge of the oxidative state of an atom gives us an idea about its positive or negative character. In themselves, oxidation numbers have no physical meaning; they are used to simplify tasks that are more difficult to accomplish without them.

The Rules:

1. Free elements are assigned an oxidation state of 0.

    e.g. Al, Na, Fe, H_2, O_2, N_2, Cl_2 etc have zero oxidation states.

2. The oxidation state for any simple one-atom ion is equal to its charge.

    e.g. the oxidation state of Na^+ is +1, Be^{2+}, +2, and of F^-, -1.

3. The alkali metals (Li, Na, K, Rb, Cs and Fr) in compounds are always assigned an oxidation state of +1.

    e.g. in LiOH (Li, +1), in Na_2SO_4(Na, +1).

4. Fluorine in compounds is always assigned an oxidation state of -1.

    e.g. in HF_2^-, BF_2^-.

5. The alkaline earth metals (Be, Mg, Ca, Sr, Ba, and Ra) and also Zn and Cd in compounds are always assigned an oxidation state of +2. Similarly, Al and Ga are always +3.

    e.g. in $CaSO_4$(Ca, +2), $AlCl_3$ (Al, +3).

6. Hydrogen in compounds is assigned an oxidation state of +1. Exception - Hydrides, e.g. LiH (H=-1).

    e.g. in H_2SO_4 (H, +1).

7. Oxygen in compounds is assigned an oxidation state of -2. Exception - Peroxide, e.g. H_2O_2 (O = -1).

    e.g. in H_3PO_4 (O, -2).

8. The sum of the oxidation states of all the atoms in a species must be equal to net charge on the species.

    e.g. Net Charge of $HClO_4$ = 0, i.e. [+1(H)+7(Cl)-2*4(O)] = 0

    Net Charge of CrO_4^{2-}=-2,

    To solve Cr's oxidation state: x - 4*2(O) = -2, 4 * 2 = 8, and 8 – 2 = 6, so x = +6, so the oxidation state of Cr is +6 (there is only one Cr).

Balancing Redox Reactions

Redox reactions must be balanced to observe the **Law of Conservation of Mass**. This process is a little more complicated than balancing other reactions because the number of electrons lost must equal the number of electrons gained. Balancing redox reactions, then, conserves not only mass but also charge or electrons. It can be accomplished by slightly varying our balancing process.

Example: Balance the reaction:

$$Cr_2O_3(s) + Al(s) \longrightarrow Cr(s) + Al_2O_3(s)$$

Solution: Assign oxidation numbers to identify which atoms are losing and gaining electrons.

$$Cr_2O_3(s) + Al(s) \longrightarrow Cr(s) + Al_2O_3(s)$$
$$3+ \ 2- \qquad\quad 0 \qquad\quad 0 \qquad 3+ \ 2-$$

Identify those atoms gaining and losing electrons:

$$Cr^{3+} \longrightarrow Cr^0 \quad \text{gained 3 electrons } = \text{ reduction}$$
$$Al^0 \longrightarrow Al^{3+} \quad \text{lost 3 electrons } = \text{ oxidation}$$

Balance the atoms and electrons:

$$Cr_2O_3(s) \longrightarrow 2Cr(s) + 6 e^-$$
$$2Al(s) + 6 e^- \longrightarrow Al_2O_3(s)$$

Balance the half reactions by adding missing elements. Ignore elements whose oxidation number does not change. Add H_2O to add oxygen and H^+ to add hydrogen.

$$Cr_2O_3(s) \longrightarrow 2Cr(s) + 6 e^- + 3 H_2O$$

Need 3 oxygen atoms on product side. This requires $6H^+$ on the reactant side.

$$Cr_2O_3(s) + 6 H^+ \longrightarrow 2Cr(s) + 6 e^- + 3 H_2O$$

AND

$$2Al(s) + 6 e^- + 3 H_2O \longrightarrow Al_2O_3{}_{(s)} + 6 H^+$$

Need 3 oxygen atoms on reactant side. This requires $6H^+$ on the product side. Put the two half reactions together and add the species. Cancel out the species that occur in both the reactants and products.

$$Cr_2O_3(s) + \cancel{6}H^+ + 2Al(s) + 6 \text{ electrons} + \cancel{3}H_2O \longrightarrow 2Cr(s) + 6 \cancel{\text{electrons}} + 3 \cancel{}$$
$$H_2O + \cancel{Al_2O_3{}_{(s)}} + 6 H^+$$

The balanced equation is:

$$Cr_2O_3(s) + 2Al(s) \longrightarrow 2Cr(s) + Al_2O_3(s)$$

Example: Balance the reaction:

$$AgNO_3 + Cu \longrightarrow CuNO_3 + Ag$$

Assign oxidation numbers to identify which atoms are losing and gaining electrons.

$$AgNO_3 + Cu \longrightarrow Cu(NO_3)_2 + Ag$$
$$1+\ 5+\ 2-\quad 0 \qquad 2+\ 5+\ 2-\quad 0$$

Identify those atoms gaining and losing electrons:

$$Ag^{1+} + 1\,e^- \longrightarrow Ag^0 \quad \text{1 electron gained: reduction}$$
$$Cu^0 \longrightarrow Cu^{2+} + 2\,e^- \quad \text{2 electrons lost: oxidation}$$

Balance the atoms and electrons:

$$AgNO_3 + 1\,e^- \longrightarrow Ag^0$$
$$Cu^0 \longrightarrow Cu(NO_3)_2 + 2\,e^-$$
$$Cu^0 \longrightarrow Cu^{2+} + 2\,e^-$$

Balance the electrons:

$$AgNO_3 + 1\,e^- \longrightarrow Ag^0$$
$$Cu^0 \longrightarrow Cu(NO_3)_2 + 2\,e^-$$

1 electron gained and 2 electrons lost. Needs to be equal so 2 electrons need to be gained.

$$2\,[Ag + 1\,e^- \longrightarrow Ag^0] = 2\,AgNO_3 + 2\,e^- \longrightarrow 2\,Ag^{0+}$$

Reduction: $2\,AgNO_3 + 2\,e^- \longrightarrow 2\,Ag^0$
Oxidation: $\quad Cu^0 \longrightarrow Cu(NO_3)_2 + 2\,e^-$

Balance the half reactions by adding missing elements. Ignore elements whose oxidation number does not change. Add H_2O for oxygen and H^+ for hydrogen

$$2\,AgNO_3 + 2\,e^- \longrightarrow 2\,Ag^0 + 2\,NO_3$$
$$2NO_3 + Cu^0 \longrightarrow Cu(NO_3)_2 + 2\,e^-$$

Put the two half reactions together and add the species. Cancel out the species that occur in both the reactants and products.

Reduction: $2 \, AgNO_3 + 2 \, e^- \longrightarrow 2 \, Ag^0 + 2 \, NO_3$
Oxidation: $2 NO_3 + \quad Cu^0 \longrightarrow Cu(NO_3)_2 + 2 \, e^-$

The balanced reaction is:

$$2 \, AgNO_3 + Cu \longrightarrow Cu(NO_3)_2 + 2 \, Ag$$

Example: Balance the reaction:

$$Ag_2S + HNO_3 \longrightarrow AgNO_3 + NO + S + H_2O$$

Assign oxidation numbers:

$$Ag_2S + HNO_3 \longrightarrow AgNO_3 + NO + S + H_2O$$
$$1+ \ 2- \quad 1+ \ 5+ \ 2- \qquad 1+ \ 5+ \ 2- \quad 2+ \ 2- \quad 0 \qquad 1+ \ 2-$$

Identify those atoms gaining and losing electrons:

oxidation: $\quad S^{2-} \longrightarrow S^0 + 2 \, e^-$
reduction: $\quad N^{5+} + 3 \, e^- \longrightarrow N^{2+}$

Balance the atoms:

Oxidation: $2 \, NO_3 + Ag_2S \longrightarrow S + 2 \, e^- + 2 \, AgNO_3$
Reduction: $3 \, H^+ + HNO_3 + 3 \, e^- \longrightarrow NO \ + 2 \, H_2O$

Balance electrons lost and gained:

2 electrons lost and 3 electron gained.
Need to be equal so find multiple: 6

Oxidation: $3[\ 2 \, NO_3 + Ag_2S \longrightarrow S + 2 \, e^- + 2 \, AgNO_3]$
$\quad\quad\quad\quad 6 \, NO_3 + 3 \, Ag_2S \longrightarrow 3 \, S + 6 \, e^- + 6 \, AgNO_3$
Reduction: $2[\ 3 \, H^+ + HNO_3 + 3 \, e^- \longrightarrow NO \ + 2 \, H_2O]$
$\quad\quad\quad\quad 6 H^+ + 2 \, HNO_3 + 6 \, e^- \longrightarrow 2 \, NO \ + 4 \, H_2O$

Put the two half reactions together and add the species. Cancel out the species that occur in both the reactants and products.

$6 \, NO_3 + 3 \, Ag_2S + 6 \, H^+ + 2 \, HNO_3 + 6 \, e^- \longrightarrow 3 \, S + 6 \, e^- + 6 \, AgNO_3 + 2 \, NO + 4H_2O$

The balanced equation is:

$$3 \, Ag_2S + 8 \, HNO_3 \longrightarrow 6 \, AgNO_3 + 2 \, NO + 3 \, S + 4 \, H_2O$$

To balance a redox reaction which occurs in basic solution is a very similar to balancing a redox reaction which occurs in acidic conditions. First, balance the reaction as you would for an acidic solution and then adjust for the basic solution. Here is an example using the half-reaction method:

Example: Solid chromium(III) hydroxide, $Cr(OH)_3$, reacts with aqueous chlorate ions, ClO_3^-, in basic conditions to form chromate ions, CrO_4^{2-}, and chloride ions, Cl^-.

$$Cr(OH)_3(s) + ClO_3^-(\, aq) \rightarrow CrO_4^{2-} (aq) + Cl^-(aq) \quad (basic)$$

Solution: Write the half-reactions:

$$Cr(OH)_3(s) \rightarrow CrO_4^{2-}(aq) \text{ and}$$
$$ClO_3^- (aq) \rightarrow Cl^-(aq)$$

Balance the atoms in each half-reaction. Use H_2O to add oxygen atoms and H^+ to add hydrogen atoms.

$$H_2O \, (l) + Cr(OH)_3(s) \rightarrow CrO_4^{2-} (aq) + 5 \, H^+ (aq)$$

$$6H^+ (aq) + ClO_3^- (\, aq) \rightarrow Cl^- (aq) + 3 \, H_2O \, (l)$$

Balance the charges of both half-reactions by adding electrons.

$$H_2O \, (l) + Cr(OH)_3(s) \rightarrow CrO_4^{2-} (aq) + 5 \, H^+ (aq)$$

has a charge of +3 on the right and 0 on the left. Adding 3 electrons to the right side will give that side a 0 charge as well.

$$H_2O \, (l) + Cr(OH)_3(s) \rightarrow CrO_4^{2-} (aq) + 5 \, H^+ (aq) + 3e^-$$

$$6H^+ (aq) + ClO_3^- (\, aq) \rightarrow Cl^- (aq) + 3 \, H_2O \, (l)$$

has a charge of -1 on the right side and a +5 on the left. Six electrons need to be added to the left side to equal the -1 charge on the right side.

$$6 \, e^- + 6H^+ (aq) + ClO_3^- (aq) \rightarrow Cl^- (aq) + 3 \, H_2O \, (l)$$

The number of electrons lost must equal the number of electrons gained so multiply each half-reactions by a number that will give equal numbers of electrons lost and gained.

$$H_2O \text{ (l)} + Cr(OH)_3(s) \rightarrow CrO_4^{2-} \text{ (aq)} + 5 H^+ \text{ (aq)} + 3e^-$$
$$6 e^- + 6H^+ \text{ (aq)} + ClO_3^- \text{ (aq)} \rightarrow Cl^- \text{ (aq)} + 3 H_2O \text{ (l)}$$

The first half reaction needs to be multiplied by 2 to equal the 6 electrons gained in the second half-reaction.

$$2[H_2O \text{ (l)} + Cr(OH)_3(s) \rightarrow CrO_4^{2-} \text{ (aq)} + 5 H^+ \text{ (aq)} + 3e^-] =$$
$$2H_2O \text{ (l)} + 2 Cr(OH)_3(s) \rightarrow 2 CrO_4^{2-} \text{ (aq)} + 10 H^+ \text{ (aq)} + 6e^-$$

Add the two half-reactions together; canceling out species that appear on both sides of the reaction.

$$2H_2O + 2 Cr(OH)_3(s) + \cancel{6e^-} + \cancel{6H^+} \text{ (aq)} + ClO_3^- \text{ (aq)} \rightarrow 2 CrO_4^{2-} \text{ (aq)} + \cancel{10} H^+ \text{ (aq)} + \cancel{6e^-} + Cl \text{(aq)} + \cancel{3} H_2O$$

$$\downarrow \qquad\qquad\qquad \downarrow$$
$$4 H^+ \text{ (aq)} \qquad\qquad 1 H_2O \text{ (l)}$$

Since the reaction occurs in basic solution and there a
side, 4 OH⁻ need to be added to both sides. Combine the H⁺ and OH⁻ where appropriate to make water molecules.

$$4 OH^- \text{ (aq)} + 2 Cr(OH)_3(s) + ClO_3^- \text{ (aq)} \rightarrow 2 CrO_4^{2-} \text{ (aq)} + 4 H^+ \text{ (aq)} + Cl^- \text{(aq)} + 1H_2O \text{ (l)} + 4 OH^- \text{ (aq)}$$

$$4 H_2O \text{ (l)}$$

Write the final balanced equation:

$$4 OH^- \text{ (aq)} + 2 Cr(OH)_3(s) + ClO_3^- \text{ (aq)} \rightarrow 2 CrO_4^{2-} \text{ (aq)} + Cl^- \text{ (aq)} + 5 H_2O \text{ (l)}$$

Identify the components of electrolytic and electrochemical systems.

Electrolytic cells use electricity to force nonspontaneous redox reactions to occur. **Electrochemical cells generate electricity** by permitting spontaneous redox reactions to occur. The two types of cells have some components in common.

Both systems contain two **electrodes**. An electrode is a piece of conducting metal that is used to make contact with a nonmetallic material. One electrode is an **anode**. An **oxidation reaction occurs at the anode**, so electrons are removed from a substance there. The other electrode is a **cathode.** A **reduction reaction occurs at the cathode**, so electrons are added to a substance there. Electrons flow from anode to cathode outside either device.

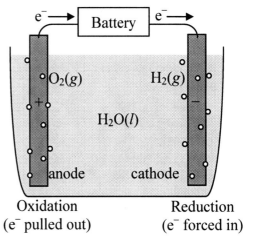

Oxidation   Reduction
(e^- pulled out)   (e^- forced in)

Electrolytic systems

Electrolysis is a chemical process **driven by a battery** or another source of electromotive force. This source pulls electrons out of the chemical process at the anode and forces electrons in the cathode. The result is a **negatively charged cathode and a positively charged anode**.

Electrolysis of pure water forms O_2 bubbles at the anode by the oxidation half-reaction:

$$2H_2O(l) \rightarrow 4H^+(aq) + O_2(g) + 4e^-$$

and forms H_2 bubbles at the cathode by the reduction half-reaction:

$$2H_2O(l) + 2e^- \rightarrow H_2(g) + 2OH^-(aq).$$

The net redox reaction is:

$$2H_2O(l) \rightarrow 2H_2(g) + O_2(g).$$

Neither electrode took part in the reaction described above. An electrode that is only used to contact the reaction and deliver or remove electrons is called an **inert electrode**. An electrode that takes part in the reaction is called an **active electrode**.

Electroplating is the process of **depositing dissolved metal cations** in a smooth even coat onto an object used as an active electrode. Electroplating is used to protect metal surfaces or for decoration. For example, to electroplate a copper surface with nickel, a nickel rod is used for the anode and the copper object is used for the cathode. $NiCl_2(aq)$ or another substance with free nickel ions is used in the electrolytic cell. $Ni(s) \rightarrow Ni^{2+}(aq) + 2e^-$ occurs at the anode and $Ni^{2+}(aq) + 2e^- \xrightarrow{\text{onto Cu}} Ni(s)$ occurs at the cathode.

Electrochemical systems

An **electrochemical cell** separates the half-reactions of a redox process into two compartments or half-cells. Electrochemical cells are also called *galvanic cells* or *voltaic cells*.

A **battery** consists of one or more electrochemical cells connected together. Electron transfer from the oxidation to the reduction reaction may only take place through an external circuit.

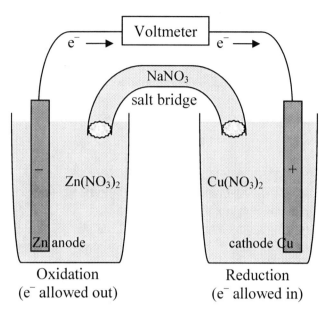

Oxidation
(e⁻ allowed out)

Reduction
(e⁻ allowed in)

Electrochemical systems provide a **source of electromotive force**. This force is also called or *voltage* or *cell potential* and is measured in **volts**. Electrons are allowed to leave the chemical process at the anode and permitted to enter at the cathode. The result is a **negatively charged anode and a positively charged cathode**.

Electrical neutrality is maintained in the half-cells by **ions migrating** through a **salt bridge**. A salt bridge in the simplest cells is an inverted U-tube filled with a non-reacting electrolyte and plugged at both ends with a material like cotton or glass wool that permits ion migration but prevents the electrolyte from falling out.

The spontaneous redox reaction $Zn(s) + Cu^{2+}(aq) \rightarrow Zn^{2+}(aq) + Cu(s)$ generates a voltage in the cell above. The oxidation half-reaction $Zn(s) \rightarrow Zn^{2+}(aq) + 2e^-$ occurs at the anode. Electrons are allowed to flow through a voltmeter before they are consumed by the reduction half-reaction $Cu^{2+}(aq) + 2e^- \rightarrow Cu(s)$ at the cathode. Zinc dissolves away from the anode into solution, and copper from the solution builds up onto the cathode.

To maintain electrical neutrality in both compartments, positive ions (Zn^{2+} and Na^+) migrate through the salt bridge from the anode half-cell to the cathode half-cell and negative ions (NO_3^-) migrate in the opposite direction.

An animation of the cell described above is located at
http://www.mhhe.com/physsci/chemistry/essentialchemistry/flash/galvan5.swf.

A summary of anode and cathode properties for both cell types is contained in the table below.

		Electrolytic cell	Electrochemical cell
Anode	Half-reaction	Oxidation	Oxidation
	Electron flow	Pulled out	Allowed out
	Electrode polarity	+	−
Cathode	Half-reaction	Reduction	Reduction
	Electron flow	Forced in	Allowed in
	Electrode polarity	−	+

The reducing and oxidizing agents in a standard electrochemical cell are depleted with time. In a **rechargeable battery** (e.g., lead storage batteries in cars) the direction of the spontaneous redox reaction is reversed and **reactants are regenerated** when electrical energy is added into the system. A **fuel cell** has the same components as a standard electrochemical cell except that **reactants are continuously supplied**.

Calculate standard cell potentials.

A **standard cell potential,** E°_{cell}, is the voltage generated by an electrochemical cell at **100 kPa and 25 °C** when all components of the reaction are pure materials or solutes at a **concentration of 1 M**. Older textbooks may use 1 atm instead of 100 kPa. Standard solute concentrations may differ from 1 M for solutions that behave in a non-ideal way, but this difference is beyond the scope of high school chemistry.

Standard cell potentials are calculated from the **sum of the two half-reaction potentials** for the reduction and oxidation reactions occurring in the cell:

$$E^\circ_{cell} = E^\circ_{red}(\text{cathode}) + E^\circ_{ox}(\text{anode}$$

All half-reaction potentials are relative to the reduction of H^+ to form H_2. This potential is assigned a value of zero:

For $2H^+(aq \text{ at } 1 \text{ M}) + 2e^- \rightarrow H_2(g \text{ at } 100 \text{ kPa})$, $\quad E^\circ_{red} = 0$ V.

The standard potential of an oxidation half-reaction E°_{ox} **is equal in magnitude but has the opposite sign to the potential of the reverse reduction reaction.** Standard half-cell potentials are **tabulated as reduction potentials**. These are sometimes referred to as **standard electrode potentials $E°$**. Therefore,

$$E^\circ_{cell} = E^\circ(\text{cathode}) - E^\circ(\text{anode}.$$

Example: Given

$$E°=0.34 \text{ V for } Cu^{2+}(aq)+2e^-\rightarrow Cu(s) \text{ and}$$
$$E°= -0.76 \text{ V for } Zn^{2+}(aq)+2e^-\rightarrow Zn(s)$$

find the standard cell potential of the system

$$Zn(s) + Cu^{2+}(aq) \rightarrow Zn^{2+}(aq) + Cu(s)$$

Solution: $E°_{cell} = E°(\text{cathode}) - E°(\text{anode})$

$$= E°\left(Cu^{2+}(aq) + 2e^- \rightarrow Cu(s)\right) - E°\left(Zn^{2+}(aq) + 2e^- \rightarrow Zn(s)\right)$$
$$= 0.34 \text{ V} - (-0.76 \text{ V}) = 1.10 \text{ V}.$$

Competency 21.0   Understand the nature of organic reactions

An **addition reaction** is a reaction in which two atoms or ions react with a double bond of an alkene, forming a compound with two new functional groups bonded to the carbons of the original double bond. In these reactions, the existing pi bond is broken and in its place, sigma bonds form to two new atoms.

Examples of Simple Addition Reactions

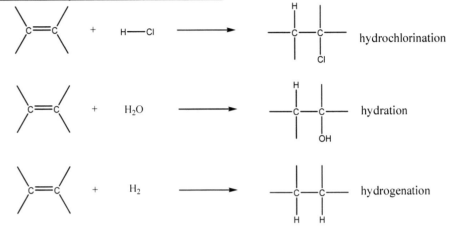

The mechanisms for these types of reactions depend on the nucleophilicity/electrophilicity of both the alkene and adding group, and the presence of solvent or catalyst.

In many cases, the first step of the reaction is the attack of a positively charged proton by the pi electrons, causing a proton transfer across the double bond. This is followed by addition of the nucleophile to the remaining cation.

Mechanism for Electrophilic Addition of HCl to 2-Butene

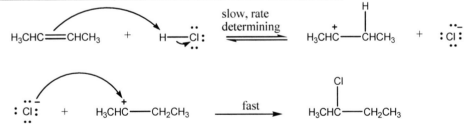

A **substitution reaction** is a reaction in which an atom or group of atoms is replaced by another atom or group of atoms. The most common types of these reactions are S_N1 and S_N2 reactions.

Examples of Substitution Reactions

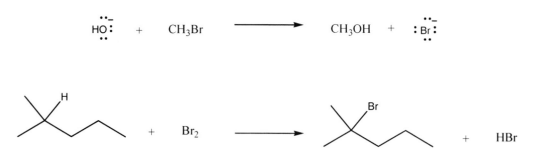

On of the most important types of substitution reaction is a nucleophilic substitution, an S_N2 reaction in which a halide is added to a molecule. These reactions can lead to a variety of new functional groups. The mechanism for these reactions involves the attack of a nucleophile on a central carbon atom. Simultaneously, β-elimination of a leaving group occurs.

Mechanism for Nucleophilic Substitution of OH⁻ to Bromomethane (S_N2 Reaction)

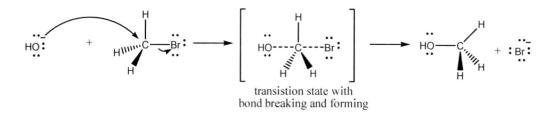

transistion state with
bond breaking and forming

The mechanism for an S_N1 reaction is a multi-step mechanism, where the leaving group is eliminated in the first step to leave a positively charged carbocation (an electrophile). The cation is then attacked by a nucleophile, followed by the final step of proton transfer to afford a neutral molecule.

An **elimination reaction** is a reaction in which a functional group is split (eliminated) from adjacent carbons. This is a reaction that can often compete with nucleophilic substitution and is highly dependent on the leaving group present in the molecule. Elimination reactions are favored by the presence of strong bases.

Examples of Elimination Reactions

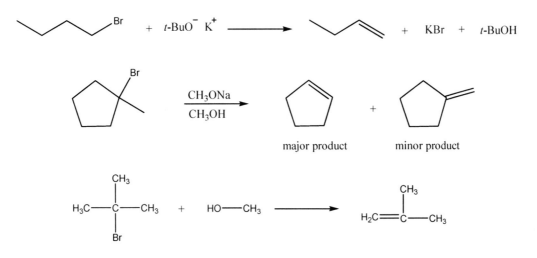

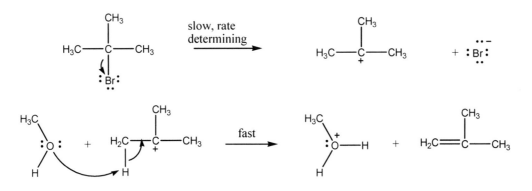

There are two types of elimination reactions, E1 and E2 reactions. The mechanism for E1 is a multistep reaction that involves the formation of a carbocation intermediate. The E2 mechanism is a series of steps, bond breaking and bond formation, that occur simultaneously. Similar to the S_N2 case outlined above, both the haloalkane and the base are involved in the transition state.

Mechanism for Elimination of 2-Bromo-2-methylpropane (E1 Reaction)

SUBAREA V.   **STOICHIOMETRY AND SOLUTIONS**

Competency 22.0   Understand the mole concept

Utilize the mole concept and Avogadro's number.

A single atom or molecule weighs very little in grams and cannot be measured using a balance the lab. It's useful to have a system that permits a large number of chemical particles to be described as one unit, analogous to referring to a dozen and having everyone interpret that as meaning 12 of something or referring to one gross as 144. A useful number of atoms, molecules, or formula units is **that number whose mass in grams is numerically equal to the atomic mass, molecular mass, or formula mass** of that substance. This quantity is called the **mole, abbreviated mol**. Because the ^{12}C isotope is assigned an exact value of 12 atomic mass units, there are exactly 12 g of ^{12}C in one mole of ^{12}C. The atomic mass unit is also called a Dalton, and "u" (for "unified atomic mass unit") or "Da" may be used as an abbreviation. Older texts use "amu." To find the molecular weight of a substance, use the periodic table to determine the molecular weight of each atom in the substance and multiply by the number of atoms of that substance present.

Example:

$$Al_2(SO_4)_3 \text{ molecular weight} = 2(26.982 \text{ u for Al}) + 3(32.065 \text{ u for S}) + 12(15.999 \text{ u for O})$$
$$= 342.147 \text{ u.}$$
$$\text{Therefore 1 mol } Al_2(SO_4)_3 = 342.147 \text{ g } Al_2(SO_4)_3.$$

It's been found experimentally that this number of atoms, ions, molecules, or anything else in one mole is 6.022045×10^{23}. For most purposes, three significant digits are sufficient, and **6.02×10^{23}** will be used. This value was named in honor of Amedeo Avogadro after his death and it is referred to as

Avogadro's number.

The table on the next page illustrates why the mole and Avogadro's number are useful. These concepts permit us to think about interactions among individual molecules and atoms while measuring many grams of a substance.

Name	Formula	Formula weight (u)	Mass of 1 mol of formula units (g)	Number and kind of particles in 1 mol
Atomic hydrogen	H	1.0079	1.0079	6.02×10^{23} H atoms
Molecular hydrogen	H_2	2.0158	2.0158	6.02×10^{23} H_2 molecules
				$2(6.02 \times 10^{23})$ H atoms
Silver	Ag	107.87	107.87	6.02×10^{23} Ag atoms
Silver ions	Ag^+	107.87	107.87	6.02×10^{23} Ag^+ ions
Barium chloride	$BaCl_2$	208.24	208.24	6.02×10^{23} $BaCl_2$ units
				6.02×10^{23} Ba^{2+} ions
				$2(6.02 \times 10^{23})$ Cl^- ions

Competency 23.0   Understand the relationship between the mole concept and chemical formulas

Write formulas and name compounds correctly

Proper formulas will follow the rules of the previous skill. (See also **0016** for writing proper formulas and naming compounds.) Here are some ways to identify <u>improper</u> formulas that are emphasized below by underlining them.

In all common names for **ionic compounds, number prefixes are not used** to describe the number of anions and cations.

> **Examples**: $CaBr_2$ is calcium bromide, <u>not calcium dibromide</u>.
> $Ba(OH)_2$ is barium hydroxide, <u>not barium dihydroxide</u>.
> Cu_2SO_4 is copper(I) sulfate, <u>not dicopper sulfate or copper(II) sulfate or dicopper sulfur tetroxide.</u>

All ionic compounds must have a **neutral charge in their formula** representations.

> **Example**: <u>MgBr is an improperly written formula</u> because Mg ion always exists as 2+ and Br ion is always a 1– ion. $MgBr_2$, magnesium bromide, is correct.

Proper **oxoanions and acids use the correct prefixes and suffixes**.

> **Example**: HNO_3 is nit<u>ric</u> acid because NO_3^- is the nit<u>rate</u> ion.

In both ionic and molecular compounds, the **less electronegative element comes first**.

> **Example**: <u>CSi is an improperly written formula</u> because Si is below C on the periodic table and therefore less electronegative. SiC, silicon carbide, is correct.

Calculate mole fraction and percent composition

A **mole fraction** is used to represent a component in a solution as a portion of the entire number of moles present. If you were able to pick out a molecule at random from a solution, the mole fraction of a component represents the probability that the molecule you picked would be that particular component. Mole fractions for all components must sum to one, and mole fractions are just numbers with no units.

$$\text{Mole fraction of a component} = \frac{\text{moles of component}}{\text{total moles of all components}}$$

The **percent composition** of a substance is the **percentage by mass of each element**. Chemical composition is used to verify the purity of a compound in the lab. An impurity will make the actual composition vary from the expected one.

To determine percent composition from a formula, do the following:

1) Write down the **number of atoms each element contributes** to the formula.

2) Multiply these values by the molecular weight of the corresponding element to determine the **grams of each element in one mole** of the formula.

3) Add the values from step 2 to obtain the **formula mass**.

4) Divide each value from step 2 by the formula mass from step 3 and multiply by 100% to obtain the **percent composition of each element**.

The first three steps are the same as those used to determine formula mass, but we use the intermediate results to obtain the composition.

Example: What is the chemical composition of ammonium carbonate $(NH_4)_2CO_3$?

Solution:

1) One $(NH_4)_2CO_3$ contains 2 N atoms, 8 H atoms, 1 C atom, and 3 O atoms.

2) $$\frac{2 \text{ mol N}}{\text{mol } (NH_4)CO_3} \times \frac{14.0 \text{ g N}}{\text{mol N}} = 28.0 \text{ g N/mol } (NH_4)CO_3$$

$$8(1.0) = 8.0 \text{ g H/mol } (NH_4)CO_3$$

$$1(12.0) = 12.0 \text{ g C/mol } (NH_4)CO_3$$

$$3(16.0) = 48.0 \text{ g O/mol } (NH_4)CO_3$$

Sum is $\overline{96.0 \text{ g } (NH_4)CO_3/\text{mol } (NH_4)CO_3}$

3)

4) $$\%N = \frac{28.0 \text{ g N/mol } (NH_4)_2CO_3}{96.0 \text{ g } (NH_4)_2CO_3/\text{mol } (NH_4)_2CO_3} = 0.292 \text{ g N/g } (NH_4)_2CO_3 \times 100\% = 29.2\%$$

$$\%H = \frac{8.0}{96.0} \times 100\% = 8.3\% \quad \%C = \frac{12.0}{96.0} \times 100\% = 12.5\% \quad \%O = \frac{48.0}{96.0} \times 100\% = 50.0\%$$

Calculate an Empirical Formula

If we know the chemical composition of a compound, we can calculate an **empirical formula** for it. An empirical formula is the **simplest formula** using the smallest set of integers to express the **ratio of atoms** present in a molecule.

To determine an empirical formula from a percent composition, do the following:

1) Change the "%" sign to grams for a basis of 100 g of the compound.
2) Determine the moles of each element in 100 g of the compound.
3) Divide the values from step 1 by the smallest value to obtain ratios.
4) Multiply by an integer if necessary to get a whole-number ratio.

Example: What is the empirical formula of a compound with a composition of 63.9% Cl, 32.5% C, and 3.6% H?

Solution:

1) We will use a basis of 100 g of the compound containing 63.9 g Cl, 32.5 g C, and 3.6 g H.

2) In 100 g, there are: $63.9 \text{ g Cl} \times \dfrac{\text{mol Cl}}{35.45 \text{ g Cl}} = 1.802 \text{ mol Cl}$

$$32.5/12.01 = 2.706 \text{ mol C}$$

$$3.6/1.01 = 3.56 \text{ mol H}$$

3) Dividing these values by the smallest yields:

$$\frac{2.706 \text{ mol C}}{1.802 \text{ mol Cl}} = 1.502 \text{ mol C/mol Cl}$$

$$\frac{3.56 \text{ mol H}}{1.802 \text{ mol Cl}} = 1.97 \text{ mol H/mol Cl}$$

Therefore, the elements are present in a ratio of C:H:Cl=1.50:2.0:1

4) Multiply the entire ratio by 2 because you cannot have a fraction of an atom. This corresponds to a ratio of 3:4:2 for an empirical formula of $C_3H_4Cl_2$.

The **molecular formula** describing the **actual number of atoms in the molecule** might also be $C_3H_4Cl_2$ or it might be $C_6H_8Cl_4$ or some other multiple that maintains a 3:4:2 ratio. You would have to know the molecular mass of the compound and compare it as a multiple of the molecular mass of the empirical formula of the compound to correctly determine the compound's molecular formula.

Competency 24.0   Understand the relationships expressed in chemical equations

Balance chemical equations

See 0016 for further explanation on writing and balancing equations.

Antoine **Lavoisier** is called **the father of modern chemistry** because he carefully weighed material before and after chemical reactions to determine that **chemical reactions do not alter total mass** . This principle is called **conservation of matter**. It does not apply to nuclear reactions. The mass of individual atoms does not change, so placing an equal number of each type of atom on both sides of a chemical equation insures conservation of matter will be represented.

Balancing equations (other than redox reactions) is a multi-step process. See **0016** for instructions and examples.

Perform stoichiometric Conversions

To convert **mass in grams to moles**:

> 1. First determine the molar mass (molecular weight) of the substance by adding the masses for each element in the substance in the substance and multiplying by the number of atoms of the element present:
>
> > **Example:** Determine the molar mass of $CuSO_4$.
> >
> > **Solution:** 1 mole of Cu = 63.5 g + 1 mol of S = 32 g + 4 mol O = 4 x 16 or 48 g = 143.5 g/mol
>
> 2. Determine the number of moles present using the molar mass conversion: 1 mol = molar mass of substance. Put the 1 mol on the top of the fraction and molar mass on the bottom of the fraction so that the grams of the substance cancel and the answer is in moles of the substance.
>
> > **Example:** If you have 315 g of $CuSO_4$, how many moles is that?
> >
> > **Solution:** 315 g x 1 mol/143.5 g = 2.20 mol $CuSO_4$

Moles to mass (grams) conversions are just the reverse of the process above. You will need to flip the conversion factor so that grams are on the top of the fraction.

Mass-mass stoichiometry problems

In a mass-mass stoichiometry problem, the mass of one compound that participates in a reaction is given and the mass of a different compound is required. Solving these problems is a three-step process:

1) Grams of the given compound (known mass) are converted to moles (known moles) using molecular mass.
2) The moles of the given compound (known moles) are related to moles of the second compound (unkown moles) by relating their stoichiometric coefficients.
3) The moles of the second compound (unkown moles) are converted to grams (unkown mass) using the molecular mass of the compound.

These steps are often combined in one series of multiplications, which may be described as **"grams of known to moles of known to moles of unknown to grams of unknown."**

Example: What mass of oxygen is required to consume 95.0 g of ethane in this reaction: $2C_2H_6 + 7O_2 \rightarrow 4CO_2 + 6H_2O$?

	step 1	step 2	step 3

Solution:
$$95.0 \text{ g } C_2H_6 \times \frac{1 \text{ mol } C_2H_6}{30.1 \text{ g } C_2H_6} \times \frac{7 \text{ mol } O_2}{2 \text{ mol } C_2H_6} \times \frac{32.0 \text{ g } O_2}{1 \text{ mol } O_2} = 359 \text{ g } O_2$$

By expressing the molecular mass of the first or given compound as moles per gram, the grams of the known cancel. By putting the moles of the known compound on the bottom with the molecular coefficient of the unknown compound on top in the second conversion the moles of the known are canceled and converted to moles of unknown. And finally, by expressing the molecular mass of the second compound as grams per mole, its moles are converted to grams for the final answer and the units (by canceling) end up as grams of the unknown.

Determine limiting reagent

The **limiting reagent** of a reaction is the **reactant that runs out first**. This reactant **determines the amount of product formed**, and any **other reactants remain unconverted** to product and are called **excess reagents**.

The limiting reagent may be determined by **dividing the number of moles of each reactant by its stoichiometric coefficient**. This determines the moles of reaction if each reactant were limiting. The **lowest result** will indicate the actual limiting reagent. Remember to use moles and not grams for these calculations.

Example: Consider the reaction $3H_2 + N_2 \rightarrow 2NH_3$ and suppose that 3 mol H_2 and 3 mol N_2 are available for this reaction. What is the limiting reagent?

Solution: The equation tells us that 3 mol H_2 will react with <u>one</u> mol N_2 to produce 2 mol NH_3. This means that 2 mol N_2 (started with 3 and used 1) will remain so H_2 is the limiting reagent because it runs out first.

Example: 50.0 g Al and 400. g Br_2 react according the the following equation:

$$2Al + 3Br_2 \rightarrow 2AlBr_3$$

until the limiting reagent is completely consumed. Find the limiting reagent, the mass of $AlBr_3$ expected to form, and the excess reagent expected to remain after the limiting reagent is consumed.

Solution: First convert both reactants to moles:

$$50.0 \text{ g Al} \times \frac{1 \text{ mol Al}}{26.982 \text{ g Al}} = 1.853 \text{ mol Al} \quad \text{and} \quad 400. \text{ g Br}_2 \times \frac{1 \text{ mol Br}_2}{159.808 \text{ g Br}_2} = 2.503 \text{ mol Br}_2.$$

The final digits in the intermediate results above are italicized because they are insignificant.

Dividing by stoichiometric coefficients gives:

$$1.853 \text{ mol Al} \times \frac{\text{mol reaction}}{2 \text{ mol Al}} = 0.9265 \text{ mol reaction if Al is limiting}$$

$$2.503 \text{ mol Br}_2 \times \frac{\text{mol reaction}}{3 \text{ mol Br}_2} = 0.8343 \text{ mol reaction if Br}_2 \text{ is limiting.}$$

Br_2 is the lower value and is, therefore, the limiting reagent.

The reaction is expected to produce:

$$2.503 \text{ mol Br}_2 \times \frac{2 \text{ mol AlBr}_3}{3 \text{ mol Br}_2} \times \frac{266.694 \text{ g AlBr}_3}{\text{mol AlBr}_3} = 445 \text{ g AlBr}_3.$$

The reaction is expected to consume:

$$2.503 \text{ mol Br}_2 \times \frac{2 \text{ mol Al}}{3 \text{ mol Br}_2} \times \frac{26.982 \text{ g Al}}{\text{mol Al}} = 45.0 \text{ g Al.}$$

50.0 g Al – 45.0 g Al = 5.0 g Al are expected to remain.

Calculate percent yield

The **yield of a reaction is the amount of product** obtained. This value is nearly always less than what would be predicted from a stoichiometric calculation because side-reactions may produce different products, the reverse reaction may occur, and some material may be lost during the procedure. The yield from a stoichiometric calculation on the limiting reagent is called the theoretical yield.

Percent yield is the actual yield divided by the theoretical yield times 100%:

$$\text{Percent yield} = \frac{\text{Actual yield}}{\text{Theoretical yield}} \times 100\% .$$

Example: 387 g $AlBr_3$ are produced by the reaction described in the previous example. What is the percent yield?

Solution: $\dfrac{387 \text{ g } AlBr_3}{445 \text{ g } AlBr_3} \times 100\% = 87.0\% \text{ yield.}$

Competency 25.0 Understand the properties of solutions and colloidal suspensions, and analyze factors that affect solubility

Account for properties of liquids (i.e., viscosity, vapor pressure, surface tension, boiling and freezing point as a function of pressure, and critical temperature).

Viscosity

Viscosity measures the ability of a liquid to flow. Liquids with high viscosity flow less easily because they have strong intermolecular forces relative to kinetic energy. The viscosity of liquids decreases with temperature because it is easier for rapidly moving molecules to flow into the spaces between them. For most liquids (water is an exception), viscosity increases with pressure because the molecules are squeezed together forcing a greater interaction, but this dependence is not as strong as the dependence on temperature.

Vapor Pressure

When a liquid is placed in an open container or a closed container that is not entirely filled, there are always some molecules at the surface of the liquid (e.g., the half-shaded molecules to the left of the diagram) which have enough kinetic energy to overcome the attraction of their neighbors and escape into the gas above the liquid. This process is known as **evaporation**. In a closed container, these gas molecules develop a pressure until a dynamic equilibrium - the rate of their return to the liquid phase by **condensation** (e.g., the half-shaded molecule on the right in the diagram) equals the rate of their escape by evaporation - is achieved: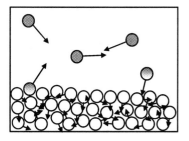

Evaporation

Liquid ↔ **Vapor**

Condensation

At equilibrium, the partial pressure of the substance in the gas phase is at its **saturated vapor pressure**. Solids are also in equilibrium with vapor and have a saturated vapor pressure. There is no real difference between the terms *gas* and *vapor*, but *gas* is often used to describe a substance that appears in the gaseous state under standard temperature and pressure and *vapor* is normally used to describe the gaseous state of a substance that is ordinarily a liquid or solid at standard temperature and pressure.

A dynamic equilibrium consists of two **opposing reversible processes** that both occur at the **same rate**. *Balance* is a synonym for equilibrium. A system at equilibrium is stable; it does not change with time. Equilibria are drawn with a double arrow.

The saturated vapor pressure of a liquid is often simply called its **vapor pressure**. This term can sometimes lead to confusion when equilibrium is not present, but equilibrium is usually assumed.

An increase in temperature raises vapor pressure (making the liquid more **volatile**) because kinetic energy opposes intermolecular attractions and permits more molecules to escape from the liquid phase. See **0007** for a discussion of the kinetic theory and **0010** for information on phase changes.

More information on vapor pressure may be found at: http://hyperphysics.phy-astr.gsu.edu/hbase/kinetic/vappre.html. A flash animation of liquid/vapor equilibrium showing how vapor pressure is measured is located at: http://www.mhhe.com/physsci/chemistry/essentialchemistry/flash/vaporv3.swf.

Surface Tension

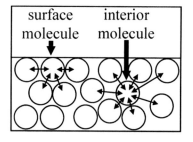

There are very few molecules in the gas phase and so the intermolecular attractive force pulling a surface molecule (labeled in the diagram) towards that direction is very weak, but there are many molecules with intermolecular attractive forces in the liquid phase. This leads to an imbalance of forces and it makes the surface molecule stick to the liquid molecules nearby more strongly. There is a net inwards pull away from the interface to minimize its surface area. This is not the case for molecules in the interior of the liquid where the forces are balanced. Surface tension is the energy required to increase the surface area of a liquid by a unit amount. Because of surface tension, there is a "film" at the interface that makes it more difficult for a solid object to "break through" the surface than to move around when it's already completely submerged. An increase in temperature decreases the surface tension because the kinetic energy acts in opposition to the intermolecular attractive forces. Chemicals with strong intermolecular attractive forces have a high surface tension. Surface tension can also be altered by adding other substances. NaOH added to water will raise its surface tension, and adding soap to water lowers surface tension (because the soap acts as a surfactant).

Boiling Point as a Function of Pressure

For a liquid in an open container, vapor pressure increases with temperature until the vapor pressure is equal to the external pressure, and the boiling point occurs at that temperature. Boiling is defined as the process of vapor bubbles forming and escaping from the liquid by breaking the intermolecular attractive forces within the liquid. Substances with stronger intermolecular attractive forces have a higher boiling point. An increase in the surrounding pressure forces molecules closer together and increases their intermolecular attractive forces. More kinetic energy is then required to break these bonds, so the boiling point of a liquid increases with increases in pressure.

Critical Point

See **0010** for phase diagrams and a complete discussion on phase changes and the critical point. In this skill, we've seen how rising temperature at a gas-liquid interface increases vapor pressure and decreases surface tension. All the liquid will become a gas if left at the boiling point long enough, but if the external pressure is increased above the vapor pressure, some material will remain in the liquid phase and the boiling point will increase. A pressure cooker is a good example of this. Finally, however, a temperature is reached at which no amount of pressure will keep the material in a liquid state. The highest temperature at which a substance can exist as a liquid is its **critical temperature**. **Critical pressure** is the vapor pressure of a liquid at its critical temperature. Surface tension shrinks to zero and there is no longer a gas-liquid interface when critical conditions are reached.

Above its critical temperature and pressure, a substance takes the shape and fills the volume of its container like a gas, but it has a density and intermolecular attractive forces similar to a liquid. This phase is called a **supercritical fluid**. Like liquids and gases, they are able to flow from one place to another.

Summary

The following table summarizes the properties of a liquid as temperature and pressure are altered. The speed and kinetic energy of molecules are only dependant on temperature as discussed in **0007**.

Effect on a liquid of an **increase** in one variable with the other constant	– = decrease, **0** = no change, **+** = increase, **NA**=not applicable					
	Average speed of molecules	Average translational kinetic energy of molecules	Viscosity	Vapor pressure	Surface tension	Boiling point
Temperature	+	+	–	+	–	**NA**
External pressure	0	0	+/–[1]	**NA**[2]	**NA**[2]	+

[1]A slight increase for most materials but a slight decrease for water at some temperatures.
[2]Not applicable. For a pure substance in a closed container at equilibrium, external pressure forces more vapor into the liquid phase. The volume of each phase is altered but conditions at the interface remain unchanged.

Identify factors involved in the dissolving process.

Heterogeneous combinations of materials are called **mixtures**. Mixtures are composed of two or more pure substances that are not chemically combined. Mixtures may be of any proportion and can be physically separated by processes such as filtering, centrifuging, or distillation.

Mixtures can be classified according to particle size.

- **Homogeneous Mixtures.** Homogeneous mixtures have the same composition and properties throughout the mixture and are also known as **solutions.** They have a **uniform color and distribution of solute (what is being dissolved) and solvent (what is doing the dissolving) particles throughout the mixtur**e.

- **Heterogeneous Mixtures.** Heterogeneous mixtures do not have a uniform distribution of particles throughout the mixture. The different components of the mixture can be identified and separated through physical processes.

When two or more pure materials mix in a homogeneous way (with their molecules intermixing on a molecular level), the mixture is called a **solution**. Dispersions of small particles that are larger than molecules are called **colloids**. Liquid solutions are the most common, but any two phases may form a solution. When a pure liquid and a gas or solid form a liquid solution, the pure liquid is called the **solvent** and the non-liquids are called **solutes**. When all components in the solution were originally liquids, then the one present in the greatest amount is called the solvent and the others are called solutes. Solutions with water as the solvent are called **aqueous** solutions. The amount of solute in in relation to the amount of solvent is called its **concentration**. A solution with a small concentration of solute is called **dilute**, and a solution with a large concentration of solute is called **concentrated**.

As more solid solute particles (circles in the figure to the right) dissolve in a liquid solvent (grey background), the concentration of solute increases, and the chance that dissolved solute (grey circles) will collide with the remaining undissolved solid (white circles) also increases. A collision may result in the solute particle either bouncing off the solid or reattaching itself to the solid. If it reattaches, the process is called **crystallization**, and is the opposite of the solution process. Particles in the act of dissolving or crystallizing are half-shaded in the figure. An animation of the solution process may be found here: http://www.mhhe.com/physsci/chemistry/essentialchemistry/flash/molvie1.swf.

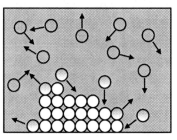

Equilibrium occurs when no additional solute will dissolve because the rates of crystallization and solution are equal.

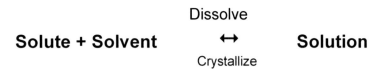

Dissolve

Solute + Solvent ↔ **Solution**

Crystallize

A solution at equilibrium with non-dissolved solute is a **saturated** solution. The amount of solute required to form a saturated solution in a given amount of solvent is called the **solubility** of that solute. If less solute is present, the solution is called **unsaturated**. It is also possible under certain special conditions to have more solute than the equilibrium amount, resulting in a solution that is termed **supersaturated**.

Pairs of liquids that mix in all proportions are called **miscible**. Liquids that don't mix are called **immiscible**.

Analyze the effects of physical conditions on the dissolving process and on solubility.

Gas solubility

Pressure does not dramatically alter the solubility of solids or liquids, but kinetic molecular theory predicts that **increasing the partial pressure of a gas will increase the solubility of the gas** in a liquid. If a substance is distributed between gas and solution phases and pressure is exerted, more gas molecules will impact the gas/liquid interface per second, so more will dissolve until a new equilibrium is reached at a higher solubility. **Henry's law** describes this relationship as a direct proportionality:

$$\text{Solubility of gas in liquid (in } \frac{\text{mol solute}}{\text{L solution}}) \propto P_{gas}$$

For example, **carbonated drinks** contain CO_2 and are bottled under high pressure, permitting the gas to dissolve into aqueous solution. When the bottle is opened, the partial pressure of CO_2 in the gas phase rapidly decreases to the value in the atmosphere, and the gas bubbles out of solution. When the bottle is closed again, CO_2 gas pressure builds up in the bottle until a saturated solution at equilibrium is again obtained. Nitrogen also increases in the bloodstream of deep-sea divers when they experience high pressures. If they return to atmospheric pressure too rapidly, large bubbles of nitrogen gas will form in their blood and cause a potentially lethal condition known as **the bends** or **decompression sickness**. The diver must enter a hyperbaric (high pressure) chamber to redissolve the nitrogen back into his blood and lower the pressure slowly to atmospheric conditions.

Increasing the temperature decreases the solubility of a gas in a liquid because kinetic energy opposes intermolecular attractions and permits more molecules to escape from the liquid phase. The vapor pressure of a pure liquid increases with temperature for the same reason (see **0025**). Greater kinetic energy favors material in the gas phase.

Liquid and solid solubility

For solid and liquid solutes, the effects of temperature are dependent on whether the reaction absorbs heat (endothermic reaction) or releases heat (exothermic reaction). Endothermic and exothermic reactions are discussed in more detail in **0012** and **0013**. The following brief analysis is applicable for the effect of temperature on solutions.

Three processes occur when a solution is formed:
1) Solute particles are separated from each other, and heat is required to break these bonds.

2) Solvent particles are separated from each other to create space for solute particles, and heat is required to break these bonds also.

3) Solute and solvent particles interact with each other forming new bonds (see **0025**), and releasing heat.

If the heat required for the first two processes is greater than the heat released by the third, then the entire reaction may be written as an endothermic process:

$$\text{Solute} + \text{Solvent} + \text{Heat} \rightarrow \text{Solution}$$

and according to Le Chatelier's principle (see **0017** and **0018**), **solubility will increase with increasing temperature for an endothermic solution process**. This occurs for most salts in water, including NaCl. There is a large increase for potassium nitrate—KNO_3.

However, heat is released when many solutes enter solution, and the entire reaction is exothermic:

$$\text{Solute} + \text{Solvent} \rightarrow \text{Solution} + \text{Heat}.$$

Solubility will decrease with increasing temperature for an exothermic solution process. This is the case for cerium(III) sulfate—$Ce_2(SO_4)_3$—in water.

The energy change associated with the process in which a solute dissolves in a solvent is called the **heat of solution**. This energy change is the net result of two processes: 1) the energy required to break the solute-solute bonds, called the **crystal lattice energy**, and 2) the energy released when the solute particles bond with the solvent molecules, called the **heat of hydration**.

Example: What is the heat of solution for KCl in water?

Solution: The crystal lattice energy of KCl, the energy necessary to break apart the KCl crystal lattice and form free ions, is represented by:

$$KCl\ (s) \rightarrow K^+\ (g) + Cl^-\ (g) \qquad\qquad \Delta H = +167.6\ \text{kcal}$$

The heat of hydration of KCl, the energy released when the free ions are hydrated, is represented by:

$$K^+\ (g) + Cl^-\ (g) \rightarrow K^+\ (aq) + Cl^-\ (aq) \qquad \Delta H = -163.5\ \text{kcal}$$

The overall reaction is endothermic, and the heat of solution is positive since more energy is required in the first step than is released by the second step.

$$KCl\ (s) \rightarrow K^+\ (aq) + Cl^-\ (aq) \qquad\qquad \Delta H = +4.1\ \text{kcal}$$

Summary

The following table summarizes the impact of temperature and pressure on solubility:

Effect on solution of an **increase** in one variable with the other constant	– = decrease, **0** = no/small change, **+** = increase, **++** = strong increase				
	Gas solute in liquid solvent			Solid and liquid solutes	
	Average kinetic energy of molecules	Collisions of gas with liquid interface	Solubility	Solubility for an endothermic heat of solution	Solubility for an exothermic heat of solution
Pressure	0	++	+	0	0
Temperature	+	+	–	+	–

Calculate concentrations and dilutions in terms of molarity, molality, normality, weight percentage, and mole fraction.

The **molarity** (M) of a solute in solution is a concentration expressed as the number of moles of solute in a liter of solution.

$$\text{Molarity} = \frac{\text{moles solute}}{\text{volume of solution in liters}}$$

Molarity is the most frequently used concentration unit in chemical reactions because it reflects the number of solute moles available. By using Avogadro's number (see **0022**), the number of molecules in a flask--a difficult image to conceptualize in the lab--is expressed in terms of the volume of liquid in the flask—a straightforward image to visualize and actually manipulate.

Rarely do we see or use concentrated solutions. The majority of solutions that we come across in our daily lives are dilute solutions. Molarity is useful for dilutions because the moles of solute remain unchanged if more solvent is added to the solution:

$$(\text{Initial molarity})(\text{Initial volume}) = (\text{molarity after dilution})(\text{final volume})$$

or

$$M_{initial}V_{initial} = M_{final}V_{final}$$

Example: What is the molarity of a 5.00 liter solution that was made with 10.0 moles of $CuCl_2$?

Solution: We can use the original formula. Note that in this particular example, where the number of moles of solute is given, the identity of the solute ($CaCl_2$) has nothing to do with solving the problem.

$$\text{Molarity} = \frac{\text{\# of moles of solute}}{\text{Liters of solution}}$$

$$M = \frac{moles}{liter}$$

Given: # of moles of solute = 10.0 moles
Liters of solution = 5.00 liters

$$M = \frac{moles}{L} = \frac{n}{V}$$

Molarity = $\dfrac{10.0 \text{ moles of } CaCl_2}{5.00 \text{ Liters of solution}}$ = 2.00 M

Answer = 2.00 M

Example: A 250 ml solution is made with 0.50 moles of NaCl. What is the molarity of the solution?

Solution: In this case we are given ml, while the formula calls for L. We must change the ml to Liters as shown below:

$$250 \text{ ml } \times \frac{1 \text{ liter}}{1000 \text{ ml}} = 0.25 \text{ liters}$$

Now, solve the problem using the equation:

$$\text{Molarity} = \frac{\text{\# of moles of solute}}{\text{Liters of solution}}$$

Given: Number of moles of solute = 0.50 moles of NaCl
Liters of solution = 0.25 L of solution

$$\text{Molarity} = \frac{0.50 \text{ moles of NaCl}}{0.25 \text{ L}} = 2.0 \text{ M solution}$$

Answer = 2.0 M solution of NaCl

Example: What is the molarity of 3.50 L of solution that contains 90.0 g of sodium chloride?

Solution: Grams must be converted to moles within the molarity equation:

$$M = 90.0 \text{ g NaCl} \times (1 \text{ mol} / 58.5 \text{ g}) / 3.50 \text{ L} = 0.440 \text{ M}$$

The **molality** (m) of a solution is a concentration expressed as the number of moles of the solute in a kilogram of solvent.

$$\text{Molality} = \frac{\text{moles solute}}{\text{mass of solvent in kilograms}}$$

Molality is a useful measure of concentration in situations where solution density (and thus, volume) is changing and the impact of this change is not important. The molarity of a solution will change with temperature because the liquid will expand or contract. Molality will remain constant. Because water typically has a density of one kilogram per liter, the molality and molarity of aqueous solutions at room temperature have roughly the same numerical value. Molality is used in calculating freezing point depressions and boiling point elevations.

Example: Calculate the molality when 75.0 grams of $MgCl_2$ is dissolved in 500.0 g of solvent.

Solution: Since m = # mol solute
Kg solvent

$$m = \frac{moles}{Kg}$$

First we need the number mol solute ($MgCl_2$)

mol = 75.0 g $MgCl_2$/ 95.3 g/mol =0.787 mol

We also need kg of solvent so 500.0 g of solvent needs to be converted to kg.

Kg = 500.0 g x 1 kg/1000 g = 0.5000 kg

Now it is just a matter of substituting into the molality formula:

molality = 0.787 mol/0.5000 kg =1.57 m

Example: What is the molality of a solution composed of 2.55 g of acetone, $(CH_3)_2CO$, dissolved in 200 g of water?

Solution: First, convert the units: 2.55 g x 1 mol / 58 g = 0.044 mol acetone, and 200 g water = 0.200 kg water.

m = 0.044 mol / 0.200 kg water = 0.22 m

The **normality** (abbreviated N) of a solution is defined as the number of **equivalents** of a solute per liter of solution.

$$Normality = \frac{equivalents\ solute}{volume\ of\ solution\ in\ liters}$$

An **equivalent** is defined according to the type of reaction being examined, but the number of equivalents of solute is always a whole number multiple of the number of moles of solute, and so the normality of a solute is always a whole-number multiple of its molarity. An equivalent is defined so that one equivalent of one reagent will react with one equivalent of another reagent.

For acid-base reactions (see **0019**), an equivalent of an acid is the quantity that supplies 1 mol of H^+ and an equivalent of a base is the quantity reacting with 1 mol of H^+. For example, one mole of H_2SO_4 in an acid-base reaction supplies two moles of H+. The mass of one equivalent of H_2SO_4 is half of the mass of one mole of H_2SO_4, and its normality is twice its molarity. In a redox reaction (see competency 9), an equivalent is the quantity of substance that gains or loses one mol of electrons.

Percent by mass or volume expresses the amount (mass) of solute present as a percentage of the total solution present:

$$\% \text{ by mass} = \frac{\text{mass of solute}}{\text{mass of solute} + \text{mass of solvent}} \times 100\%$$

$$\% \text{ by volume} = \frac{\text{volume of solute}}{\text{volume of solute} + \text{volume of solvent}} \times 100\%$$
$$\text{(or total volume of solution)}$$

Example: What is the percent by mass of a solution prepared by dissolving 4.0 g of CH_3COOH in 35.0 g of water?

Solution:

$$\% \text{ by mass} = \frac{\text{mass of solute}}{\text{mass of solute} + \text{mass of solvent}} \times 100\%$$

$$= 4 \text{ g} / (4 \text{ g} + 35 \text{ g}) = 10\%$$

Example: The label on a 500 mL bottle of hydrogen peroxide, H_2O_2, says 3% by volume. How much hydrogen peroxide does it contain?

Solution: Rearranging the volume equation above:

$$\text{Volume of solute} = \text{volume of solution} \times \% \text{ by volume} / 100\%$$

$$\text{Volume of } H_2O_2 = 3\% \times 500 \text{ mL} / 100\% = 15 \text{ mL}$$

A **Mole fraction** expresses the proportion of a component in a solution relative to the entire number of moles present. If you were able to pick out a molecule at random from a solution, the mole fraction of a component represents the probability that the molecule you picked would be from that particular component. Mole fractions for all components must sum to one, and mole fractions are just numbers with no units.

$$\text{Mole fraction of a component} = \frac{\text{moles of component}}{\text{total moles of all components}}$$

Parts per million (ppm) is frequently used when very small amounts of solute are present, such as contaminants in water. When dealing with very small amounts of solute, it is more convenient to use the expression parts per million (ppm) or even parts per billion (ppb). In comparison, a 1% saline (NaCl) solution means that there is 1 part NaCl per one hundred parts water.

Example: What is the concentration of a solution in percent, ppm, and ppb that contains 10 g of NaCl dissolved in 90 grams of H_2O?

Solution: The total mass of the solution is 10 g + 90 g = 100 g. Therefore:

Percent by weight = 10 g NaCl / 100 g solution = 0.1 x 100% = 10%

ppm = 10 g NaCl / 100 g solution = 0.1 x 1,000,000 = 100,000 ppm

ppb = 10 g NaCl / 100 g solution = 0.1 x 1,000,000,000 = 100,000,000 ppb

Analyze the effect of molecular interactions in solutions.

Intermolecular forces in the solution process

Solutions tend to form when the intermolecular attractive forces between solute and solvent molecules are about as strong as those that exist in the solute alone or in solvent alone. NaCl dissolves in water because:

1) The water molecules interact with the Na^+ and Cl^- ions with sufficient strength to overcome the attraction between them in the crystal.
2) Na^+ and Cl^- ions interact with the water molecules with sufficient strength to overcome the attraction water molecules have for each other in the liquid.

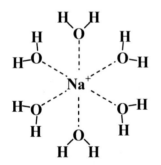

The intermolecular attraction between solute and solvent molecules is known as **solvation**. When the solvent is water, it is known as **hydration**. The figure to the left shows a hydrated Na^+ ion.

Polar and nonpolar solutes and solvents

A nonpolar liquid like heptane (C_7H_{16}) has intermolecular bonds with relatively weak London dispersion forces. Heptane is immiscible in water because the attraction that water molecules have for each other via hydrogen bonding is strong in comparison. Unlike Na^+ and Cl^- ions, heptane molecules cannot break these bonds. Because bonds of similar strength must be broken and formed for solvation to occur, nonpolar substances tend to be soluble in nonpolar solvents, and ionic and polar substances are soluble in polar solvents like water. Polar molecules are often called **hydrophilic** and non-polar molecules are called **hydrophobic**. This observation is often stated as "**like dissolves like.**" Network solids (e.g., diamond) are soluble in neither polar nor nonpolar solvents because the covalent bonds within the solid are too strong for these solvents to break.

Electrolytes and precipitates

Compounds that are completely ionized in water are called **strong electrolytes** because these solutions easily conduct electricity. Most salts are strong electrolytes. For example, all NaCl is present in solution as ions. Other compounds (including many acids and bases) may dissolve in water without completely ionizing. These compounds are referred to as **weak electrolytes** (see **0019**) and their state of ionization is at equilibrium with the larger molecule (**0017** and **0018**). Those compounds that dissolve with no ionization (e.g., glucose, $C_6H_{12}O_6$) are called **nonelectrolytes.**

[handwritten: completely ionized]

[handwritten: partially ionized]

[handwritten: no ionization]

Particles in solution are free to move about and collide with each other, vastly increasing the likelihood that a reaction will occur compared with particles in a solid phase. Aqueous solutions may react to produce an insoluble substance that will fall out of solution as a solid or gas precipitate in a precipitation reaction. Aqueous solution may also react to form additional water, or a different chemical in aqueous solution.

Solubility rules for ionic compounds

Given a cation and anion in aqueous solution, we can determine if a precipitate will form according to some common solubility rules.

1) Salts with NH_4^+ or with a cation from group 1 of the periodic table are soluble in water.

2) Nitrates (NO_3^-), acetates ($C_2H_3O_2^-$), chlorates (ClO_3^-), and perchlorates (ClO_4^-) are soluble.

3) Cl^-, Br^-, and I^- salts are soluble except in the presence of Ag^+, Hg_2^{2+}, or Pb^{2+} with which they will form precipitates.

4) Sulfates (SO_4^{2-}) are soluble except in the presence of Ca^{2+}, Ba^{2+}, Ag^+, Hg_2^{2+}, or Pb^{2+}.

5) Hydroxides (OH^-) are insoluble except with cations from rule 1 or in the presence of Ca^{2+}, Sr^{2+}, or Ba^{2+}.

6) Sulfides (S^{2-}), sulfites (SO_3^{2-}), phosphates (PO_4^{3-}), and carbonates (CO_3^{2-}) are insoluble except with cations from rule 1.

Predict the effect of solute concentration on colligative properties.

A **colligative** property is a physical property of a solution that **depends on the number of solute particles present in solution** and usually not on the identity of the solutes involved.

Vapor pressure lowering, boiling point elevation, freezing point lowering

After a nonvolatile solute is added to a liquid solvent, a smaller fraction of the molecules at the liquid-gas interface are now volatile and capable of escaping into the gas phase. On the other hand, the vapor consists of essentially pure solvent that is able to condense freely. This imbalance drives equilibrium away from the vapor phase and into the liquid phase and **lowers the vapor pressure** by an amount proportional to the number of solute particles present.

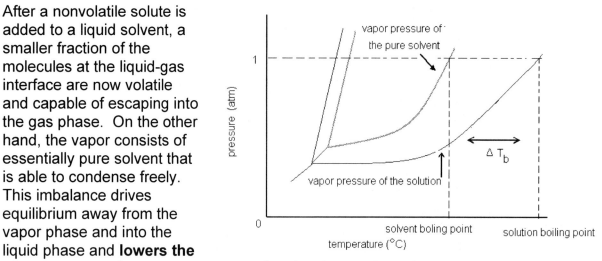

It follows from a lowered vapor pressure that a higher temperature is required to achieve a vapor pressure equal to the external pressure over the liquid (see **0025**). Thus **the boiling point is raised** by an amount proportional to the number of solute particles present.

Solute particles in a liquid solvent are not normally soluble in the solid phase of that solvent. When solvent crystals freeze, they typically align themselves with each other at first and keep the solute out. This means that only a fraction of the molecules in the liquid at the liquid-solid interface are capable of freezing while the solid phase consists of essentially pure solvent that is able to melt freely. This imbalance drives equilibrium away from the solid phase and into the liquid phase and **lowers the freezing point** by an amount proportional to the number of solute particles present.

Boiling point elevation and freezing point depression are both caused by a lower fraction of solvent molecules in the liquid phase than in the other phase. For pure water at 1 atm there is equilibrium at the normal boiling and freezing points. For water with a high solute concentration, equilibrium is not present.

Osmotic pressure

A **semipermeable membrane** is a material that permits some particles to pass through it but not others. The diagram below shows a membrane that permits solvent but not solute to pass through it. When a semipermeable membrane separates a dilute solution from a concentrated solution, the solvent flows from the dilute to the concentrated solution (i.e., from higher solvent to lower solvent concentration) in a process called **osmosis** until equilibrium is achieved. Notice that there is now more solvent on the side that originally had the higher concentration of solute.

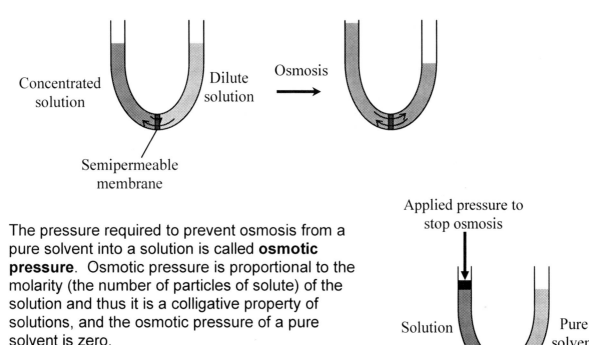

The pressure required to prevent osmosis from a pure solvent into a solution is called **osmotic pressure**. Osmotic pressure is proportional to the molarity (the number of particles of solute) of the solution and thus it is a colligative property of solutions, and the osmotic pressure of a pure solvent is zero.

A simulation of solutes and solvent molecules interacting and an animation of osmotic flow between two flexible compartments can be found at: http://physioweb.med.uvm.edu/bodyfluids/osmosis.htm.
A simulation of the osmotic pressure experiment above for NaCl, sucrose, and albumin (a protein) is located at:
http://arbl.cvmbs.colostate.edu/hbooks/cmb/cells/pmemb/hydrosim.html.
Typical changes in a pressure/temperature phase diagram after adding a non-volatile solute are found here:
http://chemmovies.unl.edu/ChemAnime/SOLND/SOLND.html.

Solve colligative property problems.

Quantitative colligative property problems typically involve a change in a property related to a solute concentration by means of a direct proportionality.

Raoult's law states that the vapor pressure of a solution with nonvolatile solutes is the mole fraction of the solvent multiplied by the pure solvent vapor pressure:

$$P^{vapor}_{solution} = P^{vapor}_{pure\ solvent} \left(\text{mole fraction}\right)_{solvent}$$

Raoult's law is often used to describe the vapor pressure change from a pure solvent to a solution using the solute concentration:

$$\Delta P^{vapor} = P^{vapor}_{solution} - P^{vapor}_{pure\ solvent} = P^{vapor}_{pure\ solvent} \left(\text{mole fraction}\right)_{solvent} - P^{vapor}_{pure\ solvent}$$

$$= -P^{vapor}_{pure\ solvent} \left(1 - \left(\text{mole fraction}\right)_{solvent}\right)$$

$$= -P^{vapor}_{pure\ solvent} \left(\text{mole fraction}\right)_{solute}$$

Different concentration units are used for other colligative properties to express a **change from pure solvent**. The following table summarizes these expressions:

Colligative property	Equation for property X $\Delta X = X_{solution} - X_{pure\ solvent}$	Proportionality constant
Vapor pressure lowering	$\Delta P^{vapor} = -P^{vapor}_{pure\ solvent} \left(\text{mole fraction}\right)_{solute}$	Pure solvent vapor pressure
Boiling point elevation	$\Delta T_b = K_b \left(\text{molality}\right)$	Solvent-dependant constant K_b
Freezing point lowering	$\Delta T_f = -K_f \left(\text{molality}\right)$	Solvent-dependant constant K_f
Osmotic pressure	$P_{osmotic} = RT \left(\text{molarity}\right)$	(Gas constant) $\square$ (Temperature)

For solutions that contain electrolytes, the change from the pure solvent to a solution is different from what is predicted by the above equations. Due to their ionic nature, these substances will dissociate to put many more ions in solution than their molal concentration would predict. The total number of ions affects the colligative properties just as the number of molecules would for a nonpolar solute.

The **van 't Hoff factor** (i) is an important factor in predicting the change in boiling point or freezing point of a solution after a solute has been added. The van 't Hoff factor is symbolized by the lower-case letter i. It is a unitless constant directly associated with the degree of dissociation of the solute in the solvent:

- Substances which do not ionize in solution, like sugar, have $i = 1$.
- Substances which ionize into two ions, like NaCl, have $i = 2$.
- Substances which ionize into three ions, like $MgCl_2$, have $i = 3$.

This pattern continues for any number of particles into which a solute dissociates.

Many colligative property problems compare one solution to another and may be solved without the use of the above expressions. All that is required for these comparison problems is knowledge of what the colligative properties are, how they are altered, and which solution contains the greater concentration of dissolved particles.

The most common errors in solving all types of colligative property problems arise from considering some value other than the number of particles in solution. Remember that one mole of glucose(aq) forms one mole of hydrated particles, but one mole of NaCl(aq) forms two moles of hydrated particles, and one mole of $Al_2(SO_4)_3(aq)$ forms five moles of them. We would expect a 0.5 M solution of glucose to have roughly the same colligative properties as a 0.25 M solution of sodium hydroxide and a 0.1 M solution of aluminum sulfate. Also remember that undissolved solids do not contribute anything to colligative properties.

Example: One mole of each of the following compounds is added to water in separate flasks to make 1.0 L of solution:

Potassium phosphate
Silver chloride
Sodium chloride
Sugar (sucrose)

A. Which solution will exhibit the greatest change in the freezing point temperature?

B. Which solution will exhibit the least change in the boiling point temperature? Be sure to explain your choices.

Solution: Determine the molecular formulas and analyze the choices for solubility and dissociation:

Potassium phosphate	KH_2PO_4	soluble in water $\rightarrow$ 4 ions
Silver chloride	AgCl	soluble in water $\rightarrow$ 2 ions
Sodium chloride	NaCl	soluble in water $\rightarrow$ 2 ions
Sugar (sucrose)	$C_{12}H_{22}O_{11}$	soluble in water $\rightarrow$ 1
molecule		

A. Of the choices, potassium phosphate forms the most ions so given that the molar concentration of all of the choices is the same, K_3PO_4 will affect the boiling point temperature and the freezing point temperature the most. For every 1 mole of K_3PO_4 that dissolves, 4 moles of ions will be present in solution.

B. Sucrose, a nonelectrolye, will have the least effect on the freezing point and boiling point temperatures because it is a molecular substance and does not dissociate into ions. For every 1 mole of sugar in solution, only 1 mole of molecules will be present.

Changes to boiling point temperature and freezing point temperature may be determined by looking at the molal concentration of the solute, according to the equations in the table above.

For **boiling point temperature changes**:

$$\Delta T_b = mk_b i$$

where m is the molal concentration of the solute, K_b is a constant specific to each solvent, and i is the number of particles or ions in solution. For water, $K_b = 0.52°$ C/m.

For **freezing point temperature changes**:

$$\Delta T_f = mk_f i$$

where m is the molal concentration of the solute, K_f is a constant specific to each solvent, and i is the number of particles or ions in solution. For water, $K_f = -1.86°$ C/m.

Example: How much will the boiling point temperature change if 31.5 grams of potassium chloride is added to 225 g of water?

Solution: First convert the units and identify the constants. KCl is an electrolyte that dissociates into two ions, so $i = 2$.

Mass of water = 225 g = 0.225 kg
Concentration of KCl = 31.5 g / 74.5 g/mol = 0.423 mole
m = 0.423 mol / 0.225 kg = 1.88 m
$K_b = 0.52°$ C/m
$i = 2$

$$\Delta T_b = mk_b i = 1.88 \text{ m } (0.56° \text{ C/m}) \, 2 = 1.96° \text{ C}$$

Example: How many grams of benzoic acid ($C_7H_6O_2$, a nonelectrolyte) must be added to 178 g of water to increase the boiling point temperature by 4° C?

Solution: First convert the units and identify the constants. Benzoic acid is a nonelectrolyte so $i = 1$.

Mass of water = 178 g = 0.178 kg
Molecular weight of benzoic acid = 122 g/mol
$\Delta T = 4°$ C
$K_b = 0.52°$ C/m

Rearranging the equation above and first solving for molality of benzoic acid:

$m = \Delta T_b / K_b i = $ 4 / 0.52° C/m x 1 = 7.69 m

Next, solve for grams of benzoic acid:

7.69 m x 0.178 kg water = 1.37 mol
1.37 mol x 122 g/mol = 167 g benzoic acid

Example: The mixture used to make ice cream does not freeze until the temperature reaches -15 to -18° C. Using ice alone, the temperature will only go down to 0° C. To reach the lower temperature needed to freeze the ice cream, salt (NaCl) is added to several 2.3 kg bags of ice. How much salt is needed to freeze the ice cream?

Solution: Each sodium chloride particle dissociates into a Na^+ ion and a Cl^- ion. Therefore, NaCl has an i value of 2. The temperature change needed is -15° C and the K_f value for water is -1.86° C/m.

Rearranging the freezing point depression expression we can determine the *molality* of the salt-ice solution that will reach -15° C.

$$m = \frac{\Delta T}{K_f i} = \frac{-15°\ C}{-1.86°\ C/m \times 2} = 4.0\ m$$

m = moles/kg, so the moles of NaCl needed can be determined from the kilograms of ice used:

4.0 mol/kg x 2.3 kg = 9.3 mol NaCl

Now, the mass of NaCl needed can be found by using the relationship between moles and molecular weight:

9.3 mol x 58.5 g/mol = 540 g of NaCl needed for every bag of ice used.

The most common errors in solving all types of colligative property problems arise from considering some value other than **the number of particles in solution**. Remember that one mole of glucose (*aq*) forms one mole of hydrated particles, but one mole of NaCl (*aq*) forms two moles of hydrated particles, and one mole of $Al_2(SO_4)_3(aq)$ forms five moles of hydrated particles.

We would expect a 0.5 M solution of glucose to have roughly the same colligative properties as a 0.25 M solution of sodium hydroxide and a 0.1 M solution of aluminum sulfate. Also remember that non-dissolved solids do not contribute anything to colligative properties.

SUBAREA VI. INTERACTIONS OF CHEMISTRY AND THE ENVIRONMENT

Competency 26.0 Understand industrial and household chemistry

Chemical concepts often involve events taking place on scales that are too small for us to see. But the application of those concepts is all around us when we work and play, cook and clean, and eat and drink.

Relating chemistry to everyday activities often requires other content in this text in combination with **strong common sense reasoning**. There are some things that many people believe they know about everyday activities that aren't true! For example, many people believe that cooks add salt when they boil water to decrease the amount of time it takes for the water to boil, but this is *false*. In reality, adding salt increases the boiling point of water (see **0025**), and so water will take *more* time to boil (see **0013**). However, once the water is boiling, the fact that it is at a higher temperature means the food will take less time to cook.

Boiling point elevation is a colligative property because more salt molecules at the liquid-vapor interface means fewer water molecules there (**0025**), shifting the equilibrium of the reaction to the left according to Le Chatelier's Principle:

$$H_2O \; (l) \leftrightarrow H_2O \; (g)$$

Therefore the vapor pressure (see **0025**) at 100 °C will decrease below 1 atm, and a higher temperature along with more time will be required for boiling. However, all of **this knowledge will go to waste if you rely on a mistaken belief** instead of reasoning through the situation.

A common example of an everyday neutralization reaction (**0019**) is the use of **antacids**. These chemicals are bases that neutralize excess gastric acid in the stomach and provide increased buffering capacity (**0019**). Gastric acid is mostly HCl.

An everyday application of the thermochemistry of reactions is in the field of **nutrition**. The energy value of food is measured in "**nutritional calories**," a unit equal to 4814 Joules. We inhale oxygen to convert organic molecules (our fuel) to carbon dioxide and water just as a flame uses oxygen to complete the same reaction, obtaining the same **heat of combustion** (**0013**).

Baking soda is a **base** that is combined with acids in cooking (such as buttermilk, vinegar, sour cream, or yogurt) to create CO_2 bubbles. These bubbles cause baked goods to rise. Bleach and ammonia are other examples of household bases used for cleaning.

In addition to **batteries** (**0020**), a common application of electrochemistry is in the prevention of **corrosion**. Corrosion is a redox reaction that oxidizes elemental metals to cations and removes their atoms from metallic bonds (**0014**).

Applications of chemistry in industry are abundant and have been used throughout this book. Ethanol is separated from a mixture of organic compounds by gas chromatography (see **0005**). Chemical technology helps keep foods fresh longer and alters the molecules in food. Processes such as pasteurization, drying, salting, and adding preservatives all prevent microbial contamination by altering the nutritional content of food (see **0001**).

Fuel refineries carry out a process called reforming. In this process, aromatic hydrocarbons are produced in a number of steps that involve dehydrogenation (removal of hydrogen), hydrogenolysis (C-C bond scission) and cyclization (ring formation) of saturated hydrocarbons. The purpose of this reforming process is to achieve **high yields** and **high rates** of production of aromatic hydrocarbons (BTX) since these materials have excellent anti-knock properties as components in motor fuels. Petrochemical plants such as refineries cost hundreds of millions of dollars to build. A more efficient plant costs less in money per gallon of fuel than one with poor efficiency. As TEL was removed from fuels, more and more of the BTX was needed. So if refiners could get more from the same plant, they could delay or eliminate the construction of costly, new facilities.

Reforming is perhaps the most important use of industrial catalysts. In the reforming process, at 770 degrees Kelvin and 10-35atm. pressure, catalysts carry out two separate and distinct roles in reforming: (a.) Dehydrogenation catalysis to break C-H bonds and (b.). Acid catalysis to break C-C bonds. Refiners need to rapidly break C-C bonds to reduce the chain lengths of the less volatile, higher molecular weight hydrocarbons to get them to the chain length for gasolines. Then they need to cyclize these and dehydrogenate them to BTX components.

The catalysts consist of metals like platinum dispersed on finely divided silica or alumina. Silica and alumina act as acids and speed the processes of bond breaking. Dr. John Sinfelt studied of rates of reaction of the catalysts in use and of bimetallic catalysts - catalysts with two metals imbedded in the silica support. He found that the presence of iridium metal, along with the platinum, gave an unexpected boost to the rate of hydrogenolysis. By speeding up the rate of C-C bond breaking, the amount of BTX components that could be produced in reforming was greatly increased. Just by changing the catalyst, existing refineries would run much more efficiently.

To find more household and industrial applications, look at www.chemcases.com

Competency 27.0   Understand the applications of nuclear reactions

<u>Power generation</u>

Nuclear power currently provides 17% of the world's electricity. Heat is generated by **nuclear fission of uranium-235 or plutonium-239**. This heat is then converted to electricity by boiling water and forcing the steam through a turbine. Fission of ^{235}U and ^{239}Pu occurs when **a neutron strikes the nucleus and breaks it apart into smaller nuclei and additional neutrons**. One possible fission reaction is:

$$_0^1n + _{92}^{235}U \rightarrow _{56}^{141}Ba + _{36}^{92}Kr + 3_0^1n$$

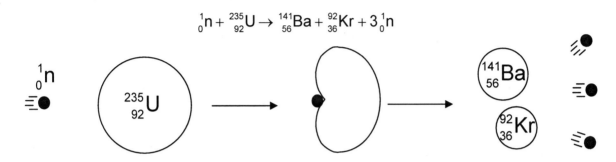

Gamma radiation, kinetic energy from the neutrons themselves, and the decay of the fission products (^{141}Ba and ^{92}Kr in the example above) all produce heat. The neutrons produced by the reaction strike other uranium atoms and produce more neutrons and more energy in a **chain reaction**. If enough neutrons are lost, the chain reaction stops and the process is called **subcritical**. If the mass of uranium is large enough that one neutron on average from each fission event triggers another fission, the reaction is said to be **critical**. If the mass is larger than this so that few neutrons escape, the reaction is called **supercritical**. The chain reaction then multiplies the number of fissions and an explosion with the violence of an atomic bomb will take place if the process is not stopped. The concentration of **fissile material** in nuclear power plants is sufficient for a critical reaction to occur but too low for a supercritical reaction to take place.

The alpha decay of **Plutonium-238 has been used as a heat source for localized power generation** in space probes and in heart pacemakers since the 1970s.

The most promising nuclear reaction for producing power by **nuclear fusion** is:

$$_1^2H + _1^3H \rightarrow _2^4He + _0^1n$$

Hydrogen-2 is called **deuterium** and is often represented by the symbol D. Hydrogen-3 is known as **tritium** and is often represented by the symbol T. Nuclear reactions between very light atoms similar to the reaction above are the energy source behind the sun and the hydrogen bomb.

Medicine

Medicine uses **X-rays** as a diagnostic tool and radioisotopes for **diagnostic radiology** and for **radiotherapy**. In diagnostic radiology, a radioisotope is introduced into the body and its location is monitored with a **gamma camera** or other imaging equipment. **Different isotopes are localized to different tissues at specific rates**. Abnormalities in internal organs, bone structure and function are found using these techniques. The isotopes typically emit only gamma rays because alpha and beta radiation are more likely to harm the patient. **Technetium-99m is a commonly used isotope for diagnostic radiology**. Many radioisotopes are used in diagnostic medicine outside the body.

Radiotherapy uses radiation as part of **cancer treatment to destroy tumors**. Rapidly growing tumors are more vulnerable to radiation damage from β particles than non-malignant tissue. Radiotherapy works by damaging the DNA of these cells. The radioactive source may be outside the body (external radiotherapy) or introduced into the body. This is common for shrinking tumors in tissues where surgery is risky such as the brain or lungs. Isotopes used for internal radiotherapy may be injected into the body as a liquid or introduced temporarily through a catheter in a sealed container. A common use of this is in treating prostate cancer.

Cobalt-60 was a common isotope for external radiotherapy, but it has mostly been replaced by linear accelerators that provide high-energy electrons (β particles) without a dangerous isotope source. It is still used to irradiate some foods to destroy bacteria. **Iodine-131 is used to combat diseases of the thyroid** and of several types of cancer. A list of isotopes used in nuclear medicine may be found at http://www.cbvcp.com/nmrc/mia.html.

Archeology

Archeology uses nuclear chemistry for **radiometric dating**. The most commonly used nuclide for this technique is Carbon-14. C-14 is mostly synthesized in the upper atmosphere where extraterrestrial radiation interacts with other molecules to produce neutrons used in the reaction:

$$_{0}^{1}n + _{7}^{14}N \rightarrow _{6}^{14}C + _{1}^{1}H .$$

Carbon-14 then decays by β-emission with a half-life of 5730 years:

$$_{6}^{14}C \rightarrow _{7}^{14}N + _{-1}^{0}e .$$

$_{6}^{14}C$ is distributed uniformly throughout the atmosphere, oceans, and living organisms because these entities all rapidly exchange carbon dioxide with one other.

Carbon-14 is present in these systems at a ratio of about 1 atom per trillion (10^9) atoms of non-radioactive carbon. However, after an organism dies, it no longer exchanges CO_2 with the atmosphere and its carbon-14 begins to decay with no replenishment. The time that has passed since biological material in plant fibers, wood, or bones was once alive may be estimated by comparing the fraction of $^{14}_{6}C$ present in the dead material to the fraction in living material.

$$t = t_{halflife} \frac{\ln\left(\dfrac{C_{sample}}{C_{living}}\right)}{\ln\left(\dfrac{1}{2}\right)}$$

where $C_{sample} \Rightarrow$ concentration in sample

$C_{initially} \Rightarrow$ concentration in living material

$t \Rightarrow$ *estimated* time before present

$t_{halflife} \Rightarrow$ half-life (5730 years for ^{14}C)

This estimate must be altered slightly by calibration curves to correct for differences in climate and cosmic background radiation over time.

Competency 28.0 Understand factors and processes related to the release of chemicals into the environment

A baby born today in the United States has an average life expectancy that is 30 years longer than a baby born 100 years ago. Significant reasons for this improvement include the manufacture and distribution of vaccines and antibiotics, an increase in our understanding human nutritional needs, and the use of fertilizers in agriculture (see **0001**). However, the benefits of these technologies are almost always accompanied by problems and significant risks.

Pesticides are used to control or kill organisms that compete with humans for food, spread disease, or are considered a nuisance. **Herbicides** are pesticides that attack weeds; insecticides attack insects; **fungicides** attack molds and other fungus. Sulfur was used as a fungicide in ancient times. The development and use of new pesticides has exploded over the last 60 years, but these pesticides are often poisonous to humans.

The **insecticide DDT** was widely used in the 1940s and 1950s and is responsible for **eradicating malaria from Europe and North America**. It quickly became the most widely used pesticide in the world. In the 1960s, some claimed that DDT was preventing fish-eating birds from reproducing and that it was causing birth defects in humans. DDT is now banned in many countries, but it is still used in developing nations to prevent diseases carried by insects. Unfortunately, its use in agriculture has often led to resistant mosquito strains that have hindered its effectiveness to prevent diseases.

Most scientists believe the emission of greenhouse gases has already led to global warming due to an increase in the **greenhouse effect**. The greenhouse effect is due to gases like CO_2 being trapped in the atmosphere close to the earth. This causes warm air to be trapped which then causes more CO_2 to be trapped. Human production of carbon dioxide from combustion of fossil fuels has increased the concentration of this important greenhouse gas to its highest level in recorded history. The precise impact of these changes in the atmosphere is difficult to predict and is a topic of international concern and political debate.

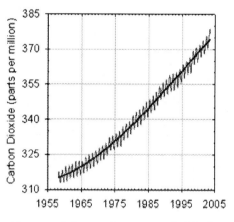

Source: Mauna Loa record, National Oceanic and Atmospheric

Rain with a pH less than 5.6 is known as **acid rain**. Acid rain is caused by burning fossil fuels (especially coal) and by fertilizers used in intensive agriculture. These activities emit sulfur and nitrogen in gas compounds that are converted to sulfur oxides and nitrogen oxides. These in turn create sulfuric acid and nitric acid in rain. Acid rain may also be created from gases emitted by volcanoes and other natural sources. Acid rain harms fish and trees and triggers the release metal ions from minerals into water which can harm people. The problem of acid rain in the United States has been addressed in recent decades by the use of **scrubbers** in coal burning power plants and **catalytic converters** in vehicles.

The ozone (O_3) layer is a region of the stratosphere that contains higher concentrations of ozone than other parts of the atmosphere. The ozone layer is important for human health because it blocks ultraviolet radiation from the sun which helps to protect us from skin cancer. Research in the 1970s revealed that several gases used for refrigeration and other purposes were depleting the ozone layer. Many of these ozone-destroying molecules are short alkyl

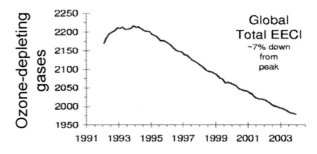

Source: National Oceanic and Atmospheric Administration

halides known as chlorofluorocarbons or CFCs. CCl_3F is one example. The widespread use of ozone-destroying gases was banned by an international agreement in the early 1990s. Other substances are used in their place such as CF_3CH_2F, a hydrofluorocarbon. Since that time the concentration of ozone-depleting gases in the atmosphere has been declining and the rate of ozone destruction has been decreasing. Many see this improvement as the most important positive example of international cooperation in helping the environment. The story of these new refrigerants is found at http://www.chemcases.com/fluoro/index.htm.

SUBAREA VII.   **FOUNDATIONS OF SCIENTIFIC INQUIRY: CONSTRUCTED RESPONSE ASSIGNMENT**

The context to be addressed by the constructed-response assignment is described in Subarea I, Objectives 0001 – 0006.

Sample Test

Directions: Read each item and select the best response.

1. A piston compresses a gas at constant temperature. Which gas properties increase?

   I. Average speed of molecules
   II. Pressure
   III. Molecular collisions with container walls per second

   A. I and II
   B. I and III
   C. II and III
   D. I, II, and III

2. The temperature of a liquid is raised at atmospheric pressure. Which property of liquids increases?

   A. Critical pressure
   B. Vapor pressure
   C. Surface tension
   D. Viscosity

3. Potassium crystallizes with two atoms contained in each unit cell. What is the mass of potassium found in a lattice 1.00×10^6 unit cells wide, 2.00×10^6 unit cells high, and 5.00×10^5 unit cells deep?

   A. 85.0 ng
   B. 32.5 μg
   C. 64.9 μg
   D. 130. μg

4. A gas is heated in a sealed container. Which of the following occur(s)?

   A. Gas pressure rises
   B. Gas density decreases
   C. The average distance between molecules increases
   D. All of the above

5. How many molecules are in 2.20 pg of a protein with a molecular weight of 150. kDa?

   A. 8.83×10^9
   B. 1.82×10^9
   C. 8.83×10^6
   D. 1.82×10^6

6. At STP, 20. μL of O_2 contain 5.4×10^{16} molecules. According to Avogadro's hypothesis, how many molecules are in 20. μL of Ne?

   A. 5.4×10^{15}
   B. 1.0×10^{16}
   C. 2.7×10^{16}
   D. 5.4×10^{16}

7. An ideal gas at 50.0° C and 3.00 atm is in a 300. cm³ cylinder. The cylinder volume changes by moving a piston until the gas is at 50.0° C and 1.00 atm. What is the final volume?

   A. 100. cm³
   B. 450. cm³
   C. 900. cm³
   D. 1.20 dm³

8. **Which gas law may be used to solve the previous problem?**

   A. Charles's law
   B. Boyle's law
   C. Graham's law
   D. Avogadro's law

9. **A blimp is filled with 5000. m³ of helium at 28.0° C and 99.7 kPa. What is the mass of helium used?**

   $$R = 8.3144 \frac{J}{mol-K}$$

   moles→g→kg

   A. 797 kg
   B. 810. kg
   C. 879 kg
   D. 8.57×10^3 kg

10. **Which of the following are able to flow from one place to another?**

    I. Gases ✓
    II. Liquids ✓
    III. Solids
    IV. Supercritical fluids

    A. I and II
    B. II only
    C. I, II, and IV
    D. I, II, III, and IV

11. **One mole of an ideal gas at STP occupies 22.4 L. At what temperature will 1 mole of an ideal gas at 1 atm occupy 31.0 L?**

    A. 34.6° C
    B. 105° C
    C. 378° C
    D. 442° C

12. **Why does $CaCl_2$ have a higher normal melting point than NH_3?**

    A. Covalent bonds are stronger than London dispersion forces.
    B. Covalent bonds are stronger than hydrogen bonds.
    C. Ionic bonds are stronger than London dispersion forces.
    D. Ionic bonds are stronger than hydrogen bonds.

13. **Which intermolecular attraction explains the following trend in straight-chain alkanes?**

Condensed structural formula	Boiling point (°C)
CH_4	-161.5
CH_3CH_3	-88.6
$CH_3CH_2CH_3$	-42.1
$CH_3CH_2CH_2CH_3$	-0.5
$CH_3CH_2CH_2CH_2CH_3$	36.0
$CH_3CH_2CH_2CH_2CH_2CH_3$	68.7

    ↑C,↑Temp

    A. London dispersion forces
    B. Dipole-dipole interactions
    C. Hydrogen bonding
    D. Ion-induced dipole interactions

14. **List the substances NH_3, PH_3, $MgCl_2$, Ne, and N_2 in order of increasing melting point.**

    A. N_2 < Ne < PH_3 < NH_3 < $MgCl_2$
    B. N_2 < NH_3 < Ne < $MgCl_2$ < PH_3
    C. Ne < N_2 < NH_3 < PH_3 < $MgCl_2$
    D. Ne < N_2 < PH_3 < NH_3 < $MgCl_2$

15. 1-butanol, ethanol, methanol, and 1-propanol are all liquids at room temperature. Rank them in order of increasing viscosity. *↑ H-bonds, ↑ viscosity*

  A. 1-butanol < 1-propanol < ethanol < methanol
  B. methanol < ethanol < 1-propanol < 1-butanol
  C. methanol < ethanol < 1-butanol < 1-propanol
  D. 1-propanol < 1-butanol < ethanol < methanol

16. Which gas has a diffusion rate of 25% the rate for hydrogen?

The rate of diffusion of a gas is inversely proportional to the square root of its molecular mass.

  A. Helium
  B. Methane
  C. Nitrogen
  D. Oxygen

17. 2.00 L of an unknown gas at 1500. mm Hg and a temperature of 25.0° C weighs 7.52 g. Assuming the ideal gas equation, what is the molecular mass of the gas?

$$760 \text{ mm Hg} = 1 \text{ atm}$$
$$R = 0.08206 \text{ L-atm / mol-K}$$

  A. 21.6 u
  B. 23.3 u
  C. 46.6 u
  D. 93.2 u

18. Which substance is most likely to be a gas at room temperature? *37°C = room temp*

  A. SeO_2
  B. F_2
  C. $CaCl_2 (s)$
  D. I_2

19. What pressure is exerted by a mixture of 2.7 g of H_2 and 59 g of Xe at STP on a 50. L container?

STP
1atm 0°C 22.4L
$R = 0.0821 \frac{L\text{-atm}}{K\text{-moles}}$

  A. 0.69 atm
  B. 0.76 atm
  C. 0.80 atm
  D. 0.97 atm

20. A few minutes after opening a bottle of perfume, the scent is detected on the other side of the room. What law relates to this phenomenon?

  A. Graham's law - *diffusion rate*
  B. Dalton's law - *pressure*
  C. Boyle's law - *volume of gas ∝ $\frac{1}{pressure}$*
  D. Avogadro's law - *volume and moles (equal)*

21. Which of the following are true?

  A. Solids have no vapor pressure.
  B. Dissolving a solute in a liquid increases its vapor pressure.
  C. The vapor pressure of a pure substance is characteristic of that substance and its temperature.
  D. All of the above

22. Find the partial pressure of N_2 in a container at 150. kPa holding H_2O and N_2 at 50° C. The vapor pressure of H_2O at 50° C is 12 kPa.

  A. 12 kPa
  B. 138 kPa
  C. 162 kPa
  D. The value cannot be determined.

23. The normal boiling point of water on the Kelvin scale is closest to:

A. 112 K
B. 212 K
C. 273 K
D. 373 K

24. Which phases may be present at the triple point of a substance?

I. Gas
II. Liquid
III. Solid
IV. Supercritical fluid

A. I, II, and III
B. I, II, and IV
C. II, III, and IV
D. I, II, III, and IV

25. In the following phase diagram, _____ occurs as P is decreased from A to B at constant T and _____ occurs as T is increased from C to D at constant P.

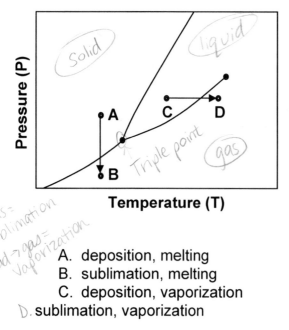

Temperature (T)

Solid→gas= sublimation
liquid→gas= vaporization

A. deposition, melting
B. sublimation, melting
C. deposition, vaporization
D. sublimation, vaporization

26. Heat is added to a pure solid at its melting point until it all becomes liquid at its freezing point. Which of the following occur(s)?

A. Intermolecular attractions are weakened.
B. The kinetic energy of the molecules does not change. √
C. The freedom of the molecules to move about increases. √
D. All of the above.

27. Which of the following occur when NaCl dissolves in water?

A. Heat is required to break bonds in the NaCl crystal lattice.
B. Heat is released when hydrogen bonds in water are broken.
C. Heat is required to form bonds of hydration.
D. The oxygen end of the water molecule is attracted to the Cl⁻ ion.

28. The solubility of $CoCl_2$ is 54 g per 100 g of ethanol. Three flasks each contain 100 g of ethanol. Flask #1 also contains 40 g $CoCl_2$ in solution. Flask #2 contains 56 g $CoCl_2$ in solution. Flask #3 contains 5 g of solid $CoCl_2$ in equilibrium with 54 g $CoCl_2$ in solution. Which of the following describes the solutions present in the liquid phase of the flasks?

A. #1 - saturated, #2 - supersaturated, #3 - unsaturated.
B. #1 - unsaturated, #2 - miscible, #3 - saturated.
C. #1 - unsaturated, #2 - supersaturated, #3 - saturated.
D. #1 - unsaturated, #2 - not at equilibrium, #3 - miscible.

29. The solubility at 1.0 atm of pure CO_2 in water at 25° C is 0.034 M. According to Henry's law, what is the solubility at 4.0 atm of pure CO_2 in water at 25°C? Assume no chemical reaction occurs between CO_2 and H_2O.

A. 0.0085 M
B. 0.034 M
C. 0.14 M
D. 0.25 M

30. Carbonated water is bottled at 25° C under pure CO_2 at 4.0 atm. Later the bottle is opened at 4° C under air at 1.0 atm that has a partial pressure of 3×10^{-4} atm CO_2. Why do CO_2 bubbles form when the bottle is opened?

A. CO_2 falls out of solution due to a drop in solubility at the lower total pressure.
B. CO_2 falls out of solution due to a drop in solubility at the lower CO_2 pressure.
C. CO_2 falls out of solution due to a drop in solubility at the lower temperature.
D. CO_2 is formed by the decomposition of carbonic acid.

31. When KNO_3 dissolves in water, the water grows slightly colder. An increase in temperature will _____ the solubility of KNO_3.

A. increase
B. decrease
C. have no effect on
D. have an unknown effect with the information given on

32. An experiment requires 100. mL of a 0.500 M solution of $MgBr_2$. How many grams of $MgBr_2$ will be present in this solution?

A. 9.21 g
B. 11.7 g
C. 12.4 g
D. 15.6 g

33. 500. mg of RbOH are added to 500. g of ethanol (C_2H_6O) resulting in 395 mL of solution. Determine the molarity and molality of RbOH.

A. 0.0124 M, 0.00488 m
B. 0.0124 M, 0.00976 m
C. 0.0223 M, 0.00488 m
D. 0.0223 M, 0. 00976 m

34. 20.0 g H_3PO_4 in 1.5 L of solution are intended to react with KOH according to the following reaction:

$$H_3PO_4 + 3KOH \rightarrow K_3PO_4 + 3H_2O$$

What is the molarity and normality of the H_3PO_4 solution?

A. 0.41 M, 1.22 N
B. 0.41 M, 0.20 N
C. 0.14 M, 0.045 N
D. 0.14 M, 0. 41 N

35. Aluminum sulfate is a strong electrolyte. What is the concentration of all species in a 0.2 M solution of aluminum sulfate?

A. 0.2 M Al^{3+}, 0.2 M SO_4^{2-}
B. 0.4 M Al^{3+}, 0.6 M SO_4^{2-}
C. 0.6 M Al^{3+}, 0.4 M SO_4^{2-}
D. 0.2 M $Al_2(SO_4)_3$

36. 15 g of formaldehyde (CH_2O) are dissolved in 100. g of water. Calculate the weight percentage and mole fraction of formaldehyde in the solution.

A. 13%, 0.090
B. 15%, 0.090
C. 13%, 0.083
D. 15%, 0.083

37. Which of the following would make the best solvent for Br_2?

A. H_2O
B. CS_2
C. NH_3
D. Molten NaCl

38. Which of the following is most likely to dissolve in water? H_2O

A. H_2
B. CCl_4
C. SF_6
D. CH_3OH methanol

39. Which of the following is <u>not</u> a colligative property? → depends on solute particles present

A. Viscosity lowering
B. Freezing point lowering —solute
C. Boiling point elevation —solute
D. Vapor pressure lowering — solute

40.
$$BaCl_2(aq) + Na_2SO_4(aq) \rightarrow BaSO_4(s) + 2NaCl(aq)$$

is an example of a(n) _____ reaction.

A. acid-base
B. precipitation
C. redox
D. nuclear

41. List the following aqueous solutions in order of increasing boiling point.

    I.   0.050 m $AlCl_3$
    II. 0.080 m $Ba(NO_3)_2$
    III. 0.090 m NaCl
    IV. 0.12 m ethylene glycol ($C_2H_6O_2$)

    A. I < II < III < IV
    B. I < III < IV < II
    C. IV < III < I < II
    D. IV < III < II < I

42. Osmotic pressure is the pressure required to prevent _____ from flowing from low to high _____ concentration across a semipermeable membrane.

    A. solute, solute
    B. solute, solvent
    C. solvent, solute
    D. solvent, solvent

43. A solution of NaCl in water is heated on a mountain in an open container until it boils at 100. ° C. The air pressure on the mountain is 0.92 atm. According to Raoult's law, what mole fraction of Na^+ and Cl^- are present in the solution?

    A. 0.04 Na^+, 0.04 Cl^-
    B. 0.08 Na^+, 0.08 Cl^-
    C. 0.46 Na^+, 0.46 Cl^-
    D. 0.92 Na^+, 0.92 Cl^-

44. Choose the balanced nuclear equation for the emission of an alpha particle by polonium-209.

    A. $^{209}_{84}Po \rightarrow\ ^{205}_{81}Pb +\ ^{4}_{2}He$ alpha
    B. $^{209}_{84}Po \rightarrow\ ^{205}_{82}Bi +\ ^{4}_{2}He$ alpha
    C. $^{209}_{84}Po \rightarrow\ ^{209}_{85}At +\ ^{0}_{-1}e$ electron
    D. $^{209}_{84}Po \rightarrow\ ^{205}_{82}Pb +\ ^{4}_{2}He$ alpha

45. Choose the balanced nuclear equation for the decay of calcium-45 to scandium-45?

    A. $^{45}_{20}Ca \rightarrow\ ^{41}_{18}Sc +\ ^{4}_{2}He$ alpha α
    B. $^{45}_{20}Ca +\ ^{0}_{1}e \rightarrow\ ^{45}_{21}Sc$ positron
    C. $^{45}_{20}Ca \rightarrow\ ^{45}_{21}Sc +\ ^{0}_{-1}e$ β
    D. $^{45}_{20}Ca +\ ^{0}_{1}p \rightarrow\ ^{45}_{21}Sc$

46. $^{3}_{1}H$ decays with a half-life of 12 years. 3.0 g of pure $^{3}_{1}H$ were placed in a sealed container 24 years ago. How many grams of $^{3}_{1}H$ remain?

    A. 0.38 g
    B. 0.75 g
    C. 1.5 g
    D. 3.0 g

47. Oxygen-15 has a half-life of 122 seconds. What percentage of a sample of oxygen-15 has decayed after 300. seconds?

    A. 18.2%
    B. 21.3%
    C. 78.7%
    D. 81.8%

48. Which of the following isotopes is commonly used for medical imaging in the diagnosis of diseases?

A. cobalt-60
B. technetium-99m
C. tin-117m
D. plutonium-238

49. Carbon-14 dating would be useful in obtaining the age of which object(s)?

A. a 20th century Picasso painting
B. a mummy from ancient Egypt
C. a dinosaur fossil
D. all of the above

50. Which of the following isotopes can create a chain reaction of nuclear fission?

A. uranium-235
B. uranium-238
C. plutonium-238
D. all of the above

51. List the following scientists in chronological order from earliest to most recent with respect to their most significant contribution to atomic theory:

I.   John Dalton 1
II. Niels Bohr 3
III. J. J. Thomson 2
IV. Ernest Rutherford 4

A. I, III, II, IV
B. I, III, IV, II
C. I, IV, III, II
D. III, I, II, IV

52. Match the theory with the scientist who first proposed it:

I.   Electrons, atoms, and all objects with momentum also exist as waves.
II. Electron density may be accurately described by a single mathematical equation. *Schrödinger*
III. There is an inherent indeterminacy in the position and momentum of particles.
IV. Radiant energy is transferred between particles in exact multiples of a discrete unit.

A. I-de Broglie, II-Planck, III-Schrödinger, IV-Thomson
B. I-Dalton, II-Bohr, III-Planck, IV-de Broglie
C. I-Henry, II-Bohr, III-Heisenberg, IV-Schrödinger
D. I-de Broglie, II-Schrödinger, III-Heisenberg, IV-Planck

53. How many neutrons are in $^{60}_{27}\text{Co}$?

A. 27 — p
B. 33 — n
C. 60 — p+n
D. 87

54. The terrestrial composition of an element is: 50.7% as a stable isotope with an atomic mass of 78.9 u and 49.3% as a stable isotope with an atomic mass of 80.9 u. Both isotopes are stable. Calculate the atomic mass of the element.

A. 79.0 u
B. 79.8 u
C. 79.9 u
D. 80.8 u

55. Which of the following is a correct electron arrangement for oxygen?

A.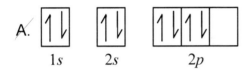

B. $1s^2 1p^2 2s^2 2p^2$
C. 2, 2, 4
D. None of the above

56. Which of the following statements about radiant energy is not true?

A. The energy change of an electron transition is directly proportional to the wavelength of the emitted or absorbed photon.
B. The energy of an electron in a hydrogen atom depends only on the principle quantum number.
C. The frequency of photons striking a metal determines whether the photoelectric effect will occur.
D. The frequency of a wave of electromagnetic radiation is inversely proportional to its wavelength

57. Match the orbital diagram for the ground state of carbon with the rule/principle it violates:

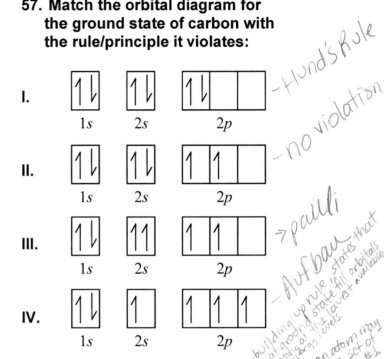

A. I-Pauli exclusion, II-Aufbau, III-no violation, IV-Hund's
B. I-Aufbau, II-Pauli exclusion, III-no violation, IV-Hund's
C. I-Hund's, II-no violation, III-Pauli exclusion, IV-Aufbau
D. I-Hund's, II-no violation, III-Aufbau, IV-Pauli exclusion

58. Select the list of atoms that is arranged in order of increasing size.

A. Mg, Na, Si, Cl
B. Si, Cl, Mg, Na
C. Cl, Si, Mg, Na
D. Na, Mg, Si, Cl

59. Based on trends in the periodic table, which of the following properties would you expect to be greater for Rb than for K?

I.   Density
II. Melting point
III. Ionization energy
IV. Oxidation number in a compound with chlorine

A. I only
B. I, II, and III
C. II and III
D. I, II, III, and IV

60. Which oxide forms the strongest acid in water?

A. Al_2O_3
B. Cl_2O_7
C. As_2O_5
D. CO_2

61. Rank the following bonds from least to most polar:

C-H, C-Cl, H-H, C-F

A. C-H < H-H < C-F < C-Cl
B. H-H < C-H < C-F < C-Cl
C. C-F < C-Cl < C-H < H-H
D. H-H < C-H < C-Cl < C-F

62. At room temperature, $CaBr_2$ is expected to be *Calcium bromide*

A. a ductile solid
B. a brittle solid
C. a soft solid
D. a gas

63. Which of the following is a proper Lewis dot structure of CHClO?

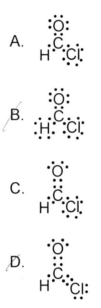

64. In C_2H_2, each carbon atom contains the following valence orbitals:

A. p only
B. p and sp hybrids
C. p and sp^2 hybrids
D. sp^3 hybrids only

65. Which statement about molecular structures is false?

A. 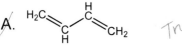 True

is a conjugated molecule

B. A bonding σ orbital connects two atoms by the straight line between them.

C. A bonding π orbital connects two atoms in a separate region from the straight line between them.

D. The anion with resonance forms (True)

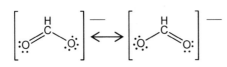

will always exist in one form or the other.

66. What is the shape of the PH_3 molecule? Use the VSEPR model.

A. Trigonal pyramidal
B. Trigonal bipyramidal
C. Trigonal planar
D. Tetrahedral

67. What is the chemical composition of magnesium nitrate?

A. 11.1% Mg, 22.2% N, 66.7% O
B. 16.4% Mg, 18.9% N, 64.7% O
C. 20.9% Mg, 24.1% N, 55.0% O
D. 28.2% Mg, 16.2% N, 55.7% O

68. The IUPAC name for Cu_2SO_3 is:

A. Dicopper sulfur trioxide
B. Copper (II) sulfate
C. Copper (I) sulfite
D. Copper (II) sulfite

69. Which name or formula is not represented properly?

A. Cl_4S ○
B. $KClO_3$
C. Calcium dihydrogen phosphate CaH_2PO_4
D. Sulfurous acid

70. Household "chlorine bleach" is sodium hypochlorite. Which of the following best represents the production of sodium hypochlorite, sodium chloride, and water by bubbling chlorine gas through aqueous sodium hydroxide?

A. $4Cl(g) + 4NaOH(aq) \rightarrow$
$NaClO_2(aq) + 3NaCl(aq) + 2H_2O(l)$

B. $2Cl_2(g) + 4NaOH(aq) \rightarrow$
$NaClO_2(aq) + 3NaCl(aq) + 2H_2O(l)$

C. $2Cl(g) + 2NaOH(aq) \rightarrow$
$NaClO(aq) + NaCl(aq) + H_2O(l)$

D. $Cl_2(g) + 2NaOH(aq) \rightarrow$
$NaClO(aq) + NaCl(aq) + H_2O(l)$

71. Balance the equation for the neutralization reaction between phosphoric acid and calcium hydroxide by filling in the blank stoichiometric coefficients.

___H_3PO_4 + ___$Ca(OH)_2 \rightarrow$

___$Ca_3(PO_4)_2$ + ___H_2O

A. 4, 3, 1, 4
B. 2, 3, 1, 8
C. 2, 3, 1, 6
D. 2, 1, 1, 2

72. Choose the equation showing the reaction between calcium nitrate and lithium sulfate in aqueous solution. Include all products.

A. $CaNO_3(aq) + Li_2SO_4(aq) \rightarrow$
$CaSO_4(s) + Li_2NO_3(aq)$

B. $Ca(NO_3)_2(aq) + Li_2SO_4(aq) \rightarrow$
$CaSO_4(s) + 2LiNO_3(aq)$

C. $Ca(NO_3)_2(aq) + Li_2SO_4(aq) \rightarrow$
$2LiNO_3(s) + CaSO_4(aq)$

D. $Ca(NO_3)_2(aq) + Li_2SO_4(aq) + 2H_2O(l) \rightarrow$
$2LiNO_3(aq) + Ca(OH)_2(aq) + H_2SO_4(aq)$

73. Find the mass of CO_2 produced by the combustion of 15 kg of isopropyl alcohol in the reaction:

hydrocarbon + $O_2 \rightarrow CO_2 + H_2O$

$2C_3H_7OH + 9O_2 \rightarrow 6CO_2 + 8H_2O$

A. 33 kg
B. 44 kg
C. 50 kg
D. 60 kg

74. What is the density of nitrogen gas at STP? Assume an ideal gas and a value of 0.08206 L•atm/(mol•K) for the gas constant.

@ STP,
1 atm
22.4 L
273 K

A. 0.62 g/L
B. 1.14 g/L
C. 1.25 g/L
D. 2.03 g/L

75. Find the volume of methane that will produce 12 m³ of hydrogen in the reaction:

$CH_4(g) + H_2O(g) \rightarrow CO(g) + 3H_2(g)$

Assume temperature and pressure remain constant.

A. 4.0 m³
B. 32 m³
C. 36 m³
D. 64 m³

76. A 100. L vessel of pure O_2 at 500. kPa and 20. ° C is used for the combustion of butane:

$2C_4H_{10} + 13O_2 \rightarrow 8CO_2 + 10H_2O$

Find the mass of butane that would consume all the O_2 in the vessel. Assume O_2 is an ideal gas and use a value of R = 8.314 J/(mol•K).

A. 183 g
B. 467 g
C. 1.83 kg
D. 7.75 kg

77. Consider the reaction between iron and hydrogen chloride gas:

$Fe(s) + 2HCl(g) \rightarrow FeCl_2(s) + H_2(g)$

7 moles of iron and 10 moles of HCl react until the limiting reagent is consumed. Which statements are true?

I.   HCl is the excess reagent
II. HCl is the limiting reagent ✓
III. 7 moles of H_2 are produced
IV. 2 moles of the excess ✓
     reagent remain

A. I and III
B. I and IV
C. II and III
D. II and IV

The limiting reagent may be determined by dividing the # moles of each reactant by its stoichiometric coefficient. This determines the moles of reaction if each rxn were limiting. Lowest result is the limiting reagent.

78. 32.0 g of hydrogen and 32.0 grams of oxygen react to form water until the limiting reagent is consumed. What is present in the vessel after the reaction is complete?

A. 16.0 g O_2 and 48.0 g H_2O
B. 24.0 g H_2 and 40.0 g H_2O
C. 28.0 g H_2 and 36.0 g H_2O
D. 28.0 g H_2 and 34.0 g H_2O

79. Three experiments were performed at the same initial temperature and pressure to determine the rate of the reaction

$2ClO_2(g) + F_2(g) \rightarrow 2ClO_2F(g)$

Results are shown in the table below. Concentrations are given in millimoles per liter (mM).

Exp.	Initial $[ClO_2]$ (mM)	Initial $[F_2]$ (mM)	Initial rate of $[ClO_2F]$ increase (mM/sec)
1	5.0	5.0	0.63
2	5.0	20	2.5
3	10	10	2.5

What is the rate law for this reaction?

rate law = k[reactants]

A. Rate $= k[F_2]$

B. Rate $= k[ClO_2][F_2]$

C. Rate $= k[ClO_2]^2[F_2]$

D. Rate $= k[ClO_2][F_2]^2$

Rate = K[ClO₂]²[F₂]

80. The reaction

$(CH_3)_3CBr(aq) + OH^-(aq) \rightarrow$

$(CH_3)_3COH(aq) + Br^-(aq)$

occurs in three elementary steps:

$(CH_3)_3CBr \rightarrow (CH_3)_3C^+ + Br^-$ is slow

$(CH_3)_3C^+ + H_2O \rightarrow (CH_3)_3COH_2^+$ is fast

$(CH_3)_3COH_2^+ + OH^- \rightarrow$
$(CH_3)_3COH + H_2O$ is fast

What is the rate law for this reaction?

A. Rate $= k\left[(CH_3)_3CBr\right]$

B. Rate $= k\left[OH^-\right]$

C. Rate $= k\left[(CH_3)_3CBr\right]\left[OH^-\right]$

D. Rate $= k\left[(CH_3)_3CBr\right]^2$

81. **Which statement about equilibrium is not true?**

A. Equilibrium shifts to minimize the impact of changes. ✓
B. Forward and reverse reactions have equal rates at equilibrium. ✓
C. A closed container of air and water is at a vapor-liquid equilibrium if the humidity is constant.
D. The equilibrium between solid and dissolved forms is maintained when salt is added to an unsaturated solution.

82. **Which statements about reaction rates are true?**

I. Catalysts shift the equilibrium to favor product formation.
II. Catalysts increase the rate of forward and reverse reactions. ✓
III. A greater temperature increases the chance that a molecular collision will overcome a reaction's activation energy.
IV. A catalytic converter contains a homogeneous catalyst. ✓

A. I and II
B. II and III
C. II, III, and IV
D. I, III, and IV

83. **Write the equilibrium expression K_{eq} for the reaction**

$$CO_2(g) + H_2(g) \rightleftharpoons CO(g) + H_2O(l)$$

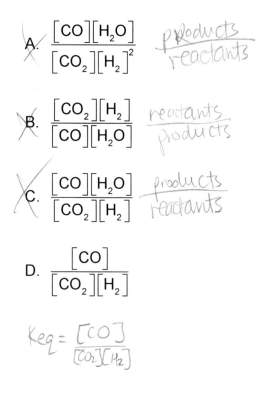

A. $\dfrac{[CO][H_2O]}{[CO_2][H_2]^2}$ products / reactants

B. $\dfrac{[CO_2][H_2]}{[CO][H_2O]}$ reactants / products

C. $\dfrac{[CO][H_2O]}{[CO_2][H_2]}$ products / reactants

D. $\dfrac{[CO]}{[CO_2][H_2]}$

$Keq = \dfrac{[CO]}{[CO_2][H_2]}$

84. **What could cause this change in the energy diagram of a reaction?**

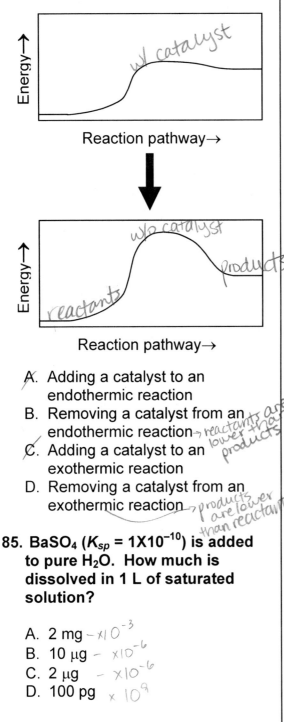

w/ catalyst

Reaction pathway→

w/o catalyst

products

reactants

Reaction pathway→

A. Adding a catalyst to an endothermic reaction
B. Removing a catalyst from an endothermic reaction → *reactants are lower than products*
C. Adding a catalyst to an exothermic reaction
D. Removing a catalyst from an exothermic reaction → *products are lower than reactants*

85. **BaSO$_4$ (K_{sp} = 1X10^{-10}) is added to pure H$_2$O. How much is dissolved in 1 L of saturated solution?**

A. 2 mg — *×10^{-3}*
B. 10 μg — *×10^{-6}*
C. 2 μg — *×10^{-6}*
D. 100 pg — *×10^{9}*

86. **The exothermic reaction 2NO (g) ↔N$_2$ (g) + O$_2$ (g) is at equilibrium. According to LeChatelier's principle:** *adding a substance either a reactant or a product will shift the rxn so as how equilibrium is established by consuming some of the added substance*

A. Adding Br$_2$ will increase [NO].
B. An increase in container volume (with T constant) will increase [NOBr].
C. An increase in pressure (with T constant) will increase [NOBr].
D. An increase in temperature (with P constant) will increase [NOBr].

87. **At a certain temperature, _T_, the equilibrium constant for the reaction 2NO (g) ↔ N$_2$ (g) + O$_2$ (g) is K_{eq} = 2 x 10^3. If a 1.0 L container at this temperature contains 90 mM N$_2$, 20 mM O$_2$, and 5 mM NO, what will occur?**

A. The reaction will make more N$_2$ and O$_2$.
B. The reaction is at equilibrium.
C. The reaction will make more NO.
D. The temperature, _T_, is required to solve this problem.

88. **Which statement about acids and bases is not true?**

A. All strong acids ionize in water. ✓
B. All Lewis acids accept an electron pair. ✓
C. All Brønsted bases use OH⁻ as a proton acceptor
D. All Arrhenius acids form H⁺ ions in water.

89. Which of the following are listed from weakest to strongest acid?

   A. H_2SO_3, H_2SeO_3, H_2TeO_3
   B. $HBrO$, $HBrO_2$, $HBrO_3$, $HBrO_4$
   C. HI, HBr, HCl, HF
   D. H_3PO_4, $H_2PO_4^-$, HPO_4^{2-}

90. NH_4F is dissolved in water. Which of the following are conjugate acid/base pairs present in the solution?

   I. NH_4^+/NH_4OH
   II. HF/F^- ✓
   III. H_3O^+/H_2O ✓
   IV. H_2O/OH^- ✓

   A. I, II, and III
   B. I, III, and IV
   C. II and IV
   D. II, III, and IV

91. What are the pH and the pOH of 0.010 M $HNO_3(aq)$?

$-\log(0.010)=2$

   A. pH = 1.0, pOH = 9.0
   B. pH = 2.0, pOH = 12.0
   C. pH = 2.0, pOH = 8.0
   D. pH = 8.0, pOH = 6.0

92. What is the pH of a buffer solution made of 0.128 M sodium formate (HCOONa) and 0.072 M formic acid (HCOOH)? The pK_a of formic acid is 3.75.

   A. 2.0
   B. 3.0
   C. 4.0 $pKa = -\log Ka$
   D. 5.0

93. A sample of 50.0 ml KOH is titrated with 0.100 M $HClO_4$. The initial buret reading is 1.6 ml and the reading at the endpoint is 22.4 ml. What is [KOH]?

   A. 0.0416 M
   B. 0.0481 M
   C. 0.0832 M
   D. 0.0962 mM

94. Rank the following from lowest to highest pH. Assume a small volume for the component given in moles:

   I.   0.01 mol HCl added to 1 L H_2O ②
   II. 0.01 mol HI added to 1 L of an acetic acid/sodium acetate solution at pH 4.0 ①
   III. 0.01 mol NH_3 added to 1 L H_2O ③
   IV. 0.1 mol HNO_3 added to 1 L of a 0.1 M $Ca(OH)_2$ solution ④

   A. I < II < III < IV
   B. I < II < IV < III
   C. II < I < III < IV
   D. II < I < IV < III

95. The curve below resulted from the titration of a _____ ____ with a _____ ____ titrant.

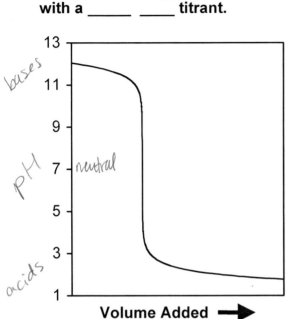

A. weak acid, strong base
B. weak base, strong acid
C. strong acid, strong base
D. strong base, strong acid

96. Which statement about thermochemistry is true?

A. Particles in a system move about less freely at high entropy
B. Water at 100 °C has the same internal energy as water vapor at 100°C
C. A decrease in the order of a system corresponds to an increase in entropy.
D. At its sublimation temperature, dry ice has a higher entropy than gaseous CO_2

97. What is the heat change of 36.0 g H_2O at atmospheric pressure when its temperature is reduced from 125° C to 40. ° C? Use the following data:

Values for water

Heat capacity of solid	37.6 J/mol•°C
Heat capacity of liquid	75.3 J/mol•°C
Heat capacity of gas	33.1 J/mol•°C
Heat of fusion	6.02 kJ/mol
Heat of vaporization	40.67 kJ/mol

A. −92.0 kJ
B. −10.8 kJ
C. 10.8 kJ
D. 92.0 kJ

98. What is the standard heat of combustion of $CH_4(g)$? Use the following data:

Standard heats of formation

$CH_4(g)$	−74.8 kJ/mol
$CO_2(g)$	−393.5 kJ/mol
$H_2O(l)$	−285.8 kJ/mol

A. −890.3 kJ/mol
B. −604.6 kJ/mol
C. −252.9 kJ/mol
D. −182.5 kJ/mol

99. Which reaction creates products with a lower total entropy than the reactants?

A. Dissolution of table salt:
$NaCl(s) \rightarrow Na^+(aq) + Cl^{\$}(aq)$

B. Oxidation of iron:
$4Fe(s) + 3O_2(g) \rightarrow 2Fe_2O_3(s)$

C. Dissociation of ozone:
$O_3(g) \rightarrow O_2(g) + O(g)$

D. Vaporization of butane:
$C_4H_{10}(l) \rightarrow C_4H_{10}(g)$

100. Which statement about reactions is true?

A. All spontaneous reactions are both exothermic and cause an increase in entropy.
B. An endothermic reaction that increases the order of the system cannot be spontaneous.
C. A reaction can be non-spontaneous in one direction and also non-spontaneous in the opposite direction.
D. Melting snow is an exothermic process.

101. 10. kJ of heat are added to one kilogram of Iron at 10. °C. What is its final temperature? The specific heat of iron is 0.45 J/g•°C.

A. 22 °C
B. 27 °C
C. 32 °C
D. 37 °C

102. Which reaction is not a redox process?

A. Combustion of octane:
$2C_8H_{18} + 25O_2 \rightarrow 16CO_2 + 18H_2O$

B. Depletion of a lithium battery:
$\overset{+1}{Li} + \overset{+4}{Mn}\overset{-2}{O_2} \rightarrow \overset{+1}{Li}\overset{+4}{Mn}\overset{-4}{O_2}$

C. Corrosion of aluminum by acid:
$\overset{0}{2Al} + \overset{+1}{6H}\overset{-1}{Cl} \rightarrow \overset{+1}{2Al}\overset{-1}{Cl_3} + \overset{0}{3H_2}$

D. Taking an antacid for heartburn:
$\overset{+2}{Ca}\overset{-2}{CO_3} + \overset{+1}{2H}\overset{-1}{Cl} \rightarrow \overset{+2}{Ca}\overset{-1}{Cl_2} + \overset{+1}{H_2}\overset{-2}{CO_3}$
$\rightarrow \overset{+2}{Ca}\overset{-1}{Cl_2} + \overset{+4}{C}\overset{-2}{O_2} + \overset{+1}{H_2}\overset{-2}{O}$

103. Given the following heats of reaction:
$\Delta H = -0.3$ kJ / mol for
$Fe(s) + CO_2(g) \rightarrow FeO(s) + CO(g)$
$\Delta H = 5.7$ kJ / mol for
$2Fe(s) + 3CO_2(g) \rightarrow Fe_2O_3(s) + 3CO(g)$
and $\Delta H = 4.5$ kJ / mol for
$3FeO(s) + CO_2(g) \rightarrow Fe_3O_4(s) + CO(g)$

use Hess's Law to determine the heat of reaction for:

$3Fe_2O_3(s) + CO(g) \rightarrow 2Fe_3O_4(s) + CO_2(g)$

A. −10.8 kJ/mol
B. −9.9 kJ/mol
C. −9.0 kJ/mol
D. −8.1 kJ/mol

104. What is the oxidant in the reaction:
$2H_2S + SO_2 \rightarrow 3S + 2H_2O$?

A. H_2S
B. SO_2
C. S
D. H_2O

105. Molten NaCl is subjected to electrolysis. What reaction takes place at the cathode?

A. $2Cl^-(l) \rightarrow Cl_2(g) + 2e^-$
B. $Cl_2(g) + 2e^- \rightarrow 2Cl^-(l)$
C. $Na^+(l) + e^- \rightarrow Na(l)$
D. $Na^+(l) \rightarrow Na(l) + e^-$

106. What is the purpose of the salt bridge in an electrochemical cell?

A. To receive electrons from the oxidation half-reaction
B. To relieve the buildup of positive charge in the anode half-cell
C. To conduct electron flow
D. To permit positive ions to flow from the cathode half-cell to the anode half-cell

107. Given:
$E° = -2.37V$ for $Mg^{2+}(aq) + 2e^- \rightarrow Mg(s)$
and
$E° = 0.80$ V for $Ag^+(aq) + e^- \rightarrow Ag(s)$,
what is the standard potential of a voltaic cell composed of a piece of magnesium dipped in a 1 M Ag^+ solution and a piece of silver dipped in 1 M Mg^{2+}?

A. 0.77 V
B. 1.57 V
C. 3.17 V
D. 3.97 V

108. A proper name for this hydrocarbon is:

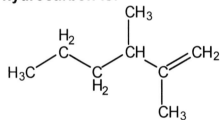

A. 4,5-dimethyl-6-hexene
B. 2,3-dimethyl-1-hexene
C. 4,5-dimethyl-6-hexyne
D. 2-methyl-3-propyl-1-butene

109.

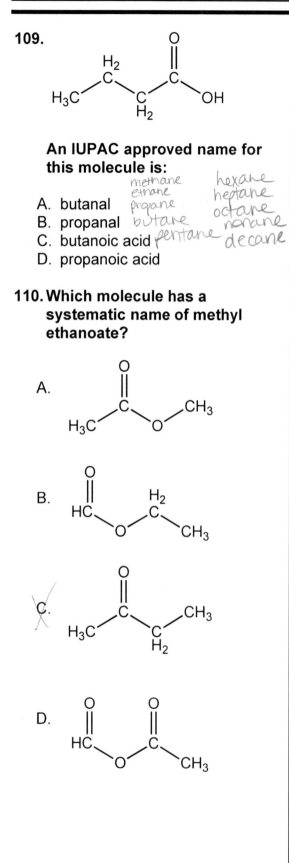

An IUPAC approved name for this molecule is:

methane hexane
ethane heptane
A. butanal *propane octane*
B. propanal *butane nonane*
C. butanoic acid *pentane decane*
D. propanoic acid

110. Which molecule has a systematic name of methyl ethanoate?

A.

B.

C.

D.

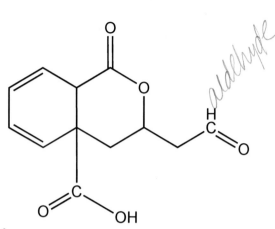

aldehyde

111.

This compound contains an:

COOH
A. alkene, carboxylic acid, ester, and ketone *R-C*
B. aldehyde, alkyne, ester, and ketone
C. aldehyde, alkene, carboxylic acid, and ester
D. acid anhydride, aldehyde, alkene, and amine

112. Which group of scientists made contributions in the same area of chemistry?

A. Volta, Kekulé, Faraday, London
B. Hess, Joule, Kelvin, Gibbs
C. Boyle, Charles, Arrhenius, Pauli
D. Davy, Mendeleev, Ramsay, Galvani

113. Which of the following pairs are isomers?

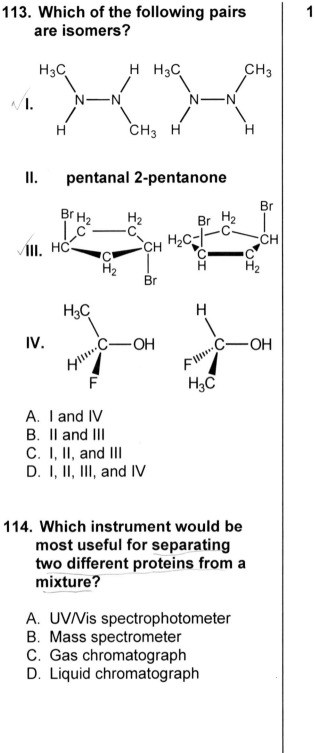

II.   pentanal 2-pentanone

A. I and IV
B. II and III
C. I, II, and III
D. I, II, III, and IV

114. Which instrument would be most useful for separating two different proteins from a mixture?

A. UV/Vis spectrophotometer
B. Mass spectrometer
C. Gas chromatograph
D. Liquid chromatograph

115. Classify these biochemicals.

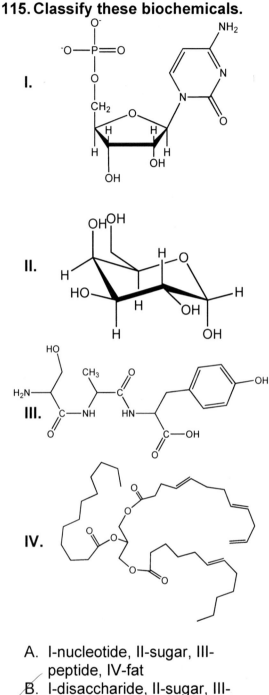

A. I-nucleotide, II-sugar, III-peptide, IV-fat
B. I-disaccharide, II-sugar, III-fatty acid, IV-polypeptide
C. I-disaccharide, II-amino acid, III-fatty acid, IV-polysaccharide
D. I I-nucleotide, II-sugar, III-triacylglyceride, and IV-DNA

$C_6H_{12}O_6$

116. You create a solution of 2.00 µg/ml of a pigment and divide the solution into 12 samples. You give four samples each to three teams of students. They use a spectrophotometer to determine the pigment concentration. Here is their data:

	Concentration (µg/ml)			
Team	sample 1	sample 2	sample 3	sample 4
1	1.98	1.93	1.92	1.88
2	1.70	1.72	1.69	1.70
3	1.78	1.99	2.87	2.20

(handwritten: 1.93, 1.70, 2.20)

Which of the following is true?

A. Team 1 has the most precise data
B. Team 3 has the most accurate data in spite of it having low precision
C. The data from Team 2 is characteristic of a systematic error
D. The data from Team 1 is more characteristic of random error than the data from Team 3.

117. **Which pair of measurements has identical meanings?**

A. 32 micrograms and 0.032 g
B. 26 nm and 2.60×10^{-8} m
C. 3.01×10^{-5} m^3 and 30.1 ml
D. 0.0020 L and 20 cm^3

(handwritten: 20mL, 0.032g, 1×10⁻⁶ µg, 1A)

118. **Match the instrument with the quantity it measures**

II. eudiometer
III. calorimeter
IV. manometer
V. hygrometer

A. I-volume, II-mass, III-radioactivity, IV-humidity
B. I-volume, II-heat, III-pressure, IV-humidity
C. I-viscosity, II-mass, III-pressure, IV-surface tension
D. I-viscosity, II-heat, III-radioactivity, IV-surface tension

119. **Four nearly identical gems from the same mineral are weighed using different balances. Their masses are:**

3.4533 g, 3.459 g, 3.4656 g, 3.464 g

The four gems are then collected and added to a volumetric cylinder containing 10.00 ml of liquid, and a new volume of 14.97 ml is read. What is the average mass of the four stones and what is the density of the mineral?

A. 3.460 g, and 2.78 g/ml
B. 3.460 g and 2.79 g/ml
C. 3.4605 g and 2.78 g/ml
D. 3.461 g and 2.79 g/ml

(handwritten: 3.460)

120. Which list includes equipment that would (not) be used in vacuum filtration.

A. Rubber tubing, Florence flask, Büchner funnel
B. Vacuum pump, Hirsch funnel, rubber stopper with a single hole
C. Aspirator, filter paper, filter flask
D. Lab stand, clamp, filter trap

121. Which of the following statements about lab safety is not true?

A. Corrosive chemicals should be stored below eye level.
√B. A chemical splash on the eye or skin should be rinsed for 15 minutes in cold water.
√C. MSDS means "Material Safety Data Sheet."
√D. A student should "stop, drop, and roll" if their clothing catches fire in the lab.

122. Which of the following lists consists entirely of chemicals that are considered safe enough to be in a high school lab?

A. hydrochloric acid, lauric acid, potassium permanganate, calcium hydroxide
B. ethyl ether, nitric acid, sodium benzoate, methanol
C. cobalt (II) sulfide, ethylene glycol, benzoyl peroxide, ammonium chloride
D. picric acid, hydrofluoric acid, cadmium chloride, carbon disulfide.

123. The following procedure was developed to find the specific heat capacity of metals:

1. Place pieces of the metals in an ice-water bath so their initial temperature is 0 °C.
2. Weigh a Styrofoam cup.
3. Add water at room temperature to the cup and weigh it again
4. Add a cold metal from the bath to the cup and weigh the cup a third time.
5. Monitor the temperature drop of the water until a final temperature at thermal equilibrium is found.

_____ is also required as additional information in order to obtain heat capacities for the metals. The best control would be to follow the same protocol except to use _____ in step 4 instead of a cold metal.

A. The heat capacity of water, a metal at 100° C
B. The heat of formation of water, ice from the 0° C bath
C. The heat of capacity of ice, glass at 0° C
D. The heat capacity of water, water from the 0° C bath

124. Which statement about the impact of chemistry on society is (not) true?

   A. Partial hydrogenation creates *trans* fat.
   B. The Haber Process incorporates nitrogen from the air into molecules for agricultural use.
   C. The CO_2 concentration in the atmosphere has decreased in the last ten years.
   D. The concentration of ozone-destroying chemicals in the stratosphere has decreased in the last ten years.

125. Which statement about everyday applications of chemistry is (true?)

   A. Rainwater found near sources of air pollution will most likely be basic.
   B. Batteries run down more quickly at low temperatures because chemical reactions are proceeding more slowly.
   C. Benzyl alcohol is a detergent used in shampoo.
   D. Adding salt decreases the time required for water to boil.

Sample Constructed-Response Assignment

Directions: Read the information below and complete the given exercise. Explain your reasoning and show your work.

126. What procedure would you use to isolate or purify an organic compound from an aqueous solution containing inorganic contaminants? Clearly describe the apparatus to be used and the steps required to accomplish this.

Answer Key

1.	C	26.	D	51.	B	76.	A	101.	C
2.	B	27.	A	52.	D	77.	D	102.	D
3.	D	28.	C	53.	B	78.	C	103.	B
4.	A	29.	C	54.	C	79.	B	104.	B
5.	C	30.	B	55.	D	80.	A	105.	C
6.	D	31.	A	56.	A	81.	D	106.	D
7.	C	32.	A	57.	C	82.	B	107.	C
8.	B	33.	B	58.	C	83.	D	108.	B
9.	A	34.	D	59.	A	84.	B	109.	C
10.	C	35.	B	60.	B	85.	A	110.	A
11.	B	36.	C	61.	D	86.	C	111.	C
12.	D	37.	B	62.	B	87.	A	112.	B
13.	A	38.	D	63.	C	88.	C	113.	B
14.	D	39.	A	64.	B	89.	B	114.	D
15.	B	40.	B	65.	D	90.	D	115.	A
16.	D	41.	C	66.	A	91.	B	116.	C
17.	C	42.	C	67.	B	92.	C	117.	C
18.	B	43.	A	68.	C	93.	A	118.	B
19.	C	44.	D	69.	A	94.	A	119.	B
20.	A	45.	C	70.	D	95.	D	120.	A
21.	C	46.	B	71.	C	96.	C	121.	D
22.	B	47.	D	72.	B	97.	A	122.	A
23.	D	48.	B	73.	A	98.	A	123.	D
24.	A	49.	B	74.	C	99.	B	124.	C
25.	D	50.	A	75.	A	100.	B	125.	B

Rationales with Sample Questions

Note: The first insignificant digit should be carried through intermediate calculations. This digit is shown using *italics* in the solutions below.

1. **A piston compresses a gas at constant temperature. Which gas properties increase?**

   I. Average speed of molecules
   II. Pressure
   III. Molecular collisions with container walls per second

   A. I and II
   B. I and III
   C. II and III
   D. I, II, and III

C. A decrease in volume (*V*) occurs at constant temperature (*T*). Average molecular speed is determined only by temperature and will be constant. *V* and *P* are inversely related, so pressure will increase. With less wall area and at higher pressure, more collisions occur per second.

2. **The temperature of a liquid is raised at atmospheric pressure. Which liquid property increases?**

   A. critical pressure
   B. vapor pressure ↑
   C. surface tension ↓
   D. viscosity ↓

B. The critical pressure of a liquid is its vapor pressure at the critical temperature and is always a constant value. A rising temperature increases the kinetic energy of molecules and decreases the importance of intermolecular attraction. More molecules will be free to escape to the vapor phase (vapor pressure increases), but the effect of attractions at the liquid-gas interface will fall (surface tension decreases) and molecules will flow against each other more easily (viscosity decreases).

3. **Potassium crystallizes with two atoms contained in each unit cell. What is the mass of potassium found in a lattice 1.00×10⁶ unit cells wide, 2.00×10⁶ unit cells high, and 5.00×10⁵ unit cells deep?**

   A. 85.0 ng
   B. 32.5 μg
   C. 64.9 μg
   D. 130. μg

D. First we find the number of unit cells in the lattice by multiplying the number in each row, stack, and column:

1.00×10^6 unit cell lengths $\times\ 2.00 \times 10^6$ unit cell lengths $\times\ 5.00 \times 10^5$ unit cell lengths

$=1.00 \times 10^{18}$ unit cells

Avogadro's number and the molecular weight of potassium (K) are used in the solution:

$$1.00 \times 10^{18} \text{ unit cells} \times \frac{2 \text{ atoms of K}}{\text{unit cell}} \times \frac{1 \text{ mole of K}}{6.02 \times 10^{23} \text{ atoms of K}} \times \frac{39.098 \text{ g K}}{1 \text{ mole of K}}$$

$$= 1.30 \times 10^{-4} \text{ g}$$

$$= 130. \text{ μg}$$

4. **A gas is heated in a sealed container. Which of the following occur?**

   A. gas pressure rises
   B. gas density decreases
   C. the average distance between molecules increases
   D. all of the above

A. The same material is kept in a constant volume, so neither density nor the distance between molecules will change. Pressure will rise because of increasing molecular kinetic energy impacting container walls.

5. **How many molecules are in 2.20 pg of a protein with a molecular weight of 150. kDa?**

   A. 8.83×10^9
   B. 1.82×10^9
   C. 8.83×10^6
   D. 1.82×10^6

C. The prefix "p" for "pico-" indicates 10^{-12}. A kilodalton is 1000 atomic mass units.

$$2.20 \text{ pg protein} \times \frac{10^{-12} \text{ g}}{1 \text{ pg}} \times \frac{1 \text{ mole protein}}{150 \times 10^3 \text{ g protein}} \times \frac{6.02 \times 10^{23} \text{ molecules protein}}{1 \text{ mole protein}} =$$
$$= 8.83 \times 10^6 \text{ molecules}$$

6. **At STP, 20. μL of O_2 contain 5.4×10^{16} molecules. According to Avogadro's hypothesis, how many molecules are in 20. μL of Ne at STP?**

   A. 5.4×10^{15}
   B. 1.0×10^{16}
   C. 2.7×10^{16}
   D. 5.4×10^{16}

D. Avogadro's hypothesis states that equal volumes of different gases at the same temperature and pressure contain equal numbers of molecules.

7. **An ideal gas at 50.0 °C and 3.00 atm is in a 300. cm³ cylinder. The cylinder volume changes by moving a piston until the gas is at 50.0 °C and 1.00 atm. What is the final volume?**

   A. 100. cm³
   B. 450. cm³
   C. 900. cm³
   D. 1.20 dm³

   $V \propto \frac{1}{P}$

C. A three-fold decrease in pressure of a constant quantity of gas at constant temperature will cause a three-fold increase in gas volume.

8. **Which gas law may be used to solve the previous question?**

    A. Charles's law
    B. Boyle's law
    C. Graham's law
    D. Avogadro's law

B. The inverse relationship between volume and pressure is Boyle's law.

9. **A blimp is filled with 5000. m³ of helium at 28.0 °C and 99.7 kPa. What is the mass of helium used?**

    $$R = 8.3144\ \frac{J}{mol\text{-}K}$$

    A. 797 kg
    B. 810. kg
    C. 1.99×10^3 kg
    D. 8.57×10^3 kg

A. First the ideal gas law is manipulated to solve for moles.

$$PV = nRT \quad \Rightarrow \quad n = \frac{PV}{RT}$$

Temperature must be expressed in Kelvin: $T = (28.0 + 273.15)\,K = 301.15\,K$.

The ideal gas law is then used with the knowledge that joules are equivalent to Pa-m³:

$$n = \frac{PV}{RT} = \frac{(99.7 \times 10^3\ Pa)(5000.\ m^3)}{\left(8.3144\ \frac{m^3\text{-}Pa}{mol\text{-}K}\right)(301.15\ K)} = 1.991 \times 10^3\ mol\ He\,.$$

Moles are then converted to grams using the molecular weight of helium:

$$1.991 \times 10^3\ mol\ He \times \frac{4.0026\ g\ He}{1\ mol\ He} = 797 \times 10^3\ g\ He = 797\ kg\ He\,.$$

10. **Which of the following are able to flow from one place to another?**

   I.   Gases
   II. Liquids
   III. Solids
   IV. Supercritical fluids

   A. I and II
   B. II only
   C. I, II, and IV
   D. I, II, III, and IV

C. Gases and liquids both flow. Supercritical fluids have some traits in common with gases and some in common with liquids, and so they flow also. Solids have a fixed volume and shape.

11. **One mole of an ideal gas at STP occupies 22.4 L. At what temperature will one mole of an ideal gas at one atm occupy 31.0 L?**

   A. 34.6° C
   B. 105° C
   C. 378° C
   D. 442° C

B. Either Charles's law, the combined gas law, or the ideal gas law may be used with temperature in Kelvin.

Charles's law or the combined gas law with $P_1 = P_2$ may be manipulated to equate a ratio between temperature and volume when P and n are constant.

$$V \propto T \text{ or } \frac{P_1 V_1}{T_1} = \frac{P_2 V_2}{T_2} \Rightarrow \frac{T_1}{V_1} = \frac{T_2}{V_2} \Rightarrow T_2 = V_2 \frac{T_1}{V_1}$$

$$T_2 = 31.0 \text{ L} \frac{273.15 \text{ K}}{22.4 \text{ L}} = 378 \text{ K} = 105 \text{ °C.}$$

The ideal gas law may also be used with the appropriate gas constant:

$$PV = nRT \Rightarrow T = \frac{PV}{nR}$$

$$T = \frac{(1 \text{ atm})(31.0 \text{ L})}{(1 \text{ mol})\left(0.08206 \frac{\text{L-atm}}{\text{mol-K}}\right)} = 378 \text{ K} = 105 \text{ °C.}$$

12. Why does $CaCl_2$ have a higher normal melting point than NH_3?

    A. London dispersion forces in $CaCl_2$ are stronger than covalent bonds in NH_3.
    B. Covalent bonds in NH_3 are stronger than dipole-dipole bonds in $CaCl_2$.
    C. Ionic bonds in $CaCl_2$ are stronger than London dispersion forces in NH_3.
    D. Ionic bonds in $CaCl_2$ are stronger than hydrogen bonds in NH_3.

D. London dispersion forces are weaker than covalent bonds, eliminating choice A. A higher melting point will result from stronger intermolecular bonds, eliminating choice B. $CaCl_2$ is an ionic solid resulting from a cation on the left and an anion on the right of the periodic table. The dominant attractive forces between NH_3 molecules are hydrogen bonds.

13. Which intermolecular attraction explains the following trend in straight-chain alkanes?

Condensed structural formula	Boiling point (°C)
CH_4	-161.5
CH_3CH_3	-88.6
$CH_3CH_2CH_3$	-42.1
$CH_3CH_2CH_2CH_3$	-0.5
$CH_3CH_2CH_2CH_2CH_3$	36.0
$CH_3CH_2CH_2CH_2CH_2CH_3$	68.7

    A. London dispersion forces
    B. Dipole-dipole interactions
    C. Hydrogen bonding
    D. Ion-induced dipole interactions

A. Alkanes are composed entirely of non-polar C-C and C-H bonds, resulting in no dipole interactions or hydrogen bonding. London dispersion forces increase with the size of the molecule, resulting in a higher temperature requirement to break these bonds and a higher boiling point.

14. List NH_3, PH_3, $MgCl_2$, Ne, and N_2 in order of increasing melting point.

    A. N_2 < Ne < PH_3 < NH_3 < $MgCl_2$
    B. N_2 < NH_3 < Ne < $MgCl_2$ < PH_3
    C. Ne < N_2 < NH_3 < PH_3 < $MgCl_2$
    D. Ne < N_2 < PH_3 < NH_3 < $MgCl_2$

D. Higher melting points result from stronger intermolecular forces. $MgCl_2$ is the only material listed with ionic bonds and will have the highest melting point. Dipole-dipole interactions are present in NH_3 and PH_3 but not in Ne and N_2. Ne and N_2 are also small molecules expected to have very weak London dispersion forces and so will have lower melting points than NH_3 and PH_3. NH_3 will have stronger intermolecular attractions and a higher melting point than PH_3 because hydrogen bonding occurs in NH_3. Ne has a molecular weight of 20 and a spherical shape and N_2 has a molecular weight of 28 and is not spherical. Both of these factors predict stronger London dispersion forces and a higher melting point for N_2. Actual melting points are: Ne (25 K) < N_2 (63 K) < PH_3 (140 K) < NH_3 (195 K) < $MgCl_2$ (987 K).

15. 1-butanol, ethanol, methanol, and 1-propanol are all liquids at room temperature. Rank them in order of increasing viscosity.

    A. 1-butanol < 1-propanol < ethanol < methanol
    B. methanol < ethanol < 1-propanol < 1-butanol
    C. methanol < ethanol < 1-butanol < 1-propanol
    D. 1-propanol < 1-butanol < ethanol < methanol

B. Higher viscosities result from stronger intermolecular attractive forces. The molecules listed are all alcohols with the -OH functional group attached to the end of a straight-chain alkane. In other words, they all have the formula $CH_3(CH_2)_{n-1}OH$. The only difference between the molecules is the length of the alkane corresponding to the value of n. With all else identical, larger molecules have greater intermolecular attractive forces due to a greater molecular surface for the attractions. Therefore the viscosities are ranked: methanol (CH_3OH) < ethanol (CH_3CH_2OH) < 1-propanol ($CH_3CH_2CH_2OH$) < 1-butanol ($CH_3CH_2CH_2CH_2OH$).

16. Which gas has a diffusion rate of 25% the rate for hydrogen?

A. helium
B. methane
C. nitrogen
D. oxygen

D. Graham's law of diffusion states:

$$\frac{r_1}{r_2} = \sqrt{\frac{M_2}{M_1}} \cdot$$

Hydrogen (H_2) has molecular weight of 2.0158 u. Using the unknown for material #1 and hydrogen for material #2 in the equation for Graham's law, the ratio of rates is:

$$\frac{r_{unknown}}{r_{hydrogen}} = \sqrt{\frac{2.0158 \text{ u}}{M_{unknown}}} = 0.25. \quad \text{Squaring both sides yields} \quad \frac{2.0158 \text{ u}}{M_{unknown}} = 0.0625.$$

Solving for $M_{unknown}$ gives:

$$M_{unknown} = \frac{2.0158 \text{ u}}{0.0625} = 32 \text{ u}.$$

The given possibilities are: He (4.0 u), CH_4 (16 u), N_2 (28 u), and O_2 (32 u).

17. 2.00 L of an unknown gas at 1500. mm Hg and a temperature of 25.0 °C weighs 7.52 g. Assuming the ideal gas equation, what is the molecular weight of the gas?

$$760 \text{ mm Hg} = 1 \text{ atm}$$
$$R = 0.08206 \text{ L-atm/(mol-K)}$$

    A. 21.6 u
    B. 23.3 u
    C. 46.6 u
    D. 93.2 u

C. Pressure and temperature must be expressed in the proper units. Next the ideal gas law is used to find the number of moles of gas.

$$P = 1500 \text{ mm Hg} \times \frac{1 \text{ atm}}{760 \text{ mm Hg}} = 1.974 \text{ atm and } T = 25.0 + 273.15 = 298.15 \text{ K}$$

$$PV = nRT \implies n = \frac{PV}{RT}$$

$$n = \frac{(1.974 \text{ atm})(2.00 \text{ L})}{\left(0.08206 \frac{\text{L-atm}}{\text{mol-K}}\right)(298.15 \text{ K})} = 0.1613 \text{ mol.}$$

The molecular mass may be found from the mass of one mole.

$$\frac{7.52 \text{ g}}{0.1613 \text{ mol}} = 46.6 \frac{\text{g}}{\text{mol}} \implies 46.6 \text{ u}$$

18. Which substance is most likely to be a gas at STP?

    A. SeO_2
    B. F_2
    C. $CaCl_2$
    D. I_2

B. A gas at STP has a normal boiling point under 0 °C. The substance with the lowest boiling point will have the weakest intermolecular attractive forces and will be the most likely gas at STP. F_2 has the lowest molecular weight, is not a salt, metal, or covalent network solid, and is non-polar, indicating the weakest intermolecular attractive forces of the four choices. F_2 actually is a gas at STP, and the other three are solids.

19. **What pressure is exerted by a mixture of 2.7 g of H_2 and 59 g of Xe at 0° C on a 50. L container?**

    A. 0.69 atm
    B. 0.76 atm
    C. 0.80 atm
    D. 0.97 atm

C. Grams of gas are first converted to moles:

$$2.7 \text{ g H}_2 \times \frac{1 \text{ mol H}_2}{2 \times 1.0079 \text{ g H}_2} = 1.33 \text{ mol H}_2 \quad \text{and} \quad 59 \text{ g Xe} \times \frac{1 \text{ mol H}_2}{131.29 \text{ g H}_2} = 0.449 \text{ mol Xe}$$

Dalton's law of partial pressures for an ideal gas is used to find the pressure of the mixture:

$$P_{total}V = \left(n_{H_2} + n_{Xe}\right)RT \Rightarrow P_{total} = \frac{\left(n_{H_2} + n_{Xe}\right)RT}{V}$$

$$P_{total} = \frac{(1.33 \text{ mol} + 0.449 \text{ mol})\left(0.08206 \frac{\text{L-atm}}{\text{mol-K}}\right)(273.15 \text{ K})}{50. \text{ L}} = 0.80 \text{ atm.}$$

20. **A few minutes after opening a bottle of perfume, the scent is detected on the other side of the room. What law relates to this phenomenon?**

    A. Graham's law
    B. Dalton's law
    C. Boyle's law
    D. Avogadro's law

A. Graham's law describes the rate of diffusion (or effusion) of a gas, in this instance, the rate of diffusion of molecules in perfume vapor.

21. Which of the following statements are true of vapor pressure at equilibrium?

    A. Solids have no vapor pressure.
    B. Dissolving a solute in a liquid increases its vapor pressure.
    C. The vapor pressure of a pure substance is characteristic of that substance and its temperature.
    D. All of the above

C. Only temperature and the identity of the substance determine vapor pressure. Solids have a vapor pressure, and solutes decrease vapor pressure.

22. Find the partial pressure of N_2 in a container holding H_2O and N_2 at 150. kPa and 50° C. The vapor pressure of H_2O at 50° C is 12 kPa.

    A. 12 kPa
    B. 138 kPa
    C. 162 kPa
    D. The value cannot be determined.

B. The partial pressure of H_2O vapor in the container is its vapor pressure. The partial pressure of N_2 may be found by manipulating Dalton's law:
$$P_{total} = P_{H_2O} + P_{N_2} \Rightarrow P_{N_2} = P_{total} - P_{H_2O}$$
$$P_{N_2} = P_{total} - P_{H_2O} = 150.\ kPa - 12\ kPa = 138\ kPa$$

23. The normal boiling point of water on the Kelvin scale is closest to:

    A. 112 K
    B. 212 K
    C. 273 K
    D. 373 K

D. Temperatures in Kelvin are equal to Celsius temperatures plus 273.15. Since the normal boiling point of water is 100 C , water will boil at 373.15 K, corresponding to answer D.

24. Which phase may be present at the triple point of a substance?

   I. Gas
   II. Liquid
   III. Solid
   IV. Supercritical fluid

   A. I, II, and III
   B. I, II, and IV
   C. II, III, and IV
   D. I, II, III, and IV

A. Gas, liquid and solid may exist together at the triple point.

25. In the following phase diagram, _____ occurs as P is decreased from A to B at constant T and _____ occurs as T is increased from C to D at constant P.

   A. deposition, melting
   B. sublimation, melting
   C. deposition, vaporization
   D. sublimation, vaporization

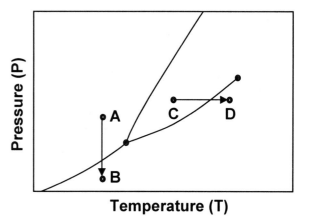

D. Point A is located in the solid phase, point C is located in the liquid phase. Points B and D are located in the gas phase. The transition from solid to gas is sublimation and the transition from liquid to gas is vaporization.

26. Heat is added to a pure solid at its melting point until it all becomes liquid at its freezing point. Which of the following occur?

   A. Intermolecular attractions are weakened.
   B. The kinetic energy of the molecules does not change.
   C. The freedom of the molecules to move about increases.
   D. All of the above

D. Intermolecular attractions are lessened during melting. This permits molecules to move about more freely, but there is no change in the kinetic energy of the molecules because the temperature has remained the same.

27. Which of the following occur when NaCl dissolves in water?

    A. Heat is required to break bonds in the NaCl crystal lattice.
    B. Heat is released when hydrogen bonds in water are broken.
    C. Heat is required to form bonds of hydration.
    D. The oxygen end of the water molecule is attracted to the Cl^- ion.

A. The lattice does break apart, H-bonds in water are broken, and bonds of hydration are formed, but the first and second process require heat while the third process releases heat. The oxygen end of the water molecule has a partial negative charge and is attracted to the Na^+ ion.

28. The solubility of $CoCl_2$ is 54 g per 100 g of ethanol. Three flasks each contain 100 g of ethanol. Flask #1 also contains 40 g $CoCl_2$ in solution. Flask #2 contains 56 g $CoCl_2$ in solution. Flask #3 contains 5 g of solid $CoCl_2$ in equilibrium with 54 g $CoCl_2$ in solution. Which of the following describe the solutions present in the liquid phase of the flasks?

    A. #1 - saturated, #2 - supersaturated, #3 - unsaturated.
    B. #1 - unsaturated, #2 - miscible, #3 - saturated.
    C. #1 - unsaturated, #2 - supersaturated, #3 - saturated.
    D. #1 - unsaturated, #2 - not at equilibrium, #3 - miscible.

C. Flask #1 contains less solute than the solubility limit, and is unsaturated. Flask #2 contains more solute than the solubility limit, and is supersaturated and also not at equilibrium. Flask #3 contains the solubility limit and is a saturated solution. The term "miscible" applies only to liquids that mix together in all proportions.

29. The solubility at 1.0 atm of pure CO_2 in water at 25° C is 0.034 M. According to Henry's law, what is the solubility at 4.0 atm of pure CO_2 in water at 25° C? Assume no chemical reaction occurs between CO_2 and H_2O.

    A. 0.0085 M
    B. 0.034 M
    C. 0.14 M
    D. 0.25 M

C. Henry's law states that CO_2 solubility in M (mol/L) will be proportional to the partial pressure of the gas. A four-fold increase in pressure from 1.0 atm to 4.0 atm will increase solubility four-fold from 0.034 M to 0.14 M.

30. **Carbonated water is bottled at 25° C under pure CO$_2$ at 4.0 atm. Later the bottle is opened at 4° C under air at 1.0 atm that has a partial pressure of 3 × 10^{-4} atm CO$_2$. Why do CO$_2$ bubbles form when the bottle is opened?**

   A. CO$_2$ leaves the solution due to a drop in solubility at the lower total pressure.
   B. CO$_2$ leaves the solution due to a drop in solubility at the lower CO$_2$ pressure.
   C. CO$_2$ leaves the solution due to a drop in solubility at the lower temperature.
   D. CO$_2$ is formed by the decomposition of carbonic acid.

B. A is incorrect because if the water were bottled under a different gas at a high pressure, it would not be carbonated. CO$_2$ partial pressure is the important factor in solubility. C is incorrect because a decrease in temperature will increase solubility, and the change from 298 K to 277 K is relatively small. D may occur, but this represents a small fraction of the gas released.

31. **When KNO$_3$ dissolves in water, the water grows slightly colder. An increase in temperature will _____ the solubility of KNO$_3$.**

   A. increase
   B. decrease
   C. have no effect on
   D. have an unknown effect with the information given on

A. The decline in water temperature indicates that the net solution process is endothermic (requiring heat). A temperature increase supplying more heat will favor the solution and increase solubility according to Le Chatelier's principle.

32. **An experiment requires 100. mL of a 0.500 M solution of MgBr$_2$. How many grams of MgBr$_2$ will be present in this solution?**

   A. 9.21 g
   B. 11.7 g
   C. 12.4 g
   D. 15.6 g

A.

$$0.100 \text{ L solution} \times \frac{0.500 \text{ mol MgBr}_2}{\text{L}} \times \frac{\left(24.305 + 2 \times 79.904\right) \text{ g MgBr}_2}{\text{mol MgBr}_2} = 9.21 \text{ g MgBr}_2$$

33. **500. mg of RbOH are added to 500. g of ethanol (C_2H_6O) resulting in 395 mL of solution. Determine the molarity and molality of RbOH.**

A. 0.0124 M, 0.00488 m
B. 0.0124 M, 0.00976 m
C. 0.0223 M, 0.00488 m
D. 0.0223 M, 0. 00976 m

B. First we determine the moles of solute present:

$$0.500 \text{ g RbOH} \times \frac{1 \text{ mol RbOH}}{\left(85.468 + 15.999 + 1.0079\right) \text{ g RbOH}} = 0.004879 \text{ mol RbOH}.$$

This value is used to calculate molarity and molality:

$$\frac{0.04879 \text{ mol RbOH}}{0.395 \text{ L solution}} = 0.0124 \text{ M RbOH}$$

and

$$\frac{0.04879 \text{ mol RbOH}}{0.500 \text{ kg ethanol}} = 0.00976 \text{ } m \text{ RbOH}.$$

34. 20.0 g H₃PO₄ in 1.5 L of solution are intended to react with KOH according to the following reaction: $H_3PO_4 + 3\,KOH \rightarrow K_3PO_4 + 3\,H_2O$. **What is the molarity and normality of the H₃PO₄ solution?**

A. 0.41 M, 1.22 N
B. 0.41 M, 0.20 N
C. 0.14 M, 0.045 N
D. 0.14 M, 0. 41 N

D. We use two methods to solve this problem. In the first method, we determine the moles of solute present and use it to calculate molarity and normality:

$$20.0 \text{ g H}_3\text{PO}_4 \times \frac{1 \text{ mol H}_3\text{PO}_4}{\left(3 \times 1.0079 + 30.974 + 4 \times 15.999\right) \text{ g H}_3\text{PO}_4} = 0.204 \text{ mol H}_3\text{PO}_4.$$

$$\frac{0.204 \text{ mol H}_3\text{PO}_4}{1.5 \text{ L solution}} = 0.136 \frac{\text{mol H}_3\text{PO}_4}{\text{L}} = 0.14 \text{ M H}_3\text{PO}_4$$

and

$$\frac{0.204 \text{ mol H}_3\text{PO}_4}{1.5 \text{ L solution}} \times \frac{3 \text{ reaction equivalents}}{1 \text{ mol H}_3\text{PO}_4} = 0.408 \frac{\text{reaction equivalents}}{\text{L}} = 0.41 \text{ N H}_3\text{PO}_4.$$

Alternatively, molarity may be found in one step and normality may be determined from the molarity:

$$\frac{20.0 \text{ g H}_3\text{PO}_4}{1.5 \text{ L}} \times \frac{1 \text{ mol H}_3\text{PO}_4}{\left(3 \times 1.0079 + 30.974 + 4 \times 15.999\right) \text{ g H}_3\text{PO}_4} = 0.136 \frac{\text{mol H}_3\text{PO}_4}{\text{L}} = 0.14 \text{ M H}_3\text{PO}_4$$

and

$$0.136 \frac{\text{mol H}_3\text{PO}_4}{\text{L}} \times \frac{3 \text{ reaction equivalents}}{1 \text{ mol H}_3\text{PO}_4} = 0.408 \frac{\text{reaction equivalents}}{\text{L}} = 0.41 \text{ N}.$$

35. Aluminum sulfate is a strong electrolyte. What is the concentration of all species in a 0.2 M solution of aluminum sulfate?

A. 0.2 M Al^{3+}, 0.2 M SO_4^{2-}
B. 0.4 M Al^{3+}, 0.6 M SO_4^{2-}
C. 0.6 M Al^{3+}, 0.4 M SO_4^{2-}
D. $0.2 \text{ M Al(SO}_4)_3$

B. A strong electrolyte will completely ionize into its cation and anion. Aluminum sulfate is $Al(SO_4)_3$. Each mole of aluminum sulfate ionizes into 2 moles of Al^{3+} and 3 moles of SO_4^{2-}:

$$0.2 \frac{\text{mol Al}_2\left(\text{SO}_4\right)_3}{\text{L}} \times \frac{2 \text{ mol Al}^{3+}}{\text{mol Al}_2\left(\text{SO}_4\right)_3} = 0.4 \frac{\text{mol Al}^{3+}}{\text{L}} \text{ and}$$

$$0.2 \frac{\text{mol Al}_2\left(\text{SO}_4\right)_3}{\text{L}} \times \frac{3 \text{ mol SO}_4^{2-}}{\text{mol Al}_2\left(\text{SO}_4\right)_3} = 0.6 \frac{\text{mol SO}_4^{2-}}{\text{L}}.$$

36. **15 g of formaldehyde (CH_2O) are dissolved in 100. g of water. Calculate the weight percentage and mole fraction of formaldehyde in the solution.**

    A. 13%, 0.090
    B. 15%, 0.090
    C. 13%, 0.083
    D. 15%, 0.083

C. Remember to use the total amounts in the denominator.

$$\text{For weight percentage: } \frac{15 \text{ g } CH_2O}{(15+100) \text{ g total}} = 0.13 = 13\%.$$

For mole fraction, first convert grams of each substance to moles:

$$15 \text{ g } CH_2O \times \frac{\text{mol } CH_2O}{(12.011+2\times1.0079+15.999) \text{ g } CH_2O} = 0.4996 \text{ mol } CH_2O$$

$$100 \text{ g } H_2O \times \frac{\text{mol } H_2O}{(2\times1.0079+15.999) \text{ g } H_2O} = 5.551 \text{ mol } H_2O.$$

Again use the total amount in the denominator $\dfrac{0.4996 \text{ mol } CH_2O}{(0.4996+5.551) \text{ mol total}} = 0.083.$

37. **Which of the following would make the best solvent for Br_2?**

    A. H_2O
    B. CS_2
    C. NH_3
    D. Molten NaCl

B. The best solvents for a solute have intermolecular bonds of similar strength to the solute ("like dissolves like"). Bromine is a non-polar molecule with intermolecular attractions due to weak London dispersion forces. The relatively strong hydrogen bonding in H_2O and NH_3 and the very strong electrostatic attractions in molten NaCl would make each of them a poor solvent for Br_2 because these molecules would prefer to remain attracted to one another. CS_2 is a fairly small non-polar molecule.

38. Which of the following is most likely to dissolve in water?

    A. H_2
    B. CCl_4
    C. $(SiO_2)_n$
    D. CH_3OH

D. The best solutes for a solvent have intermolecular bonds of similar strength to the solvent. H_2O molecules are connected by fairly strong hydrogen bonds. H_2 and CCl_4 are molecules with intermolecular attractions due to weak London dispersion forces. $(SiO_2)_n$ is a covalent network solid and is essentially one large molecule with bonds that much stronger than hydrogen bonds. CH_3OH (methanol) is miscible with water because it contains hydrogen bonds between molecules.

39. Which of the following is <u>not</u> a colligative property?

    A. Viscosity lowering
    B. Freezing point lowering
    C. Boiling point elevation
    D. Vapor pressure lowering

A. Vapor pressure lowering, boiling point elevation, and freezing point lowering may all be visualized as a result of solute particles interfering with the interface between phases in a consistent way. This is not the case for viscosity.

40. $BaCl_2(aq) + Na_2SO_4(aq) \rightarrow BaSO_4(s) + 2NaCl(aq)$ **is an example of a(n) _____ reaction.**

    A. acid-base
    B. precipitation
    C. redox
    D. nuclear

B. $BaSO_4$ falls out of the solution as a precipitate, but the charges on Ba^{2+} and SO_4^{2-} remain unchanged, so this is not a redox reaction. Neither $BaCl_2$ nor Na_2SO_4 are acids or bases, and the nuclei involved also remain unaltered.

41. List the following aqueous solutions in order of increasing boiling point.

    I.   0.050 m $AlCl_3$

    II. 0.080 m $Ba(NO_3)_2$

    III. 0.090 m NaCl

    IV. 0.12 m ethylene glycol ($C_2H_6O_2$)

    A. I < II < III < IV

    B. I < III < IV < II

    C. IV < III < I < II

    D. IV < III < II < I

C. The number of particles in solution determines the colligative properties: the greater the number of dissolved particles, the greater the boiling point elevation. The first three materials are strong electrolyte salts, and $C_2H_6O_2$ is a non-electrolyte so it will not dissociate which means it will have the lowest boiling point fo the solutions listed.

$AlCl_3(aq)$ is Al^{3+} +3 Cl^-. So $0.050 \dfrac{\text{mol } AlCl_3}{\text{kg } H_2O} \times \dfrac{4 \text{ mol particles}}{\text{mol } AlCl_3} = 0.200\ m$ particles

$Ba(NO_3)_2(aq)$ is Ba^{2+} +2 NO_3^-. So $0.080 \dfrac{\text{mol } Ba(NO_3)_2}{\text{kg } H_2O} \times \dfrac{3 \text{ mol particles}}{\text{mol } Ba(NO_3)_2} = 0.240\ m$ particles

$NaCl(aq)$ is Na^+ +Cl^-. So $0.090 \dfrac{\text{mol NaCl}}{\text{kg } H_2O} \times \dfrac{2 \text{ mol particles}}{\text{mol NaCl}} = 0.180\ m$ particles

$C_2H_6O_2(aq)$ is not an electrolyte. So $0.12 \dfrac{\text{mol } C_2H_6O_2}{\text{kg } H_2O} \times \dfrac{1 \text{ mol particles}}{\text{mol } C_2H_6O_2} = 0.12\ m$ particles

Since $Ba(NO_3)_2$ dissociates to create the most particles, the correct answer is C.

42. Osmotic pressure is the pressure required to prevent _____ from flowing from low to high _____ concentration across a semipermeable membrane.

    A. solute, solute

    B. solute, solvent

    C. solvent, solute

    D. solvent, solvent

C. Osmotic pressure is the pressure required to prevent osmosis, which is the flow of solvent across the membrane from low to high solute concentration. This is also the direction from high to low solvent concentration.

43. **A solution of NaCl in water is heated on a mountain in an open container until it boils at 100.° C. The air pressure on the mountain is 0.92 atm. According to Raoult's law, what mole fraction of Na⁺ and Cl⁻ are present in the solution?**

   A. 0.04 Na⁺, 0.04 Cl⁻
   B. 0.08 Na⁺, 0.08 Cl⁻
   C. 0.46 Na⁺, 0.46 Cl⁻
   D. 0.92 Na⁺, 0.92 Cl⁻

A. The vapor pressure of H_2O at 100. °C is exactly 1 atm. Boiling point decreases with external pressure, so the boiling point of pure H_2O at 0.9 atm will be less than 100. °C. Adding salt raises the boiling point at 0.92 atm to 100. °C by decreasing vapor pressure to 0.92 atm. According to Raoult's law:

$$P_{solution}^{vapor} = P_{pure\ solvent}^{vapor}\left(mole\ fraction\right)_{solvent} \Rightarrow \left(mole\ fraction\right)_{solvent} = \frac{P_{solution}^{vapor}}{P_{pure\ solvent}^{vapor}}.$$

Therefore, $\left(mole\ fraction\right)_{H_2O} = \dfrac{0.92\ atm\ at\ 100.\ °C}{1.0\ atm\ at\ 100.\ °C} = 0.92\ \dfrac{mol\ H_2O}{mol\ total}.$

The remaining 0.08 mole fraction of solute is evenly divided between the two ions:

$$\left(mole\ fraction\right)_{solute} = 1 - \left(mole\ fraction\right)_{H_2O} = 1 - 0.92 = 0.08\ \frac{mol\ solute\ particles}{mol\ total}$$

$$\left(mole\ fraction\right)_{Na^+} = 0.08\ \frac{mol\ solute\ particles}{mol\ total} \times \frac{1\ mol\ Na^+}{2\ mol\ solute\ particles} = 0.04\ \frac{mol\ Na^+}{mol\ total}$$

$$\left(mole\ fraction\right)_{Cl^-} = 0.08\ \frac{mol\ solute\ particles}{mol\ total} \times \frac{1\ mol\ Cl^-}{2\ mol\ solute\ particles} = 0.04\ \frac{mol\ Cl^-}{mol\ total}.$$

44. Choose the balanced nuclear equation for the emission of an alpha particle by polonium-209.

A. $^{209}_{84}Po \rightarrow \, ^{205}_{81}Pb + ^{4}_{2}He$

B. $^{209}_{84}Po \rightarrow \, ^{205}_{82}Bi + ^{4}_{2}He$

C. $^{209}_{84}Po \rightarrow \, ^{209}_{85}At + ^{0}_{-1}e$

D. $^{209}_{84}Po \rightarrow \, ^{205}_{82}Pb + ^{4}_{2}He$

D. The periodic table shows that polonium has an atomic number of 84. The emission of an alpha particle, $^{4}_{2}He$ (eliminating choice C), will leave an atom with an atomic number of 82 and a mass number of 205 (eliminating choice A). The periodic table identifies this element as lead, $^{205}_{82}Pb$, not bismuth (eliminating choice B).

45. Choose the balanced nuclear equation for the decay of calcium-45 to scandium-45.

A. $^{45}_{20}Ca \rightarrow \, ^{41}_{18}Sc + ^{4}_{2}He$

B. $^{45}_{20}Ca + ^{0}_{1}e \rightarrow \, ^{45}_{21}Sc$

C. $^{45}_{20}Ca \rightarrow \, ^{45}_{21}Sc + ^{0}_{-1}e$

D. $^{45}_{20}Ca + ^{0}_{1}p \rightarrow \, ^{45}_{21}Sc$

C. All four choices are balanced mathematically. "A" leaves scandium-41 as a decay product, not scandium-45. "B" and "D" require the addition of particles not normally present in the atom. If these reactions do occur, they are not decay reactions because they are not spontaneous. "C" involves the common decay mechanism of beta emission.

46. $^{3}_{1}H$ decays with a half-life of 12 years. 3.0 g of pure $^{3}_{1}H$ were placed in a sealed container 24 years ago. How many grams of $^{3}_{1}H$ remain?

A. 0.38 g
B. 0.75 g
C. 1.5 g
D. 3.0 g

B. Every 12 years, the amount remaining is cut in half. After 12 years, 1.5 g will remain. After another 12 years, 0.75 g will remain.

47. Oxygen-15 has a half-life of 122 seconds. What percentage of a sample of oxygen-15 has decayed after 300. seconds?

A. 18.2%
B. 21.3%
C. 78.7%
D. 81.8%

D. We may assume a convenient number (like 100.0 g) for a sample size. The amount remaining may be found from:

$$A_{remaining} = A_{initially}\left(\frac{1}{2}\right)^{\frac{t}{t_{halflife}}}$$

$$= 100.0 \text{ g } ^{15}O\left(\frac{1}{2}\right)^{\frac{300.\text{ seconds}}{122 \text{ seconds}}} = 18.2 \text{ g } ^{15}O$$

We are asked to determine the percentage that has decayed. This will be 100.0 g – 18.2 g = 81.8 g or 81.8% of the initial sample.

48. Which of the following isotopes is commonly used for medical imaging in the diagnosis of diseases?

A. cobalt-60
B. technetium-99m
C. tin-117m
D. plutonium-238

B. The other three isotopes have limited medical applications (tin-117m has been used for the relief of bone cancer pain), but only Tc-99m is used routinely for imaging.

49. Carbon-14 dating would be useful in obtaining the age of which object?

A. a 20th century Picasso painting
B. a mummy from ancient Egypt
C. a dinosaur fossil
D. all of the above

B. C-14 is used in archeology because its half-life is 5730 years. Too little C-14 would have decayed from the painting and nearly all of the C-14 would have decayed from the fossil. In both cases, an estimate of age would be impossible with this isotope.

50. Which of the following isotopes can create a chain reaction of nuclear fission?

    A. uranium-235
    B. uranium-238
    C. plutonium-238
    D. all of the above

A. Uranium-235 and plutonium-239 are the two fissile isotopes used for nuclear power. ^{238}U is the most common uranium isotope. ^{238}Pu is used as a heat source for energy in space probes and some pacemakers.

51. List the following scientists in chronological order from earliest to most recent with respect to their most significant contribution to atomic theory:

    I. John Dalton
    II. Niels Bohr
    III. J. J. Thomson
    IV. Ernest Rutherford

    A. I, III, II, IV
    B. I, III, IV, II
    C. I, IV, III, II
    D. III, I, II, IV

B. Dalton founded modern atomic theory. J.J. Thomson determined that the electron is a subatomic particle but he placed it in the center of the atom. Rutherford discovered that electrons surround a small dense nucleus. Bohr determined that electrons may only occupy discrete positions around the nucleus.

52. **Match the theory with the scientist who first proposed it:**

I. **Electrons, atoms, and all objects with momentum also exist as waves.**

II. **Electron density may be accurately described by a single mathematical equation.**

III. **There is an inherent indeterminacy in the position and momentum of particles.**

IV. **Radiant energy is transferred between particles in exact multiples of a discrete unit.**

A. I-de Broglie, II-Planck, III-Schrödinger, IV-Thomson
B. I-Dalton, II-Bohr, III-Planck, IV-de Broglie
C. I-Henry, II-Bohr, III-Heisenberg, IV-Schrödinger
D. I-de Broglie, II-Schrödinger, III-Heisenberg, IV-Planck

D. Schrödinger's equation is the equation that describes electron density, so D is the correct answer.

53. **How many neutrons are in $_{27}^{60}\text{Co}$?**

A. 27
B. 33
C. 60
D. 87

B. The number of neutrons is found by subtracting the atomic number (27) from the mass number (60).

54. **The terrestrial composition of an element is: 50.7% as an isotope with an atomic mass of 78.9 u and 49.3% as an isotope with an atomic mass of 80.9 u. Both isotopes are stable. Calculate the atomic mass of the element.**

A. 79.0 u
B. 79.8 u
C. 79.9 u
D. 80.8 u

C.

Atomic mass of element = (Fraction as 1st isotope) (Atomic mass of 1st isotope)

\+

(Fraction as 2nd isotope) (Atomic mass of 2nd isotope)

$= (0.507)\,(78.9\text{ u}) + (0.493)\,(80.9\text{ u}) = 79.89\text{ u} = 79.9\text{ u}$

55. Which of the following is a correct electron arrangement for oxygen?

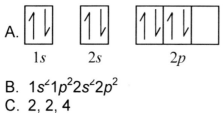

A.

1s   2s   2p

B. $1s^2 1p^2 2s^2 2p^2$
C. 2, 2, 4
D. none of the above

D. Choice A violates Hund's rule. The two electrons on the far right should occupy the final two orbitals. B should be $1s^2 2s^2 2p^4$. There is no $1p$ subshell. C should be 2, 6. Number lists indicate electrons in shells.

56. Which of the following statements about radiant energy is _not_ true?

A. The energy change of an electron transition is directly proportional to the wavelength of the emitted or absorbed photon.
B. The energy of an electron in a hydrogen atom depends only on the principle quantum number.
C. The frequency of photons striking a metal determines whether the photoelectric effect will occur.
D. The frequency of a wave of electromagnetic radiation is inversely proportional to its wavelength.

A. The energy change (ΔE) is <u>inversely</u> proportional to the wavelength (λ) of the photon according the equations:

$$\Delta E = \frac{hc}{\lambda}.$$

where h is Planck's constant and c is the speed of light.

Choice B is true for hydrogen. Atoms with more than one electron are more complex. The frequency of individual photons, not the number of photons determines whether the photoelectric effect occurs, so choice C is true. Choice D is true. The proportionality constant is the speed of light according to the equation:

$$v = \frac{c}{\lambda}.$$

57. Match the orbital diagram for the ground state of carbon with the rule/principle it violates:

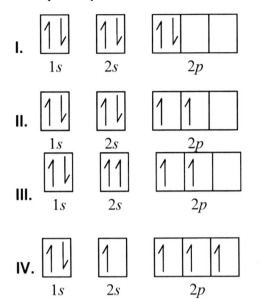

A. I - Pauli exclusion, II - Aufbau, III - no violation, IV - Hund's
B. I - Aufbau, II - Pauli exclusion, III - no violation, IV - Hund's
C. I - Hund's, II - no violation, III - Pauli exclusion, IV - Aufbau
D. I - Hund's, II - no violation, III - Aufbau, IV - Pauli exclusion

C. Diagram I violates Hund's rule because a second electron is added to a degenerate orbital before all orbitals in the subshell have one electron. Diagram III violates the Pauli exclusion principle because both electrons in the 2s orbital have the same spin. They would have the same 4 quantum numbers. Diagram IV violates the Aufbau principle because an electron occupies the higher energy 2p orbital before the 2s orbital has been filled; this configuration is not at the ground state.

58. Select the list of atoms that are arranged in order of increasing size.

A. Mg, Na, Si, Cl
B. Si, Cl, Mg, Na
C. Cl, Si, Mg, Na
D. Na, Mg, Si, Cl

C. These atoms are all in the same row of the periodic table. Size increases further to the left for atoms in the same row.

59. **Based on trends in the periodic table, which of the following properties would you expect to be greater for Rb than for K?**

    I. Density
    II. Melting point
    III. Ionization energy
    IV. Oxidation number in a compound with chlorine

    A. I only
    B. I, II, and III
    C. II and III
    D. I, II, III, and IV

A. Rb is underneath K in the alkali metal column (group 1) of the periodic table. There is a general trend for density to increase lower on the table for elements in the same row, so we select choice I. Rb and K experience metallic bonds for intermolecular forces and the strength of metallic bonds decreases for larger atoms further down the periodic table resulting in a lower melting point for Rb, so we do not choose II. Ionization energy decreases for larger atoms further down the periodic table, so we do not choose III. Both Rb and K would be expected to have a charge of +1 and therefore an oxidation number of +1 in a compound with chlorine, so we do not choose IV.

60. **Which oxide forms the strongest acid in water?**

    A. Al_2O_3
    B. Cl_2O_7
    C. As_2O_5
    D. CO_2

B. The strength of acids formed from oxides increases with electronegativity and with oxidation state. We know Cl has a greater electronegativity than Al, As, and C because it is closer to the top right of the periodic table. The oxidation numbers of our choices are +3 for Al, +7 for Cl, +5 for As, and +4 for C. Both its electronegativity and its oxidation state indicate Cl_2O_7 will form the strongest acid.

61. Rank the following bonds from least to most polar:

C-H, C-Cl, H-H, C-F

A. C-H < H-H < C-F < C-Cl
B. H-H < C-H < C-F < C-Cl
C. C-F < C-Cl < C-H < H-H
D. H-H < C-H < C-Cl < C-F

D. Bonds between atoms of the same element are completely non-polar, so H-H is the least polar bond in the list, eliminating choices A and C. The C-H bond is considered to be non-polar even though the electrons of the bond are slightly unequally shared. C-Cl and C-F are both polar covalent bonds, but C-F is more strongly polar because F has a greater electronegativity.

62. At room temperature, CaBr$_2$ is expected to be:

A. a ductile solid
B. a brittle solid
C. a soft solid
D. a gas

B. Ca is a metal because it is on the left of the periodic table, and Br is a non-metal because it is on the right. The compound they form together will be an ionic salt, and ionic salts are brittle solids (choice B) at room temperature. NaCl is another example.

63. Which of the following is a proper Lewis dot structure of CHClO?

A.   B.   C.   D.

C. C has 4 valence shell electrons, H has 1, Cl has 7, and O has 6. The molecule has a total of 18 valence shell electrons. This eliminates choice B which has 24. Choice B is also incorrect because has an octet around a hydrogen atom instead of 2 electrons and because there are only six electrons surrounding the central carbon. A single bond connecting all atoms would give choice A. This is incorrect because there are only 6 electrons surrounding the central carbon. A double bond between C and O gives the correct answer, C. A double bond between C and O and also between C and Cl would give choice D. This is incorrect because there are 10 electrons surrounding the central carbon.

64. In C_2H_2, each carbon atom contains the following valence orbitals:

A. *p* only
B. *p* and *sp* hybrids
C. *p* and *sp^2* hybrids
D. *sp^3* hybrids only

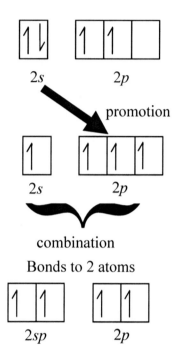

B. An isolated C has the valence electron configuration $2s^22p^2$. Before bonding, one *s* electron is promoted to an empty *p* orbital. In C_2H_2, each C atom bonds to 2 other atoms. Bonding to two other atoms is achieved by combination into two *p* orbitals and two *sp* hybrids.

65. Which statement about molecular structures is false?

A. 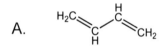   is a conjugated molecule.

B. A bonding σ orbital connects two atoms by the straight line between them.
C. A bonding π orbital connects two atoms in a separate region from the straight line between them.
D. The anion with resonance forms will always exist in one form or the other.

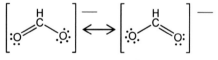

D. A conjugated molecule is a molecule with double bonds on adjacent atoms such as the molecule shown in A. Choice B and C give the definition of sigma and pi molecular orbitals. D is false because a resonance form is one of multiple equivalent Lewis structures, but these structures do not describe the actual state of the molecule. The anion will exist in a state between the two forms.

66. What is the shape of the PH_3 molecule? Use the VSEPR model.

    A. Trigonal pyramidal
    B. Trigonal bipyramidal
    C. Trigonal planar
    D. Tetrahedral

A. The Lewis structure for PH_3 is given to the right. This structure contains 4 electron pairs around the central atom, so the geometral arrangement is tetrahedral. However, the shape of

a molecule is given by its atom locations, and there are only three atoms so choice D is not correct. Four electrons pairs with one unshared pair (3 bonds and one lone pair) give a trigonal pyramidal shape as shown to the left.

67. What is the chemical composition of magnesium nitrate?

A. 11.1% Mg, 22.2% N, 66.7% O
B. 16.4% Mg, 18.9% N, 64.7% O
C. 20.9% Mg, 24.1% N, 55.0% O
D. 28.2% Mg, 16.2% N, 55.7% O

B. First find the formula for magnesium nitrate. Mg is an alkali earth metal and will always have a 2+ charge. The nitrate ion is NO_3^-. Two nitrate ions are required for each Mg^{2+} ion. Therefore the formula is $Mg(NO_3)_2$

Determine the chemical composition:

1) Determine the number of atoms for each element in $Mg(NO_3)_2$:
   1 Mg, 2 N, 6 O.
2) Multiply by the molecular weight of the elements to determine the grams of each in one mole of the formula.

$$\frac{1 \text{ mol Mg}}{\text{mol Mg(NO}_3)_2} \times \frac{24.3 \text{ g Mg}}{\text{mol Mg}} = 24.3 \text{ g Mg/mol Mg(NO}_3)_2$$

$$2(14.0) = 28.0 \text{ g N/mol Mg(NO}_3)_2$$

$$6(16.0) = 96.0 \text{ g O/mol Mg(NO}_3)_2$$

$$\overline{148.3 \text{ g Mg(NO}_3)_2/\text{mol Mg(NO}_3)_2}$$

3) Determine the formula mass

4) Divide to determine % composition

$$\%Mg = \frac{24.3 \text{ g Mg/mol Mg(NO}_3)_2}{148.3 \text{ g Mg(NO}_3)_2/\text{mol Mg(NO}_3)_2} = 0.164 \text{ g Mg/g Mg(NO}_3)_2 \times 100\% = 16.4\%$$

$$\%N = \frac{28.0}{148.3} \times 100\% = 18.9\% \qquad \%O = \frac{96.0}{148.3} \times 100\% = 64.7\%$$

Choice B is correct. Choice A is the fractional representation of the presence of each atom in the formula. Composition is based on mass percentage. Choice C is the chemical composition of $Mg(NO_2)_2$, magnesium nitrite. Choice D is the chemical composition of "MgNO$_3$", a formula that results from not balancing charges.

68. The IUPAC name for Cu_2SO_3 is:

   A. Dicopper sulfur trioxide
   B. Copper (II) sulfate
   C. Copper (I) sulfite
   D. Copper (II) sulfite

   C. Cu_2SO_3 is an ionic compound containing two Cu cations and the SO_3 anion. Choice A is wrong because it uses the naming system for molecular compounds. The SO_3 anion is 2– and is named sulfite. It takes two Cu cations to neutralize this charge, so Cu has a charge of 1+, and the name is copper (I) sulfite.

69. Which name or formula is not represented properly?

   A. Cl_4S
   B. $KClO_3$
   C. Calcium dihydrogen phosphate
   D. Sulfurous acid

A. A is the answer because the atoms in the sulfur tetrachloride molecule are placed in order of increasing electronegativity. This formula is properly written as SCl_4. B is a proper formula for potassium chlorate. Calcium dihydrogen phosphate is $Ca(H_2PO_4)_2$. It derives its name from the Ca^{2+} cation in combination with an anion composed of a phosphate anion (PO_4^{3-}) that is doubly protonated to give a $H_2PO_4^-$ ion. Sulfurous acid is $H_2SO_3(aq)$.

70. Household "chlorine bleach" is sodium hypochlorite. Which of the following best represent the production of sodium hypochlorite, sodium chloride, and water by bubbling chlorine gas through aqueous sodium hydroxide?

   A. $4Cl(g) + 4NaOH(aq) \rightarrow NaClO_2(aq) + 3NaCl(aq) + 2H_2O(l)$
   B. $2Cl_2(g) + 4NaOH(aq) \rightarrow NaClO_2(aq) + 3NaCl(aq) + 2H_2O(l)$
   C. $2Cl(g) + 2NaOH(aq) \rightarrow NaClO(aq) + NaCl(aq) + H_2O(l)$
   D. $Cl_2(g) + 2NaOH(aq) \rightarrow NaClO(aq) + NaCl(aq) + H_2O(l)$

D. Chlorine gas is a diatomic molecule, eliminating choices A and C. The hypochlorite ion is ClO^- eliminating choices A and B. All of the equations are properly balanced.

71. Balance the equation for the neutralization reaction between phosphoric acid and calcium hydroxide by filling in the blank stoichiometric coefficients.

$$\_\_H_3PO_4 + \_\_Ca(OH)_2 \rightarrow \_\_Ca_3(PO_4)_2 + \_\_H_2O$$

A. 4, 3, 1, 4
B. 2, 3, 1, 8
C. 2, 3, 1, 6
D. 2, 1, 1, 2

C. From the unbalanced equation, we determine the number of atoms on each side of the arrow. For reactants (left of the arrow): 1 Ca, 1 P, 5 H, and 6 O. For products: 3 Ca, 2 P, 2 H, and 9 O.

Since there are 3 Ca atoms on the right and only 1 Ca atom on the left, we put a coefficient of 3 in front of $Ca(OH)_2$. There are 2 P atoms on the right but only 1 P atom on the left so we put a coefficient of 2 in front of H_3PO_4. Now we have:

$$2H_3PO_4 + 3Ca(OH)_2 \rightarrow Ca_3(PO_4)_2 + ?H_2O$$

The coefficient for H_2O is found by evaluating H and then O. For H, there are 6 H from $2H_3PO_4$ and 6 from $3Ca(OH)_2$ for a total of 12 H on the left. There must be 12 H on the right for balance. None are accounted for by $Ca_3(PO_4)_2$, so all 12 H must occur on H_2O. Therefore, it gets a coefficient of 6. That also means that there are now 6 O atoms which will add to the 8 O atoms in $Ca_3(PO_4)_2$ for a total of 14 O atoms on the right. There are 8 O atoms in 2 moles of H_3PO_4 and 6 O atoms in 3 moles of $Ca(OH)_2$ for a total of 14 O atoms on the left. The O atoms balance.

$$2H_3PO_4 + 3Ca(OH)_2 \rightarrow Ca_3(PO_4)_2 + 6H_2O$$

This is choice C.

72. Choose the equation showing the reaction between calcium nitrate and lithium sulfate in aqueous solution. Include all products.

A. $CaNO_3(aq) + Li_2SO_4(aq) \rightarrow CaSO_4(s) + Li_2NO_3(aq)$

B. $Ca(NO_3)_2(aq) + Li_2SO_4(aq) \rightarrow CaSO_4(s) + 2LiNO_3(aq)$

C. $Ca(NO_3)_2(aq) + Li_2SO_4(aq) \rightarrow 2LiNO_3(s) + CaSO_4(aq)$

D. $Ca(NO_3)_2(aq) + Li_2SO_4(aq) + 2 H_2O(l) \rightarrow 2 LiNO_3(aq) + Ca(OH)_2(aq) + H_2SO_4(aq)$

B. When two ionic compounds are in solution, a precipitation reaction should be considered. We can determine from their names that the two reactants are the ionic compounds $Ca(NO_3)_2$ and Li_2SO_4. The compounds are present in aqueous solution as their four component ions Ca^{2+}, NO_3^-, Li^+, and SO_4^{2-}. Solubility rules indicate that nitrates are always soluble but sulfate will form a solid precipitate with Ca^{2+} forming $CaSO_4(s)$. Choice A results from thinking that the nitrate anion has a 2– charge instead of its 1– charge. B is correct. C assumes lithium nitrate is the precipitate. Choice D includes the reverse of a neutralization reaction. Water would not decompose due to the addition of these salts.

73. Find the mass of CO_2 produced by the combustion of 15 kg of isopropyl alcohol in the reaction:

$$2C_3H_7OH + 9O_2 \rightarrow 6CO_2 + 8H_2O$$

A. 33 kg
B. 44 kg
C. 50 kg
D. 60 kg

A. Remember "grams of known to moles of known to moles of unknown to grams of unknown." Step 1 converts mass to moles for the known value. In this case, kg and kmol are used. Step 2 relates moles of the known value to moles of the unknown value by their stoichiometry coefficients. Step 3 converts moles off the unknown value to a mass.

$$15\times10^3 \text{ g } C_4H_8O \times \underbrace{\frac{1 \text{ mol } C_4H_8O}{60 \text{ g } C_4H_8O}}_{\text{step 1}} \times \underbrace{\frac{6 \text{ mol } CO_2}{2 \text{ mol } C_4H_8O}}_{\text{step 2}} \times \underbrace{\frac{44 \text{ g } CO_2}{1 \text{ mol } CO_2}}_{\text{step 3}} = 33\times10^3 \text{ g } CO_2$$

$$= 33 \text{ kg } CO_2$$

74. What is the density of nitrogen gas at STP? Assume an ideal gas and a value of 0.08206 L-atm/(mol-K) for the gas constant.

A. 0.62 g/L
B. 1.14 g/L
C. 1.25 g/L
D. 2.03 g/L

C. The molecular mass M of N_2 is 28.0 g/mol.

$$d = \frac{nM}{V} = \frac{PM}{RT} = \frac{(1\,\text{atm})\left(28.0\,\dfrac{g}{mol}\right)}{\left(0.08206\,\dfrac{L \cdot atm}{mol \cdot K}\right)(273.15\,K)} = 1.25\,\frac{g}{L}$$

Choice A results from forgetting that nitrogen is a diatomic gas. Choice B results from using a value of 25° C for standard temperature. This is the thermodynamic standard temperature, but not STP.

A faster method is to recall that one mole of an ideal gas at STP occupies 22.4 L.

$$d\ (\text{in } \tfrac{g}{L}) = \frac{M\ (\text{in } \tfrac{g}{mol})}{22.4\,\dfrac{L}{mol}} = \frac{28.0\,\dfrac{g}{mol}}{22.4\,\dfrac{L}{mol}} = 1.25\,\frac{g}{L}.$$

75. Find the volume of methane that will produce 12 m³ of hydrogen in the reaction: $CH_4(g) + H_2O(g) \rightarrow CO(g) + 3H_2(g)$. Assume temperature and pressure remain constant.

A. 4.0 m³
B. 32 m³
C. 36 m³
D. 64 m³

A. Stoichiometric coefficients may be used directly for ideal gas volumes at constant T and P because of Avogadro's Law.

$$12\ m^3\ H_2 \times \frac{1\ m^3\ CH_4}{3\ m^3\ H_2} = 4.0\ m^3\ CH_4$$

12 g of H_2 will be produced from 32 g of CH_4 (incorrect choice B).

76. A 100. L vessel of pure O_2 at 500. kPa and 20. °C is used for the combustion of butane:

$$2C_4H_{10} + 13O_2 \rightarrow 8CO_2 + 10H_2O.$$

Find the mass of butane that would consume all the O_2 in the vessel. Assume O_2 is an ideal gas and use a value of R = 8.314 J/(mol•K).

   A. 183 g
   B. 467 g
   C. 1.83 kg
   D. 7.75 kg

A. We are given a volume and asked for a mass. The steps will be "volume to moles to moles to mass."

"Volume of known to moles of known…" requires the ideal gas law, but first several units must be altered.
    Units of joules are identical to $m^3 \cdot Pa$.
    500 kPa is 500×10^3 Pa.
    100 L is 0.100 m^3.
    20 °C is 293.*15* K.

$PV = nRT$ is rearranged to give:

$$n = \frac{PV}{RT} = \frac{\left(500 \times 10^3 \text{ Pa}\right)\left(0.100 \text{ m}^3 \text{ O}_2\right)}{\left(8.314 \dfrac{\text{m}^3 \cdot \text{Pa}}{\text{mol} \cdot \text{K}}\right)\left(293.15 \text{ K}\right)} = 20.51 \text{ mol O}_2$$

"…moles of known to moles of unknown to mass of unknown" utilizes stoichiometry. The molecular weight of butane is 58.1 g/mol

$$20.51 \text{ mol O}_2 \times \frac{2 \text{ mol C}_4\text{H}_{10}}{13 \text{ mol O}_2} \times \frac{58.1 \text{ g C}_4\text{H}_{10}}{1 \text{ mol C}_4\text{H}_{10}} = 183 \text{ g C}_4\text{H}_{10}$$

77. Consider the reaction between iron and hydrogen chloride gas:
$$Fe(s) + 2HCl(g) \rightarrow FeCl_2(s) + H_2(g) \ .$$

7 moles of iron and 10 moles of HCl react until the limiting reagent is consumed. Which statements are true?

I.   HCl is the excess reagent
II. HCl is the limiting reagent
III. 7 moles of H_2 are produced
IV. 2 moles of the excess reagent remain

A. I and III
B. I and IV
C. II and III
D. II and IV

D. The limiting reagent is found by dividing the number of moles of each reactant by its stoichiometric coefficient. The lowest result is the limiting reagent.

$$7 \text{ mol Fe} \times \frac{1 \text{ mol reaction}}{1 \text{ mol Fe}} = 7 \text{ mol reaction if Fe is limiting}$$

$$10 \text{ mol HCl} \times \frac{1 \text{ mol reaction}}{2 \text{ mol HCl}} = 5 \text{ mol reaction if HCl is limiting.}$$

Therefore, HCl is the limiting reagent (II is true) and Fe is the excess reagent.

5 moles of the reaction take place, so 5 moles of H_2 are produced, and of the 7 moles of Fe supplied, 5 are consumed, leaving 2 moles of the excess reagent (IV is true).

78. 32.0 g of hydrogen and 32.0 grams of oxygen react to form water until the limiting reagent is consumed. What is present in the vessel after the reaction is complete?

A. 16.0 g O_2 and 48.0 g H_2O
B. 24.0 g H_2 and 40.0 g H_2O
C. 28.0 g H_2 and 36.0 g H_2O
D. 28.0 g H_2 and 34.0 g H_2O

C. First the equation must be constructed:

$$2H_2 + O_2 \rightarrow 2H_2O$$

A fast and intuitive solution would be to recognize that:
1) One mole of H_2 is about 2.0 g, so about 16 moles of H_2 are present.
2) One mole of O_2 is 32.0 g, so one mole of is O_2 is present
3) Imagine the 16 moles of H_2 reacting with one mole of O_2. 2 moles of H_2 will be consumed before the one mole of O_2 is gone. O_2 is limiting. (Eliminate choice A.)
4) 16 moles less 2 leaves 14 moles of H_2 or about 28 g. (Eliminate choice B.)
5) The reaction began with 64.0 g total. Conservation of mass for chemical reactions forces the total final mass to be 64.0 g also. (Eliminate choice D.)

A more standard solution is presented next.

$$2 H_2 + O_2 \rightarrow 2 H_2O$$

First, mass is converted to moles:

$$32.0 \text{ g } H_2 \times \frac{1 \text{ mol } H_2}{2.016 \text{ g } H_2} = 15.87 \text{ mol } H_2 \quad \text{and} \quad 32.0 \text{ g } O_2 \times \frac{1 \text{ mol } O_2}{32.00 \text{ g } O_2} = 1.000 \text{ mol } O_2$$

Dividing by stoichiometric coefficients gives:

$$15.87 \text{ mol } H_2 \times \frac{1 \text{ mol reaction}}{2 \text{ mol } H_2} = 7.935 \text{ mol reaction if } H_2 \text{ is limiting}$$

$$1.000 \text{ mol } O_2 \times \frac{1 \text{ mol reaction}}{1 \text{ mol } O_2} = 1.000 \text{ mol reaction if } O_2 \text{ is limiting.}$$

O_2 is the limiting reagent, so no O_2 will remain in the vessel.

$$1.000 \text{ mol } O_2 \text{ consumed} \times \frac{2 \text{ mol } H_2O \text{ produced}}{1 \text{ mol } O_2} \times \frac{18.016 \text{ g } H_2O}{1 \text{ mol } H_2O} = 36.0 \text{ g } H_2O \text{ produced}$$

$$1.000 \text{ mol } O_2 \text{ consumed} \times \frac{2 \text{ mol } H_2 \text{ consumed}}{1 \text{ mol } O_2} \times \frac{2.016 \text{ g } H_2}{1 \text{ mol } H_2} = 4.03 \text{ g } H_2 \text{ consumed}$$

The remaining H_2 is found from:

$$32.0 \text{ g } H_2 \text{ initially} - 4.03 \text{ g } H_2 \text{ consumed} = 28.0 \text{ g } H_2 \text{ remains.}$$

79. Three experiments were performed at the same initial temperature and pressure to determine the rate of the reaction
$$2ClO_2(g) + F_2(g) \rightarrow 2ClO_2F(g).$$
Results are shown in the table below. Concentrations are given in millimoles per liter (mM).

Exp.	Initial [ClO$_2$] (mM)	Initial [F$_2$] (mM)	Initial rate of [ClO$_2$F] increase (mM/sec)
1	5.0	5.0	0.63
2	5.0	20	2.5
3	10	10	2.5

What is the rate law for this reaction?

A. Rate $= k\left[F_2\right]$

B. Rate $= k\left[ClO_2\right]\left[F_2\right]$

C. Rate $= k\left[ClO_2\right]^2\left[F_2\right]$

D. Rate $= k\left[ClO_2\right]\left[F_2\right]^2$

B. A four-fold increase in [F$_2$] at constant [ClO$_2$] between experiment one and two caused a four-fold increase in rate. Rate is therefore proportional to [F$_2$] at constant [ClO$_2$], eliminating choice D (Choice D predicts rate to increase by a factor of 16).

Between experiment 1 and 3, [F$_2$] and [ClO$_2$] both double in value. Once again, there is a four-fold increase in rate. If rate were only dependent on [F$_2$] (choice A), there would be a two-fold increase. The correct answer, B, attributes a two-fold increase in rate to the doubling of [F$_2$] and a two-fold increase to the doubling of [ClO$_2$], resulting in a net four-fold increase. Choice C predicts a rate increase by a factor of 8.

If this were an elementary reaction describing a collision event between three molecules, choice C would be expected, but stoichiometry cannot be used to predict a rate law.

80. The reaction

$$(CH_3)_3CBr(aq) + OH^-(aq) \rightarrow (CH_3)_3COH(aq) + Br^-(aq)$$

occurs in three elementary steps:

$$(CH_3)_3CBr \rightarrow (CH_3)_3C^+ + Br^- \text{ is slow}$$
$$(CH_3)_3C^+ + H_2O \rightarrow (CH_3)_3COH_2^+ \text{ is fast}$$
$$(CH_3)_3COH_2^+ + OH^- \rightarrow (CH_3)_3COH + H_2O \text{ is fast}$$

What is the rate law for this reaction?

A. $\text{Rate} = k\left[(CH_3)_3CBr\right]$

B. $\text{Rate} = k\left[OH^-\right]$

C. $\text{Rate} = k\left[(CH_3)_3CBr\right]\left[OH^-\right]$

D. $\text{Rate} = k\left[(CH_3)_3CBr\right]^2$

A. The first step will be rate-limiting. It will determine the rate for the entire reaction because it is slower than the other steps. This step is a unimolecular process with the rate given by answer A. Choice C would be correct if the reaction as a whole were one elementary step instead of three, but the stoichiometry of a reaction composed of multiple elementary steps cannot be used to predict a rate law.

81. Which statement about equilibrium is <u>not</u> true?

    A. Equilibrium shifts to minimize the impact of changes.
    B. Forward and reverse reactions have equal rates at equilibrium.
    C. A closed container of air and water is at a vapor-liquid equilibrium if the humidity is constant.
    D. The equilibrium between solid and dissolved forms is maintained when salt is added to an unsaturated solution.

D. Choice A is a restatement of Le Chatelier's Principle. B is a definition of equilibrium. A constant humidity (Choice C) occurs if the rate of vaporization and condensation are equal, indicating equilibrium. No solid is present in an unsaturated solution. If solid is added, all of it dissolves indicating a lack of equilibrium. D would be true for a saturated solution.

82. **Which statements about reaction rates are true?**

    I. **A catalyst will shift an equilibrium to favor product formation.**
    II. **Catalysts increase the rate of forward and reverse reactions.**
    III. **A greater temperature increases the chance that a molecular collision will overcome a reaction's activation energy.**
    IV. **A catalytic converter contains a homogeneous catalyst.**

    A. I and II
    B. II and III
    C. II, III and IV
    D. I, III, and IV

B. Catalysts provide an alternate mechanism in both directions, but do not alter equilibrium (I is false, II is true). The kinetic energy of molecules increases with temperature, so the energy of their collisions increases also (III is true). Catalytic converters contain a heterogeneous catalyst (IV is false).

83. **Write the equilibrium expression K_{eq} for the reaction:**

    CO_2 *(g)* + H_2 *(g)* $\leftrightarrow$ CO *(g)* + H_2O *(l)*

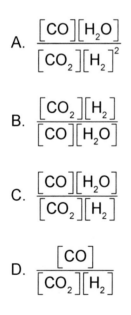

A. $\dfrac{[CO][H_2O]}{[CO_2][H_2]^2}$

B. $\dfrac{[CO_2][H_2]}{[CO][H_2O]}$

C. $\dfrac{[CO][H_2O]}{[CO_2][H_2]}$

D. $\dfrac{[CO]}{[CO_2][H_2]}$

D. Product concentrations are multiplied together in the numerator and reactant concentrations in the denominator, eliminating choice B. The stoichiometric coefficient of H_2 is one, eliminating choice A. For heterogeneous reactions, concentrations of pure liquids or solids are absent from the expression because they are constant, eliminating choice C. D is correct.

84. What could cause this change in the energy diagram of a reaction?

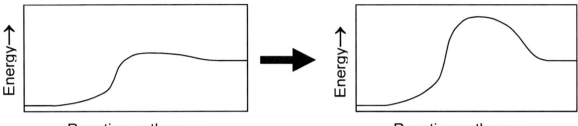

A. Adding a catalyst to an endothermic reaction
B. Removing a catalyst from an endothermic reaction
C. Adding a catalyst to an exothermic reaction
D. Removing a catalyst from an exothermic reaction

B. The products at the end of the reaction pathway are at a greater energy than the reactants, so the reaction is endothermic (narrowing down the answer to A or B). The maximum height on the diagram corresponds to activation energy. An increase in activation energy could be caused by removing a heterogeneous catalyst.

85. BaSO$_4$ (K_{sp} = 1X10^{-10}) is added to pure H$_2$O. How much is dissolved in 1 L of saturated solution?

A. 2 mg
B. 10 μg
C. 2 μg
D. 100 pg

A. BaSO$_4$ (s) → Ba^{2+} (aq) + SO$_4^{2-}$ (aq), therefore: $K_{sp} = \left[Ba^{2+} \right]\left[SO_4^{2-} \right]$.

In a saturated solution: $\left[Ba^{2+} \right] = \left[SO_4^{2-} \right] = \sqrt{1 \times 10^{-10}} = 1 \times 10^{-5}$ M.

The mass in one liter is found from the molarity:

$$1 \times 10^{-5} \ \frac{\text{mol Ba}^{2+} \text{ or SO}_4^{2-}}{L} \times \frac{1 \text{ mol dissolved BaSO}_4}{1 \text{ mol Ba}^{2+} \text{ or SO}_4^{2-}} \times \frac{(137+32+4 \times 16)\text{g BaSO}_4}{1 \text{ mol BaSO}_4}$$

$$= 0.002 \ \frac{g}{L} \text{ BaSO}_4 \times 1 \text{ L solution} \times \frac{1000 \text{ mg}}{g} = 2 \text{ mg BaSO}_4$$

86. The exothermic reaction 2NO (*g*) + Br$_2$ (*g*) ↔ 2NOBr (*g*) is at equilibrium. According to Le Chatelier's principle:

   A. Adding Br$_2$ will increase [NO].
   B. An increase in container volume (with T constant) will increase [NOBr].
   C. An increase in pressure (with T constant) will increase [NOBr].
   D. An increase in temperature (with P constant) will increase [NOBr].

C. LeChatelier's principle predicts that the equilibrium will shift to partially offset any change. Adding Br$_2$ will be partially offset by reducing [Br$_2$] and [NO] via a shift to the right (not Choice A). For the remaining possibilities, we may write the reaction as: 3 moles ↔ 2 moles + heat . An increase in container volume will decrease pressure. This change will be partially offset by an increase in the number of moles present, shifting the reaction to the left (not Choice B). An increase in pressure will be offset by a decrease in the number of moles present, shifting the reaction to the right (Choice C, correct). Raising the temperature by adding heat will shift the reaction to the left (not choice D).

87. At a certain temperature, *T*, the equilibrium constant for the reaction 2NO (*g*) ↔ N$_2$ (*g*) + O$_2$ (*g*) is K_{eq} = 2 x 10^3. If a 1.0 L container at this temperature contains 90 mM N$_2$, 20 mM O$_2$, and 5 mM NO, what will occur?

   A. The reaction will make more N$_2$ and O$_2$.
   B. The reaction is at equilibrium.
   C. The reaction will make more NO.
   D. The temperature, *T*, is required to solve this problem.

A. Calculate the reaction quotient at the actual conditions:

$$Q = \frac{\left[N_2 \right]\left[O_2 \right]}{\left[NO \right]^2} = \frac{\left(0.090\ M \right)\left(0.020\ M \right)}{\left(0.005\ M \right)^2} = 72$$

This value is less than K_{eq} (72 < 2X10^3); therefore, $Q < K_{eq}$. To achieve equilibrium, the numerator of Q must be larger relative to the denominator. This occurs when products turn into reactants. Therefore, NO will react to make more N$_2$ and O$_2$.

88. Which statement about acids and bases is <u>not</u> true?

A. All strong acids ionize in water.
B. All Lewis acids accept an electron pair.
C. All Brønsted bases use OH^- as a proton acceptor.
D. All Arrhenius acids form H^+ ions in water.

C. Choice A is the definition of a strong acid, Choice B is the definition of a Lewis acid, and Choice D is the definition of an Arrhenius acid. By definition, all Arrhenius bases form OH^- ions in water, and all Brønsted bases are proton acceptors. But not all Brønsted bases use OH^- as a proton acceptor. For example, NH_3 is a Brønsted base.

89. Which of the following is listed from weakest to strongest acid?

A. H_2SO_3, H_2SeO_3, H_2TeO_3
B. $HBrO$, $HBrO_2$, $HBrO_3$, $HBrO_4$
C. HI, HBr, HCl, HF
D. H_3PO_4, $H_2PO_4^-$, HPO_4^{2-}

B. The electronegativity of the central atom decreases from S to Se to Te as period number increases in the same periodic table group. The acidity of the oxide also decreases. Choice B is correct because acid strength increases with the oxidation state of the central atom. C is wrong because HI, HBr, and HCl are all strong acids but HF is a weak acid. D is wrong because acid strength is greater for polyprotic acids.

90. NH₄F is dissolved in water. Which of the following are conjugate acid/base pairs present in the solution?

    I. NH_4^+/NH_4OH
    II. HF/F^-
    III. H_3O^+/H_2O
    IV. H_2O/OH^-

    A. I, II, and III
    B. I, III, and IV
    C. II and IV
    D. II, III, and IV

D. NH_4F is soluble in water and completely dissociates to NH_4^+ and F^-. F^- is a weak base with HF as its conjugate acid (**II**). NH_4^+ is a weak acid with NH_3 as its conjugate base. A conjugate acid/base pair must have the form HX/X (where X is one lower charge than HX). NH_4^+/NH_4OH (**I**) is <u>not</u> a conjugate acid/base pair, eliminating Choices A and B. H_3O^+/H_2O and H_2O/OH^- (**III** and **IV**) are always present in water and in all aqueous solutions as conjugate acid/base pairs. All of the following equilibrium reactions occur in $NH_4F(aq)$:

$$NH4^+ \ (aq) + OH^- \ (aq) \leftrightarrow NH_3 \ (aq) + H_2O \ (l)$$
$$F^- \ (aq) + H_3O^+ \ (aq) \leftrightarrow HF \ (aq) + H_2O \ (l)$$
$$2H_2O \ (l) \leftrightarrow H_3O^+ \ (aq) + OH^- \ (aq)$$

91. What are the pH and the pOH of 0.010 M HNO_3 (aq)?

    A. pH = 1.0, pOH = 9.0
    B. pH = 2.0, pOH = 12.0
    C. pH = 2.0, pOH = 8.0
    D. pH = 8.0, pOH = 6.0

B. HNO_3 is a strong acid, so it completely dissociates:

$$\left[H^+\right] = 0.010 \ M = 1.0 \times 10^{-2} \ M.$$
$$pH = -\log_{10}\left[H^+\right] = -\log_{10}\left(1.0 \times 10^{-2}\right) = 2.0 \ \text{(choices B or C)}.$$
$$\text{From } pH + pOH = 14: \ pOH = 12.0 \ \text{(choice B)}.$$

92. What is the pH of a buffer made of 0.128 M sodium formate (HCOONa) and 0.072 M formic acid (HCOOH)? The pK_a of formic acid is 3.75.

    A. 2.0
    B. 3.0
    C. 4.0
    D. 5.0

C. From the pK_a, we may find the K_a of formic acid:

$$K_a = 10^{-pK_a} = 10^{-3.75} = 1.78 \times 10^{-4}$$

This is the equilibrium constant:

$$K_a = \frac{[H^+][HCOO^-]}{[HCOOH]} = 1.78 \times 10^{-4} \text{ for the dissociation:}$$

$$HCOOH \rightleftharpoons H^+ + HCOO^-.$$

The pH is found by solving for the H^+ concentration:

$$[H^+] = K_a \frac{[HCOOH]}{[HCOO^-]} = (1.78 \times 10^{-4})\frac{0.072}{0.128} = 1.0 \times 10^{-4} \text{ M}$$

$$pH = -\log_{10}[H^+] = -\log_{10}(1.0 \times 10^{-4}) = 4.0 \text{ (choice C)}$$

93. A sample of 50.0 ml KOH is titrated with 0.100 M HClO₄. The initial buret reading is 1.6 ml and the reading at the endpoint is 22.4 ml. What is [KOH]?

    A. 0.0416 M
    B. 0.0481 M
    C. 0.0832 M
    D. 0.0962 M

A. $HClO_4$ and KOH are both strong electrolytes. If you are good at memorizing formulas, solve the problem this way:

$$C_{unknown} = \frac{C_{known}(V_{final} - V_{initial})}{V_{unknown}} = \frac{0.100 \text{ M} (22.4 \text{ ml} - 1.6 \text{ ml})}{50.0 \text{ ml}} = 0.0416 \text{ M}.$$

The problem may also be solved by finding the moles of known substance:

$$0.100 \frac{mol}{L} \times \frac{1 \text{ L}}{1000 \text{ mL}} \times (22.4 \text{ mL} - 1.6 \text{ mL}) = 0.00208 \text{ mol } HClO_4$$

This will neutralize 0.00208 mol KOH, and $\dfrac{0.00208 \text{ mol}}{0.0500 \text{ L}} = 0.0416 \text{ M}$

94. **Rank the following from lowest to highest pH. Assume a small volume for the added component:**

I. 0.01 mol HCl added to 1 L H_2O
II. 0.01 mol HI added to 1 L of an acetic acid/sodium acetate solution at pH 4.0
III. 0.01 mol NH_3 added to 1 L H_2O
IV. 0.1 mol HNO_3 added to 1 L of a 0.1 M $Ca(OH)_2$ solution

A. I < II < III < IV
B. I < II < IV < III
C. II < I < III < IV
D. II < I < IV < III

A. HCl is a strong acid. Therefore solution I has a <u>pH of 2</u> because

$$pH = -\log_{10}\left[H^+\right] = -\log_{10}\left(0.01\right) = 2.$$

HI is also a strong acid and would have a pH of 2 at this concentration in water, but the buffer will prevent the pH from dropping this low. Solution II will have a pH <u>above 2</u> and below 4, eliminating Choices C and D.

If a strong base were in Solution III, its pOH would be 2. Using the equation pH + pOH = 14, its pH would be 12. Because NH_3 is a weak base, the pH of Solution III will be greater than 7 and <u>less than 12</u>.

A neutralization reaction occurs in Solution IV between 0.1 mol of H^+ from the strong acid HNO_3 and <u>0.2 mol of OH^-</u> from the strong base $Ca(OH)_2$. Each mole of $Ca(OH)_2$ contributes two base equivalents for the neutralization reaction. The base is the excess reagent, and 0.1 mol of OH^- remain after the reaction. This resulting solution will have a pOH of 1 and a <u>pH of 13</u>.

A is correct because: 2 < between 2 and 4 < between 7 and 12 < 13

95. The curve below resulted from the titration of a _____ ____ with a
_____ ____ titrant.

A. weak acid, strong base
B. weak base, strong acid
C. strong acid, strong base
D. strong base, strong acid

D. The pH is above 7 initially and decreases, so an acid titrant is neutralizing a base. This eliminates A and C. The maximum slope (equivalence point) at the neutral pH of 7 indicates a strong base titrated with a strong acid, D.

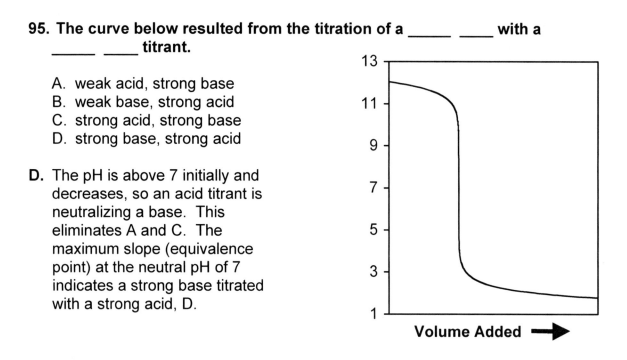

96. Which statement about thermochemistry is true?

A. Particles in a system move about less freely at high entropy
B. Water at 100° C has the same internal energy as water vapor at 100°C
C. A decrease in the order of a system corresponds to an increase in entropy.
D. At its sublimation temperature, dry ice has higher entropy than gaseous CO_2

C. At high entropy, particles have a large freedom of molecular motion (A is false). Water and water vapor at 100° C contain the same translational kinetic energy, but water vapor has additional internal energy in the form of resisting the intermolecular attractions between molecules (B is false). We also know water vapor has a higher internal energy because heat must be added to boil water. Entropy may be thought of as the disorder in a system (C is correct). Sublimation is the phase change from solid to gas, and there is less freedom of motion for particles in solids than in gases. Solid CO_2 (dry ice) has a lower entropy than gaseous CO_2 because entropy decreases during a phase change that prevents molecular motion (D is false).

97. What is the heat change of 36.0 g H_2O at atmospheric pressure when its temperature is reduced from 125 °C to 40. °C? Use the following data:

A. −92.0 kJ
B. −10.8 kJ
C. 10.8 kJ
D. 92.0 kJ

Values for water	
Heat capacity of solid	37.6 J/mol•°C
Heat capacity of liquid	75.3 J/mol•°C
Heat capacity of gas	33.1 J/mol•°C
Heat of fusion	6.02 kJ/mol
Heat of vaporization	40.67 kJ/mol

A. Heat is evolved from the substance as it cools, so the heat change will be negative, eliminating choices C and D. Data in the table are given using moles, so the first step is to convert the mass of water to moles:

$$36.0 \text{ g H}_2\text{O} \times \frac{1 \text{ mol H}_2\text{O}}{18.02 \text{ g H}_2\text{O}} = 2.00 \text{ mol H}_2\text{O}$$

There are three contributions to the heat evolved. First, the heat evolved when cooling the vapor from 125° C to 100° C is found from the heat capacity of the gas:

$$q_1 = n \times C \times \Delta T = 2.00 \text{ mol H}_2\text{O}(g) \times 33.1 \, \frac{\text{J}}{\text{mol °C}} \times (100 \text{ °C} - 125 \text{ °C})$$

$$= -1655 \text{ J to cool vapor}$$

Next, the heat evolved during condensation is found from the heat of vaporization:

$$q_2 = n \times (-\Delta H_{vaporization}) = 2.00 \text{ mol H}_2\text{O} \times (-40.67 \, \frac{\text{kJ}}{\text{mol}})$$

$$= -81.34 \text{ kJ to condense vapor}$$

Finally, the heat evolved when cooling the liquid from 100 °C to 40 °C is found from the heat capacity of the liquid:

$$q_3 = n \times C \times \Delta T = 2.00 \text{ mol H}_2\text{O}(g) \times 75.3 \, \frac{\text{J}}{\text{mol °C}} \times (40 \text{ °C} - 100 \text{ °C})$$

$$= -9036 \text{ J to cool liquid}$$

The total heat change is the sum of these contributions:

$$q = q_1 + q_2 + q_3 = -1.655 \text{ kJ} + (-81.34 \text{ kJ}) + (-9.036 \text{ kJ}) = -92.03 \text{ kJ}$$

$$= -92.0 \text{ kJ (Choice A)}$$

98. What is the standard heat of combustion of $CH_4(g)$? Use the following data:

A. −890.3 kJ/mol
B. −604.5 kJ/mol
C. −252.9 kJ/mol
D. −182.5 kJ/mol

Standard heats of formation	
$CH_4(g)$	−74.8 kJ/mol
$CO_2(g)$	−393.5 kJ/mol
$H_2O(l)$	−285.8 kJ/mol

A. First we must write a balanced equation for the combustion of CH_4. The balanced equation is:

$$CH_4(g) + 2O_2(g) \rightarrow CO_2(g) + 2H_2O(l).$$

The heat of combustion may be found from the sum of the productions minus the sum of the reactants of the heats of formation:

$$\Delta H_{rxn} = H_{product\ 1} + H_{product\ 2} + \ldots - \left(H_{reactant\ 1} + H_{reactant\ 2} + \ldots \right)$$

$$= \Delta H_f^\circ (CO_2) + 2\Delta H_f^\circ (H_2O) - \left(\Delta H_f^\circ (CH_4) + 2\Delta H_f^\circ (O_2) \right)$$

The heat of formation of an element in its most stable form is zero by definition, and the other heats of formation are found in the table, so

$$\Delta H_f^\circ(O_2(g)) = 0 \ \frac{kJ}{mol}, \text{ and the remaining values are found from the table:}$$

$$\Delta H_{rxn} = -393.5 \ \frac{kJ}{mol} + 2(-285.8 \ \frac{kJ}{mol}) - \left(-74.8 \ \frac{kJ}{mol} + 2(0) \right) = -890.3 \ \frac{kJ}{mol} \text{ (choice A)}$$

99. Which reaction creates products that have a lower total entropy than the reactants?

A. Dissolution of table salt: $NaCl(s) \rightarrow Na^+(aq) + Cl^-(aq)$
B. Oxidation of iron: $4Fe(s) + 3O_2(g) \rightarrow 2Fe_2O_3(s)$
C. Dissociation of ozone: $O_3(g) \rightarrow O_2(g) + O(g)$
D. Vaporization of butane: $C_4H_{10}(l) \rightarrow C_4H_{10}(g)$

B. Choice A is incorrect because two particles have a greater entropy than one and because ions in solution have more freedom of motion than a solid. For B (the correct answer), the products are at a lower entropy than the reactants because there are fewer product molecules and they are all in the solid form but one of the reactants is a gas. Reaction B is still spontaneous because it is highly exothermic. For C, there are more product molecules than reactants, and for D, the gas phase always has a higher entropy than the liquid.

100. Which statement about reactions is true?

A. All spontaneous reactions are exothermic and cause an increase in entropy.
B. An endothermic reaction that increases the order of the system cannot be spontaneous.
C. A reaction can be non-spontaneous in one direction and also non-spontaneous in the opposite direction.
D. Melting snow is an exothermic process

B. All reactions that are both exothermic and cause an increase in entropy will be spontaneous, but the converse (Choice A) is not true. Some spontaneous reactions are exothermic but decrease entropy and some are endothermic and increase entropy. Choice B is correct. The reverse reaction of a non-spontaneous reaction (Choice C) will be spontaneous. Melting snow (Choice D) requires heat. Therefore it is an endothermic process

101. 10. kJ of heat are added to one kilogram of Iron at 10. °C. What is its final temperature? The specific heat of iron is 0.45 J/g•°C.

A. 22° C
B. 27° C
C. 32° C
D. 37° C

C. The expression for heat as a function of temperature change:

$$q = n \times C \times \Delta T$$

may be rearranged to solve for the temperature change:

$$\Delta T = \frac{q}{n \times C} \, .$$

In this case, n is a mass and C is the specific heat of iron:

$$\Delta T = \frac{10000 \text{ J}}{1000 \text{ g} \times 0.45 \ \dfrac{\text{J}}{\text{g} \, ^\circ\text{C}}} = 22 \ ^\circ\text{C} \, .$$

This is not the final temperature (choice A is incorrect). It is the temperature difference between the initial and final temperature.

$$\Delta T = T_{final} - T_{initial} = 22 \ ^\circ\text{C}$$

Solving for the final temperature gives us:

$$T_{final} = \Delta T + T_{initial} = 22 \ ^\circ\text{C} + 10 \ ^\circ\text{C} = 32 \ ^\circ\text{C} \text{ (Choice C)}$$

102. Which reaction is not a redox process?

A. Combustion of octane: $2C_8H_{18} + 25O_2 \rightarrow 16CO_2 + 18H_2O$

B. Depletion of a lithium battery: $Li + MnO_2 \rightarrow LiMnO_2$

C. Corrosion of aluminum by acid: $2Al + 6HCl \rightarrow 2AlCl_3 + 3H_2$

D. Taking an antacid for heartburn:
$CaCO_3 + 2HCl \rightarrow CaCl_2 + H_2CO_3 \rightarrow CaCl_2 + CO_2 + H_2O$

D. The oxidation state of atoms is altered in a redox process. During combustion (Choice A), the carbon atoms are oxidized from an oxidation number of –4 to +4. Oxygen atoms are reduced from an oxidation number of 0 to –2. All batteries (Choice B) generate electricity by forcing electrons from a redox process through a circuit. Li is oxidized from 0 in the metal to +1 in the $LiMnO_2$ salt. Mn is reduced from +4 in manganese(IV) oxide to +3 in lithium manganese(III) oxide salt. Corrosion (Choice C) is due to oxidation. Al is oxidized from 0 to +3. H is reduced from +1 to 0. Acid-base neutralization (Choice D) transfers a proton (an H atom with an oxidation state of +1) from an acid to a base. The oxidation state of all atoms remains unchanged (Ca at +2, C at +4, O at -2, H at +1, and Cl at -1), so D is correct. Note that choices C and D both involve an acid. The availability of electrons in aluminum metal favors electron transfer but the availability of CO_3^{2-} as a proton acceptor favors proton transfer.

103. Given the following heats of reaction:

$$\Delta H = -0.3 \text{ kJ/mol for} \quad Fe(s) + CO_2(g) \rightarrow FeO(s) + CO(g)$$

$$\Delta H = 5.7 \text{ kJ/mol for} \quad 2Fe(s) + 3CO_2(g) \rightarrow Fe_2O_3(s) + 3CO(g)$$

$$\text{and } \Delta H = 4.5 \text{ kJ/mol for} \quad 3FeO(s) + CO_2(g) \rightarrow Fe_3O_4(s) + CO(g)$$

use Hess's Law to determine the heat of reaction for:

$$3Fe_2O_3(s) + CO(g) \rightarrow 2Fe_3O_4(s) + CO_2(g)?$$

A. −10.8 kJ/mol
B. −9.9 kJ/mol
C. −9.0 kJ/mol
D. −8.1 kJ/mol

B. We are interested in $3Fe_2O_3$ as a reactant. Only the second reaction contains this molecule, so we will take three times the opposite of the second reaction. We are interested in $2Fe_3O_4$ as a product, so we will take two times the third reaction. An intermediate result is:

$$3Fe_2O_3(s) + 9CO(g) \rightarrow 6Fe(s) + 9CO_2(g) \qquad \Delta H = -3 \times 5.7 \text{ kJ/mol} = -17.1 \text{ kJ/mol}$$

$$6FeO(s) + 2CO_2(g) \rightarrow 2Fe_3O_4(s) + 2CO(g) \qquad \Delta H = 2 \times 4.5 \text{ kJ/mol} = 9.0 \text{ kJ/mol}$$

$$3Fe_2O_3(s) + 6FeO(s) + 7CO(g) \rightarrow \qquad \Delta H = (-17.1 + 9.0) \text{ kJ/mol} = -8.1 \text{ kJ/mol}$$
$$2Fe_3O_4(s) + 6Fe(s) + 7CO_2(g)$$

However, D is not the correct answer because it is not ΔH for the reaction of the problem statement. We may use six times the first reaction to eliminate both FeO and Fe from the intermediate result and obtain the reaction of interest:

$$3Fe_2O_3(s) + 6FeO(s) + 7CO(g) \rightarrow \qquad \Delta H = -8.1 \text{ kJ/mol}$$
$$2Fe_3O_4(s) + 6Fe(s) + 7CO_2(g)$$

$$6Fe(s) + 6CO_2(g) \rightarrow 6FeO(s) + 6CO(g) \qquad \Delta H = 6 \times (-0.3 \text{ kJ/mol}) = -1.8 \text{ kJ/mol}$$

$$3Fe_2O_3(s) + CO(g) \rightarrow 2Fe_3O_4(s) + CO(g) \qquad \begin{aligned}\Delta H &= (-8.1 + -1.8) \text{ kJ/mol} \\ &= -9.9 \text{ kJ/mol (choice B)}\end{aligned}$$

104. What is the oxidant in the reaction: $2H_2S + SO_2 \rightarrow 3S + 2H_2O$?

    A. H_2S
    B. SO_2
    C. S
    D. H_2O

B. The S atom in H_2S has an oxidation number of –2 and is oxidized by SO_2 (the oxidant, Choice B) to elemental sulfur (oxidation number = 0). The S atom in SO_2 has an oxidation number of +4 and is reduced. The two half-reactions are:

$$SO_2 + 4e^- + 4H^+ \xrightarrow{\text{reduction}} S + 2H_2O$$

$$2H_2S \xrightarrow{\text{oxidation}} 2S + 4e^- + 4H^+$$

105. Molten NaCl is subjected to electrolysis. What reaction takes place at the cathode?

    A. $2Cl^-(l) \rightarrow Cl_2(g) + 2e^-$
    B. $Cl_2(g) + 2e^- \rightarrow 2Cl^-(l)$
    C. $Na^+(l) + e^- \rightarrow Na(l)$
    D. $Na^+(l) \rightarrow Na(l) + e^-$

C. Reduction (choices B and C) always occurs at the cathode. Molten NaCl is composed of ions in liquid form before electrolysis (answer C). A and D are oxidation reactions, and D is also not properly balanced because a +1 charge is on the left and a –1 charge is on the right. The two half-reactions are:

$$Na^+(l) + e^- \xrightarrow{\text{reduction at cathode}} Na(l)$$

$$2Cl^-(l) \xrightarrow{\text{oxidation at anode}} Cl_2(g) + 2e^-$$

The net reaction is:

$$2NaCl(l) \rightarrow 2Na(l) + Cl_2(g)$$

106. What is the purpose of the salt bridge in a voltaic cell?

A. To receive electrons from the oxidation half-reaction
B. To relieve the buildup of positive charge in the anode half-cell
C. To conduct electron flow
D. To permit positive ions to flow from the cathode half-cell to the anode half-cell

D. The anode receives electrons from the oxidation half-reaction (Choice A) and the circuit conducts electron flow (Choice C) to the cathode which supplies electrons for the reduction half-reaction. This flow of electrons from the anode to the cathode is relieved by a flow of ions through the salt bridge from the cathode to the anode (Choice D). The salt bridge relieves the buildup of positive charge in the cathode half-cell (Choice B is incorrect).

107. Given $E°=-2.37$ V for $Mg^{2+}(aq)+2e^-\rightarrow Mg(s)$ and $E°=0.80$ V for $Ag^+(aq)+e^-\rightarrow Ag(s)$, what is the standard potential of a voltaic cell composed of a piece of magnesium dipped in a 1 M Ag^+ solution and a piece of silver dipped in a 1 M Mg^{2+} solution?

A. 0.77 V
B. 1.57 V
C. 3.17 V
D. 3.97 V

C. $Ag^+(aq)+e^-\rightarrow Ag(s)$ has a larger value for $E°$ (reduction potential) than $Mg^{2+}(aq)+2e^-\rightarrow Mg(s)$. Therefore, in the cell described, reduction will occur at the Ag electrode and it will be the cathode. Using the equation:

$$E^O_{cell} = E^O(\text{cathode}) - E^O(\text{anode}),\text{ we obtain:}$$

$$E^O_{cell} = 0.80\text{ V} - (-2.37\text{ V}) = 3.17\text{ V (Answer C)}.$$

Choice D results from the incorrect assumption that electrode potentials depend on the amount of material present. The balanced net reaction for the cell is:

$$Mg(s) \rightarrow Mg^{2+}(aq) + 2e^- \qquad E^°_{ox} = 2.37\text{ V}$$

$$2Ag^+(aq) + 2e^- \rightarrow 2Ag(s) \qquad E^°_{red} = 0.80\text{ V (\textbf{not} 1.60 V)}$$

$$Mg(s) + 2Ag^+(aq) \rightarrow 2Ag(s) + Mg^{2+}(aq) \qquad E^°_{cell} = 3.17\text{ V (\textbf{not} 3.97 V)}$$

108. A proper name for this hydrocarbon is:

A. 4,5-dimethyl-6-hexene
B. 2,3-dimethyl-1-hexene
C. 4,5-dimethyl-6-hexyne
D. 2-methyl-3-propyl-1-butene

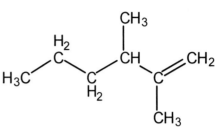

B. The hydrocarbon contains a double bond and no triple bonds, so it is an alkene. Choice C describes an alkyne. The longest carbon chain is six carbons long, corresponding to a parent molecule of 1-hexene (circled to the left). Choice D is an improper name because it names the molecule as a substituted butane, using a shorter chain as the parent molecule.

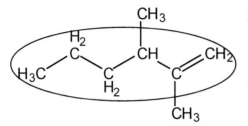

Finally, the lowest possible set of locant numbers must be used. Choice A is an improper name because the larger possible set of locant numbers is chosen.

109. An IUPAC approved name for this molecule is:

A. butanal
B. propanal
C. butanoic acid
D. propanoic acid

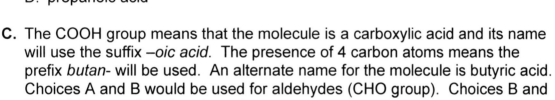

C. The COOH group means that the molecule is a carboxylic acid and its name will use the suffix *–oic acid*. The presence of 4 carbon atoms means the prefix *butan-* will be used. An alternate name for the molecule is butyric acid. Choices A and B would be used for aldehydes (CHO group). Choices B and D would be used for 3 carbon atoms:

butanal (also called butyraldehyde):

propanal (also called propionaldehyde):

propanoic acid (also called propionic acid):

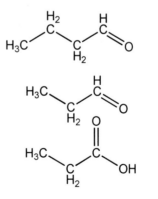

110. Which molecule has a systematic name of methyl ethanoate?

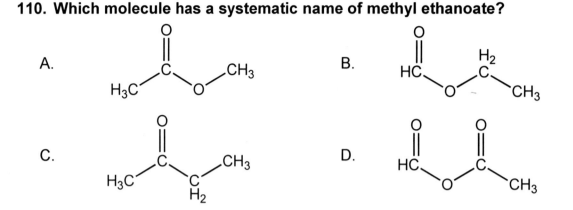

A.

B.

C.

D.

A. The suffix *–oate* is used for esters. The ester group is shown to the right. Choice C is a ketone (ethyl methyl ketone or 2-butanone). The ketone group is shown to the left. Choice D is an acid anhydride (ethanoic methanoic anhydride). The acid anhydride group is shown below to the right. A and B are both esters. The hydrocarbon R_2 with the carbonyl group receives the *–oate* suffix and the hydrocarbon R_1 with the *-yl* suffix is attached to the other oxygen. Choice B is ethyl methanoate and A is correct.

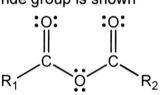

111. This compound contains an:

A. alkene, carboxylic acid, ester, and ketone
B. aldehyde, alkyne, ester, and ketone
C. aldehyde, alkene, carboxylic acid, and ester
D. acid anhydride, aldehyde, alkene, and amine

C. The derivatives are circled below:

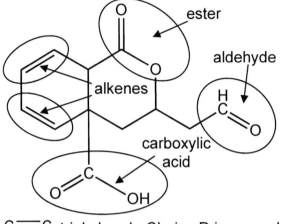

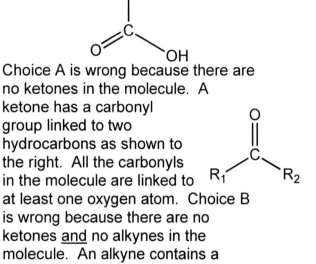

Choice A is wrong because there are no ketones in the molecule. A ketone has a carbonyl group linked to two hydrocarbons as shown to the right. All the carbonyls in the molecule are linked to at least one oxygen atom. Choice B is wrong because there are no ketones <u>and</u> no alkynes in the molecule. An alkyne contains a C≡C triple bond. Choice D is wrong because there are no acid anhydrides (shown to the left) <u>and</u> no amines (shown to the right). Amines require at least one N-C bond and there are no nitrogen atoms in the molecule.

112. Which group of scientists made contributions in the same area of chemistry?

A. Volta, Kekulé, Faraday, London
B. Hess, Joule, Kelvin, Gibbs
C. Boyle, Charles, Arrhenius, Pauli
D. Davy, Mendeleev, Ramsay, Galvani

B. Hess, Joule, Kelvin, and Gibbs all contributed to thermochemistry and have thermodynamic entities named after them. Volta, Faraday, and Galvani (choice D) contributed to electrochemistry, Kekulé to organic chemistry, London to chemical bonding, Boyle and Charles to gas laws, Arrhenius to acid/base chemistry and thermochemstry, Pauli to quantum theory, Davy and Ramsay to element isolation, and Mendeleev to the periodic table.

113. Which of the following pairs are isomers?

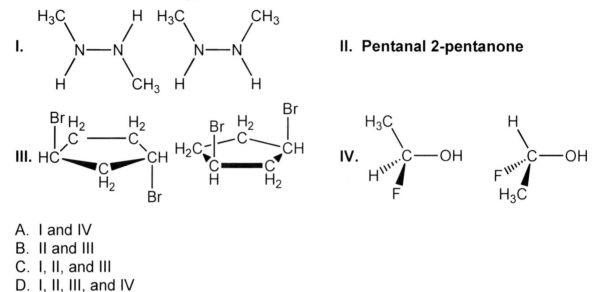

II. Pentanal 2-pentanone

A. I and IV
B. II and III
C. I, II, and III
D. I, II, III, and IV

B. In Pair I, the N—N bond may freely rotate in the molecule because it is not a double bond. The identical molecule is represented twice.

For Pair II, pentanal is

and 2-pentanone is:

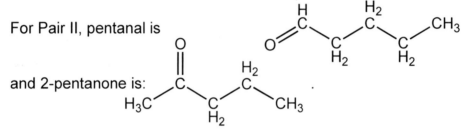

Both molecules are $C_5H_{10}O$, and they are isomers because they have the same formula with a different arrangement of atoms.

In Pair III, both molecules are 1,3-dibromocyclopentane, $C_5H_8Br_2$. In the first molecule, the bromines are in a *trans* configuration, and in the second molecule, they are *cis*. The two molecules are also viewed from different perspectives. Unlike Pair I, no bond rotation may occur because the intervening atoms are locked into place by the ring, so they are different arrangements and are isomers.

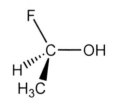

In Pair IV (1-fluoroethanol), there is a chiral center, so stereoisomers are possible, but as in Pair I, the same molecule is represented twice. Rotating the C-O bond indicates that the two structures are superimposable. This molecule shown is a stereoisomer to the molecule represented in IV. The answer is B (Pairs II and III).

114. Which instrument would be most useful for separating two different proteins from a mixture?

 A. UV/Vis spectrophotometer
 B. Mass spectrometer
 C. Gas chromatograph
 D. Liquid chromatograph

D. UV/Vis spectrophotometry measures the light at ultraviolet and visible wavelengths that can pass through the mixture, and mass spectrometry determines molecular weights. Both might be used to find the concentration of each protein, but neither is a separation technique. Gas chromatography is used for small molecules in the gas phase. Proteins are too large to exist in the gas phase. Liquid chromatography (Choice D) is used to separate large molecules.

115. Classify these biochemicals.

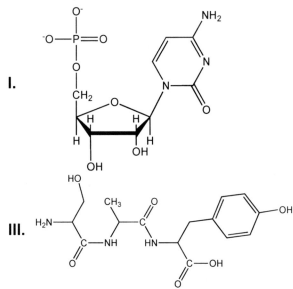

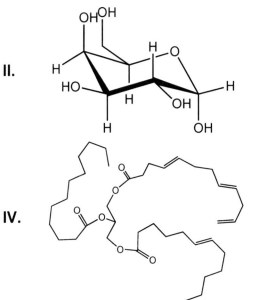

 A. I-nucleotide, II-sugar, III-peptide, IV-fat
 B. I-disaccharide, II-sugar, III-fatty acid, IV-polypeptide
 C. I-disaccharide, II-amino acid, III-fatty acid, IV- polysaccharide
 D. I-nucleotide, II-sugar, III-triacylglyceride, and IV-DNA

A. I is a phosphate (PO_4) linked to a sugar and an amine: a nucleotide. II has the formula $C_nH_{2n}O_n$, indicative of a sugar. III contains three amino acids linked with peptide bonds. It is a tripeptide. IV is a triacylglyceride, a fat molecule.

116. You create a solution of 2.00 μg/ml of a pigment and divide the solution into 12 samples. You give four samples each to three teams of students. They use a spectrophotometer to determine the pigment concentration. Here is their data:

	Concentration (μg/ml)			
Team	sample 1	sample 2	sample 3	sample 4
1	1.98	1.93	1.92	1.88
2	1.70	1.72	1.69	1.70
3	1.78	1.99	2.87	2.20

Which of the following are true?

A. Team 1 has the most precise data
B. Team 3 has the most accurate data in spite of it having low precision
C. The data from Team 2 is characteristic of a systematic error
D. The data from Team 1 is more characteristic of random error than the data from Team 3.

C. For Choice A, the data from Team 2 are closer to the mean for Team 2 than the data from Team 1 are to their mean. Therefore, Team 1's data does not have the most precision.

For Choice B, the mean from team 1 is near 1.9 μg/ml (we don't need to calculate exact values). It differs from the actual value by 0.1 μg/ml. The mean from Team 2 is near 1.7 μg/ml and is inaccurate by 0.3 μg/ml. The mean from Team 3 is not obvious, but it may be calculated as 2.21 μg/ml, differing from the actual value by about 0.2 μg/ml. Team 3's data are less accurate than the data from Team 1.

The data from Team 2 are clustered close to a central value but this value is wrong. Low accuracy with high precision is indicative of a systematic error. (C is correct).

For choice D, a lack of precision is indicative of random error, and the data from Team 1 are more precise than the data from Team 3.

117. Which pair of measurements have identical meanings?

   A. 32 micrometers and 0.032 g
   B. 26 nm and 2.60×10^{-8} m
   C. 3.01×10^{-5} m^3 and 30.1 ml
   D. 0.0020 L and 20 cm^3

C. For Choice A, the prefix *micro*— indicates 10^{-6}. 32 micrograms is 0.000032 g. For Choice B, the two measurements do not have the same meaning because they differ in the number of significant figures. 26 nm is 2.6×10^{-8} m. The symbol "n" for *nano*— indicates 10^{-9}. For Choices C and D, unit conversions between cubic meters and liters are required.

$$\text{For C: } 3.01 \times 10^{-5} \ m^3 \times \frac{1000 \ L}{1 \ m^3} \times \frac{1000 \ ml}{1 \ L} = 30.1 \ ml \text{ (C is correct)}.$$

$$\text{For D: } 0.0020 \ L \times \frac{1 \ m^3}{1000 \ L} \times \frac{(100)^3 \ cm^3}{1 \ m^3} = 2.0 \ cm^3 \text{ (D is incorrect)}.$$

118. Match the instrument with the quantity it measures:

   I.   **eudiometer**
   II. **calorimeter**
   III. **manometer**
   IV. **hygrometer**

   A. I - volume, II - mass, III - radioactivity, IV - humidity
   B. I - volume, II - heat, III - pressure, IV - humidity
   C. I - viscosity, II - mass, III - pressure, IV - surface tension
   D. I - viscosity, II - heat, III - radioactivity, IV - surface tension

B. A eudiometer is a straight tube used to measure gas volume by liquid exclusion. A calorimeter is a device used to measure changes in heat. A manometer is a U-shaped tube used to measure pressure. A hygrometer measures humidity (Choice B). Mass is measured with a balance, radioactivity is measured with a Geiger counter or scintillation counter. Viscosity is measured with a viscometer, surface tension is measured by several different techniques.

119. **Four nearly identical gems from the same mineral are weighed using different balances. Their masses are:**
3.4533 g, 3.459 g, 3.4656 g, 3.464 g.
The four gems are then collected and added to a volumetric cylinder containing 10.00 ml of liquid, and a new volume of 14.97 ml is read. What is the average mass of the four stones and what is the density of the mineral?

    A. 3.460 g, and 2.78 g/ml
    B. 3.460 g and 2.79 g/ml
    C. 3.4605 g and 2.78 g/ml
    D. 3.461 g and 2.79 g/ml

B. The average mass is the sum of the four readings divided by four:

$$(3.4533 \text{ g} + 3.459 \text{ g} + 3.4656 \text{ g} + 3.464 \text{ g})/4 = 3.460475 \text{ g (caculator value)}$$

This value must be rounded off to three significant digits <u>after the decimal point</u> because this is the lowest precision of the added values. The 4 is an exact number. This means rounding downwards to 3.460 g, eliminating Choices C and D. The volume of the collected stones is found from the increase in the level read off the cylinder:

$$14.97 \text{ ml} - 10.00 \text{ ml} = 4.97 \text{ ml}$$

The density is found by dividing the sum of the masses by this volume:

$$\frac{3.4533 \text{ g} + 3.459 \text{ g} + 3.4656 \text{ g} + 3.464 \text{ g}}{4.97 \text{ ml}} = \frac{13.8419 \text{ g}}{4.97 \text{ ml}} = 2.7850905 \text{ g/ml}$$

This value must be rounded off to three <u>total</u> significant digits because this is the lower precision of the numerator and the denominator. The first insignificant digit is a 5. In this case there are additional non-zero digits after the 5, so rounding occurs upwards to 2.79 g/ml (Choice B).

120. Which list includes equipment that would <u>not</u> be used in vacuum filtration?

    A. Rubber tubing, Florence flask, Büchner funnel
    B. Vacuum pump, Hirsch funnel, rubber stopper with a single hole
    C. Aspirator, filter paper, filter flask
    D. Lab stand, clamp, filter trap

A. Florence flasks are round-bottomed and are used for uniform heating. They do not have the hose barb or the thick wall needed to serve as a filter flask during vacuum filtration. Only a designated filter flask should be used during vacuum filtration. Every other piece of equipment could be used in filtration. A spatula is often used to scrape dried product off of filter paper.

121. Which of the following statements about lab safety is <u>not</u> true?

    A. Corrosive chemicals should be stored below eye level.
    B. A chemical splash on the eye or skin should be rinsed for 15 minutes in cold water.
    C. MSDS means "Material Safety Data Sheet."
    D. A student should "stop, drop, and roll" if their clothing catches fire in the lab.

D. In the lab, the safety shower should be used.

122. Which of the following lists consists entirely of chemicals that are considered safe enough to be in a high school lab?

    A. hydrochloric acid, lauric acid, potassium permanganate, calcium hydroxide
    B. ethyl ether, nitric acid, sodium benzoate, methanol
    C. cobalt (II) sulfide, ethylene glycol, benzoyl peroxide, ammonium chloride
    D. picric acid, hydrofluoric acid, cadmium chloride, carbon disulfide.

A. Hydrochloric acid (HCl) is a common acid reagent in high school chemistry. Lauric acid is the fatty acid $CH_3(CH_2)_{10}COOH$ also known as dodecanoic acid. Potassium permanganate ($KMnO_4$) is a strong oxidizer. Calcium hydroxide ($Ca(OH)_2$) is a strong base. These chemicals in their pure state are hazardous, but they are considered safe enough to be in high schools. Ethyl ether (Choice B) should not be in high schools because it may form highly explosive organic peroxides over time. Benzoyl peroxide (Choice C) at low concentrations in gel form is an acne medication, but the pure compound is highly explosive. Choice D consists entirely of chemicals that are too dangerous for high schools. Picric acid is highly explosive, hydrofluoric acid is very corrosive and very toxic, all cadmium compounds are highly toxic, and carbon disulfide is explosive and toxic.

123. **The following procedure was developed to find the specific heat capacity of metals:**

1. **Place pieces of the metals in an ice-water bath so their initial temperature is 0 °C.**
2. **Weigh a Styrofoam cup.**
3. **Add water at room temperature to the cup and weigh it again**
4. **Add a cold metal from the bath to the cup and weigh the cup a third time.**
5. **Monitor the temperature drop of the water until a final temperature at thermal equilibrium is found.**

_____ **is also required as additional information in order to obtain heat capacities for the metals. The best control would be to follow the same protocol except to use _____ in step 4 instead of a cold metal.**

A. The heat capacity of water / a metal at 100 °C
B. The heat of formation of water / ice from the 0 °C bath
C. The heat of capacity of ice / glass at 0 °C
D. The heat capacity of water / water from the 0 °C bath

D. The equation:

$$q = n \times C \times \Delta T$$

is used to determine what additional information is needed. The specific heat, C, of the metals may be found from the heat added, the amount of material, and the temperature change. The amount of metal is found from the difference in weight between Steps 3 and 4, and the temperature change is found from the difference between the final temperature and 0° C. The additional value required is the heat added, q. This may be found from the heat removed from the water if the amount of water, the heat capacity of water, and the temperature change of water are known. The amount of water is found from the difference in weight between Step 2 and 3, and the temperature change is found from the difference between the final temperature and room temperature. The only additional information required is the heat capacity of water, eliminating Choices B and C. Heat of formation (choice B) is only used for chemical reactions.

A good control simplifies only the one aspect under study without adding anything new. Metal at 100° C (Choice A) would alter the temperature of the experiment and glass (Choice C) would add an additional material to the study. Ice (Choice B) would require consideration of the heat of fusion. Choice D is an ideal control because the impact of water at 0° C on room temperature water is simpler than the impact of metals at 0° C on room temperature water, and nothing new is added.

124. Which statement about the impact of chemistry on society is <u>not</u> true?

A. Partial hydrogenation creates *trans* fat.
B. The Haber process incorporates nitrogen from the air into molecules for agricultural use.
C. The CO_2 concentration in the atmosphere has decreased in the last ten years.
D. The concentration of ozone-destroying chemicals in the stratosphere has decreased in the last ten years.

C. CO_2 concentrations in the atmosphere continue to increase (Choice C), but the concentration of ozone destroying chemicals has fallen (Choice D) due to international agreements.

125. Which statement about everyday applications of chemistry is <u>true</u>?

A. Rainwater found near sources of air pollution will most likely be basic.
B. Batteries run down more quickly at low temperatures because chemical reactions are proceeding more slowly.
C. Benzyl alcohol is a detergent used in shampoo.
D. Adding salt decreases the time required for water to boil.

B. Souces of air pollution (Choice A) will most likely cause acid rain.

Low temperatures decrease reaction rates, and this is also true of electrochemical reactions in batteries. At low temperature, less current is supplied and the effect will be a short life for applications that demand current. (Choice B is correct).

Benzyl alcohol (Choice C) has the formula shown to the right. Like detergents, this molecule has a non-polar region (the benzene ring) and a polar region (the hydroxyl group). But, unlike detergents, the non-polar region for benzyl alcohol is small and short. Detergents have long, "tail-like" non-polar regions that can surround oils and grease. Benzyl alcohol is sometimes included in shampoo to prevent itching and bacterial growth.

Adding salt (Choice D) increases the boiling point of water, thus increasing the time required for water to boil. It decreases the time required to cook food once boiling occurs.

Sample Constructed-Response Answer

126. What procedure would you use to isolate or purify an organic compound from an aqueous solution containing inorganic contaminants? Clearly describe the apparatus to be used and the steps required to accomplish this.

A solvent extraction is the procedure that would be used to separate different compounds in solution. This technique takes advantage of solubility differences in order to separate an organic product from impurities. For example, water and ether are immiscible solvents and will form two distinct layers, allowing physical separation utilizing laboratory equipment.

Use a separatory funnel with a stopcock and glass stopper, mounted on a ringstand, to perform the extraction. Pour the solution into the separatory funnel via the opening at the top. Then add an organic solvent such as diethyl ether or methylene chloride; the organic solvent should readily dissolve the organic compound to be purified but should not react with it, or be miscible with water. Insert the glass stopper and shake the mixture a few times. In order to vent the funnel of any gas pressure that might build up, hold the funnel upside down with the stem pointing away from people or objects; then slowly open the stopcock to release any pressure and close it again. Repeat the shaking and venting two or three times, allowing time for solute exchange. The layers will eventually separate, and two distinct layers of liquid will be clearly seen. If there is doubt, adding a bit of water to the funnel will indicate which layer is the aqueous layer and which is the organic, because the aqueous layer will increase in size when the water is added. Open the funnel's stopcock carefully to drain the bottom layer into a beaker, then drain the top layer into a second beaker. Save the purified organic layer and discard the aqueous layer, which contains the impurities.

XAMonline, INC. 21 Orient Ave. Melrose, MA 02176

Toll Free number 800-509-4128

TO ORDER Fax 781-662-9268 OR www.XAMonline.com

NEW YORK STATE TEACHER CERTIFICATION
EXAMINATION   - NYSTCE - 2007

PO#   Store/School:

Address 1:

Address 2 (Ship to other):

City, State Zip

Credit card number_____-_____-_____-_____   expiration_____

EMAIL _____

PHONE   FAX

13# ISBN 2007	TITLE	Qty	Retail	Total
978-1-58197-866-7	NYSTCE ATS-W ASSESSMENT OF TEACHING SKILLS- WRITTEN 91			
978-1-58197-867-4	NYSTCE ATAS ASSESSMENT OF TEACHING ASSISTANT SKILLS 095			
978-1-58197-854-4	CST BIOLOGY 006			
978-1-58197-855-1	CST CHEMISTRY 007			
978-1-58197-865-0	CQST COMMUNICATION AND QUANTITATIVE SKILLS TEST 080			
978-1-58197-856-8	CST EARTH SCIENCE 008			
978-1-58197-851-3	CST ENGLISH 003			
978-1-58197-862-9	CST FAMILY AND CONSUMER SCIENCES 072			
978-1-58197-858-2	CST FRENCH SAMPLE TEST 012			
978-1-58197-868-1	LAST LIBERAL ARTS AND SCIENCE TEST 001			
978-1-58197-863-6	CST LIBRARY MEDIA SPECIALIST 074			
978-1-58197-861-2	CST LITERACY 065			
978-1-58197-852-0	CST MATH 004			
978-1-58197-872-8	CST MULTIPLE SUBJECTS 002 SAMPLE QUESTIONS			
978-1-58197-850-6	CST MUTIPLE SUBJECTS 002			
978-1-58197-864-3	CST PHYSICAL EDUCATION 076			
978-1-58197-857-5	CST PHYSICS SAMPLE TEST 009			
978-1-58197-853-7	CST SOCIAL STUDIES 005			
978-1-58197-859-9	CST SPANISH 020			
978-1-58197-860-5	CST STUDENTS WITH DISABILITIES 060			

	SUBTOTAL	
FOR PRODUCT PRICES VISIT WWW.XAMONLINE.COM	Ship	$8.25
	TOTAL	

Printed in the United States
130793LV00001B/22/A